Saving the Georgia Coast

T0243909

Saving the Georgia Coast

A Political History of the Coastal Marshlands Protection Act

PAUL BOLSTER

The University of Georgia Press

ATHENS

A Wormsloe
FOUNDATION
nature book

Paperback edition, 2022

© 2020 by the University of Georgia Press

Athens, Georgia 30602

www.ugapress.org

Set in 11.5/15 Garamond Premier Pro by Rebecca A. Norton

Most University of Georgia Press titles are
available from popular e-book vendors.

Printed digitally

The Library of Congress has cataloged the hardcover edition of this book as follows:
Names: Bolster, Paul, author.
Title: Saving the Georgia coast : a political history of the
Coastal Marshlands Protection Act / Paul Bolster.
Other titles: Wormsloe Foundation nature book.
Description: Athens : The University of Georgia Press, [2020] |
Series: A Wormsloe Foundation nature book |
Includes bibliographical references and index.
Identifiers: LCCN 2019049555 | ISBN 9780820357300 (hardcover) |
ISBN 9780820357362 (ebook)
Subjects: LCSH: Georgia. Coastal Marshlands Protection Act—History. |
Wetland conservation—Law and legislation—Georgia—History—20th century. |
Coastal zone management—Georgia—Atlantic Coast—History—20th century.
Classification: LCC KFG451.7 A35197 B65 2020 | DDC 346.75804/409146—dc23
LC record available at https://lccn.loc.gov/2019049555
Paperback ISBN 978-0-8203-6257-1

To Livija "Riki" Bolster,
my wife and partner for 50 years and the Latvian girl within her.

The fate of these islands, these marshes and the waters beneath them is yet to be determined. Suffering the laws of nature since the dawn of time, this fragile zone so recently invaded by the modern human horde now awaits the laws of man.

—REID HARRIS

Contents

Illustrations

Maps and Charts

Photographs after page   188

Acknowledgments

I am indebted to many friends and family who believed I could write this book even when I doubted myself. My small Inkfingers writing group of Debby Miller, Sheila Connors, Carla Schissel, Kaaren Nowicki, and my wife listened critically to my readings and advised on how to simplify the story for the general reader who didn't live and breathe the legislative process. My family endured listening to me endlessly talk about "the book" as I researched—and still encouraged me.

My University of Georgia dissertation advisor, Robert Griffith, was a young historian who died before he had a chance to see the results of my scholarship. Whenever I was in Washington, D.C., he made time to meet and encouraged me in the work I was doing as a member of the Georgia General Assembly. He was a careful, thoughtful, and caring person, and I hope he would be pleased that his mentoring made a late but positive contribution to the history of Georgia.

During my twelve years in the Georgia House of Representatives I had the rare privilege of knowing the political leaders of the state. Most were committed to making decisions that they honestly believed were in the best public interest. In the House chamber Sidney Marcus sat on one side and George Hooks on the other; Bill Dover was at my back, and Gerald Horton at the end of the row. It was enlightening to watch them build support for proposals small and large. I am thankful to all the people who were closely involved in setting state policy and wish there was more understanding of the dedicated work required to enact legislation.

I didn't know Reid Harris when he was alive, but he left a detailed record of his work that allows us to see him. His self-published memoir of the Coastal Marshlands Protection Act is a unique contribution. Few legislators have given us this kind of insight into the legislative process. I wish more would preserve the details of their legislative life and provide us candid observations that would build the public's faith in the legislative process and government.

Beyond the work of Reid Harris, two other writers have given scholarly attention to the passage of the Act. Charles Seabrook told a concise version of the story in his carefully researched book *Salt Marsh*. Chris Manganiello completed the work of late scholar Mark Finley and his essay, "The Gold Standard: Sunbelt Environmentalism and Coastal Protection," which was published in *Coastal Nature, Coastal Culture*. Chris kindly let me read his work in its manuscript form.

It has been my great pleasure to get to know Dr. Fred Marland. His copious dusty files and long conversations filled in many of the gaps in the written documentation—but not just that. Fifty years ago he left his lab and research on Sapelo and took his scientific knowledge to public hearings. He walked the halls of the Capitol's third floor talking to legislators. He helped Reid Harris and legislators understand the science of the marsh on which public policy could rest. His engagement in the legislative process is a model for the scientists of today.

The professional archivists and librarians throughout the state have to a person been ready and eager to open their treasures to all who come looking. They have preserved much of the state's political history in document and oral form. They need more political leaders to be liberal with their papers. Mine will be there soon.

The editors at the University of Georgia Press, especially Patrick Allen, Jon Davies, and Deborah Oliver, have been very encouraging of the work and pushed for a high standard of documentation and smooth composition. Deborah did fact checking and sent me back to the sources on a number of occasions.

Above all, there would not be a book without the incredible help of my wife of fifty-plus years, Livija "Riki" Bolster. She is a far better writer than I will ever be. If you find the narrative lively, the stories enticingly told, and characters three dimensional, it is her hand that reshaped my plodding fact-based style. She has stuck with me through many expectations—the preacher, the teacher, the legislator, the homeless advocate, and now a fledgling writer—a partner and advisor in all of it.

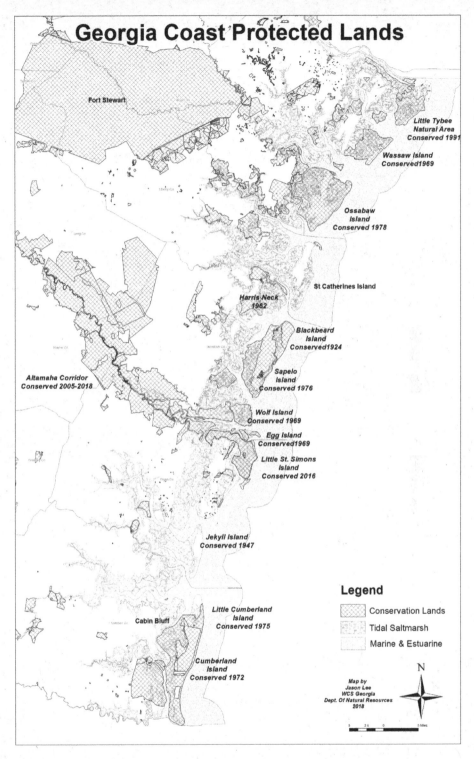

Georgia Coast Protected Lands

Fort Stewart

Little Tybee
Natural Area
Conserved 1991

Wassaw Island
Conserved1969

Ossabaw
Island
Conserved 1978

St Catherines Island

Harris Neck
1982

Blackbeard
Island
Conserved1924

Sapelo
Island
Conserved 1976

Altamaha Corridor
Conserved 2005-2018

Wolf Island
Conserved 1969

Egg Island
Conserved1969

Little St. Simons
Island
Conserved 2016

Jekyll Island
Conserved 1947

Legend

Conservation Lands

Tidal Saltmarsh

Marine & Estuarine

Little Cumberland
Island
Conserved 1975

Cabin Bluff

Cumberland
Island
Conserved 1972

Map by
Jason Lee
WCS Georgia
Dept. Of Natural Resources
2018

N

Georgia coast protected lands, 2019. (Courtesy of Jason Lee, earth ecologist,
DNR Coastal Division, Brunswick, Georgia)

Saving the Georgia Coast

Introduction

The world lies east: how ample, the marsh and the sea and the sky!
A league and a league of marsh-grass, waist-high, broad in the blade.

—SIDNEY LANIER, "The Marshes of Glynn"

My green, stubby-nosed REI kayak had taken me across the Back River from Tybee Island. I was alone (not advisable for most amateurs like myself) in the late fall when all the sunseekers were back in the city. I made a quick landfall on the slim barrier island that is the most prominent part of what the map calls Little Tybee Island. Its sandy beach is less than a mile long, but it is one of the fourteen named coastal islands that protect a hundred miles of the Georgia coast. It was the pristine sandy beach and the solitude of the island that drew me. I walked the sand and observed the shells and decaying cord grass that hinted at the animal life thriving in the waters surrounding the island. Birds sounded their call from the thick-wooded upland beyond the beach and the migrating flocks of shorebirds swarmed the sandbars at the end of the island looking for food. On that day I was the lone representative of the human race as I stretched out on the sand and watched the Atlantic's waves rhythmically slap the shore.

On another day my kayak slipped almost soundlessly through Jack's Cut into the waterway hidden by marsh grass on either side. This marsh river opened between two sandbars to accommodate the tidal flow that twice a day services the marshes reaching out behind the slim barrier island. The cut is the gateway to the expansive marsh that dominates the geography of the island. It has more than sixty hammocks that protrude above the water at high tide, but the marsh grass captures the thick black mud when the tidal waters subside. It has taken thousands of years for the sediments from Georgia rivers to build up the fertile soil of the marsh. The mud and the marsh grass cover most of Little Tybee and stretch almost as far as one can see to the edges of Savannah subdivisions.

Once through the opening, I paddled the wide, deep, and slow-flowing stream through two S turns. With my view obstructed by marsh grass, the quiet was only occasionally interrupted by the movement of birds and the splash of a fish breaking the surface of the water. My peace of mind was shattered the moment I spotted a fin sticking six inches out of the water and trailing a small wake as it moved quickly toward my tiny boat. My paddling stopped, the boat slowed, and my pulse increased with fearful anticipation. How dangerous were these waters? Beyond the beauty and tranquility of the place, I knew little about the surrounding *Spartina* grass or what lurked in the brownish water flowing to the sea. But there was no real threat from this giant mammal that topped the hierarchy of the marsh's animal life. My fellow river companion was a friendly and curious dolphin with no malicious intent. It went only slightly deeper and passed directly under my tiny craft. This animal seemed much larger than me or my boat, and I have little doubt it could have flipped me easily into the water without missing a swimming stroke. It turned out to be a friendly and majestic encounter that impressed on me the grandeur and magnitude of the Little Tybee marsh and made me want to learn more. I like to think the dolphin also enjoyed the chance encounter.

One more personal story. A friend and I, both from Atlanta, decided to camp overnight on the southern tip of Little Tybee. In late October we set up our camp on a narrow spit of sand that at one time was part of the forested barrier island. It was a long, hard, and sleepless two days for two inexperienced urbanites. While we were in the middle of the majestic beauty of the Georgia coast, the "grumpy old man boat" in which we had arrived became our obsession. Keeping the old aluminum Corps of Engineers 16-foot runabout and its 8-horsepower outboard motor from floating away with the tide presented a challenge. Foolishly, we had not brought an anchor. I found myself walking the beach at the 3:00 a.m. high tide, hoping the boat was still tied to the driftwood log. A full moon lit the sandbar after the dark clouds and their pounding rain moved out to sea. To my relief it illuminated the small boat bobbing in the waves, still tied to the log. Instead of exploring what nature had to offer, we spent most of our time pushing the boat up and down the beach to keep it safe from the tide. I knew this spot has the highest tides in the state, ranging from a normal of 6.5 feet to a spring tide of 8.5 feet, but it was sobering and awe provoking to see the water fill the space where we had a few hours earlier sat down for our evening meal. We were pure amateurs in this new place of wonder, but I like to think we were also adventurers, not as grand as John Muir who camped near here when he traveled this coast in 1867, but filled with the same spirit and awe of the nature around us. In the end, none of our boat pulling and pushing mattered, because with a dead motor we eventually needed to be towed back to "urban" Tybee. Despite the humiliating aspects of that two-day coastal wilderness experience, recalling those forty-eight hours on a coastal sandbar always brings a smile.

My experiences gave me a small insight into the lives of the first humans who came to Georgia's barrier islands some ten thousand years ago, who, as nature writer Janisse Ray puts it, paddled their canoes "through ancient maritime forests and brackish marshes, through pine flatwoods and cypress swamps."[1] In the essay from which the quote is drawn, Ray reviews Georgia's coastal literary expression as a search for a sense of place and follows closely the thoughts of Wallace Stegner, who said in his oft-quoted essay, "No place is a place until things that have happened in it are remembered in history, ballads, yarns, or monuments."[2] My camping and kayaking experiences were the beginnings of a sense of place, but as an Atlanta urbanite I needed to know more.

The central character of this book is the marsh. My hope is that it gives you a greater sense of place as a Georgian, an American, and a citizen of the world. Ray says there are four stages through which a person must pass in the search for a sense of place: first, see it; second, experience and hear its stories; third, learn and know its natural history—what is in it; and finally, settle down in it. To enact the Coastal Marshlands Protection Act of 1970, Reid Harris and his supporters would need to take enough Georgians through these stages to get ninety-eight votes in the Georgia House of Representatives to pass his bill.

John Muir, who traveled quickly through the state on his way to finding a famed place in the wilderness of the west, camped in the delta of the Savannah River when he was passing through. In his *A Thousand-Mile Walk to the Gulf* he described what he saw:

Am made to feel that I am now in a strange land. I know hardly any of the plants, but few of the birds, and I am unable to see the country for a solemn, dark, mysterious cypress woods which cover everything. The winds are full of strange sounds, making one feel far from the people and plants and fields of home. Night is coming on and I am filled with indescribable loneliness. Felt feverish, bathed in a black, silent stream; nervously watchful for alligators.

Muir saw the salt marshes as belonging "more to the sea than to the land; . . . ill defined in their boundary, and instead of rising in the hilly waves and swellings, stretch inland in low water-like levels."[3] But he did not stay long enough to hear its stories or know what was in it.

Historical novelist Eugenia Price felt deeply about her adopted home of St. Simons Island when she left it to testify in Atlanta for marshland protection. She recorded what she saw for other Georgians to see:

> I saw nothing but the first sky full of roseate light—pale blue around the edges— as the new wonder broke out of the ocean to the east and hung above the thick miasma still tucked snugly at the marsh margins, but what I heard I will never forget. . . . Soft rapid hoofbeats on the black marsh mud, scarcely rustling the dew-drenched spartina grasses, thudding, flying away from me, their beat diminishing, fading, but held to my ears by the unbelievable quiet of a marsh morning—until, unmistakably, one, then two, then three deer, invisible in the mist, splashed into the waters of Dunbar Creek and began to swim steadily to the other side. . . .
>
> . . . They had given me a set-apart moment of the kind of delight one person can never give to another person. A silence accentuated by their flying hooves and their quick swim across the salt creek—silence I will never forget.[4]

Sidney Lanier came to the coast seeking relief from tuberculosis. He hoped the salt air and sea breezes would bring a cure. He penned perhaps the most memorized and honored description of the marsh in 1895 in "The Marshes of Glynn."

> And what if behind me to westward the wall of the woods stands high?
> The world lies east: how ample, the marsh and the sea and the sky!
> A league and a league of marsh-grass, waist-high, broad in the blade,
> Green, and all of a height, and unflicked with a light on a shade,
> Stretch leisurely off, and a pleasant plain,
> To the terminal Blue of the main.
>
> Oh, what is abroad in the marsh and the terminal sea?
> Somehow my soul seems suddenly free

From the weighing of fate and the sad discussion of sin,
By the length and the breadth and the sweep of the marshes of Glynn.[5]

You can see from these few examples, Georgia writers quickly move beyond seeing to tell what they and others experience in this place ruled by tides. Price's story of the three deer crossing the marsh takes us beyond just seeing.

Beginning in 1953, a handful of young scientists, encouraged by R. J. Reynolds II, came to Sapelo Island to discover what was in the marsh; to know the tiny beasts that lived under the protective cover of the "broad in the blade" marsh grasses. The first handful built the laboratory in Reynolds's old cow barn and founded the University of Georgia Marine Institute. Over the next ten years, their research demonstrated the value of the marshland and what was in it.

John and Mildred Teal summarized the discoveries in their narrative of the marsh, *The Life and Death of the Salt Marsh*, in 1969 and provided an opportunity for the public to see into the multilayered environment scientists had been peeling open since the mid-1950s. The Teals knew the marshlands up close from their research years on Sapelo Island that began in 1955. But Mildred's literary skills enabled their readers to visit and see into the habitat. The book introduces readers to the marsh and encompasses everything from the smallest one-celled animal that lives only ten days to the large inhabitants of the sea.

> At low tide, the wind blowing across *Spartina* grass sounds like wind on the prairie. When the tide is in, the gentle music of moving water is added to the prairie rustle. There are sounds of birds living in the marshes. The marsh wren advertises his presence with a reedy call, even at night, when most birds are still. The marsh hen, or clapper rail, calls in a loud, carrying cackle. You can hear the tiny, high-pitched rustling thunder of the herds of crabs moving through the grass as they flee before advancing feet or more leisurely sound of movement they make on their daily migrations in search of food. At night, when the air is still and other sounds are quieted, an attentive listener can hear the bubbling of air from the sandy soil as the high tide floods the marsh.[6]

Often the stories of others will give a new perspective on a place. I once talked to a plumber who came to work on my elderly Tybee rental property.

His story, which my research shows was not completely factual, drew me further into this history. As high school kids, he and his friends fished freely in the marsh rivers and camped on the hammocks of Little Tybee Island. When construction people appeared with heavy equipment on the small stretch of beach, they feared "their" island needed defending from greedy Atlanta developers. He claimed he and his friends fended off development with bags of Dixie Crystal sugar. At night they mixed sugar into the diesel fuel of the equipment. This story is unlikely to be true, but it illustrates the strong sense of ownership of this place for those who grew up on this coast; their "wellbeing and survival" depended on it. They felt this was common land. While the plumber's story shows the connection between ordinary people and their marshland, there is little evidence that native coastal residents engaged in direct action in their grassroots efforts to protect the local habitat. This story nonetheless brings to mind the novel of influential counterculture environmentalist Edward Abbey, *The Monkey Wrench Gang*, about a small gang of individuals who take their love of the environment to direct action against the power lines and dams that offend them. Abbey may have dreamed of attacking a power line, but his moving portrait of the environment in *Desert Solitaire* did more to build support for the defenders of nature.[7] It is more likely the concern for bulldozers on Little Tybee brought hundreds of people to the Savannah hearing to loudly voice their opinion against mining the marsh for phosphate.

One other story, perhaps more accurate, comes from the southern end of the hundred-mile coast. In the early evening on many Fridays, ten-year-old Jack McCollough and his father put their little rowboat with its 4-horsepower motor into the Satilla River near Woodbine and headed downriver. An ebbing tide pushed them gracefully to a marsh bank somewhere near where the river widened to become the St. Andrew Sound. They set up camp on the bank and prepared to fish for trout and mullet the next day. The land was owned by the Sea Island Company and was used by the wealthy guests of the company's Cabin Bluff hunting lodge. His father maintained a good relationship with the manager in charge of the land. Sometimes Jack and his father camped on one of the islands created by the dredging of the Intracoastal Waterway that ran down the west side of Cumberland Island, and nobody seemed to know who owned these small islands. By Saturday afternoon they would have enough fish to last the week, so they would head home Sunday morning with the incoming tide. Jack went away to college and his father died in 1951, but the family fishing trips defined his view of the marsh.[8]

The sense of a place is made deeper when one learns and knows the natural history of a place. Perhaps John and William Bartram, who wrote extensively about their travels along the coast, were the first to provide this deeper look. John described in detail the plants and animals that occupied the marshes and the upland forests. Seeing the coast for the first time at age ten through a car window, Ray appreciated what she saw, but as an adult she learned more about the teeming life within the marsh. Although there are many books describing in detail the marsh ecosystem, Ray's wonder and understanding of the life in the marsh is evident in her own description.[9] It is

> full of secret life, populated as it is with marsh periwinkles, med snails, air-breathing coffeebean snails, mud fiddler crabs, purple marsh crabs, oysters, and ribbed mussels. Higher in the marsh, clapper rails build cup-shaped nests of grasses and sedges in clumps of vegetation above the high-tide line. They soften their nests with fine strips of grass, often build ramps leading into them, and sometimes even erect canopies overhead. The seaside sparrow, a bird so closely connected to the salt marsh that its abundance indicates the health of the system, . . . walks around gleaning soft-bodied spiders and sedge seeds. Sand fiddlers and wharf crabs scurry about.[10]

There are other microscopic creatures that only the scientists are likely to see and understand. In this book, I do not attempt to tell the amazing stories of the periwinkle snail or the billions of fiddler crabs that populate the marsh, but I have seen them and have watched them navigate their world. The scientists who play a major part in this book have looked into the intricate systems of the marsh for many decades and their stories made it possible for decision makers to also see its value.

Ray's last component of a "sense of place" comes from settling deep into a place. She relies on Michael Hough for this concept when he describes people with an "investment in the land because one's wellbeing and survival depend on it."[11] For people like Reid Harris, born and raised on the coast, with old roots in Brunswick and on St. Simons Island, it became imperative to communicate the precious deep sense of the marsh and protect its survival. The scientists living year-round on isolated Sapelo Island were almost religiously committed to their marsh-focused research. They came off their island to help people see more clearly the intricate nature and productive value of the marshlands. Legislative leaders seeking places on one of the study committees came to the coast to see and learn from the scientists. Reid Harris's task, and that of the many "settled-in" citizens who helped him, was to get enough other Georgians to see the marsh, hear the stories, and feel the marsh as part of themselves.

Advocates for the coast and its marshes had an opportunity to reach out to other Georgians and make this unique environment a part of the state's sense of place. With the rising popularity of family vacations in the prosperity that followed World War II, many Georgia residents had seen the marsh from Jekyll, St. Simons, and Tybee Islands, but had never seen the other 80 miles of hard-to-reach, undeveloped parts of the coast.

Somebody who had seen it and hunkered down in it had to tell the stories of the coast to make it real for others. There were opportunities at conferences and in the press to tell the stories, while magazine photographs showed the beauty of a place that belongs "more to the sea than the land." The words of Andrew Sparks, a journalist who "first published at the age of twelve," paint reverent and lyrical pictures. Dragging his readers with him, he outlined a day in the marsh.

> In twilight, the marsh is buff, gray and pale blue, faded colors, darkened by the shadow of the world turning over in bed for the night. . . .

> At night the marsh is black, humped up beside the silver water, black and furry as bear skins, black even under a sky made luminous with moonlight. The white sky and silver creeks and black marsh fill up with nighttime sounds.

> The noise at night is not only oysters even if they are the loudest things around. Fiddlers deep in their sand holes fill the incoming tide with bubbles— plop, plop, plop. Mullet jump with an unseen splash. A needle fish describes circles in the spot of a flashlight near the dock, an audible eddy, curling the water into a whirlpool. Whippoorwills sound in the distance. Up close, a mosquito hums until a slap stops the tiny noise. And oysters everywhere snap their fingers, pop their gum, click their tongues, shoot off popguns, pop, POP, poppop, pop. They make a clatter of the night, those slimy, squishy, limp, immobile oysters which in the dark seem active, almost articulate.

Morning paves the marsh with gold, sunrise reflected in every creek, ditch, and river, spreading everywhere when the tide is high, bringing color back to the green spartina.

Early sounds are lighter, brighter, a woodpecker off on some pine; .... The great marsh factory has opened up for the day, manufacturing food for bird and fish and crow and crane and crab and shrimp and man. It throbs with life, a sample of the whole world, yet like nothing else in it, this complicated net of plant and animal, this intermeshed dependency which is the marsh and which is life and nature everywhere.[12]

Using Ray's literary analysis in a book about politics may seem a bit odd; it is, however, a useful way to bring a political process into a broader cultural focus. Saving the Georgia coast was a political decision made by flawed human beings, but the literary search for a "sense of place" may be a useful way to look at what a political movement must do to succeed. People have to see, hear the stories, know the details of what is inside an issue, and be led by a few people who have settled deeply into the place. Political success is always dependent on people with passion and deep commitment to a cause. It is remarkable that during the decision time between 1968 and 1970, there were nine scheduled opportunities to step up to a microphone and tell a personal story, a scientific story, a fishing story, an engineering story, even a story of romance. At these public hearings and in the middle of the legislative debate there was a central question. How should Georgia use its coast? That question is the focus of this book. When you read the narrative of these events in Georgia's political history, look for evidence of how Georgians made a decision to protect their coast out of a sense of place.

The political history of Georgia's decision to preserve its marshlands and barrier islands unfolds in these pages. In 1968, it was hard to see and hear about the marshland. It was perhaps the most turbulent year in the country's modern political life. The Tet Offensive stoked the fire under the Vietnam antiwar movement, and the youth movement behind Sen. Eugene McCarthy in the New Hampshire presidential primary pushed President Lyndon Johnson to decline a second term. In April, James Earl Ray fired a rifle shot in Memphis that killed Martin Luther King Jr. In a restaurant kitchen, Sirhan Sirhan fired a pistol, killing Robert Kennedy, who likely would have become the next president of the United States. Street riots followed the death of King, and the youths who took to the streets at the Democratic National Convention in Chicago clashed with police in a haze of tear gas. The national politics of the year, which had seen the clash of big ideas and the specter of a country divided against itself ended with a narrow victory for Richard Nixon and an end to Democrat control of the national government. The election spelled the demise of many liberal programs, and while the clash of ideas continued into the Nixon years, there opened a small avenue for the country to pay attention to the condition of its natural environment.

The year ended with a photograph. On Christmas Eve, Apollo 8 took its fifth turn around the moon and U.S. astronauts looked up from their work to see the earth rising through the window of their small capsule. Bill Anders scrambled for a camera and captured on film what became known as the *Earthrise* photograph. Colonel Frank Borman, who commanded the first space vehicle to circle the moon, explained the impact of the moment in a recent BBC presentation. The surface of the moon in the foreground was colorless and pockmarked with craters and meteor strikes, he said, and "the contrast between the distressed moon and the beautiful blue earth was remarkable." The image of the blue and white earth helped Borman and those who saw it realize how fortunate they were to live on this big blue marble. Even after a lifetime of living with Apollo mission stories, Borman felt the photo "gave us all a sense that we live on a fragile planet, that we have limited resources, and we better learn to take care of it."[13]

Behind the noise of news stories reporting the country's turmoil, passionate conservation advocates fought for the life of the marsh. Their battles, sometimes fought with handwritten letters and well-honed testimony, were for a cause and a place that needed their protection. As Reid Harris writes, "suffering the laws of nature since the dawn of time, this fragile zone so recently invaded by the human horde now awaits the laws of man."[14] This is the story set in Georgia politics at the end of the 1960s. It is a story of how a threat to the coastal marshes galvanized fledgling organizations, scientists, common people, and government leaders to protect the future of the marshlands along the hundred miles of the Georgia coastline. It is a story about political leadership, courage, and commitment. It is also a story of how a bill becomes a law.

Chapter 1

Building Wealth on the Back of Nature

God doesn't like a clearcut. It makes his heart turn cold.

—Janisse Ray

Depending on how you count, fourteen official barrier islands and 500,000 acres of salt marsh line the hundred miles of Georgia coast. When taken as a whole, the Georgia coast has one-third of all the salt marsh on the Atlantic coast, more than any other state. The sandy beaches, dune systems, and upland forests of the islands take the direct force of the South Atlantic storms and, depending on the strength of the storm, often protect the mainland and the complex life generated in the estuaries and the marshes that developed behind them. The drinking water supply for the coast and the coastal plain comes from the Floridan aquifer that once discharged into the sea just off the coast. Fourteen rivers daily bring water to the marshes where it mixes with salt water and creates a unique habitat that spawns new life, producing more food than the best farms in the Midwest.

Protecting this precious resource in 1970 would require nine public hearings, "barrels" of letters from citizens, the creation of conservation organizations, and at least one courageous legislator. Before we dive into the decision fifty years ago to preserve this natural coastal environment, decisions that were made earlier in the state can teach some important lessons. Since the establishment of permanent European settlement on the Georgia coast, there has been an ongoing struggle to make what the natural environment offers fit what humans want to do. There has rarely been a balance in the push and pull between human desires and nature. The human use of the available natural resources has usually moved forward with slim thought for what the long-term environmental impact would be. Those who sought a balance were few in the early centuries of coastal history because the "wilderness" they encountered seemed both limitless and a wasteland without human use. Historians have recently made it clear that the coastal environment's resistance to human hopes and plans caused ownership and control of the coast to "change hands multiple times."[1]

For centuries, Native Americans occupied Georgia's coast and islands and developed an economy based on the largesse of the sea and the diversity of the longleaf pine forest. There is evidence of Native life on the coast nearly ten thousand years ago, but the total population was very small compared with the available resources and the limits of their technology. Native Americans fit the unique environment created under the thin canopy of the trees, which sustained a huge variety of grasses and other useful plants at their feet. They knew the longleaf was resistant to fire and used it to herd wild game, encourage the growth of grasses for cattle, and clear land for agriculture. Also sustaining their way of life were the buffalo and white-tailed deer that lived well on the lush grass of the forest floor, as well as the oysters, fish, and other abundant marine life. Nature for the Native Americans was not an array of resources to be exploited but "the very fabric of life," according to historian Mart Stewart in his groundbreaking study of Georgia culture and its interaction with the environment, *What Nature Suffers to Groe.*[2] While they lived off the production of their surroundings, the "wilderness" they lived in was not untouched by human hands. They learned how to use the abundant supply of fish to fertilize their corn crop and increase its abundance.

Europeans came to the coast with economic and cultural ideas they expected to impose on the people and the environment, and often found their plans didn't fit. Europeans first came in the robes of Spanish priests who tried, as they did in all of their explorations, to convert the inhabitants to Roman Catholicism. For nearly two centuries, the Spanish colonial efforts to plant colonies on the Georgia coast were focused on trade and conversion. For the time they were on the coast, they did not bring people to settle the land but sought allies among the indigenous population who knew the land and how to harvest its products.[3]

From the founding of the English colony in 1735 by a group of trustees led by James Oglethorpe, people with power and control over the coast have decided how to use its natural resources. The trustees based their decisions on philosophical ideals because the founders, whose experience was limited by knowledge of English agriculture, had little scientific understanding of the natural environment of the Georgia coast. Little thought was given to the need for balance between the hopes, dreams, needs, and desires of humans and the realities of nature. From Oglethorpe to the present day, the scientific reality of the coastal environment has often been in conflict with the efforts to produce wealth for a few or even wealth for the many. While this book focuses on the decisions Georgia's political leaders made concerning the use of coastal natural resources between 1968 and 1970 and where these protections stand today, it is useful to see how earlier generations of Georgia leaders decided to use the state's natural resources.

King George II granted Oglethorpe and his Trustees for the Establishment of the Colony of Georgia in America political control over the land between the Savannah River and the Altamaha River, expecting them to develop wealth and to push the Spanish back into Florida. Besides their military objectives, which catch most of the attention of historians, the trustees had a plan to level the distance between the wealthy and the average hardworking small farmer. They carefully selected working-class people that included fewer than a dozen individuals who had been released from debtors' prison. The colony was in fact founded by a group of English idealists who hoped to reduce class differences. Georgia was to be a new opportunity for poor, hardworking people who struggled in the English economy. They gave 50-acre land grants to settlers who needed financial support to reach the new colony and 500 acres to those who could pay their own way. Everybody was supposed to plant mulberry trees to start a silk production system and send the silk fibers back to English manufacturers. They also limited the ability of the settlers to move from parcel to parcel, sell the land, or add to their original grant. They didn't want people to accumulate wealth from increasing land values; they banned slavery because they wanted a community of yeoman farmers who did their own work, and also banned the importation of rum because it interfered with hard work.[4]

But after twenty years it was clear that the environment did not fit this ideal. The land grants were primarily in ancient longleaf pine forests that had a lush understory of wire grass. Although this looked promising for agriculture, the English didn't know that this native pine is very slow growing and characterized by a taproot that allows the tree to thrive on sandy soil. When the new homesteaders cleared the forests, the thin layer of topsoil produced crops for only a year or two, because removal of the trees also removed the restoration of soil nutrients. The resulting impoverished soil could not produce the vegetables to sustain a hardworking family farmer and a surplus to ship back to England.[5] The ideal was no match for the reality of nature.

When the king took back control of the colony in 1750, the founders' idealism soon lost out to business-minded Englishmen and plantation investors from South Carolina, who saw financial opportunities in rice and cotton production built on the institution of slavery. Rice became a significant cash crop for low-country planters who moved in from South Carolina. They transformed marshland along the rivers into diked reserves, using the river fresh water that rode on the salt water from incoming tides. Rice production took careful engineering of the water flows in and out of the fields diked by strenuous labor of African slaves. The plantation system that included cotton on the islands dominated the coastal economy from 1750 to the end of the Civil War.

The plantation economy produced commodities for which there was great demand in the English system of trade, but it required great human energy to create the diked fields and intricate understanding of the hydraulics that flooded the rice fields. The land didn't wear out because new sediments came down the rivers during the rainy season, replenishing the nutrients in the rice fields. The rivers flooded the fields before planting and watered the crops during dry seasons. The plantation needed large investments in capital for land and for slaves, but only a few people at the top of the economic order had the resources needed. The class distance between the few planters at the top and the enslaved workers widened to the extreme. In addition to the capital, it was the strength and skills of the slaves that made the system prosper. Captured slaves from West Africa brought with them an understanding of rice production in their homeland and contributed to the complex hydraulic engineering the rice fields needed to be productive. These skills, when combined with the planter's capital, transformed the natural environment.[6]

It was a high-risk business. Ships went down laden with product, and hurricanes regularly raked the coast, destroying dikes, crops, and lives. In the 130 years between the founding of Georgia and the end of the Civil War, forty-eight hurricanes lashed the coast of Georgia, sank hundreds of ships in the shipping lanes off its coast, and killed thousands who lived on remote plantations in the low country of Georgia and South Carolina. More African Americans than whites died because slaves had only flimsy structures to protect them from vicious winds and overwashing tidal surges. Following each storm there were fewer members of the elite planter class who could handle the risk catastrophic storms presented, and the class disparity grew ever wider.[7] Even as the Civil War approached, the plantation economy was on the decline. Competition from other parts of the world and the hostile low-country weather continued to drag it down.[8]

When the system of slave labor ended, the plantation system fell apart. The lack of capital in the defeated South created opportunities for the northern industrialists of the late nineteenth century. Without the slave system, the coast and barrier islands had little to contribute to the generation of wealth, becoming bargain opportunities for industrialists who had acquired amazing wealth during the Gilded Age and the first decades of the new century. They used their extreme wealth not only to build family island retreats away from the urban hustle of the industrial heartland and the financial capitals of the country but also to buy the land and extract its natural resources.

Although investment capital within the state and its economy was wrecked, Georgia did still have a major natural resource—an abundance of longleaf pine virgin forests. This slow-growing, deeply rooted, fire-resistant, hard-pine species had for centuries dominated the landscape of the coastal plain from southern Virginia to the edges of Texas. Forests of the coastal plain covered 90 million acres, of which the longleaf pine occupied 57 million.[9] This species of pine could live for hundreds of years, and its unique characteristics had been the keystone in the complex habitat that had served well the interests of Native Americans. Booming northern cities needed wood to build, and timber companies connected to Wall Street financiers were capable of an industrial-scale leveling of the forests that historian Mart Stewart called a "harvesting binge." Land and timber rights were cheap.

The new steam technology of the Industrial Age was available for a mass production system created by the new timber capitalists. Trees, hundreds of years old, fell like matchsticks to teams of sawmen and floated down the Savannah, Altamaha, Satilla, and St. Marys Rivers or rode specially built steam-powered trains to sawmills in Darien and St. Simons, where they were shipped as lumber to feed the maw of an urban construction boom in the North and even around the world. Carnegie Steel had shown Wall Street financiers the profits that can come from vertical integration of an industry. This industrial-level harvesting worked with amazing efficiency.

One traveler who had admired the massive trees in the 1870s returned in 1885 and was shocked. "Those grand forests—where are they? The trees, the grass, the cabins—where are they? Gone!"[10] The trees had moved, according to historian Albert Way. He celebrates the contribution longleaf timber made to the growth of U.S. cities and also recognizes the destruction the harvest left behind. He points out that "heart pine is revered for its strength and beauty, and the Brooklyn Bridge is a cultural, technological and economic symbol of greatness. But the stumps remaining in Georgia's coastal plain are ruins, symbolic of the destruction we have inflicted in producing those cultural gems."[11]

Like Oglethorpe and the Georgia trustees, the timber capitalists ignored the conditions of the environment that produced the bountiful harvest. The timber capitalists had a mining or extraction business model that gave no thought to replacing trees. The longleaf pine takes forty-five years to mature, but that Wall Street–driven industry had no intention of waiting around for new growth.[12] The harvesters followed a mantra of "cut and get out," selling what was left to small farmers. At the start of the extraction binge in 1870, Georgia had 18 million acres of virgin forest. By 1920, surveyors could only find 700,000 acres, and seven years later that number was down to 350,000. Historian William Boyd says that when the harvest was over "the South had sold off a large part of its natural environment and had very little to show for it." It left massive areas "denuded."[13] Gone were the trees and gone were the plant and animal habitats. The wire grass floor of the forest had supported deep biological diversity that included 192 different varieties of plants of which 122 are now endangered or threatened. Even today, the loss of the forest continues to put at risk or threaten a number of animals. The endangered animals include the gopher tortoise, the indigo snake, Bachman's sparrow, and the flatwoods salamander.[14] Restoring the longleaf forest habitat is a challenge for Georgia leaders today.

Twice during the period of the lumber capitalists and with vigorous support from the development-minded legislature, investors even attacked the Okefenokee Swamp and its surrounding forests. The state of Georgia acquired ownership of the Okefenokee when Florida joined the United States in a treaty with Spain in 1821, and the Cherokee, Creek, and Seminole nations made concessions during the following twenty years, giving the state effective control over the swamp area. State leaders supported the development of the land, which was considered "worthless." The legislature in 1890, as part of a broad sell-off of public land, completed a sale of the Okefenokee for 26½ cents per acre. The high bidders formed the Suwanee Canal Company with the goal of draining the swamp and using its rich peat soil for agriculture. They went to work digging a canal to connect the swamp to the St. Marys River. Their early efforts focused on harvesting timber. While the company had some success in extracting timber, its hand-dug excavation of a 45-foot-wide and 6-foot-deep drainage canal did not drain the swamp, nor was it useful in transporting logs. They worked hard to get through the former barrier islands that comprised the trail ridge to the east of the swamp (105 feet high in some places). After 12 miles the canal stopped just a little short of the downward slope of the sand ridge that would have connected the canal to the St. Marys River. Historians believe their failed efforts came from a lack of understanding of the ecology of the swamp on the part of both the legislative leaders and the investors.[15]

The Suwanee Canal Company closed shop in 1899, and Hebard Lumber Company took on the challenge for nearly three more decades. Hebard knew from its experience in northern forests that transportation was the critical component of the timber industry. It didn't use the old canal but committed all of its efforts to bringing the cypress and pine logs out of the swamp on temporary railroad tracks called mud lines. After nearly thirty years of intense effort, the company discontinued operation in 1927 with 40 to 60 percent of the timber still standing. The swamp didn't completely defeat the attack of the lumber capitalists, but it did show there were limits to what humans could do even with a strong will and new technology.

The company did extract 450 million board feet of lumber from the marsh, which will take the slow-growing cypress forest hundreds of years to grow replacements.[16]

The timber boom, which began in the 1870s, was not sustainable for long. By the end of the nineteenth century, most of the virgin forests were gone and the timber capitalists with them. What remained were stump fields. Land was cheap again, providing an opportunity for the men who swung the axes and guided the timber into sawmills to buy small tracts of land. The industry had paid with cash, and those who had managed to save during the boom years could buy a small subsistence farm. Like the plantation economy, African Americans had provided the muscle for the boom times, and like lower-class white foresters, some could own a small farm plot that, when cleared of stumps, provided a subsistence. There were no forest grasslands to raise cattle and the land remained demanding. As black and white workers turned to farming in the postharvest economy, the coastal plains became more racially mixed than the North Georgia uplands.[17]

The quick harvesting of the virgin forest left the state with both another hole in its economy and a change in the environment of its coastal region. The coastal industry in Darien and on St. Simons that had sprung up with the longleaf boom soon died away as new forests became harder to find.[18] The little towns that had sprung up in the boom times also withered away. With the cotton fields and the timber gone, poor farming practices of the 1930s moved the soil down the state's coastal rivers. The sediments would strengthen the marsh, but the coastal plain needed new products to offer the market.

Amid the extraction binges of the late nineteenth and early twentieth centuries, there was a glimmer of a new industry with possible lasting impact on the economy and one that was more compatible with the coastal environment. People who had prospered in the industrial expansion of the late nineteenth century had the money to invest in leisure activities. With the help of state financing in the postbellum era, private railroads and even a state-owned railway connected Georgia to the northeastern and midwestern population centers. Urban dwellers also had begun to see the need for relaxation, particularly as the belching smoke from modern industry caused a growing concern for their health. To these new sunseekers, the unpopulated

Georgia coast began to look very attractive. Railroad developers like Henry Flagler used resort hotels down the coast of Florida to improve his passenger traffic. He even tried to build a railroad to Key West. In St. Augustine he built a magnificent hotel that survives today as part of Flagler College. Georgia benefited from this rising tourism in two places: the coast and the sand hills around Thomasville.

Georgia saw the construction of a hundred thousand miles of new railroad in the 1890s, and these new tracks connected Chicago to Thomasville in Southwest Georgia. Wealthy northerners eyed the failing plantations as an opportunity to create family and business retreats. They were looking for a healthy place to relax and were interested not in the region's commodities but in the beauty nature offered. They did, however, need things to do, and hunting fit the mood of retreating urbanites. Along with the plantation's agricultural land were a few remaining stands of virgin longleaf pine around Thomasville that the timber capitalists hadn't reached. The trees stayed, as did the tenant-farming system, with the hedgerows between small plots of land acting as havens for baby quail. Leisurely hunts became part of this new resort-style plantation life. The story of how the new wealthy plantation owners stopped the march of the timber capitalists, supported scientific investigation, and preserved some of the virgin longleaf pine forest around Thomasville is beautifully told in Albert Way's book *Conserving Southern Longleaf*.[19]

Similar industrialists saw the collapse of the coastal plantation system as an opportunity to own their own island and build similar retreats isolated from the pressures of new urban life. With the complete collapse of rice production after the Civil War, newly rich captains of industry bought the underutilized islands for a song. For the middle-income beneficiaries of the new wealth there were opportunities to "take the salts" on the Georgia coast. In 1887 a railroad came from Savannah to fragile Tybee Island and hotels and cottages followed. Tybee Island saw its first hotel go up in 1889.

Early investor George Parsons bought Wassaw Island. In 1866, on his honeymoon in Savannah, he dropped the deed to the nearby 10,000-acre barrier island in his new wife's lap. His heirs would later fight to preserve the island, which may have been the least altered by humans of any of the fourteen islands.[20]

The names of the new island owners read like a list of the nation's most successful industrialists of the era. A small group of the most famous formed the Jekyll Island Club in 1886, called by *Munsey's* magazine "the richest, the most exclusive, the most inaccessible club in the world." The club controlled most of that island until 1942. The early members of the club were J. P. Morgan, William Vanderbilt, Joseph Pulitzer, William Rockefeller, Edwin Gould, and Frank Henry Goodyear. Having purchased a plantation on the Ogeechee River just south of Savannah, Henry Ford took a special interest in the use of his land to provide jobs compatible with the fragile environment. Other wealthy investors in the coast included John Wanamaker (Ossabaw Island), Edwin J. Noble of the Life Savers Co. (St. Catherines Island), Pierre Lorillard (a part of Jekyll Island), Robert C. Roebling, builder of the Brooklyn Bridge (Skidaway Island), Howard Coffin of the Hudson Motor Car Company (Sapelo, Sea Island, and St. Simons), and Asa Candler II of Coca-Cola (the northern end of Cumberland Island).[21] Philip Berolzheimer bought Little St. Simons Island in 1908, because he believed the cedar wood on the island was perfect for manufacturing his pencils, but when he saw the beauty of the island he couldn't bring himself to cut it, instead using it as a family retreat like other wealthy owners.[22]

Perhaps the most significant purchase, and the one most directly tied to the Georgia decision to protect the coast, was the purchase in 1881 of three-fourths of the largest barrier island, Cumberland, by Thomas M. Carnegie, brother and partner of steel magnate Andrew Carnegie. Although the long and somewhat complicated history of each of these islands is outside the purview of this book, owners' concern about the future use of their treasured island retreats became integral to the Coastal Marshlands Protection Act. The preservation of Cumberland and the preservation of the state's marshlands were tied closely together in the politics of the late 1960s. Lucy Carnegie, Thomas's wife, was a powerful defender of the island she had come to love. Her will created a trust for all her living children, preventing any sale of any parcel without the approval of all of the other trustees. She died in 1916, but the trust remained in effect until her last remaining daughter, Florence Perkins, died in 1962.[23]

Howard Coffin, the principal stockholder in the Hudson Motor Car Company, bought Sapelo Island, Sea Island, St. Simons Island, and other marsh islands around Brunswick beginning in 1912. These purchases controlled most of the upland in the Altamaha Delta. While he primarily used Sapelo as a retreat, Coffin, like some other wealthy owners, tried to make a little of his investment back by raising cattle. He also started a commercial oyster canning business with the dual hope of making money and creating useful work for local residents. The oyster industry worked for a while until poachers found the beds he had seeded and beat his workers to the harvest. Coffin could not find an economical way to guard the beds over thousands of acres of marsh rivers and estuaries. It is not clear if the poachers believed they had a right to the oysters growing in the marsh commons, but Coffin and his nephew William (Bill) Jones took more seriously the tourism opportunities of their vast tracts. They attracted travelers seeking relaxation who did not have the resources to buy their own island but were delighted to stay at the Coffin-Jones's "friendly little hotel" that opened on Sea Island in 1928. Persons with more fame and fortune, including President Calvin Coolidge, were willing to come to his rustic, but well-appointed, Cabin Bluff hunting lodge and reserve. The lodge was on the Cumberland River and looked across the marsh into the middle of Cumberland Island. Unfortunately for Coffin, his other investments took a huge dive with the stock market crash of 1929 and the subsequent Great Depression. One consequence was the sale of Sapelo Island to R. J. Reynolds II. Coffin did not live to see the results of his new tourism adventures, which prospered under his nephew when the cloud of the Depression lifted during World War II. These early investments in tourism give evidence of a different economic future for the coast, but this would eventually require the state to first make some difficult choices.

Following World War II, a bigger industry with lots of Yankee capital again turned its full attention to southern trees. This time the trees that caught their eye were not the slow-growing longleaf but the slash pine and loblolly pine. The new industry, interested in paper and paper products, was ready to shift capital away from the declining harvests of the Northeast and the Midwest, and as always the South was seeking new capital. The industry wanted cheap land, cheap labor, a nearly free but abundant supply of water, and a local environment that could assimilate the waste products of massive manufacturing plants. It was clearly a plus that the investors did not have to worry about a heavy regulatory environment in the South. One of the most important resources in papermaking is water, and coastal Georgia was the beneficiary of one of the most prolific groundwater supplies in the world. The Floridan aquifer covers a hundred thousand square miles over all of Florida and parts of Georgia, Alabama, and South Carolina and once flowed off the Georgia coast out into the Atlantic Ocean. But that was before the pulp and paper industry added its economic muscle to the state's booming postwar economy.[24]

The pulp and paper industry began its expansion into the Depression-racked South in the mid-1930s. University of Georgia scientist Charles Herty had solved the technical problems of making paper from the soft, fast-growing pine trees that thrived in sandy Georgia soil. Between 1935 and 1940 fifteen new plants opened; the largest, opened in 1936, was owned by Union Bag and Paper Company (later Union Camp) in Savannah. In fact, for a time in the 1940s, this plant was the largest producer of craft paper in the world. It produced a fifth of all the paper bags used in the United States, and by the 1950s the South was producing 55 percent of all the wood pulp manufactured in the country. The industry drew heavily from the Floridan aquifer. In the first year of the Union Bag plant operation it was pumping between 2 and 5 million gallons per day. The next year it was 7 million. In 1942 it was 18 million. In 1955 it was 26 million. When in 1970 it reached 78 million gallons a day, the water levels of the aquifer in Savannah were 125 feet below sea level. By then the aquifer was no longer discharging water into the ocean, and there was some evidence that water *from* the sea was beginning to flow into the cone of depression under Savannah and Brunswick. One of the fears of permitting mining operations on the coast was that saltwater incursion might destroy the value of the aquifer if the mining operation pierced the confining clay and rock protecting the sweet water. While the science of hydrology was not as advanced in 1970 as the science of the marsh, it was beginning to catch up. In future decades scientists would become more capable of advising Georgia decision makers on the dangers facing the state's groundwater supply.[25]

Boyd argues that pulp and paper production industrialized the South and in so doing changed its society and economy in a way very different from that resulting from the "cut-and-get-out" approach of the earlier timber capitalists. It combined nature and technology in new ways that had both good and bad consequences for the region. It "industrialized nature," he says. In order to feed the ravenous appetite for wood fiber of the massive mills along the coast of Georgia and South Carolina, nature had to be organized to produce a twenty-four-hour supply of trees. Most of the land was in the hands of small owners, but long-term contracts enticed them to produce the kinds of trees the industry needed and at the time the mill would need them. The industry prescribed fast-growing pines planted in straight rows, 6 feet apart, to meet a coordinated harvesting system not unlike cotton. However, this agricultural approach to forestry allowed "more timber to grow faster on less land." The trees replaced cotton as the South's cash crop. Land not good for cotton was usually very good for trees. The mills also relied on the local environment to absorb or assimilate effluent from the mills with large quantities of biological material. The pulp and paper industry, according to Boyd, was "harnessing nature as a productive force," subordinating the environment to the "dictates of industrial production."[26]

However, the paper plants threatened the coast's drinking water supply, and the tree farms were a threat to the forest biodiversity. Naturalist writer Janisse Ray describes how "the limbs and needles, the overcrowded pines drank up every inch of sky." The dense overstory allowed insufficient sunlight to sustain a wire grass habitat. The biological diversity of a longleaf pine forest gave way to a monospecies forest with few plants and animals thriving on the forest floor. Also, as with the harvesting of the longleaf virgin forest of the late nineteenth century, the clear-cut harvesting of the new industry ignored plant life that did not feed the paper mill and the flora and fauna that inhabited the earlier forest community. Ray, out of her intimate rural religion, declares that "God doesn't like a clearcut. It makes his heart turn cold, makes him wince and wonder what went wrong with his creation, and sets him to thinking about what spoils a child." A worker, she says, better be mumbling a prayer if the job he does to feed his family requires him to mow down the pine rows.[27]

Despite the loss of biodiversity and endangerment of species, Boyd credits the industrial tree farms for stabilizing land that was being destroyed by the cotton farming techniques and financing systems of the 1930s. However, the millions of acres of trees now planted in neat rows don't *vastly* improve the quality of the land, he says.

Boyd's work fits with other environmental historians who have in recent years examined closely the human impact on nature. While acknowledging the problems industry has in dealing with the waste from its plants, he agrees with Patrick Allitt, who believes a fix for environmental issues can come from the capital created by industrial development.[28] While the content of the waste continues to be a cause for concern today, both Boyd and Allitt are optimistic that industrial wealth can provide the financial resources needed to correct the damage they may have done to the natural environment.

When test wells of the Georgia Institute of Technology and those of mining companies discovered a commercial supply of phosphate below the waving marsh grass, there would be a rush to dig it up. The find, ready for digging, looked like the next natural resource that would provide wealth and jobs. The Kerr-McGee company wanted the right to extract the wealth. This 1968 phosphate find forced the state government to decide once more how it would use the natural resources of its coastal environment. To this point in its history, the state had gone along with almost every scheme offered to turn the land into wealth. The capacity of the natural environment had received little consideration by Oglethorpe's trustees, the rice and cotton producers, the timber harvesters, or the paper manufacturers. But at this point in time, some Georgians saw a different future for their coast, and the opposition to the extraction was able to tap a new level of environmental understanding.

Chapter 2

Of Archdruids, Conservationists, and Developers

Our job . . . is to prevent the lush orb known as Earth . . .
from turning into a bleak and barren, dirty brown land.

—SEN. BARRY GOLDWATER

Fast-forward. In the early months of 1969 an unusual three-way conversation took place on Cumberland Island. This conversation provides a unique and real-time opportunity to introduce the arguments that became an important part of the decisions the state had to make. The participants, David Brower, Charles Fraser, and Sam Candler, are not a complete match for all of the arguments that would arise, but they do reflect different perceptions of the environmental movement.

In the 1960s, challenges for the coastal environment were growing on several fronts. The islands were attracting people of all ages seeking beauty, tranquility, recreation, health, and well-being. More people were living on the coast, vacationing on the coast, and fishing its waters. Between 1950 and 1970 the population in the six coastal counties increased from 208,000 to 281,000.[1] Voicing concern, some predicted the population would double again in the next twenty years.

It was a time when the post–World War II industrial expansion, and the affluence that came with it, broadened the opportunities of the U.S. middle class to enjoy a higher standard of living that included vacationing. But the urban industrial expansion frightened many defenders of the natural environment. Affluent urban centers pushed by the postwar demand for housing were rapidly expanding onto farmlands and forests, showing that the muscle of a new economy had few barriers. Inevitably it would threaten the natural environment of coastal Georgia.

Although a national tide of new environmentalism had been quietly building throughout the turbulent sixties, it had not yet significantly touched Georgia. At the national level Congress had responded with the first Clean Water Act in 1963, the Wilderness Act in 1964, the Freedom of Information Act in 1964, and another Clean Water Act in 1966. One Georgia historian described this last act as a "newer more comprehensive environmentalism."[2] But federal involvement in environmental concerns was a very light touch when compared to what was to come from Congress in the 1970s.

In the late 1960s Georgians had to make a decision that would determine the future of their coast. Would they support the extraction of mineral resources that were under the marsh mud built up over the centuries? Would the state use its rivers and marshlands to help create new and expanding industries that needed to dispose of by-products in its waters? Would it follow the example of its coastal neighbors by enhancing opportunities to develop its barrier islands? Or would it use the coast to entice the growing number of vacationers to exit 1-95 before they reached the Florida line? The decision would thrust Georgia into the center of the environmental issue.

David Brower, Charles Fraser, and Sam Candler spent some hours over the course of three days sharing their views on future human use of Cumberland Island, one of the issues Georgia faced. Their conversations were recorded by John McPhee, staff writer for the *New Yorker*, who later published the give-and-take as part of his *Encounters with the Archdruid*. The conversations, which took place in the same year legislators in Atlanta were debating the issue, reflect the diversity of thinking regarding the use of the natural environment of the time, and the thoughts of the three participants paralleled what was playing out under the gold dome of the Georgia Capitol.

Brower, executive director of the Sierra Club, the force behind the 1964 Wilderness Act, and founder of several environmental organizations, was the titular archdruid. Fraser was the conservation-minded developer of Sea Pines Plantation on South Carolina's Hilton Head Island and the developer of Amelia Island Plantation on the most northern barrier island in Florida (just an easy paddle across the St. Johns River to Cumberland). The Georgia coast was an enticing gap between his two successful developments. Sam Candler was the grandson of the founder of the Coca-Cola Company and an early member of the Georgia Sierra Club group. Cumberland Island, the silent participant, the largest and most southern of Georgia's barrier islands (20 miles long and moving toward the Florida state line), was at that time owned by the heirs of Thomas Carnegie and Sam Candler's family. Charles Fraser had just completed the purchase of two slices of the Cumberland pie, two separate tracts equaling 3,117 acres, from two Carnegie heirs. Fraser wanted the island for a development like Sea Pines Plantation and his Florida Amelia Island Plantation. He did not need to own the whole island, but his dream required that he control its development. He was willing to share the profits on what he expected to be a huge financial success. However, he was not interested in moving forward unless he could prevent the urbanization that had taken place on Hilton Head outside his 5,000-acre development. He was an entrepreneur with conservation beliefs.

Brower was winding up seventeen years as the head of the Sierra Club, where he transformed the organization from a hiking club to a crusading army at the front edge of the environmental movement. In the presentations he gave as he crisscrossed the country, Brower narrated the six days of creation in which man appeared at three minutes to midnight on the last day.

> At one-fourth of a second before midnight, Christ arrived. At one-fortieth of a second before midnight, the Industrial Revolution began. We are surrounded with people who think that what we have been doing for that one-fortieth of a second can go on indefinitely. They are considered normal, but they are stark, raving mad.[3]

Brower, described by colleagues as the Isaiah of the environmental movement, was fond of pointing out in his speeches that, just in his lifetime, "mankind consumed more resources than in all previous human history."[4] In this respect his views followed best sellers of the day like Paul Ehrlich's *The Population Bomb* (1968) and Dennis and Donella Meadows's *Limits of Growth* (1972), which carried a popular message that the growth in population would outstrip the resources of the earth and cause irreparable environmental damage.[5]

Fraser, who claims a Georgia genealogy reaching back to the earliest colonials, turned the timberland his family owned on Hilton Head into what he believed was a conservation-minded development. After graduating from the University of Georgia, he focused on coastal development while seeking his degree from Yale Law School. He wanted development to respect the environment. He drew a distinction between a conservationist, which he believed he was, and a preservationist, who he said worshipped trees and sacrificed human beings to those trees. The preservationists, like Brower, were "modern druids." They "worship trees and sacrifice human beings to those trees. They want to save things they like, all for themselves." He recognized the findings of marsh scientists and their identification of the importance of the marsh as a necessary feeding ground for sea life and was willing to commit to saving 75 percent of the marsh surrounding his development. He split from preservationists when he proposed a balance between preserving the environment and the human need for recreation and the human desire to live at the edge of the sea. Fraser believed his development on Hilton Head proved that "you can take any natural area and make it available to people while at the same time preserving its beauty."[6] He was a traditional conservationist who found his intellectual roots in the "Gospel of Efficiency" that pervaded the thinking of the Progressive Era.[7] His self-interest was clear, but he also made a powerful argument for the development-oriented inclination of Georgia politics.

Sam Candler, at age thirty-eight, had lived most of his life on Cumberland Island. Using wealth generated by his great-grandfather, Coca-Cola founder Asa Candler, Sam's father had bought 2,200 acres on the northern end of the island in 1928. Sam grew up on the island's abundant oysters and shrimp, knew where to avoid the alligators, and how to kill a diamondback rattler when it encroached on his living space. He looked forward to watching his children grow up in the same natural environment.[8]

One of the foremost environmental journalists of the time, McPhee picked through the conversation between the three to tease out the difference in their points of view. While none was a nineteenth-century industrialist, the three did represent a point of view which exemplified the public policy debate going on in the state.

Fraser's hope for the island centered on his development of his two tracts. Since people would need to stay overnight to see the stars, he would build homes, a marina, stores, a conference center, and an airport that could meet their needs. He did not say it in this conversation, but there would need to be a golf course and other recreational opportunities when the island visitors were not walking on the beach or watching nesting birds. He would keep the rest of the island in a natural state. The preservation effort, he believed, would take governmental action from either the federal or state level, because his development would force property values to rise and make it inevitable that other owners would eventually sell to new developments. He might support the creation of a national seashore just to the south of his property and use environmental easements to protect the land of other owners from development (i.e., land owned by Candler and the remaining Carnegie family heirs). In this dialogue he accommodated the owners' opposition to a causeway. He believed that the population, and the supplies they would need, could get there by air freight using a small airstrip, or an aerial tram could be built to the mainland.[9]

In this conversation, Fraser appeared to move beyond efforts to persuade the current owners. He accused the Carnegie owners and Candler of wanting to preserve the environment only for themselves. He repeatedly pointed out that there were only fourteen permanent residents on Cumberland Island, or one resident every 1.4 miles. His implicit, and often explicit charge, was that the wealthy families were elitists who wanted the coastal environment all to themselves. In the three days Fraser, Candler, Brower, and McPhee explored the island, they saw no one else on the beach and no one in the woods.[10] When Fraser made this same argument in the 1969 session, it had an appeal to many Georgia legislators.

Closely connected to fledgling conservation organizations in the state, Candler made it clear the resort characteristics of the Fraser development were not "his idea of conservation." He also resisted Fraser's charge of elitism. "I am happy to have people use the island now, if they make the effort to get over here and to enjoy it," he said.[11] For the most part, Candler was a quiet observer of the discussion between Fraser and Brower, but he did make it clear to McPhee privately how he felt about his island and his place on it.

"Changes come slowly there, and leave marks on one another," he said. "There is a blending from one era to the next. Indian mounds are there. When I am on Cumberland Island, I see the same things the Indians saw. I would like to live where the Indians lived. They were closer to the earth, a part of the environment." Fraser said that after the hurricane there were no sea oats on Cumberland. "The island teaches you the value of patience. The sea oats came back. Dunes that are washed down will return. You've got to have some places that are hard to get to. I don't think this is a selfish thought. I think it's thoughtful."[12]

On one drive that the three "conservationists" and McPhee took in 1969, they sighted the clear freshwater Whitney Lake; their views diverged about the lake. Brower found the beauty of the lake in the midst of the upland forest to be irresistible. He took the position that if destruction was natural it was just fine to let it happen. Fraser was especially proud of this spot on his land. He would, however, have to bring in bulldozers to stop the marching dune that had already killed three trees and threatened to engulf the lake. Fraser maintained that he was just stabilizing the dunes and putting the lake back to its original size. Candler mused that "there's a place for development and there's a place for nature." When Fraser asked how far back his homes should be from the beach, Candler quickly replied: "the mainland."[13]

In his role as the national druid or the biblical Isaiah of the environmental movement, Brower argued that if 90 percent of the natural environment had been developed for human use the other 10 percent should be preserved in its natural state. At one point in the discussion, he said the rule should be reversed on Cumberland, 90 percent should belong to nature and only 10 percent for human use. Fraser liked this ideal as long as the 10 percent was committed to his development.[14]

Brower was at a disadvantage in the discussion because he had never been on a barrier island before. He was more comfortable in the middle of battles over pristine Rocky Mountain forests and the deep canyons cut by the Colorado River in Nevada and Arizona. He showed his lack of understanding of the coastal environment when, to Fraser's delight, he thought it reasonable that twenty thousand people could comfortably live in Fraser's Cumberland Oaks development.[15]

While the attention of the public was focused on other conflicts in an age of many conflicts, the roots of an environmental movement were sprouting. Environmental historian Adam Rome has put the causes of the fledgling environmental movement into four easily understood component parts: warnings of scientists, youth movements of the decade, middle-class women, and liberal political commentators.[16] Any list of four causes is going to be overly simplistic, but these four, like the dialogue between Brower, Candler, and Fraser, are useful for setting the scene for the beginning of the movement in Georgia. The roots of this new age in U.S. life will receive continued examination by future historians who, because of their own times, will look more closely at the human relationship with the natural environment.

Environmental movements learned many lessons from the civil rights movements of the decade. Perhaps the most important is the grassroots nature of any broad-based effort to make change in a democratic society. National leadership and national organizations focused attention on profoundly important federal legislation, but for some the power for meaningful change rested at the local level of society.[17] Studies of grassroots environmental movements echo the point that multiple local protests, focused on parks, roads, strip mines, and mountain wilderness, were critical to efforts to create "profound social change."[18] As the environmental movement matured at the end of the twentieth century, advocates sometimes split between those at the grassroots who fought for access to the "commons" and those who had more pure wilderness experience as their goal. It is clear, however, these divides disappeared when the battle lines were drawn between "industrialists" and those who broadly sought the preservation of the natural environment.[19] There are the continuing questions of whether the strength of the participatory democracy that swelled in the late decades of the twentieth century will maintain its strength as time marches forward, and whether the environmental movement will keep its base in grassroots activism.

Perhaps the most important root of the environmental awakening of the 1960s was science; that is certainly true of its arising in Georgia. The voice of scientists, warning of the damage to the natural environment, had a vital influence on the national movement. It was Georgia scientists who were ready with hard facts when the political leadership of the state turned its attention to the future of its coast.

Rachel Carson's scientific exposé on DDT in *Silent Spring* of 1962 was a sharp warning that chemicals spread into the environment had lasting effects in unexpected places and species. The book was a broader warning that human science, technology, and industrial expansion of the new economy had the power to profoundly and permanently alter the natural environment. In 1962 she gave the world a broad warning about the pollution coming from expanding industrialization:

> During the past quarter of century this power has not only increased to one of disturbing magnitude but it has changed in character. The most alarming of all man's assaults upon the environment is the contamination of air, earth, rivers, and sea with dangerous and even lethal materials. This pollution is for the most part irrecoverable; the chain of evil it initiates not only in the world that must support life but in living tissues is for the most part irreversible.[20]

Not only did the book's influence reach deep into the public consciousness, but it also challenged scientists to emerge from their labs to bring their science to bear on the issues of the day. The tide of opinion the book created would not let ecologists remain aloof from the public debate.[21]

In addition to her clarion call to arms, Carson set a high standard for research focused on the environment. Behind *Silent Spring* was deep biological research that Carson had published over her long career, which allowed the book to withstand the attacks leveled at it. Her commitment to a scientific standard of evidence is recognized today as central to the "ways environmental arguments have been constructed. It is now essential that environmental policy be evidence based."[22]

It is also important to understand that scientists and engineers had the respect and the attention of the public because Americans were racing to put a man on the moon. At the end of 1968 the astronauts of the Apollo 8 mission snapped an unexpected picture of the beautiful green and blue earth rising over the stark landscape of the moon. The public marveled over the scientific achievement but also saw the earth as the only place where humankind was able to live.

Georgia scientists were making a contribution to an expanding understanding of the fragile nature of the environment. The Georgia marshlands were the subject of a huge surge in scientific investigation coming out of the University of Georgia Zoology Department and the scientific research at its marine institute on Sapelo Island. In 1948 Eugene Odum and fellow scientist Don Scott met Richard J. Reynolds II, island owner and heir to the tobacco fortune built by his father, on a bird-watching expedition. With Reynolds's full enthusiasm and financial support, the University of Georgia Marine Institute (UGAMI) was founded in 1953. Reynolds paid for the best scientific equipment and installed it in his old dairy barn.[23] In a short time, the original results from the institute scientists grabbed the attention of the scientific community from around the world by proving that the marsh was critical to the abundant sea life along the coast.[24] While it is not entirely clear which scientist, Odum or John Teal, first concluded that the marsh produced more nutrients than it consumed, this scientific conclusion proved the value of the marsh. With each tidal cycle the marsh made a contribution to the ocean. Teal presented his findings at the 1958 institute-sponsored first international Salt Marsh Conference, declaring that half the production of the marsh and its estuaries was swept out to sea and was responsible for the food chain that sustained marine life. From Odum's own research and the work of his graduate students would come the knowledge that the marshes were producing a large amount of nutritious detritus and "outwelling," which Odum first articulated in 1968.[25]

Odum's call for the protection of Georgia's coastal environment was especially powerful at the time the state was making its decision. Indeed, he was one on a short list of scientists given credit for leading the nation's environmental movement. Donald Worster, who authored one of the early intellectual histories of the movement, *Nature's Economy*, recognized Odum's fame when he listed the intellectual leaders of the movement as Rachel Carson, Berry Commoner, Eugene Odum, and Paul Ehrlich.[26] With his brother Howard, Odum had published the first college textbook on ecology, *Fundamentals of Ecology* (1953), in which he supported the broad theory that ecosystems would find stability and remain stable and predictable if humans left them alone. Our interference with ecosystems would upset the balance and damage the natural environment. His theory dominated scientific thinking in the field until the late 1980s.[27] It was a voice of high authority when heard in the halls of the Georgia Capitol. Georgians of all political persuasions were proud of their university and inclined to listen to its leading scientist.

The thoughts of two Harvard social scientists, John Kenneth Galbraith and Arthur Schlesinger Jr., helped political leaders take an active interest in the environmental movement. They took liberal thought beyond the economic security issues of the New Deal and focused attention and government action on the "quality of life." Their newly formulated goals helped build the intellectual foundation of environmentalism. They theorized that prosperity, which resulted in new suburban homes, new time-saving appliances, and new automobiles, should also produce public goods that affluent families could enjoy. They called for government to produce clean and beautiful roads, schools, universities, parks, forests, rivers, and neighborhoods that enhanced the quality of U.S. life. This liberal argument fostered the growth of the bipartisan environmental movement that prompted action from Kennedy and Johnson but also carried over into the Nixon administration. In the 1970s, quality of life was a goal that crossed liberal and conservative lines, and still can be the foundation of bipartisan policy action today. Policies and programs that fostered quality of life in the new age of affluence struck a positive cord with the public. Politicians began to see they could move votes with environmental proposals.[28] While the battles over the constitutional rights of African Americans in Georgia and the South required most of the political energy, there were efforts, largely unnoticed, to improve the quality of life and the effectiveness of governmental services. It wasn't just northern liberals; southerners also cared about the quality of life.

Women searched for new roles and meaningful work in the 1960s. An educated generation of women, who were not yet fully engaged in the workforce, sought ways to make meaningful contributions. Many followed the national agenda to improve the quality of life and became fully committed to efforts to improve their communities. Improvements to the neighborhood park, and the neighborhood school that served their children, were largely left to mothers. Women who had busied themselves in the garden club were ripe recruits for an environmental movement, and many were available to lead. Jane Yarn brought women into the Garden Club of Georgia with programs, studying conservation rather than flower arranging. When they were called on to make a difference, they deluged the Capitol with letters.[29]

The 1960s was also a time when the nation's youths challenged the established order. From 1960 on, students were the shock troops of the civil rights movement. While the leaders of the NAACP and Martin Luther King's Southern Christian Leadership Conference provided the focus for demands for change, it was the youths of the Student Non-Violent Coordinating Committee who directly challenged the barriers to equality in the country. When Cold War warriors of the older generation sent young men to Vietnam, the youths who stayed behind organized massive resistance to the war.

Earth Day, April 23, 1970, was the coming-out party for the new environmental movement. Across the country, an estimated 20 million people participated in grassroots organized events at 1,500 universities, 10,000 schools, and numerous community-focused projects. Georgia's experience with Earth Day reflected the moderate nature of the student leadership and the conservative nature of the state's political environment. The organizers of the University of Georgia events worked hard to keep radical voices away from the mic.[30] When environmental organizations expanded their membership dramatically and grassroots movements sprang up across the country, there were only a few federal environmental laws on the books and even fewer state laws. When strip mining threatened Georgia's marshes, state officials led the fight with a little support coming from their colleagues in federal agencies. Most federal legislation regulating use of the environment did not pass Congress until the 1970s. One of the earliest reforms of the governmental process, the Freedom of Information Act (FOIA, 1964), came from the tenacious effort of David Brower of the Sierra Club. This legislation became a core tool in all the social reform movements of the decade—a clarion call for greater governmental transparency and participatory democracy. Federal legislation transformed the environmental movement because the new laws gave organizations access to the regulatory decisions through the right to obtain information (FOIA), the requirement for agencies to review the environmental impacts, the right to notice, the right to participate in a public hearing, and the right to intervene through the courts. The environmental movement of the seventies morphed into an environmental regulatory movement, with organizations exercising their rights to shape national policy and win battles at the local level.[31] But these federal tools were not available when Georgia faced the question of how to use the marsh.

Important stirring occurred at the federal level. President Johnson used his executive authority to create some small agencies to gather information that could describe what was happening to the environment. He had made environmental quality a part of his Great Society program and Lady Bird Johnson had pushed for the beautification of the federal highway system, but in 1968 legislation was limited to the Open Records Act and the 1966 Water Quality Act. It was President Richard Nixon, winning the office by a small margin in 1968, who expanded the federal government's powers and control of the national effort to improve the quality of the environment. Nixon used his executive power to create two environmental giants: the Environmental Protection Agency (EPA) and the National Oceanographic and Atmospheric Administration (NOAA). The federal legislation initiatives that started with Nixon drew the attention of the Congress throughout the 1970s. What surprises many people who are active in politics today is that most of the seminal environmental legislation passed the Congress with large bipartisan majorities.[32]

1970   Environmental Protection Agency—created by executive order
1970   National Environmental Policy Act—required impact studies
1972   Clean Water Act—required a permit to disturb the marshlands
1973   Endangered Species Act
1976   National Forest Management Act
1976   Federal Land Policy and Management Act
1977   Surface Mine Control and Reclamation Act
1980   Comprehensive Environmental Response, Compensation,
        and Liability Act[33]

Again, none of these federal agencies and tools were available when Georgia citizens mounted their defense of the marshes. None of the three men in the 1969 conversation on Cumberland Island could know that both Democrats and Republicans would significantly move the whole country forward on its environmental concerns. They likely did not think in partisan terms because party affiliation in the Georgia legislature mattered little when only twenty-six House members were Republicans. The three men did know there were two points of view under the umbrella of a growing environmentalism. One was defined by the conservation efforts of Theodore Roosevelt and Gifford Pinchot during the first decade of the twentieth century. In this Progressive Era, Republican and Democratic presidents and many reform-minded members of Congress from both parties looked for ways to improve the efficiency of the country. Pinchot, who led the National Forest Service, sought to eliminate the wasteful harvesting of the timber capitalists of the last century. The reformers recognized the everyone-for-themselves attitude led to wasteful systems of production, the prime example being the indiscriminate harvest of the nation's forests. Lack of regulation hindered productivity and damaged the land. Through scientific methods they believed government regulation of the country's forests could make them more productive. The era was known for the Gospel of Efficiency, and its leaders both Democratic and Republican did not shrink from government regulation.[34]

The other voices within environmentalism were preservationists. John Muir and others believed the "wisest use of nature was often little or no use at all." They "emphasized the recreational, aesthetic, and spiritual use of public land over an economic one."[35] They had a strong ally in Teddy Roosevelt, who loved the wilderness, and used his authority to set aside more acreage for national parks.

In the 1969 Cumberland dialogue, Fraser held up the conservation side of the argument. While recreation was not critical to progressives searching for efficiency, the early environmentalists were for the wise use of the land. Fraser was looking for a way to allow a new generation of tourists to enjoy the natural beauty of Cumberland Island. People had to get there and have a nice place to stay while they enjoyed nature. On the other hand, Sam Candler fit the preservationist model: people were welcome to enjoy his island, but they had to be willing to make the effort to get there.

Candler would have found a compatriot in Barry Goldwater's affinity for nature. Goldwater did not understand the Reagan administration's attempted reversal of the environmental regulations of the 1970s. Defeated for president in 1964, he was back in the U.S. Senate in 1969, where he fully supported Nixon's environmental program. Goldwater's political career had started with the publication of books of his nature photographs, and he gained statewide attention from a film he produced on a forty-one-day trip down the Colorado River. In the "Saving the Earth" chapter of his 1969 conservative manifesto, *Conscience of a Conservative*, a guidepost for the nation's conservative movement, he said that "our job . . . is to prevent the lush orb known as Earth . . . from turning into a bleak and barren, dirty brown land." Goldwater supported the federal government's efforts to clean up the environment and sponsored federal legislation to preserve new wilderness areas. Enlightened by his experiences in the wilderness of the west, he found common ground with Sam Candler when he wrote that "there are parts of the state of mine that should be kept for people who don't mind working to see the beauty."[36]

But neither Candler, Brower, Fraser, nor Senator Goldwater would have recognized the partisan divide that has plagued environmental politics since the 1980s. Nor could they have anticipated in 1969 the conservative free-market approach to the environmental concerns today. Historians in recent years have begun to highlight the environmental arguments that emerged from supply-side economics and free-market views of the Chicago school of economic thought advanced by Milton Friedman and others. In their defense of the "invisible hand" of a free marketplace, these economists spawned new approaches for environmental concerns. Environmentalists within the Republican political orbit looked for private-sector solutions to environmental concerns. Critics had seen some of the negative effects of federal agency control over forests, water, and land in the west and found evidence that government management led to a degraded environment. They theorized that private owners "with the right incentives" would more effectively preserve nature. Glimmers of this divide are visible in the Georgia debate over the use of its natural resources.

However, when mining threatened the marshes off Savannah in 1968, advocates had little confidence that a free-market company like Kerr-McGee was likely to become a protector of the Georgia coast. There was also little precedent and little confidence federal agencies would "save the marsh." For Georgia citizens and their leaders the marsh was a part of their sense of place. They put this local issue before their local elected officials, expecting them to do the right thing. If the marshes were going to be saved, it was up to Georgians.

There was, however, a strong flavor of the free-market environmentalist argument in the efforts to save the barrier islands from development.[37] These islands were private property, and the owners' hopes for preservation were rooted deeply in a foundation of state politics that ownership brought rights. Island owners had hunkered down deep in their land, becoming critical in the fight to preserve the nature they had learned to love. Georgia citizens had a simple idea: they wanted to save the marsh. They didn't worry much about the broad ideologies that have often split the leaders and their followers today.

Chapter 3

The Election of 1966

A free society and a democratic republic can best be preserved by the separation
of power among the legislative, judicial and executive branches of government.

—STATE REP. ROY LAMBERT

Peter Zack Geer rapped the assembled legislators to order at 9:30 on the
morning of January 10, 1967. It was an unusual meeting of the Georgia General Assembly. Senators and representatives were meeting jointly for the purpose of choosing the next governor of the state. Two candidates had survived
the primary, the primary runoff, and the general election. But neither had
received a majority of the votes.

The first task of the day was to open the returns for each of the 159 counties in order to publicly and officially tally the votes. To add to the strange-
ness of circumstances, the newly elected Speaker of the House assisted with
the task. It was rare to elect a Speaker before there was a governor. In fact,
the governors of Georgia for many decades had "helped" choose the leadership of the House and kept very close tabs on the body's daily activities. If
the governor did not like what he heard from the monitor in his office, he
would send a messenger to the Speaker with instructions. But the election
of George L. Smith as Speaker on the previous day amounted to a political
coup, organized by a small group of legislators before they knew they would
also be in charge of selecting the next governor. In light of the immense decision on that day, the creation of an independent House did not get the
attention it deserved.

With George L. Smith as Speaker, George T. Smith (it's important to
remember the difference between L and T) had no direct role to play in the
day's activities. He won the general election for lieutenant governor without

a runoff and would preside over the Senate for the next four years, but his official vote count would come after the count for governor was completed.

Emerging from a lengthy period of factious politics, Georgia was beginning to adjust its governmental and political structures to the social changes dictated by new constitutional mandates. From the 1930s, the divide between the Talmadge and the anti-Talmadge factions within the Democratic Party had dominated the election of governors. The demolition of discriminatory practices under Georgia law was beginning to take effect in everyday life. Many of the Jim Crow laws still lurked in the unused pages of the Georgia Code. Feelings stemming from the lengthy history of racial injustice could still catch fire to dominate political dialogue. While by 1966 it was clear the state would not sacrifice the existence of public education on the high altar of segregation, the feeling of resistance still ran deep among white voters.

From his second-floor office, then Governor Carl Sanders monitored the vote count as it droned on throughout the day. His four years of long days were almost over. Elected in 1962, Sanders had been one of the most active governors in recent times. He had led a reform effort intended to modernize the state's system of government and was a pivotal figure in the state's effort to adjust its policies, programs, and political structure to the earthquake that flowed down from the U.S. Supreme Court and the civil rights legislation that swept through Congress at the apex of liberal political change. He was not a liberal but managed the state in liberal times. In later years, he summarized his message in the 1962 campaign: "We are not going to tear up the educational institutions. We're not going to destroy progress in Georgia. We're going to try to moderate our position and try to preserve our state and protect everybody in this State and not allow the federal government to take us over." Sanders thought of himself as a progressive. To him, that meant you wanted to make improvements in the efficiency and effectiveness of the government.[1] In his inaugural speech he said "we revere the past. We adhere to the values of respectability and responsibility which constitute our tradition." However, he also embraced the need for movement: "change to achieve efficiency, economy and better government is both wise and justified." He would walk the line between change and traditional values.[2] According to his biographer, James Cook, Sanders maintained a public position as a segregationist but he also said, "I'm not a damned fool." He became the voice of reason that quelled the diehard leaders of full-throated resistance.[3]

Before he piloted B-17 bombers in World War II, Sanders attended the University of Georgia on a football scholarship. He returned to UGA after the war and earned his law degree. Sanders, a tall, handsome, established lawyer, was only thirty-seven when he was elected governor in 1962. Legislative efforts during four years in the Georgia House of Representatives and his four years in the Senate had earned him a leadership position as president pro tem, or second in power behind Lieutenant Governor Peter Zack Geer. The position gave him an intimate knowledge of details of the state's inner workings. Practicing law in Augusta gave him a vision of how the law shaped society and a clear understanding of the decisions of the U.S. Supreme Court.

Sanders, then state senator, was center stage when the U.S. Supreme Court's decision in *Brown v. Board of Education* blew up the network of state laws that had relegated black and white people to separate institutions. The monumental decision, which made segregation laws unconstitutional, came into unyielding conflict with the state law enacted under the leadership of Governors Talmadge and Griffin, which required closing all the public schools rather than bow to accepting integration. Sanders, like some other political leaders across the South, and most southerners, looked for a way out of the policy dilemma. At the time, Sanders had six years (three terms) in the Senate, which under the county unit system usually turned over every two years. His tenure helped him get elected by the members to lead the Senate. In this leadership position, he helped create the General Assembly Committee on Schools, better known commonly as the Sibley Commission after its chair, John Sibley, which traveled the state to hold public hearings. While a narrow majority of people testifying at the ten hearings were for closing the public schools, the commission's majority report stated that the state should let local school boards decide whether to keep their schools open. It also said that no child in Georgia should be compelled to attend an integrated school.[4] On the Eggs and Issues Tour across the state (annually sponsored for the Chamber of Commerce), Sanders went further than most other state leaders, supporting the Sibley Commission and saying clearly that "public education will be preserved." House Majority Leader Frank Twitty, who gave the House view on the tour, joined Sanders on the side of keeping the schools open.[5] Neither Sanders, nor Twitty, nor Sibley, nor any other political leader with a future in the state, called for integration. Only a few sought to stir the ugly water beneath the political surface because most saw education as the foundation for future progress and the development of new jobs and new wealth. With the help of other civic and business leaders, the tide of public opinion turned enough so that Governor Ernest Vandiver, at one point a member of the Talmadge faction, declared to the General Assembly in January 1962 that "public education will be preserved."[6]

Sanders got a huge boost from another 1962 U.S. Supreme Court decision. In *Baker v. Carr*, the justices said each election district had to be apportioned on the principle of "one person, one vote." The political changes this simple standard required would stretch across Sanders's term as governor. It would take several years and three federal district orders for Georgia to fully comply and in the process created a major shift of power. In 1940, under the county unit system where votes were allotted by county, the most populous eight counties, with 30 percent of Georgia's population, held only 12 percent of the seats in the legislature. By 1960, this imbalance skewed further. These counties now held 41 percent of the population but no more seats. Rural counties however, which in 1940 had 42 percent of the population, held 60 percent of the seats in the Georgia House. By 1960, their population had dropped to 32 percent. The disproportion of urban and rural voters only increased as more Georgians moved to the cities during the post–World War II decades of economic growth.[7] Although the simple standard would not be fully in place until the 1968 election, it was easy for the court to see how it applied to a statewide race for governor.

Almost immediately following the Supreme Court decision, civil rights lawyers filed *Gray v. Sanders* in the Atlanta federal district court to void the use of the county unit system in the election of the governor. As a leader of the Senate, Carl Sanders (no relation to James O'Hear Sanders, the plaintiff) worked hard in the 1962 session to find a compromise that would save the old system. The final result of the highly contentious debate reduced the disparity between a vote in Fulton County, the state's largest, and a vote in

Echols County, the smallest. Just one day after the legislature passed its hard-fought county unit patch bill, the three-judge panel hearing *Gray v. Sanders* overturned the law. Their decision was upheld by the U.S. Supreme Court one year later.[8] Although Sanders worked to save the old political system, he was an urban candidate for governor and the change was significantly to his advantage. The change, according to Sanders, "moved the political power from the rural counties to the metropolitan areas of the state" and especially to Metro Atlanta, which was already the center of economic power.[9] The change made Sanders the leading candidate in the Democratic primary and, while he won the election even if you used the old county unit counting system, the political calculations in future statewide elections would begin to focus on urban voters. This struck a blow to the heart of the Talmadge faction, which depended on rural county unit votes.

Putting Sanders into the context of his political times requires a short review of historians seeking to explain the central character of southern politics. In his classic study, *Southern Politics in State and Nation*, V. O. Key argued in 1949 that the region's politics were dominated by four "crippling" institutions: disenfranchisement of African American citizens; disproportion of political control; the one-party system; and Jim Crow. Key hoped there was a "way out" of a southern politics heavily based on race; if African Americans were "gradually assimilated into political life, the underlying Southern liberation will undoubtedly be mightily strengthened."[10] According to Numan Bartley, who in the early 1970s took another look at the broad subject of southern politics, Key's hope for a more liberal bent to the region when its pillars were destroyed did not materialize because the issue of race rushed to the forefront. While black voting strength increased dramatically, so did white registration. In the postwar era of Key's research, there was a brief time when a New Deal political structure showed some early signs of an economic realignment based on "common class interests" and more liberal policy. Bartley, however, concluded from his analysis of election results that the "deep racial" feelings engendered by the Second Reconstruction pushed the South's politics back to its conservative roots.[11]

Most commentators agree that Sanders and his response to the issues of the day was the most productive Georgia had seen. His broad goals included improvement in the standard of living, improvement in the state's image and improvement in the efficiency of state government, and a first-rate education for every Georgian.[12] It was an optimistic time of economic growth and the improvement of public services.

Having closely followed the Sibley Commission, Sanders was skilled at using commissions to study issues and make recommendations that became the heart of his activist legislative proposals. In his second year as governor, his legislative agenda was broad and deep and yielded one of the most impressive sets of new laws the state had seen. When the session was over, the stack of bills on his desk included a plan for education, a tax bill with new revenues, congressional reapportionment, a curb on highway billboards, prison reform, and increased funding that affected all departments. Sam Hopkins, a columnist for the *Atlanta Journal and Constitution*, claimed that "never before have such far-reaching pieces of educational legislation passed the General Assembly."[13] Sanders was proud of his administrative work, which he felt improved the efficiency of each state agency, and of his appointment of highly qualified leaders for those agencies.[14] In this avalanche of legislation was a little noticed bill (HB 730) granting new powers of independent action to the Water Quality Control Board; this launched the state on a new campaign to clean its polluted rivers. With this bill a new agency committed to environmental quality was born.[15]

The four years of Carl Sanders's governorship saw the most dramatic and far-reaching changes in public policy in the postwar era, although historians have argued he fit into a pattern that spanned governors from Ellis Arnall to Jimmy Carter (1942–74) and continued for governors who followed. Gary Roberts, who brought the work of several historians together in *Georgia Governors in an Age of Change*, contends these governors all made "promises of better education, better roads, better healthcare, better farm programs." Sanders added "jobs and industry, welfare and youth programs, recreation and tourism" as the society continued to evolve.[16] While Sanders's victory over Marvin Griffin was a classic showdown between the old politics and the new, there was even within the Talmadge-Griffin faction an understanding that a new prosperous urban Georgia was emerging, and underneath the political rhetoric, government had a critical role to play. In his essay, Bartley doesn't relinquish his belief that the New Deal political vision of V. O. Key was lost in the racial storms of the 1960s, but he asserts that over time governors came to stress the role government had to play in promoting economic growth. Bartley believes a new "public ideology came to be perceived in terms of economic growth."[17]

So what took so long to count the votes on January 10, 1966? Why didn't the voters decide who would be governor? Although legislators could only choose between Howard "Bo" Callaway and Lester Maddox, some voters, following a common voter election day feeling, didn't like either choice, had cast their ballot for "some other guy." On the most critical issue of the day, dismantling the institutions of segregation, there was not a whole lot of difference between the two front-runners. Atlanta-born, balding, and bespectacled, Maddox was also popular and notorious as a result of his resistance to the 1964 Civil Rights Act, which made it unlawful to deny any person access to "places of public accommodations." Maddox's restaurant, the Pickrick Cafeteria, was the source of his self-made middle-class status, his wealth, his pride, and his confidence. He started the restaurant with all his savings from a number of low-paying jobs and worked tirelessly to meet his boyhood dream of being a businessman.[18] He cherished the personal relationships he had developed with the patrons. Georgia Institute of Technology students from the nearby campus ordered a wing and mashed potatoes from the cheap part of the menu, knowing he would likely walk through, offering to replenish their plates from a tray of fried chicken breasts.[19]

But Pickrick was just for white patrons. The U.S. Supreme Court had said his restaurant was in the "stream of commerce," and the Congress had power under the U.S. Constitution to say who could enter his business. But at his core Maddox believed he alone had the right to say which patrons could enter his private property. The day after President Johnson signed the Civil Rights Act, African American leaders of the Atlanta civil rights movement brought the classic confrontation between these two strongly held beliefs to the door of his restaurant. Maddox resisted. It was 1964, and the massive resistance that had spread across the southern states in the 1950s following *Brown* seemed to be moderating. But Maddox and the Pickrick breathed life into the wall of resistance. While Sanders led the state's accommodation to the inevitable change, Maddox resisted with a flair that caught every headline in Georgia and many across the country. That day in July 1964, he met the civil rights testers at the door, with an axe handle in one hand and waving a pistol in the air in the other. Later, he made signed axe handles available to Pickrick customers for a $2 charge. On one occasion, when the door was not manned, he called to his staff to help him physically throw African American "intruders" out of the building. Of the sixty-five employees of the restaurant, forty-five were African American, many in supervisory positions, he said. In this first confrontation, he claims, six of his "negro cooks and bakers" helped him to shove the intruders to the sidewalk in under ten seconds. They got a bonus of $20 for each expelled body.[20]

Throughout his life and political career, Maddox maintained he was not a racist—only a believer in segregation. The distinction was not clear to people at the time, and it remains even harder for people fifty years later to understand. But for Maddox, it was likely real. He grew up in a "blue collar" neighborhood near Georgia Tech where eight or ten black families lived "around the corner" and "the black children and the white children played together without strife." In his autobiography he objects to being called a racist because a "segregationist is an individual—black, white, or any other color—who has enough racial pride and racial integrity and love for his fellow human beings to want to see all races protected and preserved."[21] Bob Short, author of the most complete Maddox biography, argues that as governor he kept his promise to be the "best governor this state has ever had and I can't possibly do that by working against any group of citizens or creating special conditions for any groups."[22]

Maddox prided himself on telling the truth even if it hurt him. The best job he had, before starting his restaurant, was with Atlantic Steel, where his father had worked. Even with his tenth-grade education (he later earned a high school diploma through correspondence courses), he moved up to supervise a small program in the plant until his commitment to the truth got in the way of his economic hopes. In his 1975 autobiography, he tells of being told to fire two employees because they had been seen riding with union organizers. Although Maddox had just added a new shift, his boss instructed him to claim there was a staff reduction. He could not tell a lie for the company.

"Then say they're no good! That they're not doing the work!"
"I can't lie about them," I said flatly.

"How you do it is up to you. But get rid of those two men!" There was a pause.

"Do as I tell you, Maddox, or you won't be working here yourself, is that clear?"[23]

Maddox quit. Maddox proudly reported seeing the two men working at the plant some years later.[24] Although his autobiography doesn't indicate the race of the two men, later he said the two men were African American.[25] He had personal relationships with African Americans, but he resisted the new antidiscrimination laws and supported people who also resisted.

Maddox did not believe his campaigns for political office were about race because he distinguished between issues of race and the issue of segregation. He focused his first campaign in 1957, against long-term mayor of Atlanta William B. Hartsfield, on crime and the failure of law enforcement to root out corruption and put a stop to the pervasive illegal lottery known as the bug. But without a doubt, his campaigns injected the issue of race into the city election. For years he had run small ads for his restaurant in the *Atlanta Constitution* under the title, "PICKRICK SAYS," where he also publicized his segregationist views and called to task the advocates of integration. In the lead-up to passage of the 1964 Civil Rights Act, he picketed at both the White House and the Democratic National Convention in Atlantic City, New Jersey. In his 1957 race for mayor of Atlanta, he criticized the long-term incumbent, William B. Hartsfield, for his "liberal" views and close relationships with African American community leaders. While race was not central to the Maddox stump speech, his listeners knew where he stood and cheered loudest when race was mentioned or inferred.[26]

The Pickrick saga ended when Maddox was forced to face the reality of a $200-a-day fine; instead of paying the fine, or allowing black patrons, he chose to close Pickrick. He eventually sold his property to Georgia Tech as part of a university expansion plan.[27] But as the restaurant door closed, a long-sought political door opened. Before 1966, Maddox had already run three times for high public office—twice for mayor of Atlanta and once, in 1962, for lieutenant governor of the state. He loved being the candidate of the "little people" against the "ultra-liberal *Atlanta Constitution*" and its "establishment" backers in the Atlanta corporate community. He knew how to run a shoe-leather no-budget campaign from his "fatigued" white station wagon packed with cheaply printed posters that just read "Maddox, Maddox, Maddox" or "Maddox Country." Traveling from one speech to the next, he stopped alongside his opponents' expensive billboards and personally nailed up his signs. He had no experience in government, no support from anyone in the Democratic Party, and no one in his campaign had worked in state government or had run a political campaign.[28] Only eight members of the General Assembly endorsed him. Although he took correspondence courses in accounting and engineering, his formal education stopped in the tenth grade when his alcoholic father lost his job at Atlantic Steel and Maddox went to work full-time. According to Bob Short, who was helping Jimmy Carter run for governor in 1966, Maddox "was a blue collar kind of guy who could communicate to blue collar. That is why he won."[29] What Maddox had was name recognition as the state's symbol of the resistance, a demonstrated belief in the sanctity of private property, a reputation as a truth teller and corruption fighter, opponent of the "establishment" and "communism," and a fervent belief in the Bible as the word of God, which he could quote freely from memory.

Many observers felt that two political parties had existed side by side under the Democratic umbrella from the New Deal forward. Maddox, as the symbol of the resistance, fit the conservative faction founded by Eugene Talmadge, inherited by his son Herman, and kept in power by Marvin Griffin. Its strength was built on the county unit system that made county bosses critical to a race for governor. The other side of the party consisted of anti-Talmadge factions that coalesced around candidates for governor. These included the New Deal supporter and founder, E. D. Rivers, Ellis Arnall in the post–World War II years, and Carl Sanders. Ernest Vandiver came from the Talmadge faction but maintained independence once elected governor. He moved away from the diehard segregationists in the Talmadge camp when confronted with the reality of public school closing.[30]

Apart from the rhetoric of segregation and anticommunism, the Maddox platform was similar in tone to the goals of Sanders. Maddox committed to improvements in elementary and secondary education, the expansion of higher education, highways, mental health, penal reform, state aid to cities and counties, economic development, and improved police pay. After the election was over, even Jimmy Carter, who failed to make the runoff, recognized Maddox's written platform was more progressive than Callaway's.[31] While it is hard to look past Maddox's views and actions on segregation, his rise from urban poverty and beliefs in the American Dream made him a more complicated political figure than his axe-handle-wielding image.

Bo Callaway, formerly a Talmadge faction Democrat, brought the first serious challenge to the state's one-party system. A graduate of Georgia Institute of Technology and West Point, Callaway helped his family establish Callaway Gardens, the 2,500-acre resort, near Pine Mountain. He was an ally of Barry Goldwater and swept into the southwest Georgia congressional seat in 1964 with the anti-Johnson, anti–civil rights, anti–Great Society landslide produced by Goldwater in Georgia and four other Deep South states: South Carolina, Alabama, Mississippi, and Louisiana. In these states, the loss of eight Democratic members of Congress prompted historian Numan Bartley to conclude the election had made "a shambles of the Democrats' New Deal coalition, and one-party politics was clearly coming to an end throughout the South."[32] In his single term in the U.S. House of Representatives, Callaway followed the Goldwater agenda and voted against Medicare, an increase in the minimum wage, aid to higher education, aid to elementary and secondary education, voting rights, equal employment, protection of civil rights workers, and aid to local governments. He also introduced a constitutional amendment to eliminate the principle of "one person, one vote."[33] As the heir to the old textile manufacturing money from Callaway Mills, and with moneyed support from the state's economic and corporate interests, his campaign had all the latest get-out-the-vote techniques, professional staff, television advertising, and authoritative polling of a modern political campaign. As all leading politicians in Georgia had been since the 1950s, and like Maddox, he was committed to a segregationist path.[34]

While candidate Callaway was confirmed by a state Republican Party convention, the Democrats conducted a party primary that included former liberal governor Ellis Arnall and former moderate governor Ernest Vandiver, one-term state senator Jimmy Carter, former lieutenant governor Garland Byrd, and Comptroller General Phil Campbell, plus Hoke O'Kelly, who always ran but nobody knew. Maddox, Democratic Party chair James Gray, and Byrd appealed to the segregationists. Ellis Arnall was clearly the "progressive" with a positive track record. He shot to the top of the handicappers' list when Vandiver quit after a mild heart attack. With Vandiver out of the race, the Talmadgeites could not agree on a candidate. Carter was the relatively unknown moderate in the race and climbed steadily as he campaigned vigorously and was said to look good on the newly important medium of television. Gray and Arnall had the best financial backing and got attention through advertising.[35]

Most pundits at the time expected Ellis Arnall to head the Democratic ticket. He was the candidate V. O. Key envisioned when he speculated a New Deal–style politics would come to Georgia. Arnall was governor during and just after World War II (1942–46). As governor, he followed the lead of former governor Ed Rivers. He supported federal programs that came from the New Deal and Democratic liberals who controlled the federal government. Arnall was more in line with the leaders of the national Democratic Party than any governor since the beginning of the New Deal.[36] During his time as governor he rescued the University System of Georgia from the political interference of Eugene Talmadge, which had resulted in the loss of accreditation. He paid off the state debt, rewrote the Georgia Constitution, eliminated the poll tax in the new constitution, supported Rep. John Greer's legislation that took the hoods off members of the Klan, gave eighteen-year-olds the right to vote, and because of the pardon scandals of the Rivers administration, passed the power of pardon and parole to a new and independent state board. He personally argued successfully before the U.S. Supreme Court that higher railroad rates on southern shipping were unlawful.[37]

But the most important change had been the demise of the all-white Democratic primary, which the U.S. Supreme Court struck down in *Smith v. Allright* in 1944. That action gave the dwindling Talmadge forces a new issue. They demanded Arnall, who was governor at the time, call a special session of the General Assembly to make the primary a completely private affair. Primus King, a black minister from Columbus, filed suit to knock down the Georgia election laws and won, despite the state's appeal to the U.S. Supreme Court.[38] In addition to the long-term structural change to Georgia politics, black votes in a special election in the 5th District helped seat a liberal, Helen Douglas Mankin, in the U.S. House of Representatives. Mankin's victory sent Talmadge into a frenzy about African American participation in the electoral process, which led to his most "blatant racist campaigns."[39]

Arnall, who by 1966 headed a large successful Atlanta law firm, had the ear of the corporate community, which made him a logical successor to Carl Sanders. His elaborate campaign apparatus was well financed, but he had been out of office for nineteen years and did not come across well on television to rural and small town voters. He started out on top but lost votes to others.[40] Arnall held the left side of the political spectrum in an election where the voters were continuing to march to the right.

Maddox, James Gray, and Garland Byrd held the right. Byrd and Garland had close connections to the Talmadge faction and appealed to the virulent segregationist vote. Gray, like Maddox, had jumped ship in 1964 and supported Republican presidential candidate Barry Goldwater. But, unlike Maddox, Gray closely shadowed the Goldwater conservative platform. The three divided the traditional Talmadge faction conservative vote.[41]

Carter climbed steadily and edged out Gray for third place, but Maddox, the symbol of the "resistance," ended up in second behind Arnall. In the primary runoff, Maddox consolidated the votes of defeated conservative candidates Gray and Byrd and probably picked up most of the moderate Carter voters who would not vote for Arnall, who was Georgia's lone representative of liberalism. Republican voters, who had no primary election, followed the advice of a few GOP strategists, who mistakenly believed Maddox was the easiest target for their guy in the general election, so they cast their votes in the open Democratic primary for Maddox, who won the primary runoff with 54 percent of the vote.[42] Bartley saw this result as a repudiation of Georgia's fledgling progressive flirtation.

The Maddox victory stunned Carl Sanders, who saw Arnall as an extension of his progressive goals for Georgia, and it shocked most other leaders within the Democratic Party. After all, Maddox had no money (his daughter had managed the campaign from a two-room office), he had few, if any, elected officials behind him, and he had no hands-on experience with governing. Sanders, despite his shock, committed to support the Democratic nominee, while others jumped to the Callaway ship, or looked for another candidate.[43] With business community backing, a slick campaign organization, and television advertising his money could buy, most people clearly expected Callaway to become the first Republican governor of Georgia since Reconstruction.

Black and white liberal activists became the wild card in what had already been a wild election. Because civil rights leaders didn't feel they would have any place to go in the general election on November 8, 1966, they began holding mass public meetings in the style of the civil rights movement. From these grassroots meetings gradually emerged the Write In Georgia (WIG) movement. The WIG movement had no money and no ready candidate, but they were determined to find a write-in candidate. They finally settled on Ellis Arnall, who never endorsed their efforts but did not ask them to cease. Hosea Williams, lieutenant to Dr. Martin Luther King Jr., used his grassroots skills to rally voters to the cause. When they could not get clear answers from Callaway supporters on issues related to the environment, a few university professors from West Georgia, including biologist Fred Marland, became engaged in the WIG movement.[44]

Bruce Galphin, editorial writer and columnist for the *Atlanta Constitution*, described the movement as "an improbable, loosely organized, underfinanced but dedicated collection of unpaid amateurs. Pros, idealists, self-seekers, soft-voiced ladies, tough worded men, professors, civil rights workers, housewives, union officials, doctors, clergymen, secretaries, businessmen, lawyers, students, Christians and Jews, whites and Negroes—as unlikely a crew of election-wreckers as ever wrote a colorful footnote in American politics."[45] Moderate Republican advisors urged Callaway to make some minor concessions to the liberal voters seeking hope under the bleak circumstances. However, Callaway, believing his new scientific polling data, remained aloof from the little-people human issues that might have turned the small margin of votes needed to win.[46]

The *Atlanta Journal* cast its lot with Callaway. Despite the pleadings of the leaders of the Atlanta Chamber of Commerce, Eugene Patterson, editor of the *Atlanta Constitution*, did not follow. But the editorial staff said that "we are simply unable to say honestly that either of the nominees available in 1966 merits endorsement by a newspaper which deeply believes the state will be on the wrong track under the principles which both have proclaimed as the lights that guide them."[47] Many voters felt the same way.

In the end the voters on November 8, 1966, did not decide the election. When rural votes reached the Capitol the day after the election, because neither of the leading candidates had a majority of the votes, neither could claim the governor's office. The write-in votes for Ellis Arnall were enough to prevent the election of either candidate. Callaway supporters urged Governor Sanders and Attorney General Arthur Bolton to call a general election runoff and filed suit to get the Georgia Supreme Court to agree with them. But Attorney General Bolton, without direction from Sanders, defended the course laid out by the Georgia Constitution: the decision lay with the General Assembly. Maddox trusted the decision to the large Democratic majority in the General Assembly. The American Civil Liberties Union argued that because the legislature was not yet constitutionally apportioned, it could not make the decision. One suit argued that Sanders should remain as governor until the next election in 1970. The three-judge panel of the Federal District Court agreed that a new election was needed, though it preferred either an immediate new election or a runoff. The U.S. Supreme Court surprised many when it heard the case and rejected the district court's argument. Justice Hugo Black, writing for the 5–4 majority, said that the Georgia Constitution unambiguously gave the General Assembly the job of selecting the new governor in this case. In dissent, Justice William O. Douglas observed that a legislature does not comply with "one person, one vote" and therefore could not decide who would govern the state.[48] This may have been one of the few times in his life when Lester Maddox agreed with the Supreme Court.

At this point, it is important to understand how George L. Smith ended up at the Speaker's podium counting votes on January 10, 1966. His election as Speaker of the House the day before represents a significant shift in control over state policy. In essence, it put the legislature in charge of the Georgia coast.

In the middle of the hot gubernatorial campaign season, Reid Harris caught a ride back to Atlanta with Elmer George, the executive director of the Georgia Municipal Association, from an interim committee meeting that had taken place in Rome, Georgia, on September 29. Representative Harris, a Brunswick attorney nearing the end of his first term in the House, complained how the governor exercised almost total control of the House of Representatives. Elected in 1964 and reelected after the first reapportionment in 1965, Harris had seen Carl Sanders masterfully control the agenda of the General Assembly. Harris was one of a new breed of post–county unit system legislators who expected to be part of the reform of state government that would come from this seismic shift of power to the urban centers. George represented city governments that sought power to address the issues of urban growth. Harris, a real estate lawyer with a deep understanding of the separation of powers in the state's constitution, chafed under a system that diminished the independence of the legislative branch.

The governor controlled who would be elected Speaker, other officers, and who would serve on and chair the committees of the House. The Speaker assigned bills to committees with the governor's blessing and therefore could largely determine a bill's fate. Knowing the sentiment behind the story, Harris had heard the joy in Governor Sanders's voice when he often recounted the following story.

> The owner of a manufacturing plant wanted to start a program that called for the support and vote of the workers. The owner told one of his foremen to approach the workers and solicit their approval.
>
> The foreman went from man to man mostly meeting with success but when he came to Billy Johns he met solid opposition. Johns wanted no part of the plan.
>
> The foreman explained the owner really needed Johns' vote.
>
> Johns could have cared less.
>
> The foreman reported to the owner that Johns was a hold out. So the owner himself went to Johns and asked for his vote.
>
> Johns said he wasn't interested.
>
> The owner asked if Johns was interested in keeping his job.
>
> Johns allowed that he needed to keep his job and now that things had been properly explained he could sure go along with the owner's plan.[49]

Harris and everyone else in the General Assembly understood the governor was talking about them.[50] In his unpublished "Memoirs for My Grandchildren," Harris tells this story as part of his recounting of the independence movement that also preserves the correspondence of the key players.[51]

In his first act as governor, Sanders had fired the incumbent Speaker of the House, George L. Smith, over loyalty, replacing him with long-time loyalist George T. Smith.[52] He had a phone installed at George T.'s Speaker's podium for ease of communication. In the four years of his term, the General Assembly never failed to pass one of Sanders's proposed bills and it never passed one he opposed. The governor kept legislators in line because he controlled the budget and the building of highways. He had significant patronage opportunities. His biographer, James Cook, observes that "the governor ran the state."[53] Perhaps the most dramatic example Cook gives is the "discipline" Sanders applied to a future Speaker of the House, Thomas B. Murphy. Having vigorously supported Sanders in 1962, Murphy was rewarded with the chair of the Standing Committee on Hygiene and Sanitation. When he opposed one of the governor's bills on the floor of the House, he got a call to come see Sanders in his office, and was urged to "get on the team." Murphy later remarked that "it just wasn't my idea of leadership," and continued his opposition when his beliefs ran counter to the governor. Soon Murphy was no longer a chairman, and his seat in the House chamber was moved to the far corner in the back row under the balcony, where it remained for the last two years of Sanders's term.[54]

Like Harris, Murphy saw the need for change. Under the singular control of the governor, the state budget passed out of committee in thirty minutes and was considered only for another thirty minutes on the House floor. According to Murphy, "you didn't change anything in the budget. Whatever the Governor sent you, you adopted, and that was it."[55] Murphy felt the state would make more progress when more minds were engaged on the state budget, the most basic document of state government.[56]

After listening to Harris complain, George asked, "why don't you do something about it?" Harris took up the challenge and, when back in Atlanta, he called a good friend, Rep. Robin Harris of Decatur, who chaired the House Judiciary Committee on which Reid served. Robin met Reid for dinner in Atlanta, and they agreed to invite a select group to Robin's house for dinner the next evening. They invited Reps. Elliott Levitas (DeKalb), Wayne Snow (Chickamauga), and Milton Jones (Columbus). All were lawyers, all were members of the House Judiciary Committee, and all came.

These five initiators, or perhaps conspirators, were later joined by Rep. Roy Lambert of Madison, another Judiciary Committee lawyer. Using Robin Harris as the source, they issued an invitation to the Democratic members of the House to meet Sunday, October 9, 1966, at 11:00 a.m. at the Stone Mountain Inn, the day after the University of Georgia–Ole Miss

Legislative Day football game. The telegram from Robin Harris said the purpose of the meeting was to discuss "legislative independence and election of speaker." The "vast majority" of House Democrats attended the meeting and agreed on a course of action. The Democratic nominee for Speaker and Speaker Pro Tem would be decided by secret ballot in a party-only caucus. Members who participated in this election would be "honor bound" to support the winner when the official vote happened on the first day of the General Assembly. The caucus meeting was set for November 13, just five days after the November 8 general election. Nobody knew at the October meeting who would win the general election, but they expected that there would be a governor elect ready to take control, and they agreed on a quick process that gave the future governor little time to interfere in selection of the House leadership.

The organizers of the October 9 meeting felt it was a great success. George L. Smith of Swainsboro, the fired former Speaker under Ernest Vandiver, attended and announced his candidacy for Speaker and was committed to voting for whoever was selected by the Democratic caucus. At that point, the organizers knew they were on the way to a House independent of the governor's control. Smith's participation and the strong support of Thomas Murphy showed that rural legislators were with the urban conspirators.[57]

The assembled members agreed to send a letter to the two general election candidates, Maddox and Callaway, calling on them to support the independent selection of the Speaker. The letter stated a commitment to the principle that "a free society and a democratic republic can best be preserved by the separation of powers among the legislative, judicial and executive branches of government." Signed by Roy Lambert as chair of the group, the letter also stated a hope that the election of the officers of the House could be "accomplished without intervention from the Governor's office in any way . . . by means of inducement of coercion, or otherwise." Maddox responded that he strongly agreed with the Georgia Constitution on the question of separation of powers. Likewise, Callaway said that "nothing is more important than an independent Legislature."[58]

When the Democratic caucus met on Sunday, November 13, there was great confusion about how the state would get a new governor. The path to an independent House was set before the election results were in, but it may have helped that there was no governor-elect who could use the future benefits of his office to interfere. In what turned out to be a close vote, the caucus selected the rural leadership of George L. Smith over the urban leadership of Robin Harris. George Busbee from Albany (governor 1977–83) defeated Tom Murphy for the newly created position of majority leader.[59] From that point forward, the legislature would have a stronger voice in future environmental policy and how the state would use its marshlands.

Carl Sanders was not a fan of the legislative independence movement. He believed that an independent House of Representatives weakened the office of the governor and made it difficult to modify state policy and operate efficient programs in an environment of change. In later years, he said he would not like to be governor when so much of the power had shifted from the executive branch.[60] Tom Murphy, no fan of Sanders, had a different view of history and later said the independence of the House put more minds to work on the issues of the state, and it was the beginning of progress for the state.[61]

George L. Smith said he would rather be Speaker than governor. He was proud to be a part of an "entirely independent law making body that chose its officers without suggestion or prompting from the Executive Branch of Government." He felt that the independent election of House officers on January 9, 1967, was the "most significant development since statehood."[62]

The next morning, January 10, at 9:30 a.m., Secretary of State Ben Fortson rolled down the center isle of the House chamber with an assistant pushing four file drawers of returns for the tabulators to count. Before they started, Rep. Mac Pickard of Columbus was recognized for a motion on a resolution to conduct a runoff election between Maddox and Callaway on January 31, 1967.[63] As everyone expected, Peter Zack Geer, before he ruled on the motion, recognized Reid Harris for a short presentation. Harris took the well and argued from a deeply held belief that the legislature had the power to go behind the Constitution and "return to the source of its power," the people from which such power came. He believed that, without a vote of the people, the governor would lack power to effectively govern the state. Yet, as he yielded the floor, he knew the issue was lost.[64]

A Maddox supporter, Geer ruled the motion for a new election out of order, basing his action on the decision of the U.S. Supreme Court and the opinion of Attorney General Arthur Bolton. Tom Murphy, a Maddox supporter, made a motion to call the question on the resolution confirming the General Assembly's power to decide who would be governor. Elliott Levitas, thinking quickly, called for the "ayes" and "nays." This, of course, was one of the objectives of all the parliamentary maneuvering. Many Democrats voted with the Callaway supporters and against the motion to "call the question," but it passed 148 to 110 and cleared the way for the final vote. While the first vote was largely procedural, it gave many thankful Maddox-committed Democrats an opportunity to tell their Callaway constituents they had tried to give the choice of governor back to the people.[65] Roy Lambert's wife, Chris, home from teaching school all day and watching the proceedings on public television, said "oh, crap," when her husband cast his vote for Lester Maddox.[66] The lawyers who started the independence movement didn't always vote together, but it gave them a common bond of experience and a trust in each other.

A few days before the November election, Callaway had asked a small number of the independence conspirators—Robin Harris, Elliott Levitas, Milton Jones, and Reid Harris—for their help when it was clear the General Assembly was going to decide the issue. Levitas, a Rhodes Scholar and young law partner of Ellis Arnall, recalled the meeting with Callaway and his staff at the Marriott Hotel in downtown Atlanta. Levitas asked to see the list of House and Senate members the staff had been working on, and he asked for the copy of the rule book. The Callaway folks had neither. Their advice was to get a list and start calling the members whose voters had gone with Callaway. If it came to a straight up-or-down vote, Levitas, who was disappointed by the lack of preparation, did not think they would win and decided their best option was to push for a vote for a new runoff election.[67]

The only other action in a long day of reading out the vote counts was Geer's other ruling that discounted 18,347 write-in votes, because Cobb and Fulton election officials failed to transmit them in a sealed envelope. By midafternoon, the final count of the citizens' votes gave Callaway 453,665, Maddox 450,626, and 52,831 certified write-in votes for Arnall.[68] No one had secured the required "50 percent plus one" to claim a majority.

Late in the afternoon, Geer started the legislature's vote to decide the governorship. Maddox needed 130 votes to win, and Rep. Tom Murphy cast the 130th "yea" vote. Just after seven o'clock in the evening the vote was completed, with Maddox capturing 182 and Callaway 66. Of interest were the votes cast for Callaway by Elliott Levitas, Reid Harris, and the Democratic majority leader George Busbee. Levitas and Busbee explained that they voted as their constituents had voted in the general election, and Harris explained his vote for Callaway the same way.[69]

At 7:18 that evening, when the vote was finished, Maddox, who had been hiding out in the state auditor's office, sent word to Peter Zack Geer that he would come to the House and make short remarks. With a Georgia State Patrol escort, he moved through the packed halls of the Capitol to Sanders's office. At the outgoing governor's suggestion, they found a Bible and a judge, and Maddox was sworn in as the next governor of Georgia.[70]

Chapter 4

Who Was in Charge?

He knew what he did not know.

—Shirley Miller

When Lester Maddox first sat down behind the governor's desk, he knew little about the inner workings of the state's agencies or its legislature. He had run a small business with sixty-five employees, so he knew about making payroll and balancing the books. Several times he had expanded his restaurant, so he also knew how to invest capital for future growth. He knew how to budget and was good with numbers. He knew how to say things that would capture the interest of the press, and he was accustomed to talking freely with the press, but he had spent little time crafting carefully worded statements (sound bites we now call them). While he was used to speaking broadly about the large public issues of the day, he hadn't created any legislation, or seen policy changes make their way through an intricate and often frustrating legislative process. He was a "political outsider" and an "unlikely governor."[1]

He knew he was an outsider elected without connections to any political establishment and believed it was a virtue to be "free from the pressures of the Democratic Party, free from the pressures of the Republican Party . . . and free of the pressure of all individuals and groups making up the political establishment."[2] Unusually free of political contributions, his campaigns were largely run out of his car with the help of his daughter who tried to coordinate his travel around the state. Most Democratic senators and representatives had voted for him to be governor, but he personally knew only six House members out of 196 and no members of the Senate. Since the success of legislative initiatives is often determined by personal relationships, he was not well equipped to be the state's chief legislator.

Fortunately, the government in place could operate on its own while its agency leaders waited for any new orders from a new governor. The inconclusive November 1966 election let Carl Sanders continue working with his usual vigor on a new budget with little help from Maddox or Callaway. He invited both in for a short consultation, but there was another Sanders budget ready to be introduced in the General Assembly in January 1967. During his activist four-year term, Sanders had used commissions to closely review the operation of state agencies, and more than thirty had completed self-evaluations. The Bowdoin Commission, named for its businessman chair William R. Bowdoin, had operated all four years and made numerous recommendations that Sanders implemented. He carefully vetted the people he chose to run state agencies.[3] He had appointed his trusted House floor leader, Arthur Bolton, to fill a vacancy as attorney general, and Bolton had just been elected to a full four-year term as the state's chief lawyer. The government that Maddox inherited was in good hands.

So on January 11, Maddox had two tasks in front of him: find people to help him, and calm the fears his flamboyant political style and his resistance to new civil rights laws had created in anxious state political leaders and the public. One of these people was Bob Short, whom he had met during the campaign. A leader in Jimmy Carter's campaign, Short had done community affairs work for both Governors Sanders and Vandiver. Short sat out the runoff at the Democratic Party headquarters but, for the sake of the future of the party, was willing to provide advice and act as the new governor's press secretary. When it first looked like Maddox would be selected, Short recruited Bill Burson to help write a speech that could be used at the hurriedly organized inauguration on January 11.

The speech, which many saw as the appearing of a "new Maddox," brought applause from the press, legislators, and business leaders. In his address, Governor Maddox fit closely the policy mold of the other governors of the era and their commitment to policies that would bring business investment and jobs to the state. He followed the policy consensus when he said the cause for the state is "the building of a greater and more prosperous Georgia with expanded horizons of opportunity for all."[4] He called for advancements in education, highway expansion, mental health treatment, penal reform, and assistance to urbanizing local governments. He struck a moderate tone on race. He recognized that people "want a public school system equal to the best in the nation, and they want every child regardless of his circumstances to where he lives to be prepared to compete on an equal basis with every other child in the country." The state's economic support would not discriminate on the basis of "race, creed, color or national origin."[5]

While the speech did not put the issue of race under the Maddox governorship to rest, it helped people have some confidence the state was not going to turn back the clock on public education. "There will be no place in Georgia during the next four years for those who advocate extremism or violence," Maddox said. And, remarkably from a states' rights proponent, he declared that "there is no necessity for any conflict to arise between federal-state authorities."[6]

Although it was not unusual for an inaugural speech, Maddox returned many times in his speech to the belief that government must be an expression of the people's will. Quoting Thomas Jefferson, he added that "the people, when given the facts and the opportunity to act on them, can be counted on to decide public matters wisely." He pledged to support the "free interchange of ideas in areas of differing opinions . . . and upon the final determination of issues by the people themselves." However, he was more specific when he encouraged the policy task forces he expected to appoint "to hold hearings to ascertain public thinking and to get citizen recommendations." Even more specific was his announcement of an open door to the governor's office on the first and third Wednesdays of each month, which became known as Little People's Day. Here he would have a chance to hear directly from people who cared about Georgia.[7] His openness to input and public hearings would give encouragement to the advocates in the environmental movement. Public hearings would be a critical tool for the protectors of the marshlands.

Perhaps it was inevitable that Governor Maddox would have a rocky relationship with the legislature. He had very little experience with legislation, and he arrived on the scene a day after the House of Representatives had declared its independence from the governor. He had supported the independence movement in a letter to coconspirator Roy Lambert prior to his selection and the convening of the new Democratic caucus.[8] The House had just elected George L. Smith, who had been relieved of the post as Speaker on the first day of the Sanders administration.[9] Bob Short advised Maddox to support the independence of the legislative branch of government and in fact, Maddox had little opportunity to do anything that would prevent the House leadership from exercising its newfound muscle. In his inaugural speech he conceded to the change in the basic relationship between the governor and the legislature. He gave little detail but proclaimed his belief in "the separation of powers of government" and said it was the legislature's responsibility to complete its reapportionment in a special session. He called the special session, but he did not make recommendations on the issue.[10] In his later years, Maddox said he was proud of the independence of the legislature, claiming that "never once during my years as governor had I so much as called a member of the House or Senate or made even a veiled suggestion as to who should be elected to any legislative office."[11]

Whether from his philosophy or lack of experience, Maddox conceded leadership over legislation to the members of the General Assembly, proclaiming to adoring supporters that "We've got more laws now than we know what to do with."[12] He quickly demonstrated he was not well equipped to be the chief legislator. In the 1967 legislative session, he announced the Sanders budget was too optimistic in its revenue projections and the legislative budget writers would need to reduce the appropriation to the University System of Georgia in order to bring revenue and expenses into balance. The legislative leaders did bring the budget into line with the governor's revenue estimate, but they also made sure the system got the funds contained in the Sanders budget.

Maddox did have good political instincts when it came to selecting legislators to work on his priorities, and he persuaded good people to work with him. One Sunday afternoon in December 1966, Tom Murphy was at home, perhaps watching a football game, when he had a call from Maddox. At first Murphy thought it was about getting a commitment to vote Maddox in as governor, which he quickly gave. But Maddox asked him to come to Atlanta for a conversation and to bring his wife, Agnes, because his wife, Virginia, wanted to meet her. Murphy had eaten at the Pickrick a few times, but he had never had a personal conversation with Maddox. After some chitchat, the likely governor asked Murphy to be his floor leader in the House. Murphy was surprised by the invitation because he had been a supporter of the independence movement, was a George L. Smith supporter in the caucus vote, and would not "support anything I didn't believe in." Murphy had established that reputation for independence when he stood up to Governor Sanders. Maddox knew Murphy's reputation for straight talk. He wanted Murphy working with him because people said Murphy had strong opinions he did not keep to himself. "If you disagree with me you'd stand up and tell me right to my face. . . . I want somebody that can make me think."[13] Murphy, who had lost a close Democratic caucus vote to George Busbee, the new majority leader, accepted the floor leader job and spent four years representing the governor. He became a key player on the House-Senate Budget Conference Committee, which considered the opinions of other members and often rewrote the governor's budget recommendations.[14]

Peter Zack Geer, who presided over the joint session and who had defeated Maddox for lieutenant governor in 1962, recommended that Maddox talk to a young rural senator from Enigma (a town on the Florida line, just a piece east of Tifton) about being a floor leader in the Senate. Bobby Rowan was elected in 1963 into the first class of senators following the demise of the county unit system. His neighbors were tobacco growers and turpentine dippers, and his hometown was so small you could throw a rock from one end to the other.[15]

All but five of the fifty-four senators were freshmen in 1964. Under the county unit system, three small rural counties elected one senator, with the required residence rotating among the counties. Each term a new senator from a new county usually occupied the seat. The end of the system opened the possibility of longevity and a political career. Their ranks included Jimmy Carter (who ran for governor in 1966) and the first African American senator, Leroy Johnson of Atlanta. Rowan, a great storyteller, was affable and popular with his fellow senators and one of the first in the body to shake Johnson's hand. He would have a long political career and continue as a friend of the governor, but his time as floor leader was rocky and limited. It also showed Maddox's lack of nuanced understanding of legislative protocols.

During Maddox's second year in office during the 1968 session, the Farm Bureau proposed that farm equipment be exempt from the state's 3 percent sales tax. Sen. Ford Spinks, who was backing the exemption, talked to Rowan about the measure and Rowan, whose district adjoined Spinks's and had mostly farmers or interests related to farming, agreed to go downstairs to speak with the governor about the issue. Murphy, whose district also represented a lot of farmers, sat in on the meeting, which did not go well. A strong fiscal conservative, Maddox said the proposal would take $30 million out of state revenue, which the state could not afford. He was unwilling to find cuts in the budget to make up the revenue. Loyal to his governor over his voters, Rowan went back upstairs, took the Senate floor, and explained the fiscal impact of the bill and dutifully explained why the state could not afford the exemption.

That was not the end of the discussion. Spinks went down to see the governor and, in an unusual move, Maddox changed his mind. Rowan learned of the "change of mind" as he sat in his seat on the Senate floor and heard Spinks announce the change and the reasons the governor now thought the 3 percent exemption would be good for the general economy of the state. Rowan never got a chance to "explain" the governor's change of mind to the Senate or his voters. He decided that same day that Maddox needed someone else to represent him in the Senate, went to the well of the Senate, and tendered his resignation as floor leader.[16] Rowan's fellow senators applauded him, signaling their lack of respect for Governor Maddox as the chief legislator.

Maddox also lost the respect of legislators because he did not discuss the appointments he wanted them to confirm before they were officially announced. Rowan usually found out from the press who the governor had nominated. On one list the governor submitted directly to the Senate, there were three nominees from Rowan's Senate district.[17] *Atlanta Constitution* columnist Eugene Patterson, no friend of Maddox, highlighted the Rowan resignation and said the governor's "one band style" was leaving him "lorn and lonesome."[18]

Maddox also lost the respect of legislators by being a little too honest about the social life in the Capitol. On the final night of the 1968 session, he roamed the halls and committee rooms on the fourth floor and discovered liquor flowing freely from a makeshift bar as part of the traditional celebration of the end of the session. The next day he expressed his outrage and shock to reporters about the celebrating.[19] While the revelation may have made Maddox look good to his conservative, churchgoing supporters, it did not improve his ability to pass legislation.

By 1968 the independence movement and Maddox's lack of legislative experience had significantly diminished his chief legislator role. However, as the chief executive he was in charge of the agencies and programs of the state. In this role Maddox had significant power as well as important characteristics that made the operation of state government go more smoothly than anyone at the time had reason to expect. He was not always right in his understanding of an issue, but he was always honest and straightforward in expressing his opinion about issues. That is what convinced Tom Murphy to work with him. To this day, Rowan believes that Maddox "didn't have a crooked bone in his body." Zell Miller, who as chief of staff was given significant responsibility in the last two years of Maddox's term, believed Maddox was "basically an honest and kind person. He was easy to work for because he delegated so much to you. His heart and instincts were largely in the right place."[20] While that characteristic often got him into deep trouble with those who disagreed, there was an honesty about Lester Maddox that people on all sides could appreciate.

The second and most significant attribute was his ability to recognize an issue that went beyond his knowledge and understanding. Perhaps the most important thing about Lester Maddox, according to Bobby Rowan, was that "he knew what he did not know." Shirley Miller, wife of former governor Zell Miller, who was often around Maddox during the two years when Zell was his chief of staff, used almost the same words to describe him: "Governor Maddox respected agency heads and he knew what he didn't know, and he was open-minded to those in his administration who did know."[21]

When Maddox took the helm, agencies and people were already in place for him to turn to. Maddox kept the Sanders people, who continued the Sanders initiatives.[22] There were highly qualified and committed people who Maddox could ask for advice on environmental issues. His tenth-grade education gave him basic math skills, and keeping the books for his restaurant and managing the expansion of his building gave him skills that would help him with line items in the budget. According to Shirley Miller, he had acquired serviceable writing skills, but relying on the science behind environmental issues was perhaps where "he knew what he didn't know." This last characteristic would yield the greatest benefit for the state.

While Maddox was pleased to rely on the expert managers Sanders had put in place during his term, one exception generated a significant confrontation between the principle the Bowdoin Commission had set out and the governor's desire to have a few loyal friends in place. The Georgia Game and Fish Commission was staffed with natural scientists who had direct responsibility for the wild areas of the state and keeping close connection the state's hunters, fishermen, and lovers of wildlife. The Bowdoin report said the commissioner of Game and Fish should be a professional wildlife manager.[23] But Maddox chose George Bagby.

Bagby came from a very different place than Maddox or any of the leaders of the early conservation cause. Born in the small town of Dallas in rural West Georgia and given Talmadge as a middle name, he was by family tradition part of the Talmadge wing of the Democratic Party. He was small in stature but large in ambition. At age thirteen he hitchhiked the 80 miles from his home to the Capitol and hung around long enough until they put him to work as a doorkeeper, and then later as a reader for the clerk of the House. The Paulding County representative let him sleep on the floor of his hotel room during the week, and on the weekends he connected with his teacher on class assignments and managed enough study during the session to graduate from high school at age sixteen.[24] After graduation from West Georgia College he enlisted in the navy during World War II. (War experience was a common denominator for many legislators.) At the end of the war he joined the Georgia State Patrol and in 1947, at age twenty-six, he was named head of the Georgia Bureau of Investigation (at the time a unit of the Georgia State Patrol). But the legislature was in his blood and, in 1948 he was elected to the House of Representatives from his home county. While there was no law against having a job making the laws and at the same time being employed to enforce the laws, Governor M. E. Thompson was high on ethics in government. He said that did not look good and fired him from the bureau. The sole gap in his legislative service was when he ran for a U.S. House seat in 1960, which he won by popular vote but lost by county unit vote. He represented Paulding County in the House for a combined thirteen years. During those years he found time for night classes at John Marshall Law School. His daughter, Judith, remembers him getting home at

2:00 a.m. from night law classes in Atlanta after hitchhiking back to Dallas. He passed the bar and started a country law practice in his hometown of Dallas.[25]

There was no more colorful figure in Georgia politics in the latter days of Marvin Griffin's governorship. At one tense point in a legislative session, Bagby took the well in the House to oppose the governor's $50 million Rural Roads Bond Program. By doing so, he joined Lieutenant Governor Vandiver's side of the dispute. From the well he told the House he had met the night before with his brother John, who worked for the State Patrol, and warned him the governor would likely fire John after this speech. From the well, Bagby assured his brother John that it would be all right, because "I've got a ham in the smoke house, I've got meal in the barrel, and I've got a hoecake in the stove. We can take care of our own." Until that speech, Griffin did not know Bagby's brother John was a state employee, but he called the director and told him to quickly correct the situation. Then he sent a letter to Bagby.

> Dear George,
> Get the ham out of the smokehouse, get the meal out of the barrel, and keep the hoecake on the stove, 'cause John's coming home.[26]

While Bagby's political experience was rooted in the conservative, segregationist, rural politics of the county unit days, he was a yellow-dog Democrat who did not follow the Dixiecrats when they stomped out of the party in 1948. He didn't align with political factions that wished to resist the civil rights changes to a bitter unproductive end. Unlike nearly all the members of the General Assembly, most of the Maddox staff, and the Sanders agency heads, Bagby supported the governor from the start of the 1966 Democratic primary.[27] He joined with other yellow dogs to help connect Maddox to the votes he needed to win in the General Assembly, which earned him the leadership of the Game and Fish Commission. He was one of the few Maddox appointees tied to the governor's political campaign and perhaps the only one who had strong connections to a very independent House of Representatives.

Choosing Bagby to head Game and Fish was not an easy appointment and precipitated one of the first political tests of the Maddox administration. The Sanders-appointed director didn't like being asked to leave and the board of the commission, which had authority over hiring the director, didn't like Maddox telling them who their new leader was going to be. They took an informal poll. Bagby lost 10–1. The commission chair, Harley Langdale, who owned a great deal of forested land in South Georgia, said the commission was going to follow Governor Sanders's Bowdoin Commission recommendation and look for a professional trained in the intricacies of wildlife management. This was a test of Sanders's reform of agency management and an education for the new governor, who hadn't informed the commission of his support for Bagby. The commission tabled the governor's recommendation for a month. One member of the board anonymously told a reporter that "we ain't gonna have no political appointment."[28]

Although a hot controversy for the fledging administration, Bagby helped calm things a little with the press. He camped in the lobby of the governor's office and told reporters he recognized the need for experts to make objective scientific decisions for the commission and felt the commission had those experts in place with two highly qualified deputy commissioners. In typically colorful language, he said the commission has "experts running out their ears" and suggested that maybe the director should be a person who can "get along with the General Assembly on money and meet the public." He also calmly made it clear he thought the members of the House and Senate were on his side.[29] Eugene Patterson, *Constitution* columnist and a long-time Maddox critic, labeled the appointment the "first great power play" and in his column told the commissioners if they "stick by their guns a good new day will dawn in Georgia's wildlife development." Even Patterson had to admit, though, that Bagby's "abilities in politics are rising above question."[30]

The boiling controversy came down to a simmer in the period before the next commission meeting. Someone took a closer look at the Bowdoin Commission report and found that the director "should have considerable political sagacity."[31] The Game and Fish Committee of the House asked the commissioners to meet with them, and while commission members were present, took a committee vote on the Bagby nomination showing nearly unanimous support. As a further inducement, the committee wrote a bill that would roll back fishing license fees and another that would strip the commission of its administrative powers, threatening to roll them out of committee if the commission rejected their colleague's appointment.[32] The commission vote on February 9, 1967, was still contentious as four members supported thirteen-year veteran of the department Howard Zeller. But in the end the commission buckled to the governor and the legislature on a 6–4 vote for Bagby. He went from the commission meeting to the governor's office to be sworn in with Appropriations Chair Sloppy Floyd present. Floyd then ordered his friend, the new "Fish Head," to come immediately before his committee.[33]

The fight over his appointment illustrated a few things about the politics of the times. While it was considered a setback for the Sanders efficiency in government reforms, it illustrated the power and leadership that rested in the state's agencies. However, it also showed the new power the legislative independence movement had vested in the General Assembly. Maddox and future governors would ignore that power at their own peril. These two circumstances gave George Bagby, with the confidence of the governor and the confidence of the General Assembly, significant influence over the coming coastal environmental decisions Georgia would make during his time as Fish Head.

Bagby loved the outdoors, and made a very natural and genuine connection to the sportsmen of the state. He was proud of his fishing skills, claiming that he had caught more fish than any other politician in rural Paulding County. His daughter Judith accompanied him on regular Saturday fishing trips. She remembers he usually finished with four or five strings of fish. On the way back home, he dropped off the strings at the homes of both black and white neighbors who welcomed the contribution to their slim rural diets. He knew from boyhood the adventure of hunting and fishing, and he understood the personal connection the people of Georgia had to their natural environment and the personal nature of legislative decisions.[34]

Bagby developed a close relationship with the department's rangers. In his first year as director, he put 80,000 miles on his agency automobile. He visited all twelve districts and held private meetings with the nonmanagement staff. After the formal meetings, rangers put on fish fries for local officials, state representatives from the area, and others. Bagby cemented lifetime loyalty from his rangers when he and his General Assembly friends swiftly moved their base annual pay from $4,000 to $7,800.[35] After the Game and

Fish appointment fight was over, Maddox made it clear the department would not be a "dumping ground for the employment of politicians seeking favors" and that he would not interfere in the policy-setting functions of the commission.[36] Like Maddox, Bagby recognized his limitations. He left the policy questions to the engineers and scientists of the department.[37] Jack Crockford, the assistant commissioner, who attended the meetings of the newly created Georgia Natural Areas Council, was the go-to person on policy. Jim Morrison, the information officer, was the journalist who could get the message out to the sportsmen of the state.[38] It was later evident that Bagby was a huge asset in any political fight.

At the start of the Maddox governorship, the state had considerable capacity to deal with many of the environmental issues arising. It was not easy to see this capacity because it was spread out across many agencies and departments. In 1970, the Governor's Bureau of State Planning and Community Affairs published a report on the state's environmental activities that listed the many agencies able to deal with "the complexity of environmental problems."[39] The report said the "problems are interrelated, which clearly pointed out the need for close coordination among agencies for a concerted attack on such things as air and water pollution, solid waste management, and pesticide control, just to mention a few." While the report, completed in the early days of the Carter governorship, pointed to the need for coordination and provided unspoken support for Carter's reorganization plans, it is also important evidence for how environmental issues were handled in the Maddox years. The capacity was impressive and close cooperation between agency heads was needed. Coordination depended more on personal relationships between agency leaders than governmental structure. Here is a list of agencies Governor Maddox had available to him to meet the environmental needs of the state.

The *Department of Public Health* was responsible for the collective health of the citizens. It could ban oyster harvesting in estuaries and coastal rivers when pollution made the oysters unsafe to eat. It governed air and water quality, sanitation, and sewage disposal systems and was administratively responsible for the *Water Quality Control Board*. Empowered by legislation under Carl Sanders in 1964, this board set water-quality standards and had some capacity to enforce those standards against industrial and municipal polluters. It operated with Director R. S. "Rock" Howard and a secretary but grew to a staff of fifty by 1970. Howard and his young engineers were in the front line of the battle to clean the state's rivers and provided critical leadership in the fight to save the marsh from mining.

Quality of food, its production, processing, and distribution to consumers was the responsibility of the *Department of Agriculture*. When Phil Campbell resigned to become U.S. Commissioner of Agriculture under Richard Nixon, Maddox appointed Tommy Irvin, his first chief of staff and a former legislator, to head the department. Irvin was one of the six House members who had supported Maddox in the general election. This opened a position for Zell Miller to become the chief of staff for the governor. The department was created in 1874 as the first such department in the country. Irvin went on to serve as commissioner of agriculture until January 2011.

The *Department of Mines, Mining and Geology* promoted the exploration and extraction of mineral resources within the state. During the Maddox years, its mission and support of the mining industry came into conflict with environmental policy. The test wells exploring for minerals on the coast and discovery of phosphate precipitated the fight over the future use of marshlands. The department and its geologist were absorbed by the Department of Natural Resources under Governor Carter.

The *University of Georgia* produced scientific research and scientists who were directly engaged in the public policy questions about the future of the Georgia coast. Eugene Odum was the best-known environmental scientist in the state, with international recognition for his writings on ecology. Much of the scientific investigation of the ecology of the marshlands in the world came from the small *University of Georgia Marine Institute* on Sapelo Island. It was established in 1953, but study of the coastal environment started as early as 1949 with the financial support of the owner R. J. Reynolds II, who had developed a strong interest in ocean science as a naval officer in World War II.

The twenty-seven *Soil and Water Conservation Districts* were created by legislation in 1937 to control topsoil erosion and the silting of the state's rivers. The water runoff from the cotton-depleted land washed down the state's rivers during the middle decades of the twentieth century and was caught in the marshes along the full length of the coast. The districts recognized the problem and sought ways to slow the erosion of the topsoil.

The *Georgia Forestry Commission*, one of the oldest state agencies, was created to protect, manage, and utilize the forest resources of the state for efficient production of timber and the growing demand for recreation. It played a significant role in shaping forestry regulations to support the expansion of the pulp and paper industry in the postwar era and was an important partner for those seeking to restore the longleaf pine forests in recent years.

The role of the public-private *Georgia Science and Technology Commission* is to give advice related to the protection of the environment. The commission helped the state coordinate its research efforts with the private sector.

The mission of the *Georgia Natural Areas Council*, created in the final legislative session of Governor Sanders (1966), was to identify natural areas of the state that might need special protection in the future. The unstated purpose was to find natural areas that might be designated as wilderness under the federal Wilderness Act of 1964, and it explored the state's rivers for federal designation as Scenic Rivers. During its short life, it fostered and coordinated the work of many advocates who sought to preserve the natural environment of the coast. The council brought together scientists and agency heads and played a significant role in the effort to protect the coast. Look for more on this unique state agency in chapter 5. Its first and only executive director, Robert Hanie, would be in the middle of the political campaign to save the marshlands.

The *Georgia Historical Commission*, operating under the supervision of Secretary of State Ben Fortson, was committed to preserving historical sites.

The *State Highway Department*, created back in 1916, showed the state's commitment to the road-building business, but in 1969 the state created an Environmental Planning Unit within its Division of Planning. The planning and construction of Interstate 95 along the coast, crossing fourteen rivers critical to the salinity of the marsh, commanded the attention of environmentalists and agency heads.

The *Department of Industry and Trade* was formed under Governor Ernest Vandiver and was central to state efforts to generate new jobs and new investment. In the post–World War II era, governors around the country, including Lester Maddox, gave primary attention to economic growth. The department committed its resources to locating new industries in the state.

While it assisted new arrivals in meeting the state's air and water quality standards, it was unlikely to push for higher standards. It worked with the Water Quality Control Board (WQCB) to establish sound balanced environmental regulations, although its central loyalty was to jobs and economic development. When decisions were made regarding Georgia's coastal environment, the department's first consideration was always the effect of the policy on current and future jobs. The agency was usually caught in the middle between expanding industry and expanding tourism.

The Savannah and Brunswick Port Authorities were merged into the *Georgia Port Authority* during this period. Expanding the ports was an important part of the state's plan for economic growth and could easily come into conflict with the efforts to preserve the environment around the two port cities. The port authority promoted the use of the state's rivers for domestic and international commerce, and its goals could easily conflict with the goals of a healthy environment.

The state agency with the most direct responsibility for the wild areas on the Georgia coast in the late 1960s was the *Department of Game and Fish*. Created in 1911, it didn't rival the Department of Agriculture in age but had a long history of looking after the natural environment. The independent Game and Fish Commission set policy for the department, promoted hunting and fishing, managed wildlife, and had a significant interest in an ecological balance. It could acquire property to protect habitat for a variety of recreational activities and saw the hunters and fishermen of the state as their prime constituents. The department attracted many recent graduates from the University of Georgia and employed many professional scientists able to advise the governor and the legislature on environmental issues. They connected to the scientists in the University System of Georgia and at parallel federal agencies. Commercial fishermen, shrimpers, and oystermen looked to the department to preserve their livelihood. The commission and its scientists would play an important role in the preservation of the Georgia coast.

The goal of the *State Parks Department*, created in 1937, was to expand outdoor recreational facilities to meet the future recreational needs of an expanding urban population. It developed plans to meet the vacationing interests of the growing number of affluent families during the good times of the postwar prosperity. It could use its acquisition powers to protect "delicate ecologically balanced areas" of the state and was a tool available for the protection of the barrier islands.

The state government had experience with developing and managing property through the use of authorities. The *Jekyll Island State Park Authority* acquired the barrier island in 1947 from the heirs of the Jekyll Island Club through a friendly condemnation. Its purpose was to give "average" Georgia families an opportunity to vacation on the beach; when the causeway to the island was completed, it was one of only three places where anyone but the wealthy could look at the Atlantic from a Georgia beach. The two other recreational authorities were the *Lake Lanier Islands Authority* and the *North Georgia Mountain Authority*. The authority's public-private development model was something the state knew how to use, and it would be an option for state control of the barrier islands.

Creation of the *Georgia Recreation Commission* under Sanders in 1963 gave recognition to a growing need for recreation and a possible business opportunity for the state. Throughout the debate over the use of the Georgia coast, its use for recreation would compete with traditional extraction and industrial uses. The commission's studies of the recreational needs of the state provided important information to state leaders making decisions. Its work strengthened the arguments of Charles Fraser and his legislative supporters.

The *Department of Education* had responsibility for implementing a science curriculum that prepared students and teachers to understand the ecological discoveries of the day.

The *Department of Law* was led by Attorney General Arthur Bolton. The department provided legal advice to all state departments. These included agencies and departments important to environmental issues, such as the Water Quality Control Board, the Air Quality Control Branch of the Department of Health, the Game and Fish Commission, and the little-known Mineral Leasing Commission. It was Bolton's job to say what the law was for the state government agencies. Bolton was in the thick of the debate over mining the coast for phosphate, and he was responsible for deciding who owned the marshlands.

This quick review not only shows a capacity to deal with the complexity of environmental issues but also shows the need for a great deal of cooperation between agencies. Governor Maddox had a number of places where he could seek advice when complex environmental issues landed on his desk, and they did land. Scientific knowledge and professional leadership existed within these agencies, and the staff was accustomed to interacting across the lines of agency authority. It was remarkable how effective agencies could be, and even more remarkable how freely Maddox permitted the agencies to exercise their authority. He allowed them to speak out in the press when controversy arose. With advocacy organizations in the very early stages of development, leadership on environmental issues had to come from independent thoughtful agency heads.

Chapter 5

Gathering the Troops

Humans must have beauty. They have to have recreation. If a man
sees and smells only pollution, he is going to be a terrible creature.

—R. S. "Rock" Howard

If you were a budding scientist and wanted to study the natural environment, you wanted to be a graduate student in the University of Georgia, Department of Zoology. By the time Maddox became governor, the state's investments in higher education under Governors Vandiver and Sanders were beginning to pay dividends. Dr. Eugene Odum, a professor in the UGA Zoology Department, had established himself and the university as the leader in the new science of ecology. Odum, with the determination to make ecology a field of study distinct from established scientific fields, and with significant collaboration with his brother Howard Thomas Odum, published the first ecology textbook in 1953, *The Fundamentals of Ecology*. By 1959 it was already in its second edition.

The University of Georgia Marine Institute (UGAMI) on Sapelo Island became the laboratory for the scientific investigation of the marsh environment and the research conducted there supported the broader ecosystem theory at the heart of Odum's understanding. With his colleague Don Scott, Odum had arranged a bird-watching trip to Sapelo back in 1948, in hopes of spotting a rare Mexican pheasant. While they peered through binoculars, R. J. Reynolds II drove up in his Jeep and engaged them in conversation. The conversation expanded over lunch with good scotch whiskey and an overnight stay at the Reynolds mansion. Scott and Reynolds stayed up late over the scotch while Odum, a teetotaler, went to bed. Reynolds confessed that his cattle business and his retreat for wealthy patrons was not paying off and asked Scott if the university might be interested in using part of the island. Reynolds created a foundation in 1952 to support a lab on the island. It took some time for the scientists to persuade the university that it needed a new research center on the coast, but a year later they had secured a $50,000 startup budget and with the foundation's help and the loan of the *Kit Jones*, a 65-foot research vessel, they were up and running by the end of 1953. While for most people at the time the coastal marshland was just something to be "developed," the scientists on Sapelo through research determined the importance of the marsh and the effect of the twice-daily tides on the marsh systems.[1]

The research conducted under the institute umbrella got the attention of scientists around the world. Over its continuing lifetime, more than a thousand scientific papers expanding knowledge of ecosystem ecology came from data collected on the island. The institute invited fifty-five scientists to the Salt Marsh Conference on the island in 1958 to discuss the early results of the research. John Teal, one of the first to come to the island to do research with his wife, Mildred, presented his evidence. Nearly half of the nutrients generated in the marsh were exported to near-shore environments, Teal concluded, and these nutrients were responsible for the well-being of marine life for as much as 5 miles out to sea. The nutrients that came from the annual life cycle of *Spartina* grass, the bacteria that digested it and marsh algae, are used by other plants and animals that create abundant life in the open waters of the estuaries. The Teals believed the marshlands produce 10 tons of organic material per acre. That makes the marsh the most productive land in the world. The most remarkable discovery coming from the collective research of the institute scientists was that the plants in the marsh consume only 55 percent of what they produce and thus leave 4.5 tons of organic material for export to the ocean. In their 1969 book, *The Life and Death of the Salt Marsh*, the Teals provided the public with a readable summary of the scientific discoveries and the productive capacity of the marshlands that came out of the small institute and its dedicated scientists.[2] When the scientists were done, the marsh clearly could no longer be considered wasteland.

While not widely known or understood outside scientific circles, the movement in scientific theory, in which Odum and the determined Sapelo scientists played a significant part, had broader implications to the society as a whole. The theory that systems in nature were greater than the sum of their parts drove forward scientific investigation. Odum wanted the public to understand the whole marsh and its relationship to the human society that held its fate. The public didn't need to understand the plankton that floated in and out with the tide in order to understand the importance of a healthy marsh. He believed in "a new kind of science focused on nature as a set of systems." His ability to simplify the message of massive scientific studies is succinctly etched above the entrance to the University of Georgia's Odum School of Ecology: "The ecosystem is greater than the sum of its parts." And Odum's message was broader than biology. His sociologist father, Howard Odum, wrote twenty-three books and two hundred articles, exploring the concept that society itself was a system of interdependent parts, where improvement in one part generated improvement in others.[3] His father's sociological theory naturally drew Eugene into a belief at the core of the environmental movement that man and nature are inseparable in the largest ecosystem, the earth. Odum, like his father, was easily drawn into a comfortable civic role of interpreting the new science for the general public, legislators, and a governor who had little opportunity in life to study science. His voice, as the state's most notable scientist, could be heard above the loud conflicted voices of the late 1960s politics.

Organizations that would form the backbone of the environmental movement in Georgia were coming together in 1967. The organizations which now have paid staff, were clearly infants when compared to the capacity to research the issues and to lobby the legislature today. However, they still had the capacity to organize volunteers into a network with the grassroots ability to impact state policy. One center of energy was the graduate students in the Department of Zoology at the University of Georgia. A few students, enlightened by their studies and encouraged by their professors, moved from the classroom to grassroots action they believed could make a difference. They could teach communities of concerned citizens the new theories of ecology and make plain the value of the marshlands proven by research scientists on Sapelo.

Steven Johnson, in his second year as Odum's graduate student, received a postcard inviting him to a meeting in Atlanta to talk about organizing a Sierra Club group. An Emory University graduate whose family came to West

Point, Georgia, in the 1830s, Johnson received the postcard from Bill Blake because when Johnson was in Colorado for a year taking undergraduate biology classes he had joined the Sierra Club out there. He liked the organization's aggressive defense of the environment. With the Sierra Club, he had hiked to the bottom of the Grand Canyon to see the sites to be flooded by dams proposed by Walter Hickel, Nixon's secretary of the interior.

Blake sent postcards to the nineteen members of the club with addresses in Georgia. At the time, most of the members of the hiking club were in California, which had ten chapters, and a few other western states. A single chapter covered the whole eastern part of the country, from Maine to the Virgin Islands. Of the ten people who showed up for the meeting in the spring of 1967, three were in the zoology department: Steven Johnson, Dick Murlless, and Richard Bailey. Blake asked if anyone wanted to head the group; when no one volunteered, Blake did. Johnson became the conservation committee chair. They planned some hikes and started a newsletter, trying to build up membership. The Georgia group was officially authorized on February 27, 1968. The core leaders, including Johnson, Murlless, Bailey, and James Richardson, had sent the Sierra Club a well-researched proposal to make Cumberland Island a National Seashore in January 1968. Secretary of State Ben Fortson endorsed the proposal, but island owners were not yet ready to give up their private control.[4] The simple, poorly attended meeting established an organization able to engage others and connect Georgia to a growing national advocacy organization.

The Sierra Club was quickly morphing from a hiking club to a national environmental advocacy organization and was committing more and more of its members' resources to direct advocacy. It had lost its tax-exempt 501(c)(3) status when it published a full-page ad in the *New York Times* opposing the Grand Canyon dams. Its national membership, stuck at seven thousand for many years, would be a hundred thousand by 1970. When Steven Johnson applied for membership in 1966, he was required to find two current members who would recommend him. He didn't know two members, but because the organization was now interested in gaining members on the East Coast, the membership committee accepted Johnson, with his Georgia address, without the required references. A new member from Georgia was a prize, and he was soon a leader in the Georgia group and able to connect the club's ardent few members to other fledgling organizations.[5]

At about the same time, the former member of Congress from the 4th District in DeKalb County, Jim Mackay, was helping some interested constituents come together around environmental issues. After only one term in Congress he had just been defeated for reelection in 1966 by Ben Blackburn but felt a responsibility to follow through on the discussions he had with constituents. On January 28, 1967, Mackay invited his former advisory group on "water and conservation" to a community discussion. Among the sixty-five people who attended was Robert Hanie, who had helped Mackay organize the meeting, and Charles Foster, the president of the Nature Conservancy out of Washington. From this meeting came a grant from the Nature Conservancy that would pay Robert Hanie for six months to help organize the Georgia Conservancy. The group, according to its official history, saw itself as a "statewide umbrella organization, dedicated to preserving resources, educating the public, and addressing a variety of issues with advocacy programs."[6] Hanie, who claimed to be a fifth-generation Georgian, was born and grew up in North Georgia's Habersham County but had a broad range of experiences in his young life. An Emory University graduate in geology, he had just been admitted to a doctoral program in American studies at Emory. He had spent 1961 to 1963 teaching geology at a secondary school in Tanzania, also visiting Nigeria, Uganda, Kenya, and the island of Zanzibar. When he returned to the United States, he taught American history at Druid Hills High School in DeKalb County from 1963 to 1965. Congressman Mackay's son was one of Hanie's students, and that relationship connected him to organizational opportunities. Prior to taking the Nature Conservancy staff position, he spent a year as a "field engineer" with the Department of the Interior's Water Pollution Control Administration.[7]

The discussion group was not officially organized as the Georgia Conservancy until May 8, 1967, but it began a tradition of a fourth-Saturday outing with a trip down Sweetwater Creek on February 25. The turnout in nine-degree weather was a good sign people were ready for an organization focused on preserving the natural areas of the state.[8]

Decisions were made in the first year that shaped the character of the early Georgia Conservancy. First, the board saw itself as an umbrella that would coordinate the efforts of other organizations doing work related to the environment. Second, it applied and received from the IRS tax-exempt status under the provisions of section 501(c)(3). This meant it could educate legislators on environmental issues but was limited to spending only small amounts of money asking legislators to take specific action on legislation or appropriations, and made the organization cautious about direct lobbying on specific issues. The third decision limited members of the organization to receiving information and participating in programs but having little say in its governance. The board selected its own members with no vote of the membership. Governance was in the hands of professionals who were at the upper end of the income ladder.[9]

Jim Mackay offered Hanie the position of executive director of the organization, but Hanie was ambitious and saw a better opportunity as executive director of a new state agency. In the last legislative session under Carl Sanders in 1966, the state created the Georgia Natural Areas Council (GNAC) to shine a spotlight on the natural areas of the state that could benefit from protection against future development.[10] This council fit the Sanders model of establishing small governmental organizations to gather the best information on an issue. By early 1967, the tiny agency with a budget of $20,000 was just being formed and in need of an executive director. Many of the same individuals who were giving life to the Georgia Conservancy, including Charles Wharton, a zoologist from Georgia State University, and Odum from UGA, are given credit for creating the GNAC and both knew Hanie from his work starting the Georgia Conservancy.[11] Wharton, probably the state's leading nature scientist, had worked for years to get such an agency. In 1963 a senator from the mountains of North Georgia and future governor, Zell Miller, created a study commission for Wharton, who gave the senator a report on areas that needed protection.[12] When Wharton was chosen as the first chair of the council, he said the purpose was "to guide the future of Georgia's remaining natural environment." And he included in that mission large areas like "mountains or the coastal islands with their salt marshes." Advocating for the creation of the council, he asked Sen. John Pennington in a letter, "will Georgia be a wasteland sprinkled with commercial tourist attractions?"[13]

The GNAC had virtually no direct powers and looked like many of the other forward-thinking Sanders efforts to study issues needing greater attention in a developing economy. Its charge to identify "natural areas" of importance to the state and give advice to other agencies was broad. The legislation defined a natural area as "a tract of land in its natural state set aside and permanently protected or managed for the purpose of preservation of native plants or animal communities or rare and valuable individual members of such communities or any other natural features of outstanding scenic or geological value." It could not protect the identified areas, but it could put an area on a list for protection and draw attention to its value. The authorizing legislation had a wonderfully expansive catch-all mandate to "take such other action as may be deemed advisable to facilitate the administration, development, maintenance or protection of the natural area system or any part or parts thereof."[14] The statutory language probably means few legislators paid much attention to the creation of this council. However, it did give Hanie and the scientists behind the council a broad range of activities from which to choose and a platform from which to sound the alarm when an environmental crisis arose.

Membership of a state board or council is usually a good indication of intent. The GNAC brought together four state agencies—the Game and Fish Commission, the Forestry Commission, the Department of State Parks, and the Soil and Water Conservation Commission—and four scientists from the state's private and public colleges and universities. Leonard Ledbetter represented the Water Quality Control Board, and the private planning association appointed former senator and defeated candidate for governor, Jimmy Carter, to the board in 1968.[15] The GNAC met once a quarter and listened to reports on targeted natural areas developed by Hanie and his assistant, Laura Carr.[16] In a report to the council at the end of 1967, Hanie expansively described its function as "the only agency in the state organized specifically as a group of scientists and professionals to advise the people of Georgia on the wise use of certain terrestrial environments."[17]

Hanie and the GNAC would become a connecting point able to bring together people and institutions. Hanie traveled 19,000 miles on forty-six field trips in the first fourteen months that the council operated.[18] But he wasn't on the road more than George Bagby. Perhaps one of the most important connections Hanie made was with Jane Hurt Yarn (wife of Charles Yarn), who was representing the Georgia Association of Landscape Design

Appraisers. In his first months as council director, Hanie described a meeting with Yarn and a "group of well informed and enthusiastic ladies who are concerned about the destruction of our visual landscape." He suggested they might serve as a "catalytic group" to enact a Georgia Coastal Wetlands Act.[19] Both Hanie and the attractive and elegant Yarn knew how to connect to people of influence, and together they would have a big impact on the outcome of events on the Georgia coast.

To the team of advocates who came together in the fight to save the Georgia coast, Yarn played an integral role. They noted her intellect and organizational skills and her passion for nature as she walked the marble halls of the Capitol. For Yarn, it began with a trip to Africa. Sitting next to her husband on the return flight over the Atlantic, she turned to him and declared she was determined to make a difference in the quality of the environment of her own country.[20]

Charlie had arranged the five-week vacation in Africa with their two sons, aged nine and eleven. Jane, concerned about the security following the Mau Mau Uprisings, was a last-minute addition to the father-son bonding trip. While building the top plastic surgery practice in Atlanta, Charlie had missed out on many childhood experiences with their older daughter but was determined to make it up with their sons. He had come home late and left early for many years and now, with three other surgeons, the practice was prosperous. Together, the family explored the wonders of the Serengeti grasslands and had seen the rolling hills of Kenya. Jane was mesmerized. She brought a stack of books along on the trip, but "never opened a one of them," Charlie declared.[21] Unfortunately, the land on the hills was wearing out from overuse and neglect. Kenya's new independence from Britain and the loss of the empire's economic clout and know-how had left few resources to be invested in the earth itself.[22]

For the rest of his life, Charlie would remember the details of the conversation with his wife on their return flight. No, he remembered, it was not a conversation or a discussion. Jane was "speaking" to him about what she was going to do when they got back home and for the rest of her life.[23] Shortly before she died in 1995, she told a reporter "I had this conversion. . . . And I decided I'm just not going to come back home and let all that good wild land be ruined after having lived in the wilderness."[24] In an article in the *Garden Gate*, the quarterly publication of the Garden Club of Georgia, she wrote that the Africa trip helped her see

> the interrelation of all life to the other. . . . Life there is in its true primitive form with predators and prey. The dependence on the water hole, the need for plant life, etc.,—the cycle of life goes on. We could have found ourselves as dependent as the hyena on these same life giving things, and we became a part of the drama for a while.[25]

A well-educated mother of three, Yarn was well known and well connected in North Atlanta's elite social circles. She was a regular on the tennis court, chaired United Way drives, and was active in her Habersham Garden Club. Born Jane Hurt, her love of nature was learned at her mother's side in the garden and on her family's farm outside of Scottsboro, Alabama. This farm girl went to Converse College in South Carolina, because her mother's people were from Greenville. In the middle of World War II, 1942 to be exact, she came to Atlanta with a roommate whose boyfriend was in the city, and the boyfriend had a friend who would go along on the double date. Charlie, the blind date, knew that first night that he wanted to spend the rest of his life with Jane. He called his mother when he got back to the Emory medical student dorm to tell her "I just met the girl I am going to marry, if she will have me." The very same night, Jane met up with her mother, who was in Atlanta for a shopping trip, and told her she had "met the boy I am going to marry."[26]

Charlie found her an unusual person who was comfortable in her own skin. She had a quick mind and was quick to let you know her opinion. Charlie remembers her being a little too outspoken, so early in their relationship he had to teach her some "diplomacy." She was very efficient and, from careful study of an issue, she knew what she wanted to communicate. She had a gentle southern style, but was always direct and honest. For Charlie she was a "truthful, straightforward person." He remembers one of Jane's friends and coactivists saying to her in a social setting, "isn't that so, Jane?" and getting the response, "frankly, no."[27] To Eugene Odum, "she was a person who could get people to work together. Her charm, skill, and patience—she had such an attractive personality—it was hard to get mad at her." Odum recognized that Jane "taught the academics how to deal with and convince the private sector."[28]

When Yarn landed at the Atlanta airport, she went right to work getting in the middle of the nascent conservation efforts, helped by her membership in the Habersham Garden Club. She first learned a lot from a design study course offered by the University of Georgia School of Landscape Design and sponsored by the Garden Club of Georgia. She took advantage of an opportunity to attend the Natural Resources Institute offered by Valdosta State and Shorter Colleges. After studying the issues, she joined the Georgia Association of Landscape Design Appraisers and led its leadership group into Bob Hanie's little office. The association had a small project to study the marshes of Glynn, which under Hanie's advice became a broader project focused on Georgia's marshes. From these simple beginnings she was asked to help Hanie organize a conference on the future of the marshes and barrier islands and very quickly was immersed in Georgia's grassroots environmental movement. But she never lost her connection to the garden club members across the state, and by 1969 she was on the board of the state organization and cochair of its conservation council. She chaired the Habersham Garden Club and focused its monthly programs on conservation and through articles in the *Garden Gate* she encouraged the other hundred clubs in every part of the state to do the same.[29] Some former members, who had tired of flower arranging and beautifying small parks, returned to the club because the group was working on something worthwhile.[30] When Yarn needed letters sent to members of the legislature, her fellow gardeners across the state responded enthusiastically. Garden clubs and the women who led them were an overlooked source of power but became a gentle but potent force in the growing environmental movement.

One environmental issue that needed attention was Georgia's polluted rivers. The Vandiver administration, in 1957, had given the Department of Public Health broad—but unspecific—authority to protect the state waters from the pollution quickly rising from rapid urban and industrial growth.[31] The Council on Water Quality created by the Georgia Water Quality Control Act was tasked with meeting and giving "advice" to the Department of Health, but it created no specific agency to actually carry out the broad mandate and no budget to hire staff. Responsibility with no budget line item meant no action. Very little changed in the state until 1964.

Another little-noticed source of power came during the avalanche of legislation passed in the second year of the Sanders administration. A bill passed in 1964 created an independent Water Quality Control Board with all the powers and the mandate of the 1957 act, but with teeth.[32] While it remained under the umbrella of the Department of Health as a division for administrative purposes, the board was instructed to "set water quality standards, issue and revoke permits for the discharge of sewage, industrial and other wastes in the waters of the state." It set rules related to both the surface and underground waters of the state. The 1964 act declared it to be state policy that water resources be "utilized prudently to the maximum benefit of the people in order to restore and maintain a reasonable degree of purity." The phrase "reasonable degree" gave the agency discretion and established a protocol that first sought cooperation. Perhaps the most important aspect of the new law was that it granted independence to the board and control over policy and staff.[33]

Sanders appointed R. S. "Rock" Howard in 1964 as director of the work of the WQCB and to employ a group of professional engineers with the mission to clean the state's rivers. Georgia was behind other states in fighting pollution, but it was about to catch up. Sanders had hired a fighter.[34] Howard was a large, athletic man with an engineering degree from Clemson University, where he had pitched for the baseball team, quarterbacked for the football team, and boxed intercollegiately. His boxing career spanned high school in Savannah, Clemson University, and the U.S. Navy, where he was his ship's champion. He was 6' 4" with long arms and large hands—or fists, depending on the need of the moment. Somewhere along the line his size, his boxing career, and his personality appropriately earned him the nickname Rock.

Howard graduated from Clemson during the Depression. He quickly took a job teaching and coaching in Brunswick, buying a little house on St. Simons Island where he experienced the coastal environment firsthand. He spoke three languages and was assigned to espionage during World War II. Howard never revealed to anyone his war experience specifics. Returning from the war, he also returned to Brunswick and worked for the State Health Department under a small federal grant intended to reduce malaria and yellow fever. When Georgia had a chance to send an engineer to a new Harvard University masters program in sanitary engineering, Howard was first on the list. Having obtained his graduate degree, he returned to the South and spent nineteen years in Albany, Georgia, as the health engineer for Southwest Georgia. Because both the work and money were slim, he was also the Daugherty County engineer and the warden at the county prison farm. The warden's job came with a pickup truck and a house, which significantly stretched the combined $12,000 a year salary. His education and experience made him the best person in Georgia to lead the state crusade for clean water.[35]

In 1964 Georgia had nearly four hundred industrial plants, only one of which was treating its wastewater. That plant was built by the U.S. Army Corps of Engineers during construction of the dam for Lake Allatoona in 1947. Only a few cities and towns were doing even minimal treatment of their sewage before dumping it into a nearby river. Georgia had invited industries to bring jobs to the state, but it had not held them accountable for the resulting pollution.[36] An environment that could absorb waste was an asset when recruiting industries. The pulp and paper industry had assumed it was its right to fill the rivers with the effluent from its many mills.

Leonard Ledbetter was the first engineer Howard hired. Ledbetter really had no interest in working for a government agency when he got a phone call from Howard at Georgia Tech. The work Ledbetter had done as a graduate student with an Alabama Water Commission was enough to interest Howard, and the offer of a free lunch in the state cafeteria was enough to interest Ledbetter in a further conversation. Howard, driven by a cause, convinced Ledbetter to reverse his private-sector plans. He committed to join an agency where the only other employee was the secretary. But Rock Howard's "charisma and deep commitment to the mission" was hard to resist. Ledbetter graduated on Friday with a master's degree and walked into the WQCB office on Monday. At the start, to prove to themselves they could make a difference, they selected ten plants and ten municipalities to see what could be done. If they had no success, Howard and his engineers would quit.[37] Howard told his staff how to conduct themselves when doing the government's business: never take a cup of coffee from anyone, and don't go to lunch with them. Instead, go into the field and ask for the compliance plan for meeting new standards.[38]

The authority under the legislation was broad, but "maintain a reasonable degree of purity" left room for industrial engineers to argue. Howard, however, was not particularly tolerant of their arguments. The WQCB's budget was insufficient to take deep-pocketed polluters to court, so he tried not to go there. The agency could not impose civil fines for violating orders. He found it quicker and more efficient to take his data to the local community through the front pages of the state's newspapers. Reporters would keep in touch with him because they knew he had a good story editors would like. When he used descriptive language not usually used in public the reporters appreciated his candor and protected his public image. His large personality was hard to ignore.[39]

Some time after the 1965 Savannah River federal enforcement conference, engineers from Union Camp (formerly Union Bag and Paper Company), the largest paper mill in the world at the time, came to Atlanta to discuss the waste discharged from their Savannah plant. The engineers sat across the conference table from Howard's engineers, who had determined the water standards they expected from the plant's discharge. The engineers for the company argued those results could not be "reasonably" achieved with the technology available. They went back and forth for over half an hour. Howard, leaning back in his chair with his hands behind his head, reached the end of his patience. He brought his large boxer hands from behind his head and crashed them on the table. It silenced the conversation. He demanded, "what time is it?!" They all looked perplexed, first at the clock on the wall, and then back at Howard. "It is 1967 and we have the science and engineering that will soon put a man on the moon. Get out of my office and don't come back until you have a solution that meets our standard." The story became legendary within the agency, and Howard's leadership motivated his small staff.[40]

Howard knew Georgia was no longer a small-town, old-fashioned, row-crop farming state with so much water it did not need to care about pollution. He had inherited "hundreds and hundreds of problems" that were ignored by the "last generation." He clearly had in mind the pulp and paper plants scattered across the state. He knew that towns recruiting new industry were not "prepared with adequate sewage treatment plants to accommodate industry and a rapidly increasing population." He wanted the state to be selective in the industries it was seeking, and he wanted to help communities be ready to meet the environmental needs of those new industries.[41] Howard was able to help voters see the social and economic implications of pollution, but he also had a holistic view of the impact of the environment on people: "Humans must have beauty. They have to have recreation. If a man sees and smells only pollution, he is going to be a terrible creature. We will have more mental and physical illnesses."[42]

He also believed in the public's right to know and to speak. In 1966, he took his message across the state through local public hearings to hear from communities how they wanted to use their rivers. He would set standards based on a system of classification. Howard went beyond the federal mandate, which covered only interstate rivers, to set standards on streams flowing within the state only.[43] He came away from the hearings convinced the people of the state would support efforts to end pollution. After the hearing experience, he told Robert Hanie he was optimistic that, with the support of the people, Georgia could "make great strides" against the water pollution issues.[44]

Of the top ten industrial polluters targeted in the early days of Howard's tenure at WQCB, many were willing to work out a compliance plan once they saw the agency was reasonable but, if ignored, would take action in the courts. The owner of a mining company in Cartersville met Howard and Ledbetter as they walked into the courthouse. The owner wanted to see if they were serious, but now he was willing to resolve the issue. They worked out a clean-up plan and together went to the judge for approval.[45] In some cases they created partnerships between industry and municipalities that resulted in the construction of a treatment plant serving the interests of both.[46] They preferred to negotiate compliance and were willing to give reasonable time to meet the water standards.

Not often, but enough times to be remembered fifty years later, the board's crusade ran into stiff local political resistance. Howard and the agency ignored local politics and stepped into the ring the courts provided. Most memorable was the case against a dye and fabric finishing plant in Swainsboro. The company's attorney was George L. Smith (at the time still Speaker of the independent House of Representatives). Smith, who vigorously defended his client, kept Leonard Ledbetter, then assistant director for industrial waste, on the witness stand for ten hours challenging his expertise. At one point, the Emanuel County judge hearing the case told Smith privately that he was tired of seeing Smith pass laws in Atlanta, and then argue they didn't apply to his local community. Smith, knowing the judge was going to rule against his client, said he would move to have a jury trial on the issue. The judge, showing the power of a Superior Court judge, responded that he would then direct the jury's verdict. The judge gave the parties six weeks to cool off and think through the issue. Before the deadline expired, the company agreed to the WQCB's proposal that they pay a third of the cost of a city treatment plant, and that Swainsboro would treat the plant's waste. The board also provided a state grant to pay for a third of construction of the plant.[47] Howard was "reasonable," as the statute suggested, but he did not back down from a fight.

As one might expect, the settlement in Swainsboro wasn't the end of the story. Beating the Speaker in his home county made Howard, Ledbetter, and their board a little nervous. A call came from the Speaker's office, asking Howard and Ledbetter to come see him at the Capitol. The meeting was a surprise for the agency men: the Speaker hoped they understood he had to fight for his client, but their campaign to clean the state's waters was the right thing for Georgia. They had his full support. "How can I help you do your job?" he said. The answer was always a budget that fit the challenge. Although Smith promised more funds in the next budget, he had a heart attack and died before he could fulfill his commitment.[48]

During its first five years, the WQCB investigated more than five hundred municipal and industrial polluters. The investigations included nearly every river in Georgia, but it was the lower Savannah, its estuaries, and its marshes that drew Howard's special attention.[49] Howard was not happy when Ralph Nader sent a team to Savannah that produced *The Water Lords* exposé in 1971.[50] He felt Nader's environmentalists should stay in Washington and clean up the waters of northern Virginia, but the book spotlighted the extent of the pollution in both the river and the marsh. Its most shocking revelation was that fish from the ocean could not swim past Savannah because its waters had insufficient oxygen to support marine life. The fish that tried were asphyxiated. Howard was a hero to the writers because he had put Union Camp, American Cyanimide, and Continental Can on the front pages of the Savannah newspapers, and not in a good way. He singled out Savannah for its failure to treat waste before it was dumped directly into the river. The river had the lowest classification in the state as "industrial or navigational," but it still could not meet the clean water standards. According to the Water Quality Control Board and the U.S. Army Corps of Engineers, it seldom met the minimal oxygen content of three parts per million.[51] Nader's book also burst the myth that the pollutants dumped in the river bypassed the marsh and went directly into the Atlantic. It highlighted Eugene Odum's opinion that the estuaries are fragile and that "a relatively small added input can cause the system to go anerobic, which means that it becomes, biologically speaking, useless." The sulfuric acid discharge from American Cyanimide went into the south branch of the river, and tidal flows moving through the south branch circulated throughout the marshes between Savannah and Tybee Island.[52] If there was a Georgia hero in Nader's book, it was Rock Howard.

So, how did Lester Maddox relate to Howard and the mission of the Water Quality Control Board? First of all, the WQCB and its mission was the brainchild of the previous governor. There was no visible environmental plank in the Maddox election campaign, nor was it an issue that reached the level of public discussion during the campaign. Early in 1967, Howard and Ledbetter received a request to come talk to Maddox about their work. Maddox addressed them as "Mr. Rock and Dr. Ledbetter." After brief introductions and a short explanation of the mission, Maddox said he did not know much about the nature of the program or the issue, but he would support them in "the good work" they were doing. Even more important to the engineers, the governor made it clear he would never politically interfere with their efforts to clean up the rivers. Then he asked, "what do you need from me?" The answer, as always, was budget support. Maddox said he would help with that, and there is evidence that he did. By the end of the Maddox governorship, the staff of the WQCB had grown to fifty, and it was still operating independently.[53]

Ledbetter recalls one event that gives insight into the governor's approach to environmental issues. The board had provided one third of the funds to construct a treatment plant to a small town in West Georgia, and a state school in the town had also paid another third of the cost. The community wanted the governor to speak at the dedication and the governor's office asked Mr. Rock for a speech. A staff member wrote a speech they thought the governor would be comfortable giving, which focused on pollution and the fragile nature of the environment. The staff writer attended and reported back that Governor Maddox read the first paragraph, then put aside the carefully drafted text, and warned the audience about the pollution of the mind and the threat that communism represented to the public order and the spirit of the country.[54] The governor was clearly more comfortable with his broad ideology than the details of environmental policy, but he was not likely to interfere with the work of others who knew more about it than he did.

If Rock Howard was the hero of Georgia's efforts to clean its rivers, Reid Harris is the man most responsible for saving the marshes. Harris was just thirty-one when he was first elected to the Georgia House in 1964. He was born into a family deeply rooted in coastal Georgia and in the leadership of the Brunswick community. His father, Myddleton "Mid" Harris, was a hard act for any child to follow. Mid went to work in the middle of the Depression (1937) as a runner for the First National Bank of Brunswick; through very hard work, thrift, and personal enterprise, he ended his career as the president and the largest single stockholder. At one point Myddleton was president of the school board, on the board of the Presbyterian Church, and on the board of the Brunswick Port Authority. He was instrumental in expanding the Colonel's Island Terminal Port, which became the most active automobile importation center in the state. The auto port, across the river from Brunswick, needed to be in an incorporated municipality to bring a railroad line to the dock area, so Myddleton helped get the legislation done. Recognizing his inspiration and work, the Brunswick business establishment named the new town—which had no residents but just ships and cars—Mid, Georgia. Myddleton also found time to create a Kiwanis Club for Brunswick and to serve on the R. J. Reynolds Research Foundation. Reid's older brother, Myddleton Jr., was second in command at the bank and became the chair of the board of the Georgia Bankers Association in the late

1960s, when Reid was in the legislature. The bank and the family had a close relationship with the Alfred Jones family, owner of the Sea Island Company and the Cloister, a five-star resort. Myddleton Jr. had a long-term seat on the board of the Sea Island Company and took his turn as president of the local Chamber of Commerce.

As bank president, Myddleton Sr. had a role in the Carnegie family struggle over the future of Cumberland Island. Before the Carnegie Trust, established by the family matriarch Lucy Carnegie, was dissolved in 1962 by the death of the last direct heir, Georgia law changed to require the trust to be managed by a Georgia bank. In 1957 the First National Bank of Brunswick became the trustee for all Carnegie land on Cumberland. Many of the direct heirs, no longer closely connected to the island, responded favorably to a proposal to strip-mine part of the island because geologists had discovered titanium under its wooded uplands. The bank, meeting its fiduciary duty under the trust agreement, asked for mining proposals and awarded a twenty-year contract to the Pittsburg Paint Company. Lucy Ferguson, one of the direct heirs and a Cumberland lover, took the trust to the Georgia Supreme Court for its actions. The court vacated the contract because its life would go beyond the likely life of the trust.[55] While the recent history of Cumberland is well documented in a number of books, the deep connection of the Harris family to the coastal issues is important to understand.

Bright as a child, Reid Harris pulled more in the direction of the arts than the core business of the family. He was an enthusiastic and accomplished pianist. In his early school years he went to Glynn Academy an hour early so he could play its grand piano before classes started. Since he grew to his full 6' 4" height in high school, the tallest person in his graduation class, he spent the first two years of high school on the basketball team, but not the last two. His yearbook shows music to be of greater interest to him than sports. He participated in the glee club all four years and he is at the school's grand piano as the accompanist for the Girls Septets. The time saved from sports went into his love of writing, and in his senior year Harris became the editor in chief of the school newspaper.[56] He dreamed more of being a concert pianist or a southern writer than a forward for a championship boys' basketball team.[57]

Mid Jr. was seven years older than Reid, and when their mother left the boys home alone, Mid would sometimes lock Reid in an upstairs closet, or on one occasion hang him out of the second-story window of their home. And drop him.[58] In an unpublished, highly autobiographical novel, Harris has the main character following his brother off the dock into a fast-moving stream and nearly drowning.[59]

In his high school years, Reid was a favorite babysitter for his two nieces. They loved it when their mom, a single mother, went out for an evening, because Uncle Reid would come in with his Donald Duck act. He could perfectly mimic the Disney character and, using the voice, read favorite stories—backward.[60]

Harris graduated from Glynn Academy in 1948 and left home in the fall to attend the University of North Carolina, Chapel Hill. Halfway there, he turned his car around and returned to Brunswick—to see Doris Nelms. He was sitting on the front steps of her home on St. Simons Island when she came home in her nursing uniform. The visit was a surprise to Doris and the reason for the visit an even greater surprise. Would she marry him? The answer was, yes—but not until he finished college and had a financial plan to support marriage and a family. Harris turned his car back to Chapel Hill and finished his degree in political science.[61]

The marriage to Doris was postponed by another obligation: serving in the military. Harris served in an intelligence unit of the army and was assigned to the Army Language School at the Presidio of Monterey, California, where he became proficient in Russian. For the rest of his life, he could hold a conversation in the difficult language. Although Harris had not met all of Doris's security requirements, he did have a seat in the new law school class at Emory University when they married in the fall of 1955.[62]

In 1958 he became a first-year lawyer at the respected firm of Conyers and Gowen in Brunswick. Albert Fendig, who was one year behind Harris at Glynn Academy, recalls they were both sent to the damp, insect-ridden basement of the Glynn County Courthouse to do what many first-year associates did—search titles. The search required the young lawyers to trace the title back to a King's Grant, which was the beginning of the chain of title to most property on the coast.[63] There is no record of what Harris thought of this assignment, but the search must have had some appeal, because real estate law became the focus of his law practice. He had also read many "King's Grants" and knew they didn't usually include the marsh. Fellow lawyers described Harris as rooted in the intellectual issues that formed the foundation of Georgia law.

Harris likely did not see the connection at the time of how searching musty documents would yield a core idea in his legislation to save the coast. However, understanding what the king of Great Britain granted would become critical to the question of who owned the marsh.

Chapter 6

Let's Dig Up the Marsh

Making landfills with ooze and silt dredged from
the sea floor or elsewhere is sheer nonsense.

—Rep. Arthur Funk

When Reid Harris packed up his things from his Atlanta hotel room after
the first forty-day session of his third two-year term and headed back to
Brunswick, it was likely with a great sense of accomplishment and with
palpable excitement about getting back to his family and law practice. He
had been in Atlanta every week for almost three months. He had made the
trip home nearly every weekend and his family came to Atlanta a few times
during the session. He had kept his legal cases active but used a legislative
privilege to postpone the trials on those cases that could not be settled by
phone from the legislative anterooms. He knew from past years that most
of his clients respected his legislative service and for the most part had
waited patiently for his attention. Occasionally his partners filled in for him,
but that was not good for the long-term relationship, and he respected his
partners' concern about his lack of revenue production.[1] Rep. Dean Auten,
who served the Brunswick district from 1976 to 1986 confirmed the difficulty
of running a business while serving a district remote from the Capitol.[2]

One friend and real estate broker remembers completing a sale, but the
buyer wanted Harris to do the closing. The answer was no. Harris was on
his way to Atlanta for the session. The refusal didn't end the friendship or
the business relationship, but the agent was unhappy because "he needed
the commission."[3] His friend and fellow conspirator Roy Lambert, who had
a solo law practice, knew the cost of legislative service. When the session
let out early on Friday afternoons, Lambert made a beeline to his Madison

law office so he could spend the weekend catching up on his clients' business. Since Lambert's office was closer than Brunswick, he could handle a few emergencies during the week, but, like Harris, he stayed overnight in Atlanta.[4] Most of all, Harris was excited about waking up every morning next to his wife in their comfortable and beautiful St. Simons Island home. He knew the rushed weekend trips home didn't let him love and cherish his family as he had promised to do.

His wife and three sons keenly felt the sacrifice each Sunday afternoon when he backed the car out of the drive for the seven-hour drive to the capital. They carried on without him, but he missed out on the pleasures of parenting and felt he put too heavy a burden on his wife to run the household and take care of the family all week. It was 305 miles to Atlanta, almost the longest trip of any legislator in the state, and although there was an active evening life that surrounded each session, there were many lonely nights.

Despite the personal burden of his public service, Harris left the session with a great sense of satisfaction for the contribution he was making to the quality of life in his state and his community. After years of dramatic change in the makeup of the legislature, there seemed to be a new team of members seeking to modernize Georgia law and address public issues in a straightforward and creative way. Harris's role in the fight for the legislative independence of the House had shifted power in the state to the legislative branch, and in the process he had made close friends and gained respect from members across the political spectrum. On the floor of the House, he was a lawyer for members who needed help wording amendments, even if he opposed the amendment.[5] Power in the legislature had not come to him by appointment or by election to a position of leadership. He wasn't an officer, a governor's floor leader, or the chairperson of a committee large or small. His influence came from persuasion and hard work. He knew something about all 196 members and had an index card on each to remind him of their occupation, special interests, hometown, and legislative engagement.[6] He was a key member of the House Judiciary Committee, which handled a large percentage of the bills introduced each year. The committee had managed the work on a new appellate code and the revision of the Georgia Constitution that had been on the state's Bar Association want list for a number of years.

He was part of the team of lawyers who had worked these bills through the House and the Senate.

The passage of the 1968 Surface Mining Act enhanced his reputation among his colleagues and brought recognition from people statewide interested in restoring mined-out kaolin pits and protecting the environment. From this experience, he knew how long it took to gather support for a significant piece of legislation and the satisfaction it brought to have his ideas govern a part of the state's business.

Ideas for legislation came from personal experience. Yearly trips to Florida to see family had taken him past "the slime pits, the bleak landscapes the mining left in its wake after the phosphate had been extracted."[7] On one visit he read in the local newspaper a child had drowned in one of the unsecured lakes mine operators left behind. Harris became determined to force mining companies in Georgia to restore the land when the extraction was done. When a fellow legislator from South Georgia brought him a small bag of phosphate rocks he had picked off the ground near the Florida border, he knew it was not long before phosphate miners would be coming to his state. For a few days Harris carried the rocks in his suit pocket, fingering them, and thinking. He then went to Legislative Counsel and had a resolution drawn authorizing an interim study committee to look into the issue and bring recommendations to the next session. This was 1966. The resolution went into committee but never received a hearing on the floor. Patience and persistence, he learned, were keys to legislative success.[8]

Early in the 1967 session, Harris learned a member close to Speaker Smith had requested his resolution be buried in committee. Soon Harris was sitting next to Rep. Paul Nessmith on the House floor for a private conversation. As reported by Harris it went like this:

"Can't go for that, young man," he said. "Be harmful to my business."
"I thought you were in the business of selling heavy equipment," I said.
"Sell a lot to kaolin miners," he explained.
"If the mining were regulated, the miners would have to clean up their sites. It would take more, not less equipment," I said.
"Hadn't thought of that," he said. "You going to introduce your resolution again?"

"Plan to. Are you going to fight me again?" I asked.

"Nope. Bring me a copy before you drop it in the hopper this time and I'll sign on as a co-sponsor."[9]

Harris knew if a more experienced legislator's name was early on the list of sponsors the measure would have a better chance of passing. This time it passed without significant opposition. The study committee, which included WQCB director R. S. "Rock" Howard, traveled to mining sites during the interim.[10] Howard was the chief architect of efforts to clean up the rivers and organized the committee's investigation. Harris made sure their visits included the phosphate mines and stagnant ponds in north Florida. Later Howard assisted with the drafting of the Surface Mining Act for introduction in 1968 and had Harris's back during the legislative process.

When the Surface Mining Act was introduced at the beginning of the 1968 session, Harris's name appeared first on the bill. It was immediately followed by veteran legislators. Harris carefully reviewed the House members who outranked him in years of service and picked Paul Nessmith as second signer because he usually appeared only on noncontroversial legislation.[11]

The details and provisions of this legislation provide insight into the structure and intent of Harris's future efforts to save the marsh and as such are worth a close look. While the bill's purpose was to promote an "efficient and productive mining industry," it also had an environmental purpose: to "advance the protection of fish and wildlife and the protection and restoration of land, water and other resources affected by mining" and assist the state in the "reduction, elimination or counteracting of pollution or deterioration of land, water and air attributable to mining." It was okay to remove the "overburden" (material covering the deposit) to get to the valuable minerals, but before the state licensed the extraction, the miner needed a Mined Land Use Plan, showing how the land would be restored. This Mined Land Use Plan was the heart of the bill, for it required after the mining was complete, the site "shall be consistent with the land use in the area and the mine and shall provide for reclamation of the affected land." The bill also created a board to issue licenses, enforce its provisions, and oversee the implementation of the plan. It was also important that a board dealing with mining include representatives recommended by the Game and Fish Commission and the Water Quality Control Board.[12] Later, a similar board to monitor a spe-

cific environmental task would be part of Harris's future legislation directed
at saving the marsh. This bill fit the Progressive Era model of conservation.
It required miners to use nature efficiently and to use some of the resources
extracted to return the land back to where it was when they started. When
the mining companies wanted to extract minerals from the marshlands, one
of the big questions would be whether they could restore it after it was destroyed in the mining operation. Can you regrow a marsh?

The usual last section provided for an effective date, that is, a starting
date, an issue that later would be important in the Coastal Marshlands Protection Act. Many legislative battles have been fought over this seemingly
benign section because it is the point of transition between the old practice
and the new. Approved on February 15, 1968, the Surface Mining Act did
not take effect until January 1, 1969. The governor could begin appointing
members of the board and that board could issue rules as soon as the governor signed the bill.[13] However, the mining operations begun in the months
remaining in 1968 would not be affected by the provisions of the bill. It also
did not anticipate mining of lands covered twice daily by tides.

One could argue that this was the first Georgia environmental law of
the new era. It gave Harris experience devising a regulatory framework that
could control the use of a natural resource of the state and, like the Water
Quality Control Board, an agency that could enforce its rules. It also recognized the need for coordination between state agencies responsible for the
natural environment, and it fostered cooperation through membership on
the board. A board also helped to balance the private interests at stake. But
the effective date of the bill made it a nonplayer in the 1968 battle to save
Georgia's coastal marshes from the hydraulic dredge.

As Harris left the legislative session, all seemed right with his world. He
was in line to be the new president of the Brunswick Bar Association and
was well liked by other lawyers in town.[14] He had a wonderful wife he loved
deeply, three boys to parent (the youngest, Doug, was born in 1967 and still
in diapers), a prospering law practice, and popularity with the voters of his
district. His election to a new term in the fall seemed almost certain. Re-
publican-leaning voters remembered he stood up for their rights to pick the
state's governor, and his vote for Bo Callaway had reflected their will. He
even had a little statewide recognition, a plus that puts a spark in any poli-

tician's eye. The next two years would test all of that, and the tests were not long in coming.

In his suit pocket Harris carried a telegram from the managing partner of Conyers, Fendig, Dickey, and Harris. Albert Fendig Jr. had called an unusual partners meeting for 8:30 a.m. Saturday, the morning after his arrival from Atlanta. When he walked into Fendig's office, all of the partners were gathered. Nobody was talking. Something was up, and it was not the celebration of his return or the landing of a large new client. As Harris recalled, Fendig was the only one to speak.

> Placing his cigar carefully in the ashtray on his desk and averting his eyes from mine the spokesman cleared his throat. "We've decided that you are not to run for the General Assembly again."
> I was stunned. I looked around the room. All eyes were cast toward the floor. "Do you understand what I said?"
> A surge of anger hit me. "How can I not understand?"
> "Well, what is your response?" His voice was cold.
> "You want a response just like that?" I asked. "Not possible right now."
> "When will it be possible?"
> "I'll give you a reply Monday morning," I said and walked out of the room.[15]

Reid's best advisor was his wife, Doris. Her advice was direct. "You can't even think of staying with the firm. What will they do to you in the future? Risks, risks, to heck with the risks, you can make it on your own."[16]

He tried to compromise by committing not to run in 1970 and give up part of his income from the firm, but that went nowhere. They agreed that he would leave the firm on June 1 after he resolved or passed on the work he had already lined up. Harris's father, Myddleton Harris, board chairman and president of the First National Bank of Brunswick, voiced support of his son, saying simply "Do what you think is best. I will send as many clients as I can to your new office."[17]

Sources do not provide a clear reason for the firm's decision. Most likely the reason was economic. Small-town law firms needed partners who made a strong contribution to the income of the firm, and a partner in Atlanta working on state business didn't fit that definition. Former Brunswick representative Dean Auten (1976–86) remembered that the financial complaints of his insurance agency partners during a period of his most intense legislative activity led him to sell part of his business at a loss.[18] That is the way Albert Fendig III remembers the decision regarding Harris's partnership in the law firm. Fendig III had developed a strong international litigation practice and remembers most decisions being left to his father and to Tom Dickey. He did not attribute "politics" to the move to ask Harris to leave the General Assembly but believes it was rooted purely in the fact that a small firm could not subsidize a partner who was deeply engaged in the legislative process.[19] If Harris had doubts about the motives for the decision, he kept them to himself when he published his account of the events of 1968.

His second test would be getting reelected. There was no challenge from the Dickey-Fendig firm. Albert Fendig III, who people always thought would have a political career like his uncle Charles Gowen, who had founded the firm and held the seat for many years, had no interest in politics at this point in his legal career.[20] Harris did pick up an opponent in the Democratic primary. It was not a huge worry because Harris had solidified his popularity. His vote for Callaway earned him a free ride from the Republicans.

The third challenge to his comfortable and successful life emerged from a meeting that took place in Governor Maddox's office on May 24, 1968. On that date, the Kerr-McGee Corporation, represented by Charles Gowen—who had moved from Brunswick and the Fendig law firm in 1962 to join Atlanta's most prominent firm, King and Spalding—met with the governor and the Mineral Leasing Commission. On behalf of Kerr-McGee, Gowen asked the state commission to advertise for bids on a lease of 72,000 acres of marshland as well as the open estuary known as the Wassaw Sound, including the seafloor off the beach and out to the 3-mile limit. They included marshes around Little Tybee Island and Cabbage Island, which they owned, and the marshes around Wilmington Island, part of which they controlled by an option. Kerr-McGee planned to strip the overburden, pile it up on an island, sandbar, or marsh, and dig out the phosphate ore lying just above the limestone and protective clay layer just above the freshwater aquifer. In part, the proposal had real estate implications because the dredged marsh material could be used to create new waterfront property.[21] The word got out because Maddox invited two reporters to the meeting. According to Reid Harris, the front-page news on May 25 "would change life forever."[22]

Kerr-McGee's ownership of Little Tybee Island, Cabbage Island, and its option on Wilmington Island made the proposal very real and limited the possible bidders to one. The corporation had recently purchased a little-known Georgia corporation established by Jim Williams, Fanjo, which owned Little Tybee. Kerr-McGee quietly bought Cabbage and Petit Chou Islands directly from Williams. Williams, a small-time local antique dealer and consultant with development ambitions, would later become famous as a leading character in the historic Savannah melodrama narrated in John Berendt's best seller, *Midnight in the Garden of Good and Evil*. According to Berendt, Williams used the proceeds from his first venture in the historic preservation of some townhomes to purchase Cabbage for $5,000. Some old hands said it was a foolish investment because it had been on the market a year earlier for half that price and because only 5 of the 1,800 acres were above the high-tide line. You could not build a house because there was insufficient elevation above the high-tide mark. But Williams added considerably to his small but growing wealth when in 1968 he sold Cabbage for $660,000.[23]

Very few people knew about Kerr-McGee's interest in the minerals on the Georgia coast prior to May 24, 1968. State geologist and mining engineer Jesse Auvil worked as a private consultant for Kerr-McGee beginning in February that year. At the request of the Department of Mines, potentially commercial deposits of phosphate had been identified earlier by the Engineering Extension Service of Georgia Tech.[24] Auvil had not shared with other governmental officials his research done under the private contract, so the news came as a shock to Rock Howard and George Bagby.

Georgia law that would govern Kerr-McGee was slim to nonexistent. In 1885, Georgia had joined other coastal states in a rush to find and mine phosphate. Their nineteenth-century laws were only designed to *attract* miners to the coast by protecting their claim. If someone discovered phosphate on the Georgia coast, they only needed to verify the "claim" with the secretary of state and obtain the rights to mine the phosphate within 5 miles of the discovery. Further, the law stipulated that no one else could stake a claim within 20 miles.[25] Georgia's Surface Mining Act had not anticipated mining the ocean floor, nor would it go into effect until January 1, 1969. Clearly, no existing laws prevented Kerr-McGee from strip-mining the islands it owned, but it was not clear who owned the surrounding marsh. Jack Crockford, deputy director of Game and Fish and a member of the newly created Surface Mining Board, emphasized these points to the Natural Areas Council. Kerr-McGee "owned the land and could be mining it at the present time."

He had "little confidence of halting the mining through legal means."[26] No law protected the marsh.

Just three months before Kerr-McGee's plans became known, Odum had proposed that the federal government prevent the dredging of the marsh. At an all-day meeting on Jekyll Island, the federal Water Quality Control Administration held an open hearing to collect information for its National Estuarine Pollution Study. The Georgia Pulp and Paper Association told them there was no need for new laws, but Odum urged the federal agency to prevent any dredging and filling of the marsh because it would drastically reduce seafood production of the entire coastal zone.[27] The record of this meeting was used to educate Rock Howard and Attorney General Arthur Bolton, but there was no definitive legal help available.[28]

Perhaps with good legal advice from Gowen, who had practiced law on the coast for more than two decades, and from the lawyers of the state's most prestigious corporate law firm, Kerr-McGee had decided to resolve any issues of ownership through the request for a lease of the surrounding marshlands. Gowen certainly knew that title companies would not insure a title to the marsh. A fee simple purchase of land from the state was subject to much more public scrutiny, and the lease option held out the possibility of a quick and quiet transaction.

Quiet, however, it wasn't. Public discussion of the Kerr-McGee proposal exploded after the meeting with the Mineral Leasing Commission on May 24 made front-page news the next day. The company plan to remove the overburden meant dredging between 70 and 120 feet below the marsh or ocean floor. According to Kerr-McGee's vice president T. F. Seale, who was in the meeting with the governor, the dredged material could be used to create a lot of oceanfront property similar to drive-in, boat-in lots along the New Jersey and Florida coasts. They wanted a large area to make the mining operation "as competitive as possible" and estimated the phosphate ore would be four to five times the ore currently mined in Florida. Gowen told the Mineral Leasing Commission that the lease applied to the bottom of Ossabaw and Wassaw Sounds and all the marsh surrounding the two estuaries. He declared that the mining operation would create the "first class beach development on Little Tybee" that Savannah deserved.[29]

Seale told the commission the mining operation would not "do anything to damage fish and wildlife." The company, which had been launching oil drilling platforms off the Louisiana coast since 1946, said its extraction operations "did not bother the shrimp . . . it's actually helped them." Kerr-McGee speculated that 1,500 jobs with a $10 million payroll could come from the mining operation if a phosphate finishing plant were located in Savannah.[30]

As governor, Maddox chaired the Mineral Leasing Commission, and was favorably disposed to the idea. The proposal ostensibly fit the consensus among recent Georgia governors committed to developing new wealth and new jobs. In the May 24 meeting, Maddox commented on the proposal: "This looks like something good to me. If we can protect the industry already there, work out a good lease, and get some royalties for the state, I'm for it." After some explosive comments from Rock Howard and words of caution from Attorney General Arthur Bolton in the meeting, Maddox did admit that "the question on everybody's mind is what damage would be done." He agreed the commission should advertise for bids but made it clear the bids "could be rejected if such a lease were found not in the state's best interest."[31] Like most governors at the time, he was quickly enthusiastic about the opportunity to create new wealth but wanted to hear more.

WQCB director Rock Howard had attended the meeting uninvited. He reacted with the loudest cry of anguish, both in the meeting and afterward to reporters. He knew firsthand what phosphate mining had done to the land in Florida. He told the commission that the proposed mining operation "will destroy forever nursing grounds for shrimp and fish and ruin the estuaries now under study by oceanographers." He asserted that "we're trying to bring the shellfish back in there and a dredging operation will destroy them." Furthermore, he had *not* been informed of the mining proposal beforehand, and his agency had primary responsibility to keep the waters of the state clean. He would need time to review the impact of the mining proposals on the state's waters.[32]

Other officials in the meeting were concerned but did not express their concerns as vigorously as Howard. George Bagby and Secretary of State Ben Fortson reported having "reservations." In his capacity as attorney general, Bolton raised the issue of who actually owned the marsh. "Before we could advertise for bids," he warned, "we must know what we're dealing with."[33]

Maddox did two important things in the May 24 meeting that would become essential elements of the environmental movement when it blossomed in the 1970s. Sensing a need for broader public discussion, Maddox appointed a subcommittee headed by the attorney general to review the proposal. It is not clear who in the meeting suggested holding public hearings on the lease—it was a central part of Rock Howard's approach to environmental issues—but Maddox fully supported the idea.[34] After all, he thought of himself as the "little people's" governor who listened to what everyday people had to say. The press also reported that in the meeting Maddox made it clear he wanted to get input from scientists.[35] The resulting hearings gave an opportunity for a broad array of shocked opponents to voice their concerns and rally environmentalists across the state to defend the coast. The state's environmental advocacy organizations were tiny, but the hearings gave them an opportunity to magnify their voice so the public could hear and respond to their cry for help.

University of Georgia scientists soon expressed their concern to Maddox. E. L. Cheatum, who Eugene Odum had recruited to the university to head its Institute of Natural Resources, wrote the governor in June to urge caution because "any activity involving dredging and filling . . . could affect the biological productivity of the estuaries." Cheatum urged the governor to mobilize information bearing on the lease.[36]

Maddox did one more thing that was unusual for the times. He took up the university in its offer to gather information, asking George Simpson, the chancellor of the University System of Georgia, to create a commission of scientists to study the impact of the Kerr-McGee proposal and report back to him. His call for an impact study foreshadowed the National Environmental Planning Act of 1970, which opened the environmental decision-making process to grassroots involvement and scientific review during the 1970s. Impact statements in the future would require public comment and thus offer opportunity to rally public support for or against a proposal. But in 1968 Georgia did its study because Lester Maddox wanted it.

The wheels of the opposition moved quickly. With conservation organizations still in their infancy, state governmental officials led the first wave of opposition and alerted the public of the threat to the coast. Rock Howard was the first to sound the alarm, but George Bagby was not far behind. They spoke with unusual candor and independence for state agency heads. There was no waiting for the governor to stake out a position. Despite his initial enthusiasm, Maddox did not limit the public discussion or try to muzzle his agency heads. On this environmental issue, Maddox gave state officials, whom he respected for their knowledge, the freedom to speak their minds.

Maddox asked his commissioner of Game and Fish to brief him about the issue. George Bagby had fished Georgia waters since he was a young boy but knew little about technical environmental issues. He asked advice from Leon Kirkland and Jack Crockford, the agency's top professionals. Kirkland "went ballistic." He knew about the effect of phosphate on fish populations. "Leon got very upset. When they walked into the Governor's office, Bagby said, 'Chief we have a problem.' Kirkland got Bagby upset, and together they got the Governor upset."[37]

At first, Jim Morrison, the information director for the Game and Fish Commission, knew only a little about environmental issues. He first heard about the mining proposal from Jane Yarn and Tom Lowndes, the latter a friend from the Game and Fish staff. They were on the third floor of the Capitol, just outside the entrance to the House chamber where lobbyists gather and Yarn was in the early days of her efforts to educate legislators on environmental issues. It was the beginning of a productive partnership.[38]

Morrison, a writer trained at the Henry W. Grady School of Journalism (now the Henry W. Grady College of Journalism and Mass Communication) at the University of Georgia, viewed himself as an "excellent propagandist." Not only did he have the will of a propagandist, but his position at Game and Fish also gave him tools any propagandist would need. Morrison aired weekly fishing reports that were syndicated on seventy-five radio stations across the state, he edited the *Game and Fish* magazine with a circulation of 35,000, and he could flash a press release to two hundred newspapers in the state, all of which amounted to an impressive reach in the predigital age. He stayed in close communication with the Georgia Outdoor Writers Association. Using Kirkland's knowledge of the fragile coastal environment and under his direction, Morrison immediately cranked out a news release that hit the newspapers and laid plans to have Kirkland participate in the radio feeds. These fish reports were not supposed to be political, but the shows were popular with sportsmen in rural areas, and station managers tolerated a little discussion of public policy. Over the next two years in every small town, people read Morrison's news about the threats to the Georgia marshlands, with all the scientific bases carefully covered.[39]

Rock Howard wasted no time outlining his objections in a letter on May 28 to Attorney General Arthur Bolton, the point person to gather information on the proposal. Howard shared his objections with the press as well.[40] His two lines of argument, which would remain consistent throughout the public debate, focused on the artesian aquifer and the potential damage to the shellfish industry. The mining operations, he insisted, would damage the shellfish breeding grounds. He had seen the "slime waste" in Florida when he served on the Surface Mining Study Committee. The by-product accumulated in the Florida holding ponds occasionally broke through the dikes to damage local water supplies, he reported. Howard later wrote that he was "not opposed to industry but we ought to make sure that such exploits won't leave a community in utter desolation, either above ground or below the surface of our waters."[41] Howard quickly took the issue to his Water Quality Control Board, which joined the fight against the mining proposal. Phosphate mining can't be done, he pointed out, with the "equipment now being used without transgressing our coastal water guidelines and hurting the fish and game waters."[42]

Howard dispatched Leonard Ledbetter, the board's assistant director, to review the phosphate mining in north Florida that Howard had seen himself in 1967 and to a deep mine near a North Carolina marsh. Ledbetter came back with a report spotlighting the negative impact of phosphate mining on local water resources. The North Carolina mine was pumping millions of gallons from its pits to keep the mine dry for giant excavation equipment resulting in lowering the surrounding water table.[43] Kerr-McGee would need to show more detail on its mining techniques if it expected permits from Howard's Water Quality Control Board.

Charles Wharton, the Georgia State University biologist who chaired the Georgia Natural Areas Council, told Governor Maddox that the council was unanimous in its opposition to mining the coast. He pointed to recent ocean farming experiments that could create a whole new industry producing food from the sea and urged adequate study for a "higher and better economic use . . . as well as keeping it in an aesthetically pleasing condition, some of these natural treasures that belong to all Georgians."[44]

Vernon Henry, director of the UGAMI on Sapelo, wrote Robert Hanie, director of the GNAC, that "something must be done to prevent what will surely be the destruction of property that admittedly cannot compare with mineral extraction for a short term economic gain, but is most assuredly more valuable on a long term basis." He urged Hanie to organize the opposition to mining the marsh. Henry volunteered to join an ad hoc committee he hoped Hanie would form to get land conservation legislation passed.[45] Ossabaw Island owner Eleanor "Sandy" West also urged Hanie to action when she wrote him on June 9 that "the possibility of mining is so awful that it doesn't bear thinking about."[46]

Immediately on reading the May 25 news report on the meeting, Rep. Arthur Funk of Savannah, who had been Rock Howard's math teacher, shot off a telegram to Governor Maddox urging him "to make haste slowly. . . . Making landfills with ooze and silt dredged from the sea floor or elsewhere is sheer nonsense." He was also the first elected official to record his opposition. Funk joined Howard with an early warning that dredging the overburden could puncture the Floridan aquifer and cause seawater to seep into Savannah's freshwater supply and much of the coastal plain.[47]

Georgia scientists played a critical part in the public debate over the Kerr-McGee mining proposal. They explained the science of the marsh to Reid Harris and the leadership of the state agencies. They held press conferences, wrote lengthy letters to help leaders understand the marsh, and showed up at public hearings armed with science-based testimony. They recognized this was a teachable moment for the public, and their status as employees of the state university system did not inhibit them from providing information or opinions.

Apart from the UGA zoology students and professors, most of the state's scientific activism in 1968 came from a unique brotherhood of scientists living at the University of Georgia Marine Institute on Sapelo Island. At a time when scientists and engineers were getting ready to put a man on the moon, their work was closely followed and highly respected. There were eight and sometimes nine permanent faculty members living on the island, but their ranks swelled in the summer as researchers came from universities across the country and around the world. A ferry motored them across the silent marsh.

Fred Marland spent 1966 at West Georgia College before his former colleague from Texas A&M University, Vernon Henry, the acting director of the institute, asked him to join the Sapelo research team. John Hoyt, a geologist researcher, came to Sapelo in 1960 after a stay in South Africa where he saw giant dredges destroy the country's dunes and beaches looking for diamonds. Dirk Frankenberg grew up in Marshfield, Massachusetts, where he had played in the marsh as a boy and as an adult saw it disappearing.

Tall, with piercing blue eyes and an impeccable memory of people (including their middle initials), Marland saw the institute as a monastery where each person had his or her own catechism, but all were united in a commitment to the marsh and estuary surrounding Sapelo. They shared ideas and critiqued each other's work as they moved up and down the halls, searched the library, tested in the lab housed in the old barn, or shared a seat on a small boat headed into the marsh. Their families were with them, but for the scientists the only distraction from their research was the beauty of their environment.[48]

They knew the results from researchers who came before them. Founded in 1953 by R. J. Reynolds Jr., who loved the sea and ships and longed for more knowledge of Georgia's estuaries and coastline, the institute had turned out marsh ecology research that was respected by scientists around the world.[49] Georgia decision makers had fifteen years of careful scientific research to guide their public policy decisions.

When the threat came from phosphate mining, they all took the vow to "save the beautiful landscape." Marland and fellow scientist Tom Linton remembered Kerr-McGee from their days at Texas A&M. They had watched the company's assembly line in Port Arthur launch oil-drilling platform after oil-drilling platform into the Gulf of Mexico weekly. They knew the oilmen of Kerr-McGee as Texas "roustabouts." Marland characterized the company's approach as bullish: if something was not working, "you get a bigger hammer and hit it again harder."[50] Kerr-McGee had an attitude, but so did Linton and Marland. The scientists of Sapelo were not going to let some "Texas roustabouts" destroy their islands and marshes.

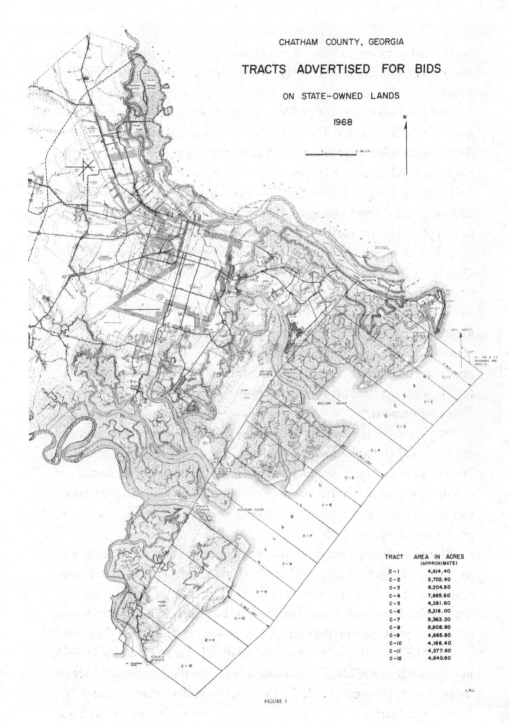

Kerr-McGee proposed leasing area. (From "A Report on the Proposed Leasing of State Owned Lands for Phosphate Mining in Chatham County, Georgia to the Chancellor of the University System of Georgia," 1968, appendix A-4, p. 41)

The scientists on Sapelo had heard rumors of coastal mining proposals in early 1968, but no one had asked for their opinions or for the result of their scientific studies. Vernon Henry wrote to Rep. Harris on February 27 asking for information on the proposed mining of Little Tybee Island. He had read the Surface Mining Act and wanted to know if permits had been issued and "who would judge if the company has returned it to the natural state." He needed Harris's "help in this cause—and it has come to that—is earnestly solicited."[51]

Few people knew about the actual Kerr-McGee proposal prior to the meeting on May 24. Gowen formally requested a meeting in a letter dated May 17.[52] And no one outside the Georgia Department of Mines knew any details on the proposal. Assistant Attorney General Don Hartman, who provided the Mineral Leasing Commission with legal advice, was handed the Kerr-McGee form of the lease before the meeting but had not had time to read it. However, he did alert Jack Crockford, deputy commissioner of Game and Fish, about the meeting and someone, probably Crockford, alerted Howard.

Hartman feared it might get rushed through because Governor Maddox and the nongovernmental members of the Mineral Leasing Commission were reportedly excited about the prospect of new investment and new jobs. Shortly before the May 24 meeting, Jack Crockford called Linton, who was the oyster expert at the UGAMI, alerting him of the threat and asking for help. Linton talked to Director Henry, and the next morning Linton, Henry, and Marland drove to Crockford's new Trinity-Washington office in Atlanta, at Crockford's request. Howard joined the meeting; together they devised several emergency strategies. The scientists would spread the word to all of their colleagues and begin assembling the relevant research. They would seek help from colleges and federal agencies. They would all work to get the information to the press ASAP. Jim Morrison would be key to getting the details out to the press and would use the pages of his magazine to help the average person understand the scientific impact of the mining operation. As the meeting was breaking up, the scientists were told that copies of a map outlining the proposed twelve-lease bid area of 72,000 acres to be strip mined were being printed next door in the Department of Transportation basement printing office. The offset printer was spitting out copies right that minute. After some introductions, the printer said it was okay for Marland to take two of the 3-by-2-foot copies.[53]

On their way back to Sapelo, the scientists went by way of Savannah and gave one of the maps to John Burk, a trusted employee and close friend of newspaper publisher Charles Morris, the owner of newspapers in Augusta, Savannah, and Jacksonville. Burk passed the map on to one of his reporters, and it eventually ran on the front page of the *Savannah Morning News*.[54] Burk kept Morris's deep-sea fishing boat in top condition, and when the publisher, an avid ocean angler, next felt the urge to wet a line, Burk arranged the trip, which gave him the opportunity to talk with Morris about the threat to his fishing grounds. In turn, the publisher made sure his reporters stayed on the mining proposal and gave the opposition support on the editorial page. The scientists took advantage of their news pipeline—feeding information to Leon Kirkland and Jim Morrison, which Morrison would get out through his "propaganda machine."[55]

Back home on Sapelo, Marland and Linton drafted letters to colleagues around the country asking for scientific data and analysis that could help avoid a "potential catastrophe for the Georgia Estuaries and nearshore area." They believed the "dredging and removal of these marshes and beaches preclude all other desirable uses as nursery grounds for fish and shellfish, aquaculture, boating, sport fishing, water skiing, water fowl hunting, bird watching, etc. We believe that the landscape should be preserved, and that the greatest benefit to the citizens of this country would require that the marshes, beaches, and near shore environment be spared of strip mining." They appealed to their colleagues to send any "ammunition" that would help defeat the Kerr-McGee proposal.[56]

Concerned they would not be able to completely stop the mining proposal, the scientists were scrambling. In a May 31 letter to Attorney General Bolton, Marland outlined requirements the state could impose on Kerr-Mc-Gee that might give the company second thoughts and might give the attorney general leverage with the governor if outright opposition was not possible. He suggested that Kerr-McGee be required to give the Mineral Leasing Commission, Rock Howard, the U.S. Army Corps of Engineers, the University of Georgia Natural Resources director, and all affected landowners a two-month notice plus detailed plans before dredging could begin. The plan should contain details of where and when the dredging would start and where the material would be put. Additionally, the plan should be published in both local and statewide newspapers. He sent Bolton a copy of *The Proceedings of the Georgia Public Meeting of the Nation's Estuaries* held on February 29, 1968, on Jekyll Island. He included in his letter a quotation by Director Henry from his February 27 letter to Rep. Reid Harris: "Our coastal environment is one of the state's most valuable natural resources. They work for us at no overhead cost—and their productivity can be markedly increased through understanding how they operate and enhancing the process already established by nature."[57]

Marland argued that there would be no trees or corn growing on top of the mud dredged from the marsh. He speculated that offshore pits as deep as 150 feet in diameter might lead to the erosion of Tybee Beach and the beaches of Hilton Head. He asked the state to require Kerr-McGee to pay for any beach erosion their offshore mining operation might cause. He also reiterated grave concern for the aquifer.[58]

Just days after the May 24 meeting in the governor's office, Marland also sent a plea for help to the U.S. Department of the Interior.[59] He got help. Fred Singer, deputy assistant secretary of the Department of the Interior, responded to Marland's plea by setting up a committee of department agencies to help defend Georgia's marshlands. As a result, a permit from the U.S. Army Corps of Engineers would be required for "any kind of dredging on the coast." He said the U.S. Army Corps of Engineers' authority and the Fish and Wildlife Coordination Act "give us sufficient input to protect any national interest which may be involved in the proposed operation." He told Marland that the regional representative of the Federal Water Pollution Control Administration would convene a meeting in Atlanta on June 13 to coordinate efforts with state officials.[60]

All the key Georgia players in the mining fight were on the twenty-five-person invitation list for the June 13 meeting: Odum, Howard, Crockford, Ledbetter, Jim Henry, Fred Marland, and Tom Linton. Howard Zeller, who left Georgia Game and Fish when Bagby got the top job, coordinated the meeting and the follow-up as the regional director of the Federal Water Pollution Control Administration. Nonstate agencies included the U.S. Army Corps of Engineers, the U.S. Fish and Wildlife Service, the

Bureau of Sport Fisheries and Wildlife, the U.S. Geological Survey, and the Bureau of Outdoor Recreation.[61] While only a small number of these federal agencies appeared at the public hearings later in the summer, the state leaders knew they had the backing of their federal colleagues and would follow their lead when regulatory opportunities became clear. Kerr-McGee also had a good understanding of how to get things done in Washington because its powerful founder, former senator Robert Kerr of Oklahoma (1949–63), had earned the title as the Uncrowned King of the Senate. Kerr's friend had been another powerful senator and majority leader, Lyndon Johnson, now sitting in the White House. But this did not deter the professionals in government agencies who understood the need to protect Georgia's coastal environment. There is also no evidence that the president, who had his own environmental agenda, interfered in the work of the federal agencies. Georgians were reaching for a bigger hammer.

Eugene Odum was part of the public debate at almost every step. Through his interest in the work of the fledgling Georgia Conservancy, he met Jane Yarn, who encouraged him to get involved.[62] His first foray into the public fray was a joint news conference held with the Georgia Conservancy. They presented a petition signed by twenty-five scientists opposing the strip mining. Both the scientists and the conservancy argued mining on the coast would "seriously damage marine life and jeopardize coastal development." Odum cautioned that their opinion was "based on information available," although he declared that "there is every reason to believe that extensive pollution, damage to sport and commercial fishing, reduction of potential protein food resources, and damage to recreational areas and aesthetic value would result should unrestricted strip mining be allowed over large stretches of the Georgia coast line." It was a "dangerous precedent" to "hastily" sell the estuaries that belonged to the people of Georgia. He called for careful study as any lease needed restrictions and cautions.[63] While Odum and the conservancy made clear their opposition to quick action, they did not slam the door on a cautious, studied plan of mining options.

Odum enlisted his graduate students to join the fight. He divided the rural counties in South Georgia among the students and asked them to offer free public seminars in those areas on the value of coastal marshland. He encouraged the activism of the zoology students and supported their efforts to organize the Georgia Sierra Club group.[64]

Forces on the other side of the issue were mounting their defense of mining. At the invitation of Jim Hall, the staff of the Brunswick business coalition, Committee of 100, nearly all the principal local business players in the state's decision gathered on the second floor of the National Bank of Brunswick on July 24 in a private meeting. The committee's membership included heavy industry, real estate development, hospitality; the committee worked closely with the Brunswick Chamber of Commerce. Hall had invited T. F. Seale, senior vice president of Kerr-McGee and attorney Gowen to present their plans. Local Reps. Reid Harris and Richard Scarlett, and Sen. Ronald Adams were joined by the Brunswick city manager, its director of planning, the county administrator, and the head of the Brunswick Port Authority, as well as David Maney, director of the Coastal Area Planning and Development Commission. Reid Harris drew state agencies to the meeting, including the Game and Fish Commission, represented by Rock Howard and Jack Crockford. There were three representatives from sport and commercial fishing and two island owners, Bill Torrey (whose family owned Ossabaw Island) and Bill Jones of the Sea Island Company. The young scientists from Sapelo met beforehand with Reid Harris at his office in the bank building and walked across the street with him for lunch at W. T. Grant's department store. They were forming a close-knit team with Harris. The Sapelo scientists present were John Hoyt, Fred Marland, Dirk Frankenberg, James Howard, and Thomas Linton.[65]

It was a full house. All the key players except the governor were present. No reporters were present, and no written historical record is known to exist of the meeting beyond Fred Marland's firsthand recollections. Sen. Ronald Adams cordially introduced attorney Charles Gowen, who continued to represent Kerr-McGee on behalf of the King and Spalding law firm.[66] Gowen was the perfect person to pitch the project to the Brunswick business community. A respected community leader for most of his adult life, he had personal connections to almost all of the businesses in the community. He represented Brunswick in the Georgia legislature from 1939 to 1960 and was the managing partner of the Dickey law firm in the city prior to joining King and Spalding in 1962. The community was proud of Gowen, who had even been a candidate for governor in 1954.[67] It was Gowen who had hired Reid Harris in 1958 right out of Emory Law School. As a lawyer himself, Harris understood that a lawyer was responsible for representing the best interests of his client, and throughout the next two-year battle over the future of the coast he never publicly criticized Gowen for doing just that in this case.

According to Marland, Gowen spoke softly about the economic benefits of the Kerr-McGee proposal, the strength and experience of the extraction company, and how it was good for Georgia to welcome "good folks" who had contributed much to Texas as the initiator of oil production in the Gulf in 1947. Some at the gathering had expected that T. F. Seale of Kerr-McGee would provide details on how the dredge and fill process would work and how the slime waste material would be disposed of. However, neither Seale nor Gowen presented any expected engineering or scientific detail on their planned mining operation.[68]

Marland, who had carefully organized the Sapelo response to Kerr-McGee, was neither soft-spoken nor deferential at the closed July 24 meeting. He was quick to describe the potential damage that would come to the whole coast if the mining proposal went forward. He characterized the deal as a Texas boondoggle, "like the Yazoo Land Fraud" of 1794.[69] After the meeting Marland wrote to Reid Harris to thank him for getting state officials to attend the meeting and hoped he "wasn't too vituperative in questioning Mr. Gowen." It was not quite an apology, but he did recognize that Gowen was a person of "great inner sensitivity" and felt he would be against the proposal if he were not representing his client.[70]

The views of those present at the meeting would be made very clear through various channels during the summer and before the final Savannah public hearing on September 30. In August, Arthur Bolton asked the scientists from Sapelo for their analysis of the mining proposal. Most had attended the Brunswick meeting on July 24 and expressed disappointment in the lack of detail offered by Seale regarding what they viewed as an experimental mining operation. Each scientist drew from his particular discipline.

Geologist John Hoyt, who had been studying the movement of sediments along the coast since 1960 with fellow UGAMI colleague Jim Henry, published a 1967 scientific paper on barrier island formation. In his letter to Bolton he warned that deepening the ocean floor off the barrier islands in order to reach the phosphate-rich material would diminish the cushioning effect of underwater land. "The waves will act directly on the shore and rapid erosion will ensue," requiring expensive beach refurbishing. To prevent beach erosion, Kerr-McGee should be required to fill the offshore holes with material from farther out to sea and restore the sea bottom to its original state, not unlike the requirements of the Surface Mining Act. A jetty out to sea from the barrier islands, which Seale had proposed to protect the mining operation, would disrupt the natural movement of sand and sediments from north to south and stimulate more beach erosion downstream. In his letter, Hoyt then turned his attention to the problem of the removal of the marsh overburden and the layer of phosphate ore, concluding it was not economically feasible to fill the resulting holes. This in turn meant that the marsh "can never return to its ecological role of producing nutrients and nursing grounds for coastal organisms." In his final, nonscience-based argument that came from living on Sapelo, he stated his belief that the marsh and the beauty of its barrier islands would be needed for the future recreational needs of a growing population and others seeking quality and beauty in their lives. The "value of the coastal islands and marshes for their recreation and attendant fisheries industry suggests that modification and destruction of these areas are hardly in the best interest of our people," he concluded.[71]

In his letter to Bolton, Dirk Frankenberg bemoaned the lack of detail shared with the group in the July 24 meeting. Seale's "casually stated opinions" were insufficient to predict the effects of the mining operation. From the information Kerr-McGee had made available to date and presented at the meeting, it was "impossible to arrive at a very clear picture of the planned operations . . . and unfortunately one cannot adequately assess the potential harm of Kerr-McGee's operations without knowing what the operation will be." As a marine ecologist who had studied the oxygen content of the estuary and marsh waters, he believed the additional sediments added to the water from dredging would critically reduce the oxygen content and overpower the respiratory systems of oysters and other bivalves. The environment of the marsh was a delicately balanced ecosystem, he argued, that if disturbed by sediments from the dredging could result in the explosion of "unexpected and often noxious plants." He said the wastes from the processing plant were toxic and feared they would not be piped far enough out to sea to keep them from returning to the Georgia coast. It was inevitable that the mining would destroy some part of the marsh, with the resulting reduction in food supply to the marsh diminishing the "number of organisms that depend on it." He expressed concern for the aquifer and believed a $1,000-a-day fine for breaching its ceiling was grossly inadequate to compensate the state and local cities for the damage it would do to the coast's clean water supply. If the proposal were to go forward, Kerr-McGee needed to prove with "hard data" that its process would prevent damage to the coast or adequately compensate the state so that any damage could be repaired.[72]

Marine geologist James Howard had "a great deal of uncertainty" regarding the mining proposal. Since the mining process could affect a public natural resource, he did not buy the Seale argument that the details of the mining process were privileged or private information. Ecosystem scientific understanding made it unlikely that material could be removed from a system without altering the whole system. Strip mining in Kansas might alter the scenic beauty with a refuse pile, he pointed out, but it would not otherwise alter the surrounding environment. The one detail that did come from the Brunswick meeting, the 3-mile waste pipeline, was another concern for Howard. Scientific studies off the North Carolina coast showed sediments dumped offshore were pushed back to the coast by "long currents." If the toxic material got into the flow along the Georgia coast, "each beach and estuary south of the source will receive some share of this material." He called for a minimum five-year moratorium to allow for sufficient scientific research on the "potential problems of this venture."[73]

While the University System of Georgia study Maddox requested continued its slow progress, the public was going to have a chance to express its views on the mining proposal and the value of the marsh. Two public hearings were scheduled.

Chapter 7

Coming in Loud and Clear

Take a message to the Governor from the people of Chatham County.
Tell him we say phooey on phosphate.

—EDWARD NESTOR, Chatham County resident

The public hearings at the State Capitol on September 16 and in Savannah on September 30, 1968, gave state officials like George Bagby and Rock Howard an opportunity to shape the public will. The response at these hearings was loud and clear.

George Bagby led a parade of fifty speakers to the podium in the Appropriations Room in the Capitol, the stately chamber that had previously housed the Georgia Supreme Court. He had been in the well of the House many times, and he was comfortable at a podium. His speech, written by his publicist Morrison, had the feel of a Eugene Talmadge stump speech, and Bagby's language honored the giant of Georgia politics who gave him his middle name. He had no soft words for the Kerr-McGee lease bid. It would "destroy an extensive portion of the Georgia coast for seafood production and sport fishing." He referred to the Bible story of Jacob and Esau: "Georgia would be selling its birthright for a bowl of soup." The company would be "taking Georgia taxpayers' property for a pittance." He pointed out that Kerr-McGee's ownership of the islands made them the only possible bidder on the lease.[1] It was not enough to just oppose—Bagby drew on his populist roots when he painted the proposal as a real estate scheme intended to create oceanfront property the average Georgian would never afford. Kerr-McGee proposed to pay the state $2 million a year for twenty years ($40 million), while the value of fill dirt at the lowest rate of 3 cents per cubic yard equaled $124 million. If we figure the fill dirt at the highest DOT rate of 15

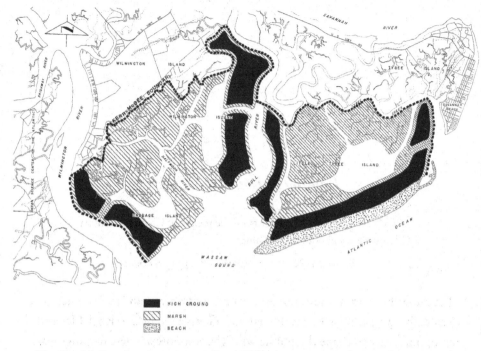

HIGH GROUND
MARSH
BEACH

The Kerr-McGee plan to convert marsh to bulkhead communities, figure 5 of the land-use plan presented by the engineering firm Thomas and Hutton at the Savannah hearing, September 30, 1968. (From "A Report on the Proposed Leasing of State Owned Lands for Phosphate Mining in Chatham County, Georgia to the Chancellor of the University System of Georgia," 1968, appendix A-4)

cents per cubic yard, that would make the fill dirt Kerr-McGee was getting worth $622 million. He disparaged the tiny return to the state. Banging his fist on the podium, he wound up his speech with his department's conclusion: the Kerr-McGee bid was the "greatest giveaway program of Georgia's state-owned lands that has been proposed since the famous Yazoo Fraud. The boondoggle is an outrage to the people of Georgia."[2] Not long after the hearing, he responded to a letter with the same bulldog tenacity. He was "opposed to moving one shovelful of earth off the Georgia coast." His department would "continue to oppose this proposition with all of our vigor."[3]

Representing the Georgia Sierra Club, Steven Johnson recalls that Bagby delivered the speech like a "fired-up" country preacher. The graduate student, who was next in line to deliver the judicious comments of the club, regretted having to follow the commissioner's flamboyant take-no-prisoners style.[4]

Rock Howard, who had led the state's opposition from the start, did not preach like Bagby, but his testimony, written for both the Atlanta hearing and the following one in Savannah, marshaled evidence gathered by his engineers. While he mentioned the aesthetic value of the marshlands, his "grave concern" and public responsibility was for the quality of the water in the marsh and in the aquifer, which in many places was less than 100 feet below the level of the sea. The quality of water in the marsh was currently meeting the standard adopted under the direction of the U.S. Water Pollution Control Act of 1965. These standards, he argued, were protecting such "existing uses as recreation, fishing and propagation of game and fish, including the harvesting of shrimp, crabs and shellfish"[5]

Citing the district chief of the U.S. Geological Survey, he pointed out that even test wells exceeding a depth of 70 feet would serve as a "direct pipe line for ocean water to move into the fresh water zone." Saltwater intrusion into the aquifer near Beaufort, South Carolina, had already caused the town to install a surface water treatment plant at a cost of $5 million. It was questionable if the "destruction" of the marsh was in the interest of the people of Georgia, but Howard's responsibility was clear. He would need a "definitive" plan in order to issue a permit, and Kerr-McGee had not given him such a plan. The state should not make a hasty decision before knowing that the dredging operation was compatible with other beneficial uses. He called for a study that might take up to five years.[6]

Charles Gowen again had the unenviable task of representing his client in a room filled with opposition. His was the only voice supporting the lease. He said the Mineral Leasing Commission should consider it in the public interest to mine the phosphate and should focus on the compensation the state would receive. He contended the opposition was due to a lack of information, but Kerr-McGee could not be expected to invest the "hundreds of thousands of dollars" needed to develop the information unless it was first granted a lease on the state lands. In a distinctly lawyerly way, Gowen stood the lack of detail argument on its head. He announced that his client had hired a Savannah engineering firm to work on "concepts," and they knew the project would not go through unless they "demonstrate to state and federal agencies that mining can take place without causing pollution of the water and air."[7] It seemed like the same point made two months earlier in Brunswick: Trust us. We will take care of the environmental questions.

Jane Yarn had helped Robert Hanie recruit more than fifty people to give their testimony. Yarn's list of expected speakers included the usual state and federal officials but also ordinary citizens who had joined the Georgia Conservancy. Her list is instructive of the broad opposition to the mining proposal.[8] While the record of the testimony created by a court reporter at the request of Arthur Bolton has been lost, we do know who Jane Yarn and Robert Hanie expected to speak. There were federal and state officials representing recreation, water resources, and public health. The health department said it did not see any air pollution issues connected to the mining, but Ogden Doremus—Savannah attorney and founder of the Izaac Walton League—stated that air pollution could be a threat from the release of sodium fluoride.[9]

The hearing in Atlanta revealed that local governments along the coast had been talking throughout the summer and were ready to state their opposition to the mining proposal. David Maney, executive director of the Coastal Area Planning and Development Commission, which covered nearly the whole coast, stepped into the well of the House and stated his opposition with confidence. He presented a resolution adopted by his commissioners stating that the people of the coastal counties were opposed to the lease of state land for phosphate mining.[10] Maney, in his prepared remarks, explained that the state of Georgia had created the Area Planning and Development Commission structure to develop comprehensive plans for orderly growth and development of the area. His testimony recognized the threat to the beaches of the coast identified by the Sapelo scientists and the importance of the natural areas as a storm barrier: "desecration of the marsh surface would remove this buffer and permit shoreline erosion and increase coastal flooding." He recognized that the "tremendous financial worth" had not been realized and asked for more time for the local planning effort to determine how best to utilize the "property owned by the citizens of the State of Georgia."[11] He might have been the first to raise the issue of who owned the marsh at a public hearing. Maney would continue to seek ways to protect the economic and social interests of the coast and become an important participant in the efforts to preserve the marshlands.

Representatives of private organizations who were opposed to the lease also attended the meeting. Two representatives of the seafood industry brought forth their industry-wide fears. Witnesses came from the Garden Club of Georgia, the Georgia League of Women Voters, the American Society of Landscape Architects, and the Georgia Conservancy. When Mrs. Alan Mather spoke at the hearing, representing 2,300 members of the Georgia League of Women Voters, she was cautious but showed a deep understanding of the issues. The league didn't know the answer to the mining question, she said, but urged "utmost consideration of estimated benefits and possible deleterious effects of the proposal." Mather pointedly asked if the leasing commissioners present at the hearing knew if the benefits of the lease "justified disturbing or destroying an ocean bed and marshes which it took centuries to build?" While the league did not take a clear position, the detailed questions Mather asked reflected information provided and concerns raised by the scientists.[12]

Yarn's Garden Club of Georgia members were represented by Mary Helen Ray, who read an official statement representing the board of directors. They had not stopped with a public statement but in the November/December 1968 issue of the *Garden Gate*, the club's bimonthly magazine, urged its 22,000 members to individually write to Governor Maddox and the members of the Mineral Leasing Commission. That issue also listed the names and mailing addresses of all the commission members.[13] Yarn put herself down as fiftieth on the list of speakers—this was possibly the first occasion she spoke in a public forum. Her husband Charlie said "her knees were knocking" when she got up to speak.[14]

Just plain citizens also showed up. Thomas Lowndes, from Tucker, Georgia, was there with his wife. In June he had written Maddox, who responded that "I realize the value of this coastal region and assure you that I do not want to see it harmed."[15] As a child, Mrs. Lowndes had visited her aunt on the marsh banks of the Altamaha River, and the couple loved their visits there together. Lowndes enjoyed hunting, fishing, and camping by a fire in the woods. As a boy he explored the open woods along Buford Highway in DeKalb County. Lowndes was connected to the issue through an intricate network of people, which included Jim Morrison of Game and Fish, the Georgia Conservancy in which he was an active member, and Bob

Hanie, who asked him to take off work from his private-sector job to testify. Lowndes recruited David Nelson, the president of the North DeKalb Jaycees, who later provided a list with telephone numbers for all the Jaycee local presidents on the coast. He felt passionately enough to later drive by himself to Savannah to participate in the hearing there also.[16]

The scientists came to Atlanta to share publicly the analysis they gave Arthur Bolton in private. The public discussion was a critical opportunity to spread the scientific understanding of the value of the marshland. Dirk Frankenberg presented a lengthy paper with scientific data on the likely impact of mining on the oxygen levels in the Wassaw Sound. His paper, to be published by the *Bulletin of the Georgia Academy of Science*, showed oxygen levels would be depleted if mining disturbed the marsh sediments (oxygen-demanding material) and could result in a spectacular fish kill. The mining of the Wassaw Sound "is capable of jeopardizing the historic commercial and sport fisheries of the Savannah region." He bluntly advised that the state should not go forward with the lease of the marshlands.[17] His colleague from the UGAMI, John Hoyt, never missed one of these opportunities, and this time he made a presentation on the importance of the marsh to oyster production.

Federal scientific colleagues, who had met with their Georgia counterparts earlier, brought the same message to the hearing. They confirmed the importance of the marshes and the estuaries as nurseries for the shrimp, the crabs, and the fish that could be harvested from the sea. They were greatly concerned with water quality standards and how mining would impact them. John R. Thoman, director of the Southeast Region of the Federal Water Pollution Control Administration, declared that "the tragedy of wetland and estuarine destruction caused by dredging and filling operations is evident along the nation's shoreline." He pointed specifically to a current mining moratorium in Florida. He also emphasized the financial benefits that came from the fishing industry and tourism, which both depended on the health of the marshes.[18]

Legislators included Reid Harris, Mike Egan, and Tom Palmer from Fulton, and Sen. Frank Downing and Sen. Bill Sisk from Savannah. Sen. William Searcey from Chatham County was not at the hearing, but when he spoke to the press he urged caution. A private meeting with Kerr-McGee officials was unable to allay his fears. He put his concerns on the record: "Mining could seriously affect the fresh water supply, lead to widespread pollution and destroy breeding grounds for shrimp and 85 percent of other fish life in the area." He went on to brand Kerr-McGee an outsider, which resonated with many of the opponents. "The Kerr-McGee people don't live here" he said. "I am thinking about the residents of the Savannah area."[19] Opposition in Savannah appeared to be building.

However, at the time of the September 16 Atlanta hearing, local officials from Chatham County and Savannah were still not taking a firm position on the lease proposal. The county government had adopted a resolution characterized as "wait and see," and commission chair Robert Lovett told the press he had faith in the outcome of the University System of Georgia study. His statement did caution that mining the marsh could pollute local waters. Savannah mayor Curtis Lewis, who had been the most supportive local official of the lease, often described as the lone local optimist, said he had a "reversal" and was now concerned about the effect the dredging would have on the city's water supply. As a recently elected Republican mayor, he may have been thinking about the cost of a plant to purify surface water if the city could no longer rely on its wells that drew water from the aquifer.[20] The Savannah Port Authority, at that time a local authority operating the port, was also reserving judgment.[21]

By the time the Bolton subcommittee came to Savannah for the second hearing two weeks later, the public had made up its mind. They expressed it loudly at what turned out to be a two-day, standing-room-only meeting. Even though the release of the impact study was still pending, there was no more "wait and see" left as far as the public was concerned. The crowd showed up, and the witnesses were nearly unanimous in their opposition to the lease. The hearing on September 30 was first planned for the community room at Savannah Electric and Power, the independent electrical utility serving the city, and arranged by state Rep. Arthur Gignilliat, who was in the management of the local utility. Bolton had required that those who wished to speak at the meeting submit a written application ten days in advance, but, smart elected official that he was, seeing the overflow crowd at the meeting waived that requirement and permitted walk-ins to get the microphone. The morning hearing opened in the community room with

Kerr-McGee representatives speaking first. Governor Maddox did not attend the hearing, but he was clearly listening from Atlanta. When Bolton adjourned the hearing for lunch, he announced it would reconvene at the DeSoto Hilton Hotel, where all the folding doors were opened to create what was then the largest public space in the city. Even so, Bolton extended the hearing to a second day so that all interested speakers (nearly 100) could express their opinions.[22]

And express them they did. "Chatham County residents, coastal officials, scientists and conservation agency spokesmen lashed out with a spirit akin to religious fervor against a proposal to mine for phosphate in coastal waters," the *Atlanta Constitution* reported. Edward Hestor, noting Governor Maddox's favorite term of disgust, "phooey," instructed commission members to "take a message to the governor from the people of Chatham County. Tell him we say phooey on phosphate." Dr. William H. Tailor, the mayor of Darien, pointedly wore a flaming red coat "as a token of the hell we will raise if you grant this lease of Georgia's underwater lands."[23]

The *Savannah Morning News* reported a story told at the hearing by Abraham Eisenman of Savannah: when he was a young man, "he was once rowing through the marshes with a girl and she told him it was the wrong time and wrong place. 'I can say the same thing of this proposal.'" Eisenman didn't want the people of Chatham County to be stuck with problems while the commissioners in Atlanta were "busy making money, making deals, making history." Judge John W. Underwood of Hinesville was similarly concerned that "a roll of bills was dangled before this commission—one dollar bills wrapped in a large bill."[24]

Rock Howard, who grew up in Savannah and boxed there, came to testify. Although he gave much the same testimony as he had delivered in Atlanta, at this second gathering he was also jousting with Union Camp about Savannah River pollution. Unimpressed by the presentation made by a Savannah engineer on behalf of the mining company, he declared that Kerr-McGee "wouldn't have much chance of getting a permit based on your statement."[25]

George Bagby had a new speech, which again circulated throughout the state in the November/December issue of *Game and Fish*. His speech, written by Jim Morrison, again delivered rhetoric unusual from a high state official: "Kerr-McGee is a company that wants to *rape* the Georgia Coast." And he continued the outsider argument: "Kerr-McGee and its owners are the people who will profit by exploiting our state owned lands." He asked if the people at the hearing thought the company would spend its real estate profits in the state. Painting a picture of an arrogant corporation that had not once offered to the Game and Fish Department any explanation of its plans, he demanded full details before any lease could be granted.[26]

Bagby had new economic numbers on the value of the seafood and sport-fishing industries. He estimated the loss of value to the state by 2020 to be $60 million. He saw a great future for the tourism industry from the 5.5 million people who would be driving past Savannah on the soon-to-be-completed Interstate 95 and noted these tourists didn't want to get off the highway to see a phosphate mine or a new subdivision. Neither did he think the tourists or the buyers of fancy oceanfront property would be interested in swimming in "chocolate brown water left by dredging."[27] Bagby's argument fit the development-focused consensus of Georgia politics, but it shifted the object of development away from heavy postwar industry to a growing industry that had a future to add more to the state's wealth.

At one point, Bagby veered off his speech to challenge how Kerr-McGee could possibly restore a mined marsh: "Anybody that proposes to put themselves in God's place and build a marshland . . . buddy, you've got a mighty big job ahead of you." The *Savannah Morning News* reported that Bagby told the story of a legislator with a similar dilemma: "He [Bagby] had a sheep shears in one hand and a skinning knife in the other. . . . And he said if he used the shears he'd get wool twice a year, but he reminded the leasing commission members at the hearing that when you take a knife to the resources of Georgia and you skin it one time, then you ain't gonna get no more wool."[28] He reiterated scientists' predictions about the precious marshes: "once destroyed, they can never be rebuilt."[29]

Bagby covered almost all the points the scientists had made in their letters to Bolton, but they also attended the hearing to bring their scientific knowledge of the marshland to the public debate. John Hoyt specified that Kerr-McGee's deep holes in the offshore ocean floor would erode the beaches; pumped out the specified 3 miles, toxic wastes would still return to southern beaches; and the marsh's nutrient-producing capacity would be permanently damaged by the deep holes in the estuary floor.[30]

At the time of the hearings, the scientists were still not sure the governor would deny the lease. Jack Crockford had told the board of the Council on Natural Areas on July 8 that because of Kerr-McGee's ownership of the land, he had "little confidence of halting the mining through legal means" and urged a focus on the terms of the contract to keep damage to a minimum.[31] As a stopgap, Hoyt presented a suggested list of requirements he had worked on with Fred Marland, to be part of any lease. The list of provisions in Hoyt's testimony included the following:

1. Return of the ocean floor to the original topography (not unlike the requirement in the Surface Mining Act).
2. Lessee payment for refurbishing Tybee Island and Wassaw Island beaches.
3. Removal of the jetty when mining was done.
4. Maintenance of waste products on land where it can be treated.
5. Maintenance of the protecting sediments on top of the aquifer.
6. A fair price for fill material.[32]

These provisions show considerable collaboration between the state agencies and the scientists and were intended to demonstrate the full public cost of the extraction company's proposal. The opposition was reaching for a hammer bigger than the one wielded by the Texas roustabouts they faced.

Fred Marland, in his testimony, reviewed the scientific contribution of the UGAMI from its founding in 1953. He offered a brief lesson on the development of the ecosystem ecology that emerged from the research done on Sapelo and from Odum's new scientific theory. He presented his own research: "Assuming one square mile or 640 acres of marsh are strip mined each year, 1,672 tons of organic matter would be lost from production from the most fertile landscape in the world."[33] Georgia's marshes were actually producing more organic material than the marshes in northern states. Perhaps the audience of average Georgians at the hearing didn't need to understand the science behind the conclusion, but they could understand that "once filled, the restorative and life giving capacities in the way of food and oxygen would be lost."[34]

"There's got to be some way to keep the breeding grounds from being destroyed," Reid Harris told reporters earlier in June. "I feel like we'll see the breadbasket of the Atlantic Seaboard destroyed if we don't do something quickly." At the Savannah hearing he made the point that Georgia's marshes could not be protected under current state laws.[35] If they succeeded in stopping Kerr-McGee's proposal, the next, more difficult step was to regulate how the marsh could be used in the future. This would not be easy in a state committed to the rights of private property and to growing its wealth.

It is again unfortunate a complete record of the testimony given in Savannah does not exist. The newspaper in Savannah did report that there were nine hours of testimony on September 30 and that thirty-one speakers remained to be heard on the second day of testimony. However, the reporters heard no additional information on the mining "concept" that attorney Gowen had promised in Brunswick and Atlanta, and Kerr-McGee's local engineering firm, Thomas and Hutton, said it needed more information in order to begin work on a design.[36] They showed a land-use plan illustrating how the marsh overburden could be used to make upland building sites, but that carried little favor with the crowd (see map, p. 122).

Perhaps the most alarming opinion offered was when former Sen. Frank Downing warned commissioners the giant hydraulic dredges were likely to find "the bomb" if they started digging in the marsh.[37] Most in the audience knew this was a reference to the atomic bomb ejected from a U.S. Air Force plane off Tybee Island in 1958 but never found.[38]

The public hearings and the unusually large participation made it clear the public wanted state officials to save the marshes. Some people were still waiting to see what the University System of Georgia impact statement would say, but Governor Maddox, just days after the final hearing, told Bob Cohn of the *Savannah Morning News* there would not be any mineral exploration on the coast "any time in the foreseeable future." The information presented to him and at the two public hearings had "dimmed" his enthusiasm for coastal mining. Cohn surveyed the members of the Mineral Leasing Commission: Ben Fortson and Arthur Bolton were clearly against the lease; two other members thought it was a good proposal but said they would follow the clear public will expressed at the Atlanta and Savannah hearings.[39] Testimony of three young scientists (Frankenberg, Hoyt, Marland) "had more of an impact on the Georgia Mineral Leasing

Commission in the last month than anything else said by the opposition," reported Cohn, who followed the issue daily.[40] The hearings demonstrated that public officials listen when the message is loud and clear.

The University System Report on Proposed Leasing, organized by George Simpson, chancellor, was close to an environmental impact statement before the National Environmental Policy Act of 1970 required one. It came from a distinguished group of professors and summarized research from the most prestigious universities in the University System of Georgia. It was written at the request of the public-school-dropout governor deciding whether to grant a lease for 25,000 acres of marshland touching on the Wassaw Sound. The number of acres in the Kerr-McGee lease bid was down from the original 72,000 but still included acreage off the Wassaw and Little Tybee beaches. Maddox wanted to know the effect of the mining proposal on water supply, the environment, and the economy. The report, delivered to the governor in late November, summarized the state's request for proposals, bid documents, and the public comments of Kerr-McGee, the sole bidder.[41]

Eugene Odum served on the advisory committee for the study and was responsible for the lengthy environmental analysis printed in full in the appendix. His paper summarized the views of environmental scientists, including those from the UGAMI. Like most reports approved by a committee, the conclusions steered to the middle ground, and lacked the clarity of thought Maddox might have liked or might have come from advocates of a particular point of view. The report was not as clear as Sapelo scientists had been both in their letters and their public testimony.

At some point following the Savannah hearing, Kerr-McGee changed its mining concept regarding the disposal of the toxic waste resulting from the washing process. The scientists had objected vigorously to the 3-mile pipeline that would dump the waste in the ocean. Faced with the strong scientific evidence that offshore currents would push the waste back to the southern barrier islands, they agreed to develop a disposal and storage process on the land. This was a partial win for the scientists. But Kerr-McGee didn't explain how it would dispose of the toxic waste if the ocean was not available.

The report projected three possible uses of the overburden. To obtain 3 million tons of phosphate ore per year, the goal of an efficient mining operation, the hydraulic dredges would need to remove 36 million cubic yards of overburden for every 7.5 million cubic yards of ore. That meant that 40.4 million cubic yards (93 percent) was available to backfill. But fill what? The first option of the report was to use all the material to create upland on which new homes could be built. The homes would be surrounded by deepwater channels and look like many coastal developments from Miami to Portland, Maine.[42] Under this option, no marsh would remain. Fred Marland, in his closing statement to Arthur Bolton the day before the Savannah hearing, pointed out there was no termination date on the "lease" of the land created from the excavated material and that Kerr-McGee would in essence "own" this new oceanfront land. The land would be arranged in "key and lagoon" communities where residents could "park a car in the front yard and a boat at the back." The payment to the state for this new land would be 20 cents per acre.[43]

The second option was to backfill the holes left by the dredges and hope that over time the marsh and its ecosystem would be restored.

The third option would obviously be a compromise between the first two: some marsh restoration and some waterfront property for residential or recreational use. This recommendation showed the characteristics of any report from any committee—on one hand there is this and on the other there is that. This has also been the criticism of many environmental impact studies.

The scientific question at the heart of the last two options was whether the marsh *could* be restored. The Sapelo group was almost unanimous that it could not be done. But Odum talked to ten leading scientists and concluded that there was no conclusive answer: "in general scientists felt that there was no overriding reason why the marsh could not be rebuilt." One scientist called restoring the marsh a "ridiculous idea," but another, showing no great enthusiasm for the proposition, said "I could rebuild a marsh if I had to." They said it would take at least ten years to turn material used to make dikes into new marsh and were not sure how productive the resulting marshlands would ultimately be. There was one scientific example from Sapelo, where Light House Creek and marsh had been diked off for a number of years. It changed chemically to form an acidic sulphide crust known as cat clay, or extremely poor soil that could support no life, neither animal nor plant.

Then it was flooded when the dike was removed. In this one case, the marsh slowly reestablished itself over a period of six years, but the sediment soil in the marsh had never been disturbed.[44] The report, therefore, remained somewhat ambiguous on this critical question.

There was a great deal of healthy academic discussion in the 226-page report and it gave a clearer understanding of the proposal than appeared in press accounts, but Governor Maddox likely turned first to the conclusion when handed the report:

1. The phosphate on the coast was "a potential major mineral resource."

2. Kerr-McGee was capable of mining it if the state did not make it cost prohibitive.

3. The areas diked for mining would remove "extensive areas" from the production of food for marine life and would remain unproductive until mining ceased.

4. The aquifer would sustain minimal damage, and the demand for water would not overburden the freshwater supply of the community.

5. Water pollutants are "amenable to control" except for the oxygen-depleting sediments released from dike construction and offshore dredging.

6. Offshore currents would not be disturbed.

7. Offshore mining that required jetties would alter coastal erosion patterns and lessen the movement of sand to the southern islands.

8. Cost-benefit analysis was inconclusive due to many unknown factors.

9. Georgia lacked a "clear public policy on how to manage and use its coastal resources, including leasing of its tidal bottoms." This comment must have seemed strange to a governor faced with a decision. This was, perhaps, the central question for the political institutions of the state regarding the lease, and eventually the legislation that followed.

10. The report recognized that the state had a number of agencies with conflicting interests and responsibility regarding the decision and complained that there was no "effective mechanism" to resolve the differences.

11. The last conclusion certainly left Maddox scratching his bald spot or looking for his bicycle.

> In order to realize the full benefit from this major mineral resource and at the same time protect in so far as possible other desirable and valuable use of estuaries, it is the opinion of this Committee that (1) a more effective mechanism for reviewing and monitoring conflicting interests be established and (2) that a clear public policy on management and use of all of Georgia's coastal resources must be formulated as a basis for leasing state-owned tidal lands in this area.[45]

Even Kerr-McGee could find passages in the report it could highlight for the governor, noting that

> A lease of the type proposed could be granted without any necessary significant damage to the natural environment other than in the immediate area of operations. At the places where mining is actually carried out, the marshes and ocean floor will be taken out of use for some years so far as the economic production of shrimp, oysters and other seafood are concerned. The natural beauty will also be damaged to some extent. Other hazards discussed in the report could, if proper precautions are taken, be either avoided or kept within reasonable bounds.[46]

Kerr-McGee did highlight the "could" language limitation, and the report went on to say that no mechanism currently existed in state government to supervise the operation. While the mining "could" be done without breaching the aquifer, who would be watching the dredge operator, or his boss?[47]

The report, as would be expected from an academic institution, called for continuous study of the coastal environment and economics of the region. It suggested that a state agency coordinate the research and recommended that the mission of the Ocean Science Center of the Atlantic, created the previous year, be given this responsibility.[48] This recommendation shows the growing influence of the center, whose director served as one of the coordinators of the report, while the UGAMI on Sapelo had no representation among the report compilers. The report shows some of the political sand under the Sapelo brotherhood was shifting.

The report frustrated the governor. Like most chief executives he wanted the report and the scientists behind it to be definitive in order to make his decision clear. Fred Marland had a phone report from a friend who was in the room when the impact report was presented to the governor. Maddox allegedly complained: "Odum doesn't want to make the decision." At some point in the decision process, Maddox told his administrative assistant, Zell Miller, "I want to hear from those young scientists on Sapelo."[49] Their opinion was certainly definitive.

Maddox's closest advisor, George Bagby, waited a year before he publicly let fly his own opinion on the University System of Georgia report. He was provoked by the legislative testimony of a geologist from the state Department of Mines, Mining, and Geology. The geologist told a later Coastal Islands Study Committee that the university impact statement supported mining the phosphate. It was "a valid proposition if handled properly." Bagby, never subtle about his opinions, called the report "a complete whitewash." He couldn't remain silent when after a year the report was still being used to give support for mining the marsh. The report failed to "properly evaluate the wildlife resources that would be lost if they came in there and mined the phosphate." Rock Howard, who had also remained silent on the report, said he was in complete agreement with Bagby.[50]

After reviewing the report in early December—probably not all 226 pages and very likely after consulting with Bagby—Maddox concluded: Georgia has the "finest marshlands in the world" and with the report "we couldn't be assured of sufficient safeguards" to "guarantee" the mining operation would not do more harm than good. He showed his frustration with the report, which was not yet made public, because it said we can do the lease and it also said we can't do the lease. He appreciated the Kerr-McGee proposal because it forced the state government to look carefully at the value of its offshore lands. He encouraged people to keep working on safeguards but said that, even with safeguards, feeding grounds for fish and wildlife would be lost.[51] While Maddox never said it clearly at the time, he did have a different vision for how the state could use its coastal resources. His vision would be tested again before his four-year term was up.

Just a few days following the delivery of the impact report, the Mineral Leasing Commission met, and at the meeting the attorney general offered a very undramatic resolution to the mining lease proposal: the response time in the Kerr-McGee proposal of November 30 had expired. That helped shift some of the responsibility to the lateness of the University System of Georgia study. The commission did give serious attention to the recommendation that the Ocean Science Center of the Atlantic be designated by legislation as the agency to continually review conflicting issues on how to best use coastal resources. Perhaps in response to the governor's frustration, Chancellor George Simpson defended the neutral position of the report, saying that he did not want a University System of Georgia committee making decisions for the state. Rather, decisions were the job of the commission and the governor.[52] Perhaps this was also a warning to the scientists, all University System of Georgia employees, who had taken clear positions on the mining question.

This Kerr-McGee mining lease proposal was finished, but the phosphate still lay under the marsh, and the company had not given up on its desire to mine it. That didn't come until later. The state had made one immediate and important decision by valuing the marshlands more than the phosphate under them. Yet there was no law protecting the marshes from dredging, filling, and developing. Enticingly beautiful hammocks were still reachable by causeways built from marsh mud. Kerr-McGee had proposed taking a large area of the marshland for its own use, but there were also other smaller owners at the edge of the sea who could see the significant value of expanding their private property into the marshland. After all, their property deed said the marsh around their land was theirs, and the county kept expecting them to pay taxes on it. Although the state had turned down this mining proposal, the state had not yet decided the future of the coastal marshlands or the barrier islands that defended them from the sea.

Chapter 8

The Conference on the Future of the Marshlands

Each of us are related to the family of man which is kin to the family of earth.

—ROBERT HANIE

When the lovers of the coast came together in October 1968, the Kerr-McGee mining lease was still on the governor's desk. In the midst of the mining threat, their purpose was to urgently plan for the future of the coast. They were called together for the Conference on the Future of the Marshlands and the Sea Islands of Georgia.

The island owners came because they were worried—with good cause—about rising taxes, roads and bridges bringing tourists, and the state action of eminent domain that might take their property, and with it the peace and beauty their islands gave them. The scientists came bringing sixteen years of pioneering work on the value of estuaries and the barrier islands, which would inform the people who attended. People from national conservation organizations offered their help. So did landscapers, environmental folks, people interested in parks and open space both local and national, archeologists, and, most prominently, the Garden Club of Georgia, the Nature Conservancy, and the Sierra Club. The conference connected all the parties that would need to work together in the coming years and as such was a preview of future collaboration. Collectively they hoped the state would decide the future of its coast based on its intrinsic value in a natural state. Surprisingly, the presenters and organizers came from the public sector. However, they knew private owners would be critical about the decisions that needed to be made. And made very soon.

Changes were coming to the coast. The Georgia Department of Transportation had already planned the right of way of Interstate 95 with eighteen interchanges as the focus of future coastal development. It was a de facto plan for the coast, and construction of I-95 had begun in McIntosh County. People on vacation were encouraged and expected to turn off the highway, and it was hoped that retirees from the colder parts of the country would look for a new home close to the sea.

The organizers who worked closely on the details of the gathering for more than a year were David Maney, director of the Coastal Area Planning and Development Commission; Fred C. Marland, scientist with the University of Georgia Marine Institute (UGAMI) on Sapelo Island; and Robert Hanie, director of the Georgia Natural Areas Council (GNAC). The three met several times to craft an agenda and develop the invitation list that represented all the key interests. Maney, as director of the Coastal Area Planning and Development Commission, had brought the voice of local government to bear on the mining issue, and his commission was most directly responsible for planning the coast's future. Marland, who during the mining fight demonstrated his ability to organize the scientists who worked for state and federal agencies, understood the scientific information that needed to be in the room during the conference. Hanie, in his short time with the GNAC, had visited several of the island owners and had selected Wassaw Island for the first Certified Natural Area. Because of his close connection to the Georgia Conservancy, the GNAC and its Coastal Committee were beginning to show some capacity to coordinate the parties interested in the conservation of the coast. Marland brought the scientists and agency staff, Hanie brought the island owners, and Maney brought the local coastal leadership.[1]

The conference was by invitation, but the information was public. Andrew Sparks witnessed the interaction between participants and reported the critical points of the presentations in a lengthy article for the *Atlanta Journal-Constitution Magazine*. He opened his article by comparing most other Atlantic seacoasts, where "beaches have become metropolis and strip cities, a tight packed, shoulder to shoulder line of motel, hotel, restaurant, bar, beach home, store and filling station," to the tranquil and unspoiled natural environment of the Georgia coast. In colorful language he informed readers that people gathered at the conference were "pressured by a hurricane force of would-be developers who see the coast as an unbuilt Florida. Ready and waiting to roll in a tide of millions."[2] This conference was the perfect opportunity to add his journalistic contribution to the conservation efforts of others.

The Cloister, the Spanish-style hotel designed by Addison Mizner on Sea Island and Georgia's best hope for a five-star resort, hosted and provided all the meals for the two-day conference at no charge: Bill Jones (Alfred W. Jones Sr.), president of the Sea Island Company and owner of the Cloister, sponsored the conference at Maney's request. Jones sat in the front row and for two days listened intently. He, like other representatives of families who owned part or all of the islands, had a long and personal history with the islands and surrounding marshlands. He was in his early twenties when his first cousin, automobile magnet Howard Coffin, asked him to manage the Sea Island property and his other coastal real estate. Coffin, a founder of the Hudson Motor Company in Detroit, had plenty of capital to invest. The tranquil island of Sapelo, Coffin's first investment in 1912, was his retreat from the pressures of the business world, a place of peace and relaxation nestled in its marsh environment. However, like other beneficiaries of the country's rapidly expanding economy, he liked to make a profit. Coffin's investments expanded to include Sea Island, where cattle once grazed. Together the cousins, Jones and Coffin, opened the Cloister in 1928, as "a friendly little hotel" and he bought and restored a century-old hunting club and its 20,000 acres, known as Cabin Bluff, on the mainland across from Cumberland Island. The Depression hit Coffin hard. When he died in 1937, there was little left of his fortune. With no direct heirs, he left his entire estate and the responsibility for his coastal enterprise to his young cousin and business partner, Bill Jones Sr. In the face of devastating losses, Jones struggled to keep the business going.[3] Forced to find capital to keep the enterprise afloat, he sold Sapelo Island to R. J. Reynolds Jr. at a fire-sale price.

The early beginnings of coastal tourism in the late nineteenth and early twentieth centuries had opened four of the fourteen barrier islands to the possibility of a new tourist and development boom. Jekyll Island (acquired by the state in 1947), St. Simons Island, Sea Island, and Tybee Island were all connected to the mainland by causeways and bridges, had hotel rooms to fill, lots to sell, and were generally ready to receive the tourists who were expected to peel off I-95. These islands were ready for development.

But the wealthy families who owned other islands were gathered in the opulent Cloister ballroom to gain a better understanding of their options. All appeared deeply committed to preserving the natural environment they had grown to love.

A brief review provides context. The Parsons family was not at the conference. Their connection to Wassaw Island went back slightly more than a century to 1866. It was the oldest on the coast. The Parsons heirs, who managed the island through a trust, wanted the island to stay wild and free and would only sell if it remained so.[4] They had discussed possibilities with the Nature Conservancy and would follow closely the discussion at the conference. The Parsons Family Trust would be the first to act on the conference's outcome.

Although the wealthy investors of the Jekyll Island Club were no longer connected to the Georgia coast, other investors were very present. Henry Ford still held his plantation on the Ogeechee River just south of Savannah. The Torrey family still owned Ossabaw, and their daughter Eleanor Torrey "Sandy" West would tell her story at the conference. Edwin Noble, who made his fortune from LifeSavers and other candy, had given control of St. Catherines Island to a family-run foundation. R. J. Reynolds Jr. had died before he had executed his intention to preserve Sapelo Island either by a transfer to the state of Georgia or through other means. His third wife, Annemarie, owned the island and was having discussions with George Bagby about its future. The Little Cumberland Island Association was represented by wealthy industrialist Ingram H. Richardson. He had created a unique owners' association that controlled development on the island based on strict conservation principles. The Candler family owned the northern tip of Cumberland Island.

The future of Cumberland Island, the largest of the fourteen barrier islands, was up in the air when the conference convened. The long and somewhat complicated history of how that island became part of our national park system and its partial designation as wilderness is beyond the scope of this book. However, a decision about the future of Cumberland was actively in the minds of the heirs of Thomas and Lucy Carnegie in 1968. The demise of a trust put forty-four heirs into a complicated discussion of what would become of the island and thrust them into the middle of the political debate over the future of the state's coastal environment.

During the conference, which preceded the Brower-Fraser-Candler conversation on Cumberland (see chapter 2), the rumor spread that Charles Fraser had a contract to buy two of the ten parcels that came from the Carnegie family subdivision of the trust holdings. One of his tracts was at the north end just south of the Candler holdings, and the other was on the south. He was already discussing a partnership with other heirs that would allow a private, conservation-oriented development like his Hilton Head Sea Pines Plantation to go forward.[5] When the conference opened, it was not just speculation that the developers were coming for the Georgia coast.

Two owners present at the start of the conference were Clifford and Eleanor Torrey (Sandy) West. Clifford was a documentary filmmaker; his film featuring the environment of their beloved Ossabaw Island, was shown during the conference. He also brought his reel-to-reel high-end tape recorder, from which was made a transcript of all the conference presentations. Sandy West's life on Ossabaw began when her father, Henry Norton Torrey, of Michigan, purchased it in 1924 as a family retreat. He had married the granddaughter of John B. Ford, founder of the Pittsburg Plate Glass Company and Sandy's great grandfather (no relation to Henry Ford). Sandy's passion for saving the coastal environment came from a lifetime of intimate connection to the natural environment of her family land. Sandy and Clifford had formed a trust in 1961 for the purpose of protecting the island from development.[6]

When Sandy took the microphone, she felt a grave responsibility because "whatever happens to one of these large islands involves the other islands and, as a consequence, the entire coast of Georgia, and perhaps the eastern coast of the United States." They had worked for a decade, she said, to find a solution that would work for all of the islands and their owners, but found some people were "interested in just birds, just pine or just marshland. We simply have not been able to find any all-encompassing, all thoughtful overall plan that considers all assets and all resources and recognizes the importance of their inter-relationship." The solution was "unavoidably dependent on politics."[7]

The owners had interests in the islands that went back for generations. They feared they would not be able to maintain the family connection to their islands, that the environment they loved would be destroyed by the oncoming pressure of development. County and state officials were eyeing the islands for opportunities to create wealth, jobs, and more tax dollars. With Georgia's economic growth bringing more people to the state, the new prosperity now gave them the means and the desire to also enjoy the beauty and peace wealthy owners had enjoyed for generations. The post–World War II governors of Georgia were gradually hammering out a political consensus that focused governmental policy on the generation of new wealth from the state's resources. For the most part, Lester Maddox fit into this consensus, and his commitment to growth worried most island owners. Economic growth and the appetite for greater growth could easily threaten those who wanted to preserve the coast for its beauty, peace, and tranquility. The environment was clearly in the crosshairs of people who embraced the unprecedented economic growth Georgia was experiencing.

Beyond the speakers, owners representing Cumberland, Little Cumberland, St. Simons, Sea Island, Ossabaw, and St. Catherines attended. The scientists from the UGAMI participated, as did scientists from the University of Georgia, Georgia State University, Emory University, the University of Florida, and Shorter College. Charles Wharton, the most distinguished biologist from Georgia State University and chair of the Georgia Natural Areas Council, and Eugene P. Odum were recognized as the scientists behind the council's creation.[8] Government agencies included the National Park Service, the Federal Water Pollution Control Administration, the Georgia Game and Fish Commission, the University System of Georgia Board of Regents, and the Georgia Ports Authority. Beyond the national presence of the Nature Conservancy, the representation from Georgia conservation organizations was slim. Only the Audubon Society and the Sierra Club appear on the invitation list, but the local Marshes of Glynn Society was represented.

Jane Yarn was there. In addition to representing the Garden Club of Georgia and the Society of Landscape Architects and Appraisers she gave many volunteer hours helping Hanie with the arrangements. More importantly, Yarn sat next to Thomas Richards of the Nature Conservancy at dinner, whom she had met at an earlier garden club evening. But this dinner conversation hatched an island acquisition plan that moved quickly when the conference ended. Rep. Reid Harris, who had a big part to play, was joined by his Glynn County colleagues from the General Assembly, Rep. Richard Scarlett and Sen. Ronald Adams.[9]

Creating a vision for the future was the role Robert Hanie gave to himself. He was a good writer and he loved the microphone. Despite no direct powers to preserve natural areas, his presence was felt all over the state in the first fourteen months of his tenure as director of the GNAC. Ingram Richardson, owner of Little Cumberland Island, who introduced Hanie as the keynote speaker, heaped praise on the fledgling Natural Areas Council. He said that 1,337 natural areas had been earmarked, and ten of these were now formally protected. The level of protection is a little hard to understand given the GNAC's lack of regulatory authority. Richardson was pleased Hanie had made a visit to Little Cumberland and all eight members of the council had visited Wassaw Island "to find out for themselves what this area was and . . . its significance." He credited Hanie with interesting Governor Maddox in conservation and let the audience know that the governor, at Hanie's invitation, would soon be joining twenty-five businessmen for a hike down Sweetwater Creek, where Maddox wanted to create a 4,000-acre "wilderness" park just outside Atlanta.[10]

Hanie's job as keynote speaker was to summon the participants to a vision for the coast, and he sought to center their thoughts on the idealism of the day. He titled the speech "The Yellow Submarine" and drew inspiration from the Beatles' 1968 hit song "Yellow Submarine," which he also quoted in part. We are all interconnected, he emphasized. Through the lyrics, Hanie pointed the conference attendees to the high ideal that "each of us are related to the family of man which is kin to the family of earth."[11]

For Reid Harris, this conference was an opportunity to gather support for the legislation he planned to introduce in the 1969 General Assembly session. Humorously taking up the image raised by Hanie, Harris said that conference participants "must come up from the yellow submarine" and deal with the practical realities of the Georgia political environment. He felt Georgia was at a critical decision point and "must find the right direction to move in or lose one of our greatest assets." He committed to three legislative actions. The first, patterned after the recent legislation in other states, was to give the state control over dredging, filling, or other uses of the "wetlands." His comments revealed his shift from using state zoning law as the foundation of marsh preservation. The control, he believed, should start at the local level where zoning law could be used but local permits would need the approval of a state board. He did not like the membership composition of the state Mineral Leasing Commission, which he felt left the balance of power with private members "who are not in any way connected with state government." While Harris did not give details on the membership of the board, which indicates what interests control any regulatory legislation, he was clearly committed to a board with strong state agency representation.[12]

His next item of business was the matter of ownership: who owned the marsh?[13] The state's decision makers had not directly confronted this central question during the mining controversy, but Harris knew, from his early days as a young real estate attorney searching titles in the basement of the Glynn County Court House, that ownership of the marsh was in doubt unless you could find a specific grant from King George II in the original title. He knew title insurance companies seldom insured title to the marsh. He also knew Kerr-McGee, which held title to Little Tybee Island, could mine the upland without any interference, but mining the marsh surrounding that upland—and accounting for 90 percent of the island—was questionable. With access to advice from King and Spalding, Kerr-McGee probably also knew this and thus included all of the marshes around its owned islands in the lease proposal. This issue was also likely understood by Attorney General Arthur Bolton, but when the University of Georgia presented the governor with its impact study, there was no mention of this central question of the state's ability to control use of the marsh. Harris believed the law was on the state's side, the state *did* own the marsh. So his second piece of legislation would be to call on the administration to make an official, legal determination of who owned the marsh.[14]

This third initiative would be a study. Reid Harris called for an estuarine study committee to be created to work with nearby coastal states to determine their mutual interest in the coast. He believed greater understanding of the economic and recreational potential of the undisturbed marsh would lead to better decisions, and his trusted scientific friends at the UGAMI supported the need to do more research.[15] There would be good material to study because a national estuarine study authorized by the 1966 Clean Water Act would also be complete. The Department of the Interior, responsible for the study, held a public hearing on Jekyll Island on February 29, 1968. At times in the legislative decision process, motions are made to study an issue in order to deliberately sidetrack an issue because delay usually has a negative effect on the outcome. However, study committees can also be used to produce information, as Harris had done with one in the passage of his 1968 Surface Mining Act, giving him good reason to have confidence in the process. With the leadership of the state government more securely in the hands of the legislature, study commissions provided an effective way to illuminate complicated decisions and they gave the public a chance to participate.

As in the public debate of the mining lease, the scientists were front and center at the conference, providing a solid foundation for the political arguments that would come. The governor had indicated to the press that he was opposed to mining the marsh, but nobody at the time knew for sure what he would do when all the facts were in. Vernon J. Henry, as the director of the UGAMI, introduced the conference participants to the work his cloistered scientists were doing. He welcomed the "gathering of the clan" and gave bold voice to the scientists he led. He hoped the conference would "provide an effective means of coordinating our several efforts to provide the best possible means of preserving our coastal areas . . . not for our lifetime, but for succeeding generations unnumbered." It has taken thousands of years to build the marshes, Henry declared, and we should "not allow man's inherent proclivity to change his environment to lead us into unwise decisions that could destroy these areas forever." He said the scientists were just beginning to understand the "magnitude and potential value of the coastal areas" and outlined research goals that would, over time, help leaders make "reliable judgments" related to the use of its resources in the future.[16]

Fred Marland summarized the results from the scientific research conducted by the UGAMI in the waters around Sapelo Island. His own studies confirmed the work of others, including Odum. The marsh was exporting a great deal of plant material to the open estuaries and the continental shelf. His studies showed that each acre of marsh produced 2.5 tons of organic material that was the "basis of the food chain for fin-fish and shellfish."[17] This basic science provided the central argument for preserving the marsh.

Of all the scientists who spoke, Marland was the most direct in his opposition to the Kerr-McGee mining proposal. He had been out front and vocal on the issue from day one. He declared it was such an "absurd, nonsensical proposal on its face that I don't see how any human being could agree with it. It is a total destruction of a living marsh . . . of a resource." It is "an upheaval, and outrage to our being. This strip mining proposal is shameful!"[18] Above all, Marland showed the fervor of the Sapelo scientists in opposition to mining the coast.

John Hoyt, an institute geologist who also testified at the mining hearings, presented his theory and understanding of how the barrier islands were created. He and Vernon Henry had investigated the geologic origins of the Georgia barrier islands and sought to increase the participants' appreciation for the unique natural area created over millions of years. The islands resulted from a combination of the sea delivering sand and its collection into dunes. What usually happened around the world was that lagoons developed behind the dunes. But in Georgia a large amount of sediment was carried down the fourteen rivers flowing to the coast, and the lagoons were filled over time to create marshlands.[19]

Hoyt's presentation included charts and discussion of movement of the Georgia coastline over millions of years that he illustrated to be a direct result of the level of the sea. He said the most westward location was the Wicomico Formation, now called Trail Ridge, which paralleled the coast along the eastern edge of the Okefenokee Swamp. The swamp, he said, used to be salt marsh until the ocean receded when the sea level dropped by 100 feet to where it is today. In Hoyt's day, Trail Ridge was no longer continuous, but left behind sand ridges that once were "magnificent barrier islands." Hoyt, working with other geologists, identified five ridge lines that had each once been barrier islands of the Georgia coast.[20] The Hoyt presentation is perhaps more important today than it was in 1968, as Georgia officials and environmental organizations target land for the preservation of habitat and seek opportunities for the future of the marshlands to migrate with rising sea levels.

Eugene Odum, who was at the time deeply engaged in producing the impact study Governor Maddox had requested, simplified the broad new theory of marsh ecology to give the nonscientific audience a strong foundation for their conservation advocacy. He gave particular support for Reid Harris's proposed legislation. He predicted the rapid rise of an "urban-industrial

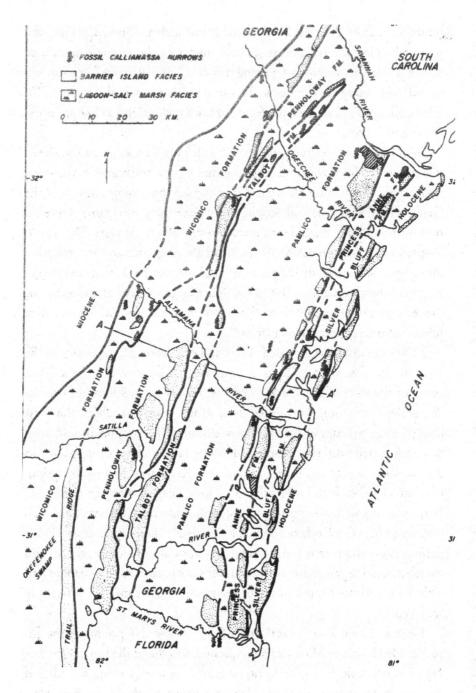

Coastal geology, 1968. (Courtesy of Dr. John Hoyt, geologist, UGA Marine Institute, published in the "Conference on the Future of the Marshlands and Sea Islands of Georgia," 1968)

environment" that "yields no biological necessities" (i.e., food and oxygen), which would arrive along with a new "invasion "of "hordes of Americans storming down into this area." Odum hoped the assembled group would develop a plan to protect the productivity of the state's estuaries and marshes:

> The solution here is to designate the basic component of the estuary as "protective" in order that other parts of the system can be exploited more directly. In Georgia, the salt marshes are the biological heart of the estuary, they must be protected so that the open water portion of the system can be used for seafood harvest, recreation, transportation, mineral regeneration and other needs of human society. If the marshes are safely in a protective category, then the sea islands can also be saved.[21]

Odum's focus on the marsh as the productive heart of the coastal environment gave credence to Harris's legislative focus on the marsh.

Odum had practical advice for the assembled island owners. He asked them not to wait too long for a long-term protective solution for their revered islands. He prodded them with the fact that R. J. Reynolds Jr. intended to give Sapelo Island to the foundation he had created but died of lung cancer before the transaction was complete. He worried Sapelo could be lost to development. He proposed they might help form a "marsh bank" in the form of a foundation that could receive charitable gifts of marsh acreage protected through easements. The use of environmental easements and land acquisition would become a significant tool in the state's effort to preserve biodiverse habitat held in private hands. But perhaps most importantly, he encouraged them to form an island owners association that could have professional staff and collectively manage the challenges coming from the state and private developers.[22]

At the conference, Thomas Richards, president of the fifty-year-old Nature Conservancy, described the practical role his organization could play in the future of the coast. His organization had perfected the preservation tool of an environmental easement. Two of his board members, Richard Pough, a past president, and Ingram Richardson, conference chair, also attended. He advised the assembled leaders they would need a thoughtful plan that could inspire broad political support, and he praised Reid Harris for his support of conservation and his commitment to pass legislation protecting the marsh. He wished they had a Reid Harris in Virginia. He also offered to private owners the knowledge and experience of his organization if they were interested in protecting the coastal environment they currently controlled. His approach differed from Odum's marsh bank idea; in Richards's formulation, the government rather than a nonprofit would be the long-term protector of the marsh, and the transaction did not have to be all charitable. He gave several examples of how the Nature Conservancy had already facilitated a transaction that had moved private property to a protective status of a governmental agency. Each future project, he said, would be under the direction of a local committee that raised funds to cover the cost of a transaction. The conservancy was especially interested in areas that "have scientific or educational values; areas that can be used for parks and open-space activities, or for general open-space purposes," and the Georgia coast certainly fit their interests. In other words, he was interested in the Georgia barrier islands, their estuaries, and marshes. At the end of his remarks, he issued a challenge: "Go out and find a tract of marshland and let us help you put together the package that will enable it to be preserved."[23] Jane Yarn, who sat next to him at dinner, took this as a personal challenge.

The conference had three immediate outcomes. The island owners determined they needed to act together or at least coordinate their efforts. A motion made by Bill Jones Sr. to form the Georgia Islands and Marshland Owners Association for the purpose of opening up communications was passed. Owners also agreed to have representatives of all the owners meet in the near future.[24]

The second outcome started with an Egg. Jane Yarn was the first to act on the opportunity Tom Richards presented. Energized by her private conversations with Richards, and taking up the Nature Conservancy's offer to help, Yarn quickly moved toward buying an island. She immediately started talking to real estate agents. Egg Island, this tiny island in the delta of the Altamaha River, is so small it is not even a dot on Georgia's official highway map. The small bit of upland and extensive marsh was once owned by Howard Coffin and the Sea Island Company. Pollution flowing down the river had significantly reduced the value of its oyster beds, and the owner, in the oyster-processing business, was ready to let it go. A Brunswick sports club heard about the availability of Egg Island, but it had little value to a club looking for land to hunt deer. Very few deer could survive on the small amount of upland on what was said to be a 700-acre island. Yarn, who had a vacation home on St. Simons and a husband who adored her, liked to hunt. She knew members of the local hunt club and she could speak their language. Before the year was out, she had connected the Nature Conservancy to the owners, and now had an option to buy the island. She just needed to raise the $28,000. She came home and told Charles, "I'm going to buy Egg Island." With Richards's help, she raised the needed money.[25]

A year after the conference, Yarn brought Andrew Sparks of the *Atlanta Journal and Constitution Magazine*, who had sympathetically covered the Conference on the Future of the Marshlands in detail, to report on a small but extraordinary expedition to Egg Island. The expeditioners included Yarn's husband, Charles; Bill Jones Sr., who provided a lunch of fried chicken, baked apples, ham sandwiches, and cupcakes from the Cloister; Yarn's friend Alma Shepherd, a member of the Habersham Garden Club and whose husband owned a large paving company; Mrs. George Niles, vice president of the Habersham Garden Club; and John Hoyt, who arrived by boat from Sapelo. The small party, engaged in a fun-filled day trip, gave Sparks and a photographer from his paper another opportunity to bring public attention to the need and opportunity to preserve other coastal islands. For Yarn, Egg "was only a first step" and in fact it was the start of Georgia's history of acquiring direct control over its coastline. Yarn had an amazing capacity to bring people together. By this point, she had formed the Coastal Reserve Committee and was raising $80,000 to complete the Nature Conservancy's purchase of nearby Wolf Island, and Yarn herself was on the national board of the Nature Conservancy.[26] The small island acquisition showed other owners what they could do and it became the seaward beginning of a preservation corridor that would eventually extend 40 miles up both banks of the Altamaha River.

Hoyt came on the excursion to help the small expedition understand what was happening to the island and to give Sparks an opportunity to explain it to his readers. The island had no dunes to absorb the impact of the open-ocean waves, although Jones recalled having seen dunes that protected the upland when he visited twenty-five years earlier. Hoyt said he believed sea rise from melting glacial ice had likely caused the beach and dunes to erode to the point where waves washed through marsh grass. At one point in time, Hoyt said, the shore of Egg was a mile out to sea. He actually expected the sea to recede again, but scientists around the world were beginning to look at the effects of a warmer climate. He explained the marsh ecosystem as "everything in the water . . . goes back to something that is feeding on the grass." He said there is less food for sea life the farther you move from the shoreline. When Jones asked what would happen if the marsh all went away, Hoyt's answer was definitive: no fish.[27]

The little expedition as reported in the *Atlanta Journal and Constitution Magazine* was a grand success. It added to the public's understanding of the value of the marsh at a time when the outcome of the protective legislation was still in doubt. For Yarn, "Egg Island was a catalyst, the first acquisition of land on the coast by a conservation organization."[28] The little island gave people hope that it would be possible to save the coast and start a long productive history of habitat acquisition. Hoyt and his colleagues would have an opportunity to explain the issues directly to the members of the Georgia General Assembly who were about to consider a Reid Harris bill to regulate the use of the marshlands.

The third outcome of the conference was the preservation of Wassaw Island. Lying just 14 miles south of Savannah and with a 5½-mile beach, it was clearly in the crosshairs of development interests as well as one of the targets of the Kerr-McGee mining lease. Wassaw, George Parsons's 1866 purchase, had been controlled by a family trust since 1933. The trustees felt an obligation to "maintain this unique area in its natural form." In 1967 it became a registered National Landmark and the Georgia Natural Areas Council gave it the first official certification from the state agency. The family passion for the island shows in the reflection Parsons's grandson Joseph Parsons gave to historian Buddy Sullivan. He worshipfully describes his long walks through the maritime forest near the salt marshes: "rising at sunrise to see the dewy freshness of warm spring mornings, the chatting of the multitude of birds that sounded like a noisy aviary . . . the evenings that brought forth the fragrance of Honeysuckle."[29]

When representatives of the Parsons family attended the first meeting of the Islands and Marshland Owners Association on December 10, 1968, in New York City to hear reports from the conference, they were looking for support and long-term answers.[30] The island was under a serious threat from Savannah business interests considering a Hilton Head–type development with a beach to enhance the city's tourist draw. The Parsonses were looking for a way to keep their island out of the urbanization pushing out from Atlanta and soon coming down I-95. They had expressed opposition to the mining lease, and with the help of Robert Hanie had Governor Maddox to dinner on the island just before he decided against the lease. The dinner with representatives of the Parsons family was on November 9, after the final Savannah Kerr-McGee hearing and included Eugene Odum and Charles Wharton.[31] Andrew Sparks had helped stir public interest in the island with a long article, "Wild Wassaw," in the *Atlanta Journal and Constitution Magazine* in June 1968.[32]

But development interests continued to swell. In 1965, the Savannah Metropolitan Planning Commission, with the full support of the Savannah Chamber of Commerce, approved a grand development plan with a bridge connecting Skidaway Island on the north side of Wassaw Sound to the city across the Black River (possibly the inspiration for Johnny Mercer's "Moon River" and later renamed to honor the Savannah-born artist). In search of money for the bridge they wrote to Governor Sanders that the purpose was expansion of recreational facilities and that "by 1975 we will need this and other islands to keep pace with the healthy growth that the State of Georgia is now feeling." On Skidaway's 21 square miles they forecast a new town of fifty thousand residents.[33] When that was accomplished, they planned to construct a Skidaway to Wassaw causeway. With its 5 miles of unmolested sandy beach, Wassaw would be a prize for the creation of a new coastal state park and high-end residential development.[34] Developer Charles Fraser himself had recommended it.

The key to the ambitious plan was the construction of the bridge across Black River. Most of Skidaway was owned by Union Camp, which until 1953 had used it to supply pine timber for its Savannah mill. The trees were no longer part of the company's supply chain plans and after twenty years had enhanced the real estate value of the island. The company offered to contribute 500 acres of its holdings to the state for a new state park *if* the state would build the bridge. Despite the offer and the support of the Planning Commission and the Savannah Port Authority, the bridge was not an easy sell. When Governor Sanders turned down Union Camp, it organized a local committee to sell the voters on a general obligation bond. In 1967, the company sweetened its deal by adding another 500 acres so the state could compete for the location of a new federal oceanographic research center. This contribution for the research center was matched by the wealthy Roebling family, who had owned a plantation on the northern edge of the island since 1934. With these opportunities on the table and the full support of the business community, the Chatham County Commission, enticed by the prospect of new real estate taxes, proposed a referendum on a $3.6 million general obligation bond. The voters bought the deal. The construction of the bridge was completed in 1969 and named for Robert Roebling.[35]

In their nightmares, the Parsons family could see invading automobiles speeding across the marsh. They knew the tranquility of their island was vulnerable to development pressures coming from Savannah, from Fraser, and perhaps from the state looking for new park land. Fortunately, the causeway coming from Skidaway floundered when the state's highway engineers tallied the cost of bridging the deep channel in the middle of Wassaw Sound. The Parsonses dodged the causeway bullet for a time and the fight with Kerr-McGee seemed to be over, but a number of studies under way could revive the direct causeway and increase the pressure for development. The newly elected Republican mayor of Savannah, J. Curtis Lewis, was a developer with interest in coastal properties, and local legislators were pushing the state to buy the island for a state park that carried the implication of condemnation. While Lester Maddox had a pleasant dinner on Wassaw with family members in November 1968, shortly before he killed the Kerr-McGee mining lease, he still did not have much of a record on conservation.[36] The Parsonses also knew from communication with other owners and their contact with Robert Hanie that Cumberland Island owners were exploring federal options for their island. The role of the Nature Conservancy, carefully laid out by Tom Richards at the October 1968 conference and the known success of Jane Yarn in protecting Egg and Wolf Islands, put the Nature Conservancy on the top of their exploration list.

On a trip to Washington in March 1969, a family friend and Parsons Family Trust board member Philip B. McMasters entered the Department of the Interior offices after 5:00 p.m. and found John Gottschalk still at his desk in the U.S. Fish and Wildlife Service. He told Gottschalk that the family was willing to give Wassaw Island away. Through a series of meetings between April and October, which included Tom Richards, cautiously, with the help of local attorney Edward Hester, they developed a transfer plan. Wassaw Island would be sold to the Nature Conservancy for $1 million and then transferred to the U.S. Fish and Wildlife Service.[37]

The transfer plan did not stay a secret. Negotiations between the Parsons Family Trust and the Nature Conservancy leaked to the business leadership and in late September 1969 the Savannah Chamber of Commerce "assailed" the plan, with local politicians not far behind. The Chamber proclaimed that the deal with the conservancy would mean the island would be closed to future public use, thus ending the geographic expansion of Savannah and Chatham County and the creation of a new beach. Its board voted unanimously to oppose the actions of a private landowner. Most elected officials from the area fell in behind the Chamber. Chatham County commissioner and the future Democratic mayor of Savannah John Rousakis had opposed the mining proposal, but he urged the state to purchase the island as a future recreational site. Even Rep. Arthur Funk, who had also vigorously opposed Kerr-McGee, fired off a telegram to Governor Maddox urging him to acquire the island before the current deal went through.[38] The *Savannah Morning News* editors could see both sides: the need for a coastal beach and the need to preserve wild areas so people could escape from their urbanized environment. They saw the need for a wildlife refuge and hoped the outcome would serve "man as well as animals."[39] The politics did not stop with a simple telegram. Locals appealed to Rep. Paul Nessmith, of nearby Statesboro, who chaired the legislatively created Coastal Islands Study Committee; Nessmith jumped right onto the issue. He insisted the people of Georgia should determine "what will be done with the state's coastal islands." In a letter he asked Charles Ewing, attorney and Parsons family member, to hold off on the transaction until his committee had a chance to visit the island and study the issue. It wasn't an inviting request, since Nessmith had already told the press he felt Wassaw "should be in the hands of the people of Georgia rather than the Conservancy."[40]

Savannah's local business and political leaders pressured Maddox, but they got a cool and unenthusiastic response. He said he would hold "final judgment," but he complained in classic Maddox exaggeration: "We have a lot of recommendations coming in to buy islands, even some off the coast of Africa. This thing can get ridiculous."[41] Maddox, at heart a fiscal conservative, had just completed the investment of $835,000 to buy a significant portion of Sapelo Island from R. J. Reynolds's widow (Annemarie Winston Schmidt Reynolds) at a bargain price (estimated to be worth $2 million). Reynolds was interested in selling to the state because she wanted to honor her husband's wishes and investment in the UGAMI. Bagby flew to Switzerland to close the deal with "found" money.[42] Wassaw was different from Sapelo for Maddox because he respected the wishes of private owners whenever possible. The governor had proved his commitment to the rights that went with private property. He saw a way to have a good result without state interference in a private transaction. He believed the state could use more recreational development and it needed to protect its wildlife. Always honest, he said "I just don't know what to do about it."[43]

Savannah mayor J. Curtis Lewis wasn't giving up. In a last-minute effort to turn things around, he told the city council they could use local bonds to buy Wassaw and pay them back in the same way the Jekyll Island Authority paid for that state acquisition. If necessary, Lewis, who had experience investing in oceanfront property, would buy the island himself as an agent for the county and with the support of local banks. This sound financial scheme, he said, would overcome the governor's wariness. As secretary of the Coastal Islands Study Committee, local state Rep. Joe Battle said he would ask the committee to get control of the beach, which then could be used by the campers at the new state park on Skidaway.[44] It wasn't clear in Battle's remarks how the campers on Skidaway would get across the sound to the new beach.

Maddox did nothing, and the conservancy deal was announced October 22, 1969. The Nature Conservancy, with the help of the Parsons family friend, found a kind lady who donated 3,000 shares of IBM stock to finance the transaction. The conservancy covered the island with an easement, ensuring it would remain in a natural state committed to the protection of wildlife and available for scientific observation. Those who said Savannah needed another beach got a beach: the Wassaw beach would be open to public use, although the deed stated that "no roadway or bridge can ever be built to the island." When the protections were all in place, the island was handed to the U.S. Fish and Wildlife Service for a bird sanctuary and scientific observation. The deal included a provision that the Parsons family and their heirs would have exclusive use of 180 acres in the center of the island.[45]

The announcement did not silence the opposition. Outraged by federal interference in their development plans, the Savannah boosters sent a delegation to see Governor Maddox. The chair of the board of the newly created Ocean Science Center of the Atlantic, Laurie K. Abbott, declared the transaction had violated four federal and state laws. He said that either the U.S. Department of the Interior would need the approval of the U.S. Congress or transfer of the island would need approval of the Georgia General Assembly. None of these approvals were obtained, and the department did not have authority to act on its own, he insisted. Battle, who was in the meeting with Maddox, acknowledged that the Parsonses had a right to do what they wanted with their private property, but he also argued that "the federal government does not have the right to accept land without due process of law." Despite Abbott's vigorous opposition to the federal government, Battle conceded that if the public got access to the island's beaches and there were some nature trails, it would be a "satisfactory" outcome.[46]

Maddox, for his part, turned the hot political mess over to his cool Attorney General Arthur Bolton. Maddox, like many a highly experienced politician, agreed with the influential delegation to ask Bolton to "proceed with all due haste" to protect the interest of the state and go to court against the federal government if necessary.[47] The issue, however hot in Savannah during September and October, disappeared from the local front pages when the U.S. Department of the Interior simply ruled that a gift to the federal government was legal in every respect.[48] There was no contrary legal theory developed from Bolton's "due-haste" investigation.

A few important conclusions came from the Wassaw story. Perhaps most important was the validation of the Nature Conservancy's approach to saving natural areas in Georgia even when under political pressure. Within a year after what became known as the Conference on the Future of the Marshlands and the Sea Islands of Georgia, several of the most vulnerable barrier islands were in hands committed to protecting them. Yet, the lines remained drawn. Political support at the state level to advance a business and jobs development agenda was strong—and potentially sufficient to override the energy and determination of those who fought to conserve the coastal environment. Additionally, while their legislators organized and committed to the development side of the decision scale, it was still not clear where Maddox's thumb came down on the scale when the land was private property. The marshlands were still not protected under any Georgia law, and it was unclear who could stop a coastal owner, large or small, from destroying the ecosystem scientists knew was the most productive land on Earth. To reach that goal of protection would take more people to understand its value.

Chapter 9

A Bill Takes a Breath

We don't want anyone up here in Atlanta telling us what to do.
—REP. CHARLES JONES

A bill takes its first breath when it is introduced. Reid Harris knew when he introduced HB 212 on January 23, 1969, the legislative process included many opportunities for it to die. At the heart of the process was the ever ticking legislative clock that the Georgia Constitution set at forty days. It is always easier to use the intricate steps of the process to kill a bill than it is to get something new into the laws of the state. Harris also knew, or would soon know, this bill had unmovable opposition from established industries while its conservation cause supporters were untested. He felt the ecology wave was coming, but was it strong enough to push through legislation on an issue that only one other more progressive coastal state had very recently done? The Georgia legislature had no history of passing environmental laws and nobody had ever seen "environmental legislation." But he knew from the Kerr-McGee mining battle that the people of Georgia were willing to fight to save their coast, to protect their "place."

Kerr-McGee had brought the coast to the front pages of the news and stirred the conscience of state leaders who had responsibilities for the coastal environment. At the end of the mining fight, Governor Maddox had thanked Kerr-McGee for bringing coastal resources to the state's full attention, and Reid Harris felt the request to dig up the coast could be a catalyst for legislation that would protect it. The threat to the coast was clear. The public had taken advantage of the hearings and voiced a simple idea: they preferred marshes to mining. As the UGA student campaign button said, they wanted their officials to "Save the Marsh." To meet that mandate there would need to be a law to replace the Phosphate Act of 1885 or the Mineral Leasing Act of 1945. No state law protected Georgia's marsh, and federal law was thin. Were Georgia legislators ready to lead an environmental cause only just emerging in other parts of the country?

Reid Harris was ready to draft a marshland protection bill that gathered the best practices he could find from the few states with some marsh protection. The island owners were organized and ready to respond to the political forces at the state capital having a different vision for the future for their islands. But they worried their voices would not be heard in the development-focused politics of the state. Jane Yarn was ready to call on her connections with the owners, and especially with the Garden Club of Georgia members. George Bagby was ready to lead the state's sportsmen into the fray. Having spoken loudly during the mining fight, the scientists were ready to share their knowledge of the marsh with legislators looking for understanding. The earlier mining debate had gotten the press ready, but no one really knew if the public supported the state government regulating the use of the marsh. And no one knew for sure who owned it.

Development interests were also ready. Kerr-McGee had not given up and had a powerful law firm ready to represent its interests. On January 15, Charles Fraser had closed on the purchase of a fifth of Cumberland Island from two financially strapped Carnegie heirs and was looking for support to develop his land and open the coast to public use and private development. The sale surprised environmental advocates and the other parts of the Carnegie family, compelling them to decide whether they wanted to see their island developed or protected.[1] The fate of Cumberland Island would not be finally decided in the 1969 legislative session, but the debate over its future would be hotly contested in legislative proposals. The owners looked disorganized, vulnerable to local pressures, and as rich carpetbaggers, easy targets. The state didn't want to restrict the capacity of the ports, and industrial interests still had hopes for expanded capacity in Brunswick and Savannah, which might require using parts of existing marshland. Like earlier governors and their supporters, the current leaders of the state were committed to growing wealth and good-paying jobs and were always looking for ways to meet this goal. They had a governor who had the same goal. Like most

Georgians, business leaders didn't want new restrictions on the use of their property. Maddox agreed with that. The rights of property owners were always central to any effort to regulate land use, and private property rights usually won the day. The lines were drawn.

The future of the Georgia coast was on the table in the 1969 session of the General Assembly. Would the state look for wealth and jobs from the usual sources of industry and urban development? Would its coastal islands look like heavily developed Hilton Head, Amelia Island, the New Jersey coast, or the Florida islands, or would the miles of unmolested beaches, clean water, and soothing ocean breezes be the attraction that would feed people's minds and the engines of the state's infant recreation industry?

Harris knew that the detailed language of a bill matters and that it takes hard work to get it right. The bill had to avoid trampling on the inviolate principle of private property and still effectively protect the marsh. That would not be easy. There was no model legislation from the National Association of State Legislatures, and federal legislation would not come for another year.

The U.S. Department of the Interior was still completing the study of the estuaries authorized by the 1966 Clean Water Act, so its detailed state by state review of laws was not yet available (published March 25, 1970). The federal study would develop model legislation for possible use in Maryland, but this was not available to Harris. John and Mildred Teal were completing their own survey of the thin list of state laws protecting the marsh, but their book, *The Life and Death of the Salt Marsh*, would not be published until later in 1969.[2] The proceedings of the National Estuarine Pollution Study hearings held on Jekyll Island in February 1968 could be of some help.[3] Harris's own work on the Surface Mining Act would be of greater help. He wrote to state governments to ask for copies of their relevant legislation, but only Maine and Massachusetts gave any significant protection to their marshes, and none of their statutes seemed to fit his approach. Fred Marland had also given him copies of relevant state legislation.[4] In the Massachusetts law passed in 1965, Harris found a significant preservation role given to local government. If local regulation prevented the owner from using his property, they were entitled to compensation. The 45,000 acres of marshland remaining in Massachusetts was small compared to the 500,000 acres on the coast of Georgia, and in 1970, there were applications in process to reduce that further.[5] Neither of Georgia's coastal neighbors with similar coastal marshland acreage had any laws or regulations on the books to protect their critical habitat, and those states were open for business when developers came proposing barrier island development. Both Florida and South Carolina had a variety of agencies with some responsibility for the estuaries and marshlands, but these were not unlike what Georgia already had in place.[6] Harris had given up on the idea that the state zoning laws could help.[7] Georgia had given its cities and counties constitutional control over zoning matters in what was known as Amendment 19, and wrestling some of that power back would likely trigger a battle with the Association of County Commissioners and the Georgia Municipal Association.

Central to the bill, and to the cost of preserving the marsh, was Harris's belief that the state of Georgia owned almost all of it. He firmly believed that when Georgia declared its independence from George II it claimed as its own the well-established property laws of England. Under those laws, even though he may have granted ownership of the land, the king owned the navigable streams and tidewaters. After the grant was executed, the king still owned the land under the tide and held it in trust for public use. Harris believed that when the American Revolution ended the rights of the king, the thirteen colonies acquired his rights and the same public trust that had existed under English law. Most of the land on the coast tracked back to a colonial grant from King George II, but unless the grant included a specific grant of the marshland, it was the state's and held for public use. He explained this belief to Virlyn Slayton, the lawyer in the Office of Legislative Counsel, who would help him through nineteen drafts and amendments to the bill. The state's ownership of the marsh was the most critical concept in the bill.[8]

Harris had given the conceptual details of the bill to Jim Morrison of the Game and Fish Commission, and Morrison had summarized them on the front page of the departmental magazine for its 35,000 readers. The intent, said Morrison, was to make sure the mining threat "will never happen again." He reinforced the belief that the state owned most of the marsh, but he also stated the department's willingness to expand its program to purchase critical acreage that might prove to be in private ownership. Commissioner Bagby was always looking for ways to expand the state's ownership of land for sportsmen, and Morrison said a $1 million appropriation would be enough to acquire marshes with proven titles in private hands. When state money was available, it was always easier to buy land than regulate land in private ownership. The editorial pledged that the department and Commissioner Bagby would fully support the legislation and urged the state's sportsmen to get involved because "the time to act is now."[9] There were several concepts in the first draft that would be consistent goals throughout the long legislative process. The first in importance was the definition of the marsh, which would determine the reach of the bill's regulatory power. The definition had three measures of what was marsh:

1. a lengthy list of plants the biologists from the UGAMI had determined only grew in a salt marsh,
2. the content of the soil common to the marsh, and
3. an intricate calculation of the tide-influenced land "ranging from 5.6 feet above the mean sea level and below."[10]

In his first draft of the new legislation, Harris created an independent Coastal Wetlands Protection Board, under the Game and Fish Commission, and protected its composition for effective implementation.[11] He wanted state agencies on the board that had environmental responsibilities: the State Game and Fish Commission, the Water Quality Control Board, the Georgia Natural Areas Council, the Surface Mining Land Use Board, and the Health Department. During the mining fight, he had seen the risk of having private interests on boards making important public decisions; choosing agencies that had openly opposed mining of the coast effectively jump-started a debate over board members.[12] While the issue of this Coastal Wetlands Protection Board and state permitting would be a subject of debate throughout the process, Harris intended from the start to put the control in the hands of conservation-oriented state agencies.[13]

The preamble, which provides some arguable indications of legislative intent, stayed consistent throughout the House process but later drew attention in the Senate. The "whereas" section of findings, which few people read and is seldom used today, was an important opportunity to explain the purpose of the bill as well as the broader reasons for conservation. Its purpose was

1. To protect the habitat marine life and wildlife needed to survive;
2. To declare, as the scientists showed earlier, the marshlands were the "richest provider of nutrients in the world";
3. To provide a buffer against flooding, erosion, and pollution;
4. To provide much-needed outdoor recreation;
5. To acknowledge the marshes were seriously threatened by industrial and commercial development; and
6. To use the state's police powers to protect the welfare, health, and safety of its citizens.[14]

The authority of the state to protect its marshlands was based on its police powers.

Central to this first draft of the bill was the provision that "no person shall remove, fill, dredge or drain or otherwise alter any wetlands in this state without first filing a written notice of intent." To do so would require a permit from the Coastal Wetlands Protection Board. It required local governments to review applications for compliance with local laws. But it gave the power to issue the permit to the state board.[15]

One issue, largely unnoticed throughout the process, was judicial enforcement of the provision of the bill. It gave to the Superior Court of the county where a violation occurred "jurisdiction to restrain a violation of this act *at the suit of any person*." This simple provision tucked into a long lawyerly procedural paragraph was parallel to national environmental efforts to give the public access to the judicial system in all of the federal legislation that passed in the 1970s. It overcame the "standing" issue that often blocks advocates who could not show direct damage from getting the violations of the law in front of a judge.[16] It is a provision that environmental advocates dearly wish was in the law today.

Also, the provisions on local governmental procedures required a public hearing before any decision on any application for a permit.[17] Perhaps this came from Harris's participation in and close observation of the powerful effect of the Atlanta and Savannah mining hearings. The public hearing became a significant part of advocates' national agenda in the 1970s and gave opportunities to be heard to local environmental movements around the country. Public hearings would play a significant part in the passage of the bill and would be used effectively to bring public pressure on the future of the largest and perhaps the most important barrier island, Cumberland.

HB 212 was finally ready for introduction on January 23, ten days into the legislative session. Harris's cosponsors reflected the support he felt he would need and they included a number of old allies. He was joined by Representatives Levitas, Lambert, and Robin Harris from the small group of legislative independence conspirators. These were also close friends from the House Judiciary Committee. Four Republicans—Mike Egan and Haskew Brantley of Atlanta, and George Waley and Joe Battle of Chatham County—showed the bipartisan nature of the bill and followed the national trend that environmental concerns were bipartisan issues. In addition to Waley and Battle, the Chatham-Savannah delegation showed strong community and business support for the bill when Reps. Arthur Funk and Arthur Gignilliat signed on. Supporting the bill also were Larry Thompson, a Democrat who shared a district with Levitas, and Dorsey Matthews. One of the few real farmers in the House, Matthews told Fred Marland in the hall of the Capitol that all farmers in their hearts are conservationists; his firm support showed there was not an urban/rural split on the bill.[18] But perhaps the cosigner who would have the most impact on the future of the coast was a Harris ally on the Surface Mining Act, Paul Nessmith of Statesboro.[19]

Speaker of the House George L. Smith sent HB 212 to Philip Chandler, chair of the State Institutions and Properties Committee on which Harris served. Chandler decided the bill and all of its complexities needed a public hearing. A public hearing on a bill isn't always a good thing. Understanding the bill is important, but it is not the only objective of a hearing. The chair's call for a public hearing often meant that he had heard opposition from some quarter and it usually alerted legislators that the bill was controversial. The opposition had obviously made their objections known to the chair. A hearing eats time on the ticking forty-day clock, which in the case of HB 212 already stood at thirty days. Yes, you have an opportunity to showcase the support for your bill and more fully present its rationale, but opposition to the bill gets the same opportunity. If the outcome is balanced, legislators whose job is to make decisions often do not want to choose sides.

On Tuesday, February 11, the House chamber, rarely used for hearings, was at full capacity. It is an impressive and historic room, with 30-foot-high tray ceilings, a rich carpeted center aisle, and rows of hand-carved polished cherry desks from the 1890s, one for each of the then-196 House members. Thirty-four speakers filled three hours with their testimony.

Intense opposition came from Reid Harris's hometown, Brunswick. It came from the business community or, rather, the established leadership of the town. It included most of the local city and county elected officials, the Glynn County Chamber of Commerce, the Brunswick-Glynn County Real Estate Board, the Brunswick Port Authority, Brunswick Pulp and Paper, the Hercules Powder Company, the Sea Island Company, the Glynn County Commission, the Commissioner of Roads and Revenue of Glynn County, and most of the lawyers and bankers who did business with them. Even the Central Labor Council, which represented all the unionized plant workers, was opposed to the bill. The local Lion's Club resolution stated the bill would be too restrictive on industry. The exception to this list of naysayers' who's who in Brunswick was Myddleton Harris Sr., Reid's father, who was worried about his son but was clearly still supportive.[20] This community of leaders had nurtured Reid into adulthood. The son of the most prominent banker in town, he had also helped lead the Chamber of Commerce as the chair of its legislative affairs committee prior to running for office.[21] His former law firm had work from all of these leaders, and his new one-person law office needed their business. But his community stood up at the hearing and with united voice opposed his approach to the preservation of the marshes of Glynn.

Harris sat in the front row of the House chamber, listening carefully. Albert Klingel of the Savannah Port Authority presented opposition from Savannah: ports should be represented on the board, and the state's Department of Industry and Trade should also be on the board to protect future development opportunities. The Georgia Ports Authority went deeper when it passed a resolution on February 18 calling for the defeat of the Harris bill, which subordinated "all other uses of wetlands to the interests of conservation." Its concern was that HB 212 would prevent the expansion of the port, and it wanted to leave land-use decisions that might affect the future of the port under the zoning powers of local government.[22] Many presenters had similar views: The state should use the coast to generate new wealth and jobs.

John McNicol, president of Brunswick Pulp and Paper, said it would be an unconstitutional "taking" of land without payment and it will "lessen the opportunity for employment." When Rep. Paul Nessmith of States-boro asked what McNicol planned to do with the company's 17,000 acres of marsh, he said they planned to grow pine trees on it.[23] The company's plan for the marsh stood in stark contrast to the hopes of conservationists.

A labor union leader whose members worked for all the big industries in Brunswick stood in the House chamber and not so subtly threatened Harris with political opposition in the next election because the bill would cost jobs.[24]

The most interesting and telling opposition came in the form of a letter to the Brunswick Chamber of Commerce from the manager of Hercules Powder, Stan Fenelon. The plant had been at the same location for sixty years but foresaw a future need to dispose of dirt coming from the stumps it processed on land near the plant. In the prior year it had swapped some land that was to be part of a Brunswick urban renewal project for marshland "owned" by the city. On this newly acquired marshland, Hercules planned to begin dumping the excess dirt and believed, rightly, that the bill would interfere with its plans. The future growth of the plant, the manager threat-ened, would have to go to another community. Harris was curious as to who had guaranteed the title to the marsh, but he probably privately rejoiced be-cause exactly such situations showed the need for his bill.[25]

Harris had certainly anticipated that a core argument against the bill would be based on property rights—and the testimony did not disappoint. Prior to the hearing, Mayor Ralph Croft of Brunswick had said the bill was a "taking" of property without due process. Most of the opposition at the hearing revolved around this issue. The *Atlanta Constitution* reported Har-ris's consistent nemesis of the bill, Rep. Robert Harrison, an attorney from a neighboring district that included Camden County and the small coastal city of St. Marys, was "vociferously opposed." Harrison cried out: "We're talking about property rights! Property rights are equal to the right of lib-erty. If you take away that right you can take away other rights!"[26]

Jim Morrison, the publicist for Georgia Bagby at Game and Fish, was disappointed that not a single Savannah resident attended the legislative hearing. He noted later in the summer of 1969 that the hearing had a strong turnout of "home grown Kerr-McGee" industries and commercial interests, but opposition to the mining of the Savannah marsh had not produced support for the legislation that proposed a permanent Georgia solution. Morrison published letters expressing gratitude for his boss's "courageous stand against those who would ruin our precious resources in the name of 'progress.'"[27]

The day after the hearing, Harris responded that the property rights argument was "ridiculous."[28] He knew the bill's definition made a careful distinction between marsh and marsh upland. Its bedrock foundation was on the legal principle that the public owned the marsh. In politics, not everyone is willing to accept the logic of a legal argument, but as a scholarly lawyer with deep real estate experience he was fully comfortable with this central point in the public debate. Harris's bill did not authorize taking any private land, but would regulate the use of what the state owned.

He had already introduced House Resolution 75-184, calling on the attorney general to do a title search along the coast to see which properties had an insurable title to the marsh. Representative Nessmith joined him in authoring the resolution.[29] Morrison, the ever-alert publicist for Game and Fish, was quoted repeating Reid's belief that "not a lawyer on the Georgia coast will certify a deed to any marshland."[30] Although the resolution passed the Natural Resources Committee, Harris did not push for its passage in the House.[31] He felt it gave a strong invitation to Attorney General Bolton, and he trusted Bolton to step into the issue and help settle it in favor of conservation.[32] HB 212 would fully occupy his time for the remainder of the session.

Harris's supporters who came to testify include many of "the usual suspects" and more. The landscape architects, urged on by Jane Yarn, spoke. Beyond the hearing, Harris knew Yarn was on the phone and writing letters every day behind the scenes. On the first day of the legislature, he had met with the executive committee of the Georgia Federation of Women's Clubs and knew they would support the bill throughout the process.[33] Yarn came to the hearing with Mary Helen Ray, first vice president of the Garden Club of Georgia, who spoke from a well-prepared text approved by the executive committee. Robert Hanie did his part at the hearing, declaring the GNAC's "complete" support for the bill. He said his agency "recognized the marshes and islands of the Georgia Coast to be a unique and irreplaceable natural resource." It was "an intact outdoor museum, a museum without walls where people work and play, hunt and fish, and derive a living from its bounty." Never shy about framing the issue as a grand vision, he called for "a new direction and principal regarding the utilization of our natural resources."[34]

From Rabun County in the northeastern corner of Georgia, Marie Mellinger came to give her support. She had worked for a time for a U.S. Department of the Interior wildlife refuge in Savannah and had written a manual on the identification of coastal plants and a book on the wildlife of Rabun County. She spoke on the need to conserve the natural environment of the coast.[35]

Support came from Harris's neighbors on St. Simons Island. Harris had asked noted author Eugenia Price to speak for the marshes. She and Joyce Blackburn, her companion and business partner, watched the sun set over those marshes each evening. After they moved to the island in 1961, Price used its history in her first novel, *The Beloved Invader*, which became a trilogy celebrating their new home. On her first day she knew she loved the marsh more than the beach. "Marshes are like a desert—changing color with the changing light."[36] At work on her second novel, Price was hesitant to break her concentration, but at Joyce's urging she flew to Atlanta for the hearing. Before she left, they started a petition drive on the island to support the bill. They easily gathered 250 names, but they were disappointed to discover that one employer had signed the names of all of his employees. Despite this mishap, the petition Price carried with her had well over two hundred names of neighbors.[37] Both Price and Blackburn were taken aback by the negative reaction of some of their neighbors. When Price lined up for the Delta Airlines flight back to Brunswick, she felt the "unanimous cold shoulder" of the Brunswick businessmen who all knew her but had been on the other side at the hearing. This experience was hurtful enough that she described it in her *St. Simons Memoir* nine years later.[38] While the distinguished author at the height of her career felt the sting of rejection from the business leaders, there is little doubt that Reid Harris, who was an integral part of the community leadership, felt the sting even more strongly.

For Price and Blackburn, the hearing was not one shot and you're done. They helped reenergize the local Marshes of Glynn Society, which formed in 1963 to protect the Brunswick view of the marsh from commercial development. Now the organization focused its attention on supporting the legislation. Price served as one of the new board members alongside one of the original society members, Hoyt Brown, a retired shop foreman from Hercules Powder. Sen. Ronald Adams of Brunswick, another of the original founders, was also on the board. The new chairman, William Lust, declared they were committed to the "wetlands bill" that was "a tremendous step in the right direction." He said that some parts of the bill may need changes, but he criticized local industry leaders for not committing to marsh preservation and coming forward with amendments to improve the bill. Brown reiterated Harris's point that the bill did not take any private property.[39] Both Price and Brown would insert their voices in the debate as the bill moved through the legislative process. It was certainly comforting to Harris that he still had a few friends back home when the leaders of his community turned so uniformly against his effort to protect the marsh.

The scientists also testified at the hearing. Eugene Odum, as usual, caught the attention of the press with his plain talk. He noted that when people start talking about motherhood and apple pie and property rights you ought to be looking for vested interests. In an argument that veered from Georgia political orthodoxy, he said that property rights were important but they come in second in importance to the interest of the "whole society."[40] He labeled the owners of the coastal manufacturing plants as "Scalawags and Carpetbaggers" who cared little about the Georgia environment.[41]

Dirk Frankenberg of the UGAMI, with his friend and colleague Marland, came to the hearing to remind the legislature of the science behind the 1968 decision not to mine the marsh. Frankenberg had provided critical scientific research on the oxygen levels that resulted from disturbing the marsh dirt during the debate over the mining lease. Disturbing the marsh, he said, threatened the oxygen supply of all the species that started their life and lived their life in the marsh.[42]

The committee heard support from the Sierra Club and the Georgia Conservancy, but when Chairman Chandler was bringing equally divided testimony to a close, Harris sat at his front-row desk "feeling totally dejected" and worried about the damage the negative testimony had done. He wondered if he could keep the bill alive.[43] Just after the closing gavel fell, there was a stir in the back of the room, a voice was heard, and down the center aisle rolled the distinguished and long-serving Secretary of State Ben Fortson. Fortson had been in office for twenty-three years and was honored for sitting on the state seal when Georgia had three governors competing for control in 1948.[44] He had been unable to walk after an automobile accident in 1926 and had a special compartment constructed in his wheelchair for the seal. As he rolled down the center aisle, the state seal rolled with him. As one of the founders of the Izaac Walton League which had promoted clean rivers and creeks and as a member of the Mineral Leasing Commission, Fortson had been a firm opponent of the Kerr-McGee lease.[45]

In his book, Harris recalls the dramatic moment.

"Mr. Chairman."

"Why, yes Mr. Secretary."

"May I speak briefly to this gathering?

"Sorry I arrived a little late. I didn't know about the roster."

"Certainly you may speak, Mr. Secretary. Ladies and Gentlemen, I present to you, Georgia's esteemed Secretary of State."

"I won't need a microphone, Mr. Chairman, spoken to larger crowds than this and was heard.

"For the record, let me make one thing abundantly clear. I wholeheartedly endorse Rep. Harris' House Bill 212. I wouldn't change one dot or an i or cross on a t.... As your Secretary of State, I say to you that we must stop the encroachment on our marsh, and I must tell you of a dereliction of my duty to you. Few people know that among the titles I hold by virtue of my office is that of Surveyor General. In that capacity I have been woefully negligent.

"Over the years I should have made it my business ... to determine the extent of the state's ownership of the coast. I haven't done so, haven't requested the funds to do so. Now, because of my failures, Rep. Harris here has taken on the tough job. Mr. Chairman, this bill was placed in the right committee. You are dealing with state property here on this. I implore you and the other committee members to take quick action in giving this bill a 'do pass' recommendation. I solicit your aid in supporting it through the House. Should this measure fail, the coast will quickly suffer dire consequences."[46]

The hearing ended. The impact of the testimony was unclear. Chairman Philip Chandler, a home builder from Milledgeville and member of the

House since 1959, immediately squelched the spirit generated by the secretary of state's impromptu speech.[47] He announced that the bill would be placed in a subcommittee for further consideration and named that subcommittee. He charged the nine members, who included Harris and bill cosponsor Paul Nessmith, to report back to the full committee by the following Wednesday.[48] Harris knew more days would click off the clock.

Harris still had strong editorial support. Two days after the hearing, an *Atlanta Constitution* editor wrote that the hearing "once more illustrated the growing importance of man's use of his environment." The editor argued that the bill was not seizing private property but instead was "moving with care, and with concern for a great natural treasure."[49] Harris also felt the support when he met with the members of the Islands and Marshland Owners Association on February 15 in Savannah. As their attorney, he explained the new bylaws for the organization, but the meeting also gave him a chance to explain the wetlands bill and ask them to contact members of the Georgia House of Representatives in its behalf. An invited guest at the gathering, Dave Maney passed out a booklet summarizing the key points from the Conference on the Future of the Marshlands and said he was very pleased to have this association to work through.[50] The minutes do not show the board taking official action on HB 212, likely because of the organization's nonprofit status, but the meeting left individual island owners well informed on the implication of the bill for the preservation of the islands and put the owners in a position to take individual action.

Harris knew that subcommittees often were where bills often went to die a quiet death. Subcommittees could hold bills as the clock continued to tick down the days. The outlook appeared even more bleak when, on the next day, subcommittee chair Chandler showed him the bill jacket. Two sponsors from Savannah, Rep. Arthur Gignilliat, high up in the management of Savannah Power and Light, and Joseph Battle, a Savannah electrician, had crossed their names out as sponsors.[51] The two defections revealed industry opposition in Savannah as well as Brunswick.[52] He had lost the support of Gignilliat and Battle, but was encouraged when Rep. Herbert Jones, a Republican from Savannah, having heard the news of his colleagues' defection, quickly pledged his support as a subcommittee member.[53]

Shortly he received a letter from his father saying he was not personally concerned about the bill, but that Brunswick's business leadership was concerned and it might be a good idea to come home to meet with them on the next Saturday. Harris certainly knew the pressure on his father was real. The bill clearly needed CPR. After meeting with the Brunswick Chamber of Commerce and talking to members of the Committee of 100, Harris knew the bill required big changes to revive its faint heartbeat. He got out a red pencil and yellow pad and went to work the evening after he returned from Brunswick.[54]

When the subcommittee met again, he and legislative counsel Virlyn Slayton had a new substitute ready. He had crossed out sections 3 and 4 of the original bill (which created and empowered the Coastal Wetlands Protection Board) and placed the responsibility for issuance of any permit fully on the local government. The "whereas" section, the public hearing, the public notice, the public right of enforcement, and the buyout provision all stayed the same. However, in order to protect the state's interest in the marsh, he added different teeth to the bill, an obscure way to reach the goal. The substitute required the applicant, after receiving a permit from the local government, to file a certificate with the secretary of state showing a title insurance policy warranting that the applicant owned the marshland slated for disruption and had clear, guaranteed title to the marshland involved in the permit.[55] This provision was at the heart of his lawyerly understanding and, while it looked like a significant regulatory retreat, state ownership of the marsh was still vigorously asserted. Harris felt the title insurance requirement actually made the bill stronger: no title insurance, no permit to disturb the marsh.[56] He also delayed implementation of the legislation by moving the effective date from April 1 to July 1, 1970.[57] The extension of the effective date could encourage quick action to beat the deadline, but owners still had to worry about the title issue. While not everyone understood the impact of the new language, it was carefully crafted by a polished attorney exercising his legislative craft.

The bill also got a new name—no longer the Wetlands Bill, it became the Coastal Marshlands Protection Act. Rock Howard had suggested the more lyrical "marshes, a term" that "we use commonly and about which poetry is written."[58] Even Howard, the engineer, understood the value of connecting the bill to Georgia's literary history. This was no change in substance, but it brought with it remembrances of Sidney Lanier's "The Marshes of Glynn," which, in earlier days, every schoolchild in Georgia, including most members of the legislature, was required to recite. It is likely Howard could do just that.

Harris lightened the bill's political baggage by adding six general exemptions: the highway department, state and federal navigation agencies, public utilities regulated by the Georgia Public Service Commission (Georgia Power and Atlanta Gas Light), railroads, water and sewer projects, and private docks on pilings above the marsh. Reid took some criticism for these exemptions but felt they "would not appreciably weaken the bill."[59] He also knew from experience that these well-connected interests could generate considerable opposition in the back rooms of the House. The exemptions reflected an astute understanding of politics in Georgia at the time: don't get in the way of the agencies most directly tasked with growing the state's wealth if you could help it.

Chandler's appointed subcommittee—which had a number of Harris supporters, including Al Burruss, Paul Nessmith, Howard Rainey, and Harris himself—met and unanimously approved the new iteration. When the full State Institutions and Property Committee met to discuss the bill on February 24, it heard favorable comments from members Paul Nessmith, Arthur Funk, and Bill Simms. One representative asked the central question: "how can you deed something that is not yours?" The following morning, the committee made a "do-pass" recommendation to the House.[60] The newspapers reported the final vote of the committee as unanimous.[61]

Coming out of committee, the bill was not as strong as the original draft, but it still had the support of the Game and Fish Commission, the secretary of state, conservationists, and a unanimous committee vote in its back pocket. The press reported it had been "lacerated" by amendments and "limped" out of committee, but an *Atlanta Constitution* editor reiterated that the legislation, in whatever its final form, was "needed to regulate the development of Georgia's marshlands areas on a reasonable basis."[62] Eugene Odum repeated his support when he wrote Harris to thank him for a copy of the substitute, which he said would be "a great step forward even though it may not be all that everyone wished for."[63] The substitute clearly limited the capacity of the state to look at the details of every permit but may have completely prohibited any private disruption of the marshlands because only a very few owners could get title insurance for their so-called right.

With one significant barrier cleared, Harris turned his attention to the full House. He had ten legislative days to get Speaker George L. Smith to take his bill off the general calendar, where all the bills out of committee were accumulating, and call it to the full House for consideration and action. If it did not happen in that ten-day period, the additional barrier of the House Rules Committee would be added to the process. At the time, the committee set the list of bills the Speaker could consider only in the last ten days of the session. Legislation often bogged down in the committee of the logjam late in the session.

However, there was the press of other legislation that could also determine the future of the coast. Development interests along the coast, harboring their own ideas about how the barrier islands could contribute to the wealth of the state, were plotting with members of the legislature to further their goals. There were investors interested in getting a piece of the coast, and Charles Fraser, with his out-front personality and flamboyant style, was at the center of that effort. He had developed a good relationship with Rep. Robert Harrison of St. Mary's in Camden County and with development-oriented county commissioners. Harrison introduced a series of bills that would undercut the support for HB 212 while assisting Fraser in developing his newly acquired property on Cumberland Island.

Fraser had tried to play nice with the Carnegie and Candler heirs in order to acquire control of development on the entire island. He believed, as is apparent from the 1969 conversation with David Brower, that the island could be used in various ways. Part, he said, should be left in a natural state and given to a preservation organization like the Nature Conservancy. Part should be devoted to recreation in a manner similar to what the North Georgia Mountains Authority was doing at Unicoi State Park in the North Georgia Mountains. And part—the 3,000 acres he owned—should be developed for vacationers and permanent residents. He had proposed cooperation with other owners through a system of strong easements and nonprofit structures as well as a for-profit corporation over which other island owners would have minority control. He was disappointed in the unplanned development of much of Hilton Head outside his 5,000-acre Sea Pines development and believed that Cumberland Island could give him a second chance at a development with conservation values.[64] But his aggressive style and public insults alienated most of the leadership of the remaining four Carnegie family groups who, with the Candlers, still owned 85 percent of the island. Nancy Carnegie Rockefeller summed up the family feeling in a letter to Fraser that showed the Carnegie family was getting ready to fight the commercial development of Cumberland:

> What right have you to criticize the Carnegies and their 84-year stewardship of Cumberland Island? If it had not been for the four generations of Carnegies, the island would not be in its 100% natural state. Not one of them destroyed a single thing in 84 years, nor allowed anyone else to, and we are not going to, now.[65]

Mary Bullard, in her book on Cumberland, says Fraser saw the Carnegies as hypocritical modern environmentalists who were "selfish, rich, upstarts" with no "sense of history" before their own time on the island. Friends of his family, he said, went back to American Revolutionary War general Nathaniel Green, when the Carnegies "were still herding sheep."[66]

While Harris waited for the Speaker to call HB 212 for the House debate, Cumberland caught on fire in the General Assembly. Fraser's Camden County allies saw the new private development bringing new investment to the island and lusted for the tax revenue that would come with it. Fraser boldly speculated that private development on the island would double or quadruple the tax revenue of Camden County within ten years. While the Camden County commissioners had some long-term relationships with segments of the Carnegie family, they were quick to join Fraser's efforts to break Carnegie-Candler control of the island. During the 1969 session, Representative Harrison was a constant opponent of HB 212 and Rep. Richard Scarlett, a lawyer holding the other Glynn County seat in the House, also took the side of the business establishment.

On March 4, Harrison introduced HB 688, to create a state authority titled the Camden County Recreation Authority. He wanted the state government to assert control over the development of its coast. In the Senate, Ford Spinks introduced an identical bill, SB 229.[67] Spinks, whose farm-oriented district centered in Tifton, chaired the Senate Committee on Business, Trade, and Commerce, and he gave Fraser an opportunity to speak before his committee. While Fraser was before the Senate committee arguing for the private-sector development of Cumberland, supporters and opponents battled in the February 11 House public hearing over the wetlands bill. Fraser told the Senate committee the island should be developed with "multiple uses that included ecological conservation preserves," but argued that other parts of the island should be developed by the private sector, which he claimed would be more efficient than a government agency like the National Park Service.[68] Spinks didn't get deeply involved in the issue but likely found Fraser's private-sector argument appealing. Perhaps his reticence came from Sen. Roscoe Dean, whose district included Cumberland. Dean said he did not like the Spinks bill and probably did not like another senator messing around in his district, but when a reporter asked his opinion of the Spinks bill he simply predicted "there would be another day."[69] He clearly intended to get even with his colleague for getting into his local politics.

The bills created a state Camden County Authority with the power to issue bonds, purchase real estate, build roads and bridges, and surprisingly, given Harrison's concerns for public property rights, the authority to condemn property. The new authority opened the possibility for realizing the long-held hope of Camden County commissioners for a road connecting Cumberland Island to the mainland. Fraser's allies in the Senate did not stop with one bill, but a week later introduced SB 260 to amend the statute governing the North Georgia Mountains Authority (NGMA) to expand its jurisdiction to the whole state. This already-established authority had the same development powers as the Camden County Recreation Authority, and its executive director was Fraser's publicist, Hugh B. Masters, who was making presentations across the state promoting Fraser's views of the recreational potential of Cumberland. The NGMA already had Unicoi State Park, nestled in the North Georgia mountains, under construction as a multipurpose recreational development with a conference hotel, cabins, campsites, a lake, and mountain trails. It was a model for how Fraser envisioned the development of the recreational part of his Cumberland plan. Some legislators were excited about a similar state-owned recreational development on Cumberland.[70]

Fraser argued that average Georgians should have access to pristine Atlantic beaches. He had offered the remaining owners an opportunity to partner with him on an environmentally sensitive private development plan, but the owners did not take kindly to his effort to control the future of *their* island. His plans and his leadership style frightened the owners, who had been accustomed to managing the island without interference from outside the family.[71] At the wedding reception of one of his Sea Pines managers to a Carnegie bride, Fraser showed up with his plans for the island and rolled them out on a picnic table to make his sales pitch.[72] Fraser then shifted to a political strategy that found support when he scolded the Carnegie family members as rich elitists with few roots in the state's history. Fraser liked to contrast the late-arriving Carnegies to his family history—his birth in Hinesville, Georgia, and his proud family colonial Georgia roots. Fraser charmed the leadership of Camden County at a dinner organized by Rep. Robert Harrison, and in early January 1969, he sponsored a luncheon in Atlanta to which Harrison invited people he thought would help.[73]

While Fraser gathered coastal developers and local governmental officials on his side, the Carnegies and the Candlers, with political resources of their own, were not idle. They organized their collective efforts through the Cumberland Island Conservation Association, which met for the first time on January 3, 1969. Sam Candler was named chairperson of the executive committee. To help them fight the Fraser-backed bills they hired a young Atlanta attorney, Thornton Morris, who early in his legal career (at the same firm as Reid Harris) had done legal work for Robert Ferguson, the husband of Carnegie heir Lucy Ferguson. Morris regularly updated the association members on the activities related to the bills.[74] Ferguson had for a short time represented Camden County in the state legislature, and Lucy adeptly made the rounds at the evening social events to express their concerns about the bills and make their own private-property arguments.

Just days after Harrison introduced his first bill, Joe Graves, a young fourth-generation member of the Johnston family faction of the Carnegie heirs, wrote to the emerging conservation organizations to ask for help. In letters to the Sierra Club, the Georgia Conservancy, the Nature Conservancy, the Little Cumberland Island Association, and the Georgia Natural

Areas Council, he stated the family desire and commitment to preserving Cumberland "as nearly as possible in its present natural state." He said the legislation introduced to benefit Charles Fraser and commercial development had created "alarm and concern" among the remaining owners. He recognized that nonnative owners were at a disadvantage in the legislative process and asked for assistance from the conservation groups.[75]

Joe Graves didn't know the fledgling conservation groups, but Sam Candler did. He had family connections he was willing to use and, in addition to Jane Yarn, he was the best owner connection to the conservation advocates.[76] He was an early member and supporter of the Sierra Club and volunteer staff for the Georgia Natural Areas Council at the same time as Steven Johnson. He also had a close connection to Jane Yarn and Reid Harris through his leadership of the Islands and Marshland Owners Association. In 1971 he paddled some of Georgia's most scenic rivers with Steven Johnson and helped report the results of their survey to the GNAC. The Georgia Sierra Club group had strong connections to Cumberland. Shortly after receiving the national Sierra Club's recognition, and after their first official meeting on December 9, 1967, the New York office asked them to investigate the possibility of Cumberland Island becoming a national park. In January 1968, the leaders of the group (all of whom were in the UGA Zoology Department) visited the island and wrote a lengthy report to the national board recommending that Cumberland become part of the National Seashore.[77] One of the authors of this report was the son of Ingram Richardson of the Little Cumberland Island Association. They had sent an early draft to a number of Cumberland owners to solicit their input, but in 1968 most were holding out for preservation under their own ownership. It took a while, but the Georgia group received a full go-ahead from the national leaders to actively work for the preservation of Cumberland.[78] When the owners were looking for help to keep Fraser's supporters at bay in the legislature, the Georgia Sierra Club group was a ready and willing ally.

Charles Fraser engaged in a full-throttle campaign to draw public opinion to the side of what he saw as controlled development. By the middle of the 1969 legislative session, he had ceased trying to get the Carnegie heirs to partner with him. Andrew Sparks, the conservation writer for the *Atlanta*

Journal and Constitution Magazine, as a guest on the Sea Pines company small airplane, flew low over the coast from Hilton Head to Cumberland and heard Fraser's full-blown plans for the remaining, privately held but undeveloped, barrier islands. He said Wassaw was best positioned to be the Hilton Head of Georgia, but that was already in the hands of the U.S. Fish and Wildlife Service. He nominated Ossabaw and Sapelo for ecology research opportunities, but even suggested there could be what he called a Golden Isles string of state or federal parks on all the islands in the barrier chain. He wanted most of Cumberland to remain in a wild state, protected by environmental easements or leases with the current owners who did not want to sell, or with a wilderness-guarding organization like the Nature Conservancy. But on his portion of the island there would be villas and cottages for families to rent, bike and walking trails, a golf course, a tennis center, and a medical center with a year-round doctor.[79]

Fraser, in attack mode, aligned himself with the business and political interests of Camden County, predicting that "Cumberland is not going to stay as it is today because there are too many external pressures."[80] He warmed the hearts of local officials by asserting that Cumberland should generate jobs and taxes for the local community. He directly criticized the private Cumberland owners for working with other large landowners in the county to keep their taxes low and "paying just a pittance" to support the local government. This was a direct hit on the owners who, Thornton Morris had advised, would be seeing a sharp rise in taxes when the local tax assessors included the Fraser purchase price in the evaluation of other land on the island.[81] Belittling the Cumberland owners was clear evidence Fraser had given up on them as partners.

Morris, looking for help to fight the Harrison bills, met with Richard Smith, president of the Georgia Conservancy. He was surprised by the lack of support from that quarter. He felt the organization was on the fence and waiting to see how Fraser's public access to the coast argument played with the legislature.[82] He reported back to the Cumberland Island Conservation Association that Smith was "quite disturbed over the increased activity around the State . . . for support of the Authority bills." Morris felt the Conservancy was supporting the island owners, "but will not go so far publically as will cause it to lose its tax exempt status as a non-profit corporation."[83]

Shortly after Harrison's bills were introduced, the advocates for preservation met to determine their strategy. It is not clear who called the meeting, and there is no list of all who were present, but we do know legislators from both the House and the Senate, conservation organizations, representatives from the Johnston branch of the Carnegie family, George Bagby, and Thornton Morris attended. The consensus was to support a resolution authorizing a joint House and Senate study committee focused on the islands and marshlands. The study would allow more time to take other action that would protect the coast. The resolution gathered support from both sides of the debate. This study approach, when combined with the efforts of family and friends, prevented action on the Harrison Cumberland bills during the 1969 session. However, they would be available to consider and could be quickly passed in 1970, the second session of the term.[84]

Paul Nessmith, a prominent signer on the Coastal Marshlands Protection Act and a supporter who helped Harris get his bill out of committee, was the primary author of the Coastal Islands Study Committee resolution, HR 82-218. Nessmith represented the persuadable middle ground in the debate over the future of the coast. He and Harris had worked together on the earlier study committee resulting in the passage of the 1968 Surface Mining Act. But Harrison was also a sponsor of the study committee resolution and had development rather than preservation on his mind. Harris went along with the study committee; in fact he had proposed a similar study in his remarks at the Conference on the Future of the Marshlands. It also fit the recommendations of the University System of Georgia impact study. Harris would later make sure that Thornton Morris became a member of the committee in order to guard the interests of the Cumberland owners.[85] Nessmith, despite his support of marshland protection, showed his support for the consensus public policy of expanding the state's wealth. He was interested in "development" of the coast because it could add "hundreds of millions of dollars to our state's economy and revenue." Unsympathetic to the island owners, he took Fraser's position that they were a "few wealthy non-resident families" who enjoyed the islands with a few close friends.[86] Both sides of the debate over the future of the coast saw how the study could benefit them. It passed with a unanimous vote in both the House and the Senate. In the period between the 1969 and 1970 sessions, the study committee would work on the issue of the future of the islands, allowing the legislators to put the Harrison bills out of their minds and focus on the remainder of the 1969 session.[87]

Because they could not fight every battle, conservation advocates went along with legislation that expanded the scope of the Ocean Science Center of the Atlantic (OSCA). HB 570 was a project of Rep. Charles Jones, the Democratic majority whip from Hinesville with gubernatorial aspirations. His coauthors were Representatives Scarlett, Nessmith, and Harrison. All but Nessmith opposed HB 212. Jones was opposed to the heavy regulatory approach of HB 212, believing that a planning process would have a better result. Like Harris, he could return to the advice of Eugene Odum, who had supported the development of a detailed plan for the coast. This was part of Odum's presentation at the Conference on the Future of the Marshlands, and there were detailed recommendations in the University System of Georgia impact study. The study called for the scope of the OSCA to be expanded so it became the nonregulatory center to research and plan for the future of the coast. Since Jones had been the author of the 1967 legislation creating the center on Skidaway Island, it was natural for him to want to see the center grow. The 1969 bill authorized creation of marine resources extension centers to make recommendations on the use of the state's "off shore lands, waters, and resources." The OSCA was to coordinate plans of other state agencies with responsibilities on the coast.[88] The legislation foreshadowed the day when marine research, which for nearly two decades had been focused on Sapelo Island, would shift to Skidaway. Over time it would become the UGA Skidaway Institute of Oceanography and the center of coastal research for the state, but at the time it was also designed to steal support from the Coastal Marshlands Protection Act. For Jones in 1969, planning and research was a better way to go than the regulatory action Harris had proposed in HB 212.

Rep. Robert Harrison of Camden County was not only a supporter of commercial development on Cumberland, he was a persistent opponent of the Marshlands Protection Act. Harrison's law firm did significant legal work for the Gilman Paper Company, which operated in St. Mary's. Richard Scarlett, who held the other House seat in Glynn County, partnered with Harrison in all the efforts to defeat HB 212. Scarlett's family went back five generations in the county, his father had served as the federal judge for the area, and he was a member of one of the two large law firms in Brunswick. In short, he had deep establishment credentials. Together they introduced two more bills designed to take care of the "marsh business" and would leave the control of marsh use to the local governments as the Brunswick business leaders wished. The first bill, HB 511, permitted the Mineral Leasing Commission to lease the state's lands and water bottoms for "mining, dredging or otherwise removing sand, clay, muck, silt, or minerals for fill materials."[89] This bill may have been prompted by the advisory letter Attorney General Bolton issued to two Chatham County contractors who were removing fill material from the state-owned marsh without a permit from the commission. They needed a lease to take what belonged to the state. One of the construction contractors was owned by the mayor of Savannah, Curtis L. Lewis. By this simple advisory action, the attorney general was asserting the state's ownership claim of the marsh.[90] While the bill required input from the Ocean Science Center of the Atlantic, the Game and Fish Commission, and the Water Quality Control Board, it put the Mineral Leasing Commission in a stronger position regarding future use of the marsh. It was clearly aligned with the interests of Kerr-McGee. It gave no public notice or right for the public to be heard and Harris aggressively labeled HB 511 a "gutting bill."[91] The bill did not come out of committee, however.

While neither of Harrison's Authority bills reached the floor of the House for a vote, they did provide legislators who opposed HB 212 an opportunity to favor a different approach that might avoid choosing sides, thus providing some cover with their constituents. These alternatives gave legislators an explanation for a "no" vote in the coming floor fight and did not fully offend the public will to "save the marsh."

It was not until Thursday, March 5, 1969, that Speaker George L. Smith told Harris he would call his bill.

On that day, the Speaker had committed to a long list of bills, calling Harris's HB 212 toward the end of the day. Often members had personal commitments that could drag them away from their duties at the end of a long day and, as the afternoon wore on, members started leaving. Some members went outside to participate in or watch the anti–Vietnam War rally that Georgia State University students had organized on the steps of the Capitol.

When the Speaker finally called the bill, Rep. Elliott Levitas warned his friend Harris that "the House is light." He advised Harris to ask the Speaker to postpone action until the next day. But Harris felt it important to get the bill through the House so there would be enough legislative days left in the session to work with the senators. He knew they didn't like getting big bills in the final days.[92]

The *Atlanta Constitution* reported that Harris's "voice quivered slightly" with the emotion of the moment when he took the well to give his closing argument. He covered the key points but kept his remarks short so more members did not leave before voting. He explained that the business community in Brunswick was opposed to the bill, but he felt the future of the marsh was too important to wait for their minds to change, and the "public interest" of the state was more important than his local politics. He said the Georgia marsh was fragile but also the most productive land in the country and maybe the world. It sustained the sea life that supported the state's fisheries and was the first defense against storms. He did not want his state to follow the destructive path taken by the states and large urban areas along the coast northeast of Georgia. To blunt the argument he knew was coming, he said local government did not have adequate regulatory or zoning capacity to control the destruction of the marsh and that this bill was giving them the authority they needed.[93]

When Harris yielded the floor, Rep. Mike Egan, the leading Republican from Atlanta, gave a brief seconding speech, reminding legislators that people should prove they own the marsh before they start "messing it up."[94]

Coastal lawyers Robert Harrison, Richard Scarlett, and Charles Jones— all on retainers from the big paper mills—spoke against the bill. They contended that public opinion guided by local advocates would be sufficient to protect the marsh. Harrison, who seemed unbothered by the state condemning land on Cumberland, made his usual argument that HB 212 infringed on property rights and it would restrict the use of 20 percent of the land in Camden County. Scarlett focused his remarks on the damage the bill would do to Glynn County's industrial recruitment efforts.[95]

Democratic Whip Charles Jones, a lawyer from Hinesville who represented both Liberty and McIntosh Counties, strongly opposed the bill. All of the local governments on the coast are against the bill, he said. As a fifth-generation owner of marshland that traced its legal title back to King George II, he pulled out the anti-Atlanta argument: "We don't want anyone up here in Atlanta telling us what we can do."[96] His family had migrated to the Midway area from New England when Georgia was still a colony of the British Crown. Jones had sold part of the family land in Riceboro to International Paper, a company that built a paper mill on a small creek in the early 1960s.[97]

The Speaker intoned: "The question now is, shall House Bill 212 by committee substitute, now pass? The Clerk will unlock the machine."

But before the voting machine was opened, Robert Harrison yelled out, "Mr. Speaker, I have an amendment."

Harris was stunned. The clerk read the amendment. Someone objected, and the Speaker called for a show of hands. The amendment was rejected.[98]

The Speaker ordered the committee substitute adopted without objection and ordered the machine unlocked. Everybody looked up at the red lights and the green lights of the voting board. The lights told Harris it was close, but he wasn't sure of the result. After a minute that surely seemed to him like an hour, the Speaker locked the machine and announced: the "ayes" were ninety-six and the "nays" fifty-nine, meaning the bill had failed to receive a "constitutional majority" and was therefore lost. The Georgia House in 1969 had 196 members. The state constitution required an affirmative vote of at least half of all members (ninety-eight) to adopt a law. The vote left Reid two votes shy of having his bill transmitted to the Senate for consideration. Levitas was right—it was a bad time to have a vote on the bill. The machine reported forty members had not voted.[99]

Harris sat quietly in his seat as the House members left for the day. He knew the fight was not over, but he could look ahead and see the intense effort it would take to get another vote. He would need the approval of the Rules Committee to get the bill back to the floor. The first step was to get the printout of the vote to see where his problems and opportunities were. The next would be a motion to "reconsider" that would be in order the next day.

In a very small notice, an *Atlanta Constitution* editor asked, "will two gentlemen stand up for beauty?"[100]

In analyzing the printout the clerk's office provided, Harris was likely pleased to see, despite the position of the local governments, that he had won a slim majority of the members who represented the five coastal counties. He had six "yes" votes to five "no" votes, with one absentee. He had strength from Republicans, who broke thirteen to nine in his favor, with two absences. He probably did not pay attention to the fact that he did have two future governors with him, Joe Frank Harris and George Busbee, but probably did notice Tom Murphy, Maddox's floor leader, was not. While Murphy often voted independently of the governor, Harris did not know where Lester Maddox came down on the bill. Future U.S. Sen. Sam Nunn voted "aye." With him were the African American members who voted ten to one for the bill, with just two absentees. He did note with some pride that all the members of the gang of six (the legislative independence conspirators), his close allies and friends, voted with him. If he had looked at the vote of Rules Committee members, he would have been encouraged. Seventeen supported the bill with only five "no" votes.[101]

The next day following a failed vote, a reconsideration motion was in order and the vote to reconsider the bill went easily his way. Members usually give a second chance, and so the votes didn't tell much about the final outcome. The bill still had to go through the House Rules Committee before it would be called on the floor. The Rules Committee met in one of the larger rooms on the fourth floor with the twenty-nine members arrayed behind a table and along the wall on one end, and the lobbyists and legislators seeking their favor on the other. The line of legislators usually spilled out the door and into the hall.

On the first day before the committee, George Busbee, the chair, asked Harris if he had seen the telegram that Rep. Richard Scarlett had given him from the Brunswick city attorney. Scarlett, who also represented Brunswick, was trying to keep the bill off the House floor, and the city of Brunswick was continuing its fight against the bill.

> "I see. Strange—he's been seated in the House chamber in the seat next to me most of the day. Maybe it slipped his mind," I said with a smile.
> "You think so?" said Busbee.
> "I doubt it," I replied.[102]

In the telegram, the city attorney said that Harris's bill would interfere with development and many years of planning on city projects and that local zoning could take care of any issues related to the marsh. Harris responded to the chair's inquiry about the issues in the telegram by pointing out that the marsh did not encroach on the projects outlined in the telegram and Brunswick had available upland that could be used for future expansion of industry.[103]

The House Rules Committee put the bill on the calendar the first day, Monday, March 9, but calling the bill on the House floor was at the discretion of the Speaker. So the exercise had to be repeated. Each afternoon, Harris went to the Rules Committee, took his turn in the line of legislators requesting bills, and received a favorable committee recommendation each day. Doggedly, each day he went to the Speaker's podium and asked for the bill to be called, but the Speaker had other priorities. There was always the possibility that opposition views were being heard in the Speaker's ear. Finally, on March 14, he heard the Speaker call HB 212 to the floor and recognized "the Gentleman from Glynn" to present the bill. To Harris even after waiting more than a week the call felt "sudden," but he was confident he had enough votes, and he relished the opportunity to once more educate the members on the value of the marsh.[104]

Always "keep it short" was the rule of presenters in the well. Harris knew to keep it short.

He also knew that many communities still believed the marshlands were worthless and only valuable if filled and built on. He acknowledged commercial interests and industrial interests in his hometown were opposed to the bill and used his willingness to buck these interests to demonstrate the importance of the decision. In remembering his speech years later, he was sure he reminded the members of the beauty of the landscape and its value to the Georgia seafood industry. At the end, he made it personal, saying he "believed with my whole heart and soul that the legislation before them was vital, needed legislation."[105]

When the debate was over, Representative Harrison was again ready with an amendment. It added to the exemption list high land to the west of the salt marsh. Harris had seen the amendment before and had no objection because it supported his intention to avoid the regulation of private property.

The Speaker then called for a vote, but he did not order the clerk to unlock the machine. He asked those in favor of the passage of the bill to raise their hand and the clerk to count the hands. He then asked those opposed to raise a hand and the clerk counted. This was an unusual procedure on the final passage of an important bill, and Harris didn't know if it helped or hurt. The Speaker might have been protecting the voting record of some House members who had left early on a Friday afternoon, and Harris had to go along with that direction.

Again a light House threatened the bill. The Speaker announced the vote: the "ayes are 97 and the nays are 30."

Harris must have sunk deep in his seat or lowered his head onto his desk. Not again! Another light House! How could he have lost after his full-time work on the bill for the last six months? All the people who said they were with him! He couldn't lose the marshes by *one vote*. Could he move for a roll call?

But then the Speaker said, "the Speaker votes aye."

After a long moment of silence across the chamber, Speaker George L. Smith added that "this bill having received a constitutional majority has *therefore passed*." By unanimous consent, the Speaker ordered it transmitted immediately to the Senate for consideration.[106]

Applause swept the chamber.[107]

Reid Harris, high school senior, at the piano with the Septets of Glynn Academy, 1948. (Glynn Academy Yearbook, *The Glynn High Tide*, 1948, from the Glynn County Library)

Lester Maddox and Thomas B. Murphy. (Courtesy of the University of West Georgia)

Reid Harris with legislative leaders on the House floor. (Reid Harris Papers Related to the Coastal Marshlands Protection Act, Richard B. Russell Library for Political Research and Studies, University of Georgia Libraries)

LBJ Heads Off Dock Strike

President Invokes Labor Law

WASHINGTON (AP) — President Johnson invoked the Taft-Hartley law to head off a longshoremen's strike scheduled to begin at Atlantic and Gulf ports at midnight Monday.

The President set up a three-man arbitration board headed by David L. Cole, of Paterson, N.J., a professional arbitrator.

Immediate effect of Johnson's action unkown in Savannah. Page 8B.

Other members are Msgr. George Higgins, director of the Social Action Department of the National Catholic Welfare Conference and also a labor arbitrator who lives in Washing-

Staff Photo by Buddy Rich

DESOTO HILTON BALLROOM CROWDED FOR PHOSPHATE MINING HEARING
Session On Kerr-McGee Proposal To State Will Continue Today

A packed house in the Savannah DeSoto Hilton ballroom hearing on the phosphate lease, September 30, 1968. (Clipping from the front page of the *Savannah Morning News,* October 1, 1968)

Painted portrait of Jane Yarn, at the Jane Yarn Interpretive Center, Tallulah Falls State Park.

Sapelo acquisition ceremony, 1969. *Left to right*: George Bagby, Virginia Maddox, Ruth Bagby, Annemarie Winston Schmidt Reynolds, Lester Maddox, and Boisfeuillet Jones. (Courtesy of Judith Bagby and Tommy Bagby)

Lester Maddox, Robert Hanie, and business leaders hiking down Sweetwater Creek in 1968. (Courtesy of the Georgia Archives, RG30-8-43)

Lester Maddox signing the bill into law. (Courtesy of Michael Harris)

Chapter 10

A Long Year Two

You can send this to the governor, Mr. Clerk.
—Speaker George L. Smith

When Speaker George L. Smith ordered the center door of the House chamber opened so he and Lieutenant Governor George T. Smith could see each other and bring their gavels down simultaneously to end the 1969 meeting of the General Assembly (*sine die*), the future of the coast remained unresolved. Following long-held tradition the Speaker ran—or pretended to run—out of the chamber, leaving the decision resting in the hands of two interim study committees: one led by a senator focused on the marsh and one led by a member of the House focused on the islands.

On day 34 of the 1969 session, HB 212 passed the House by a slim margin, or more accurately, with no margin at all. The debate on the Coastal Marshlands Protection Act shifted to the Senate, but time was swiftly running out on the first year of the two-year session. While the leadership could stretch the calendar by adjourning for the weekend, appropriations hearings, and holidays, the state constitution granted each annual session only forty official days. It was not remarkable for a bill to pass both houses in a single session, but that treatment was usually reserved for uncontroversial measures with broad-based support, emergencies, budgets, or minor revisions of existing laws. With property owners digging or filling the marsh for their own interest, Reid Harris felt the urgency. However, since the mining threat was off center stage, others didn't know enough about the marsh to put the bill into the narrow category of an emergency. And rarely did bills considered controversial reach the governor's desk over the course of just one year.

Lieutenant Governor George T. Smith presided over the Senate and wielded the power to assign bills for committee review. As with the informal politics of the House, a wrong assignment could kill a bill, whereas a good assignment could insure its passage. Harris had asked George T. to assign the bill to the Judiciary Committee, but George T. crossed up his plan when instead he assigned the bill to the Committee on Industry and Labor.[1] Opponents of HB 212 were likely pleased because the industrial and business leaders of the state kept close relations with members of that committee and its chair, Sen. Al Holloway of Albany. After all, at that moment Holloway was also president of the Georgia Chamber of Commerce.

Harris was not pleased. He had good friends and supporters on the Judiciary Committee who included Sen. Bob Walling, an attorney and a Georgia Tech engineer, who had held a House seat from DeKalb County in the prior legislative session. Harris and Walling knew each other from the House, and Walling, who at one point in his life lived in Brunswick and was an active member of the Georgia Conservancy, signed on as the sponsor of HB 212 in the Senate. From the beginning of his legislative service, Harris had served on the House Judiciary Committee and worked closely with lawyers in the Senate. They passed a new Appellate Practice Act, and Harris served on a subcommittee that revised both the Georgia Criminal Code and the Georgia Corporate Code. He knew his friends on the Senate Judiciary Committee would listen and help him. However, he "had a terrible feeling the bill would die" in Holloway's committee.[2]

Holloway, a former bomber pilot, served his first term in the Senate in 1957 under the county unit system. Reg Murphy, columnist for the *Atlanta Constitution*, described him as a "well to do business man" who, as president of the Georgia Chamber of Commerce, carried a "big business tag."[3] Fellow senator Bobby Rowan remembers Holloway's big, jovial personality that cemented friendships after a long legislative day was over. "He was my friend and I voted with him when he had the ball and he voted with me when I had it," recalled Rowan. Since the Senate was only one third the size of the House, friendships made a larger difference. Ethics restrictions were also more lax, and the limited formal restrictions permitted a member of the legislature to also serve in a leadership role in a business organization.[4]

Leadership seemed to come naturally for Holloway. He headed a bomber group in the European theater and finished World War II as an air force captain with a Distinguished Flying Cross. From his days as a young insurance claims adjuster working in Albany for his brother's company, he created a place of significance in the leadership of the Albany community. That's where he met his second wife, whose father owned an engineering and equipment supply business in Albany, giving him the opportunity to develop his business management skills. As the years passed, the business gave him time and resources to invest in public service.[5]

Harris may not have known that Holloway had sea breezes in his lungs. Although Holloway represented landlocked Dougherty County, his roots connected him to a different coast. He was born in York County, Virginia, near the Chesapeake Bay where his father was a commercial fisherman. He caught fish in seine nets, turned them into cat food, and raked oysters from the banks of marsh creeks. The sea life of the marsh was the mainstay of the family budget. Scientists would not need to tell Senator Holloway how the tides of the Chesapeake Bay nurtured sea life.[6]

As a small-business owner, however, Holloway usually stayed close to the state's business interests. At a time when state policy gave full support for the development of Georgia resources and the expansion of its wealth, there was not much distance between the business agenda and the position of state leaders. Holloway was not only a committee chair with life and death power over bills in his committee, but he was also a coalition builder and a leader in the Senate. There were often conflicts with Sen. Hugh Gillis, the leader of the rural faction. While some might describe it as a feud, the differences between the two men were based in the priorities for state investments: one saw investments in rural communities as a top priority, while the other saw the state's economic future in urban areas.[7]

At the beginning of the 1969 session, the Senate Democratic Caucus met to organize an independent Senate much like the House had done in 1967. It differed in that the Senate's head (lieutenant governor) was elected by the people, rather than by members of the Senate, and the rules needed to leave some of its power with the lieutenant governor. They adopted bylaws giving a Democrat-controlled Policy Committee the power to select the chairs of

Senate committees and to make recommendations on important legislation. Since there were only seven Republicans in the Senate, those recommendations always carried the day. One Democratic Caucus vote had an important impact for the Coastal Marshlands Protection Act. Holloway was elected majority leader. He joined Lieutenant Governor Smith in the responsibility of selecting five members of the Policy Committee. In addition to his control of his Committee on Industry and Labor, Holloway had a great deal of influence with the chair of the Rules Committee, which would decide if HB 212 would reach the floor of the Senate.[8] Unlike Harris, Holloway had more than persuasion power.

Holloway also had two unique friends who would play powerful roles in the political history of the state. Arranged by district number, the seating on the Senate floor made James Earl Carter—future governor and future president—Holloway's deskmate during Carter's one Senate term following the 1964 reapportionment (due to the demise of the county unit system). They sat together because their districts joined, and they stayed together on issues because their constituent interests usually aligned. They became close friends in the Senate and remained close during Carter's years as governor (1971–75). Holloway was also firmly connected to the House through his Atlanta legislative housemate. George Busbee represented Albany in the House and had won a tight contest with Tom Murphy for majority leader in the first independent House Democratic Caucus of 1966. Busbee would become governor following Carter. There was a lot of influence concentrated in their two-bedroom Atlanta apartment, and the differences between the House and the Senate had an easy and informal avenue of communication. While Busbee was not a prominent supporter of HB 212, Holloway certainly knew about the Coastal Marshlands Protection Act before it ever reached his committee.

Commissioner of Labor Sam Caldwell was probably another reason Holloway was chair of this committee and handling most of the Labor Department's business. The commissioner, whose agency had offices in every corner of the state, had an effective political base because he could help House and Senate members who had significant African American constituents. He had a generous number of African American employees in the district offices around the state who were willing to "volunteer" to go door to door when Commissioner Sam's friends in the legislature needed votes in a critical election.[9] This relationship likely helped Holloway in his bid to become majority leader.

Harris received a notice from Holloway that the last meeting of the Industry and Labor Committee would be on March 24, 1969, just two days before the end of the 1969 session. During the meeting Sen. Armstrong Smith, a Republican from East Point, where he owned a paint manufacturing business, argued the bill should be given a "do pass" to the full Senate. A chemist by training, Smith had connections to Brunswick, where he had managed the Dixie Paint and Varnish Company for more than ten years. He argued in the committee meeting that pollution posed an immediate threat to the coastal area.[10] Smith confirmed the strong Republican support for the bill.

But Holloway had decided when it hit his committee there would not be time to give the bill, which could impact the state's economic future, the attention it would need. Harris also knew HB 212 had little chance of passing with only a two-day window remaining in the session. Holloway later admitted to having "fears" the bill would not be flexible enough to protect both the marsh and economic development. Given the late date of the House action, Holloway didn't need the usual "study committee" excuse for a delay.[11]

Either out of a desire to lower the heat building around the bill, or from a sincere desire to understand its effect on the state's economy, Holloway authored the creation of a study committee resolution, which passed the Senate before the final day. The *Atlanta Constitution* editorial did not surrender a focus on marsh protection; it criticized Holloway for labeling the bill as complicated and said the "responsibility for any such exploitation of the Georgia marshlands during the next year now rests squarely with Sen. Holloway."[12] Holloway drafted and passed a resolution creating a Coastal Marshland Study Committee, but it only passed the Senate.

So he could control the process, Holloway asked to chair the interim study committee appointed by Lieutenant Governor Smith. Smith appointed a strong committee that included Senators John Riley of Augusta, Turner Scott of Thomaston, Bob Walling of DeKalb, and Bob Smalley of Griffin.[13] The committee had no representation from the coast. With this study committee, Holloway seemed to be legitimately seeking answers to his questions and perhaps giving bill supporters time to make their best case.

During the summer, Harris anxiously waited for Holloway to announce his plans. It was September before Holloway finally notified Harris that the study committee would hear from the Sapelo scientists on October 17 and would hold a public hearing in Brunswick the next day.[14]

"We must gather our forces and put up a better fight next year," wrote Jane Yarn to Reid Harris after the 1969 session. She praised him as a "wonderful inspiration" and greatly appreciated his courage and hard work—and then she and other supporters got to work. In the period between sessions, supporters promoted the legislation through teach-ins, presentations to civic groups, seminars, and a massive letter-writing campaign.[15] Yarn was true to her word, using her connections to promote a letter-writing campaign from women's organizations that included the League of Women Voters and the 22,000 members of the 199 local chapters of the Garden Club of Georgia. Yarn was a new member of the latter's executive committee, and as cochair of its Conservation Council she was behind the Garden Club of Georgia's adoption of HB 212 as part of its official legislative agenda. The club had a history of writing to members of the legislature and encouraged all of its members to write individually. In fact, it had published instructions in the *Garden Gate* on how to write an effective letter to a member of the legislature.[16] Yarn was very pleased the board of the Garden Club of Georgia gave her freedom to present environmental issues on their behalf. She reported to the board that in 1969 she had spoken to the Sportsman's Federation, the annual Forestry Shade Tree Conference, women's clubs, churches, Scouting groups, and the three-day Conference on Environmental Quality in order to promote passage of HB 212.[17]

Yarn found ways to educate her Northside Atlanta friends and the Atlanta business community. She arranged for Clifford West's new film on the natural environment of Ossabaw to be shown at the High Museum in Atlanta, followed by a discussion of the issues facing the coast. The film was "powerfully presented to Atlanta's power structure. . . . It was a deeply moving and disturbing experience for many of them, this select body of movers and shakers and builders." She used her long-term relationships with numerous Atlanta organizations to connect to influential friends who could support her efforts. One of those who attended the High showing was the president of the Atlanta Chamber of Commerce, Rawson Haverty. Eugene Odum developed a resource list for her to use with the film to educate audiences across the state.[18]

The zoology graduate students at the University of Georgia helped spread the scientific knowledge of their professors across the state. Joyce Murlless, whose husband was a student of Don Scott (a founder and early UGAMI researcher), helped the graduate students write an elementary-school curriculum explaining the new science of ecology and the value of the marsh to sea life. They sent the curriculum to every elementary science teacher in the state. Joyce, who was working on a master's degree in education, also went to nonscience classes at the university, even drama classes, to present the arguments for the marsh in ways more understandable than presentations by her husband's graduate school colleagues. Together the zoology students developed a one-page "WHY SAVE OUR MARSH" flyer (all words and no graphics) that was cheaply reproduced in quantity, distributed to classes, and sent home with students throughout the state. They printed "Save the Marsh" campaign buttons and distributed six thousand bumper stickers.[19]

The students' efforts to educate the public about the bill and the environmental issues across the state got help from Jane Yarn. In the *Garden Gate*, the Garden Club of Georgia published the contact information for the graduate students willing to make environmental presentations to clubs all over the state.[20]

By 1969 the Georgia Sierra Club group was a fully recognized unit of the Sierra Club's Eastern U.S. club, and authorized to make the preservation of Georgia's coast its first major advocacy initiative. Steven Johnson represented their views at public hearings and kept up with the work of the Georgia Natural Areas Council, as he and Sam Candler joined the council staff midway through 1969.[21]

By December, the Athens-based graduate students had plans to get the marsh protection issue in front of students when they returned for the winter quarter. A Sierra Club film night on January 19, 1970, netted 110 students. Their activities had a broader objective—to get statewide participation on Earth Day on April 22. There was a loose connection and overlap between the Sierra Club organizing and the Save the Marshes Committee. Generally, many of the same UGA students were behind both. Committee members were also faculty, undergraduate students, and townspeople; Richard Murlless was chair.[22] The major Save the Marshes Committee event was a community forum on January 28 that was termed a "three-way discussion" among Eugene Odum, Dirk Frankenberg, and Rep. Robert Harrison. It was more accurately two against one. This forum, which drew the attention of sympathetic student reporters from the *Red and Black*, the campus newspaper, had predictable content, but it served the organizers' purpose of bringing student attention to the marsh issue. It is not clear what student support Harrison expected in response to his usual argument that HB 212 infringed on the rights of local government and individual property rights.[23]

Jane Yarn had forged a strong relationship with the UGA graduate students. The next Sierra Club event advertised Yarn as the featured speaker in Atlanta on February 4, at the parish house of All Saints Episcopal Church. At this point, Yarn had become a headliner for her work with the Nature Conservancy in preserving Egg and Wolf Islands. Close coordination between conservation advocates was again evident. Organizers piggybacked on the trip they were making to Atlanta to testify at the final Senate hearing on HB 212.[24]

Yarn was quickly becoming a significant public voice for the conservation movement. Early in January 1970, she had received the Conservationist of the Year Award from the Georgia Wildlife Federation. Her acceptance speech urged awareness of environment and natural beauty.

> I think all of us are concerned with the world around us, our total environment. But I think some of us might have been submerged too long in our special lives, such as the city, to where a shell or a façade has been formed between us and our total environment. Many of us just can't see our relationship to the world around us.[25]

She clearly understood the role of the state's politics. She told Bob Harrell of the *Atlanta Constitution* that in environmental advocacy "all roads lead to the Gold Dome of the Capitol."[26]

Yarn used her understanding and her ability to convince legislators, both Democrats and Republicans, of the importance of environmental issues. "As she maneuvered in what was, at that time, essentially a 'man's world,' Yarn grew infamous for using her charm to hide a blistering wit, which caught many opponents off guard." One environmental advocate admitted that "we were all a little in love with her."[27]

More than just becoming a public spokesperson for the cause, Yarn was well on her way to organizing a direct lobbying arm for conservation. Informally organized with the cooperation of the Georgia Sierra Club group, they gave it an academic-sounding name: the Planning and Conservation League of Georgia. It was not limited by the 501(c)(3) worries of the Georgia Conservancy. It was under this umbrella the Sierra Club provided testimony to the Senate Industry and Labor Committee. Yarn had the board of directors of the Garden Club of Georgia give the loose lobby network their full endorsement.[28] During the 1970 session the loose collaboration of the league acquired a little more structure and a new name: SAVE, for Save America's Vital Environment. This was not a membership organization at this point, but rather a gathering of all the people Yarn knew who wanted to directly contact legislators on environmental issues. She didn't want to be held back by IRS 501(c)(3) restrictions. If there were any expenses, Yarn paid them. Jim Morrison, even as an employee of the Game and Fish Commission, had the freedom to be a regular member of the informal group that began coordinating environmental lobbying.[29] The Garden Club of Georgia board also gave its endorsement to SAVE and were ready to ask their members to write letters to their own legislators and to critical legislative leaders on the issues SAVE identified.[30] The Cumberland Island owners were pleased to hear from their lobbyist Thornton Morris that SAVE would have their backs in the ongoing battle over the future of their island.[31] SAVE, under Yarn's informal organizational style, provided an opportunity for environmental advocates to coordinate their efforts to influence legislators.

The Sierra Club itself, unlike the Georgia Conservancy, could lobby directly for the passage of HB 212. Because the national organization had lost its 501(c)(3) tax-exempt status over its fight to stop a dam in the Grand Canyon, it was free of the direct lobbying fears that restricted the Georgia Conservancy. The Georgia Sierra Club group put a "Lobbyist Wanted" notice in its newsletter, asking people interested in the job or in volunteering to contact Steven Johnson. They were looking for a person to make direct contact with legislators, keep community advocates informed, and get needed information out to the public through the press. The Georgia group was to channel its lobbying efforts through Jane Yarn and the Planning and Conservation League.[32] While there is no solid evidence of the success of this new venture, the Sierra Club linked student intensity to the work of other advocates.[33] Saving the marsh and HB 212 was the connection point and a beginning for broader environmental advocacy in the state focused on the state legislature.

Other supporters were also busy. Fred Marland made presentations to organizations. He was invited by Deborah Adams, wife of Brunswick senator Ronald Adams, to speak to the Brunswick chapter of the American Association of University Women. While many of the members' husbands were likely part of the Brunswick business establishment, "This Beleaguered Earth: Can Man Survive?" was the organization's national study, and members wanted to know more about the value of the marsh. Marland also traveled to Thomasville to speak to another group of well-educated women on the same issues.[34]

Like the UGA student effort, spreading knowledge was the intention of a seminar Dave Maney of the Coastal Area Planning and Development Commission organized shortly after the 1969 session ended. He worked closely with the UGAMI and the Marshes of Glynn Society to present the public seminar at Brunswick Community College titled "Marshland, Not Wasteland." The program warned that marshlands along the Atlantic were rapidly disappearing due to contamination, and in New Jersey and New York there were "virtually no marshes left." The seminar recognized the need to "strike a reasonable balance between the various users of the marshlands." The speakers included John Hoyt, Fred Marland, and Tom Linton from the UGAMI, Leonard Ledbetter from the Water Quality Control Board, and a speaker from Game and Fish. All supported HB 212 and clearly hoped knowledge would blunt some of the most vocal local opposition.[35]

During the time between sessions, reporters also kept the issue before their readers. They made some effort to keep the coverage evenhanded, but writing about the coastal environment created more knowledge and understanding that would bring political support in indirect ways. In particular, the *Atlanta Constitution* provided institutional support to reporters Jeff Nesmith and Andrew Sparks to dig deeper into the environmental issues.

In his "Salt March" series, Nesmith highlighted the ongoing efforts of Rock Howard and the WQCB to reduce the pollution coming into the marshes from coastal rivers. To demonstrate the pollution effects of the industry along the rivers. Howard used population equivalent data, comparing pollution generated by industry to the equivalent in people pollution. The plants in Savannah, led by Union Camp's paper mill, dumped pollution into its river equal to the untreated sewage of a city of 900,000 people, and the twice-a-day tides pushed the pollution back up the river and into the adjacent marshes. Howard was particularly frustrated with the chemical plant owned by American Cyanamide, which emptied 1 million pounds of raw sulfuric acid into the Savannah River each day.

In high gear in the fall of 1969, Rock Howard's continuing campaign to clean Georgia's rivers contributed to the rising public awareness of environmental issues facing the coast. He had worked closely with federal counterparts to clean up the lower Savannah River. His water quality colleagues at the U.S. Department of Health, Education, and Welfare had investigated the river in 1965 and collaborated with Howard on a pollution enforcement conference on the problems created by the Union Camp discharges and the unprocessed sewage from the city. In cooperation with Howard's engineers, they had found the pollution had created a dead zone where no animal life could survive. The conference is not formal but brings together the parties involved to work out solutions; it led to a plan to clean up the Savannah River. Howard had monitored the river closely after the 1965 plan of action and found there was still an animal life dead zone in the river.

In 1969, Howard put the Savannah River back in the news. The Federal Water Pollution Control Administration, with Howard's cooperation and data, called a new enforcement conference in September 1969. Data on the river showed that the cleanup effort over the past four years had made little progress. The Union Camp mill was still producing 70 percent of the oxygen-devouring material going into the river, the equivalent of a city of 800,000 people, only a slight improvement since the plan of action was established. What grabbed most of the public's attention was that fish still could not swim upriver past the dead zone. During the Kerr-McGee mining fight, Georgia scientists had also shown that very little of the pollution went into the ocean—some went directly into the marsh, and the tides brought much of what did make it out to sea back into the marsh. The scientists knew that oxygen levels in the marsh were closely balanced and that new material could severely affect the marine life coming from the marsh. While the passage of the 1966 federal Clean Water Act still left enforcement largely in the hands of the states, the South's pulp and paper industry would eventually need to process the biological material it discharged so it didn't absorb all of the oxygen in the rivers. The September 1969 pollution enforcement conference put the pollution of the river on the front pages of the *Savannah Morning News*, and this time Union Camp produced a costly plan to pump the effluent across the river and clean it in aeration ponds before it was released back into the river.[36] While it did not touch upon the issues of heavy metals, which would become a concern in later years, the control of biological components of the effluent would make it possible by 1972 for fish once again to swim past Savannah.[37]

Several environmental disasters got the nation's attention in 1969: Santa Barbara, California, suffered a 200,000-gallon oil spill, and the Cuyahoga River near Cleveland, Ohio, caught fire. In Georgia, the dead river downstream of the Union Camp plant did even more to increase public interest in conservation. It demonstrated that the pulp and paper industry's use of the local environment to flush pollutants would need to change in the future. The attention to the Savannah River conference also increased statewide support for the Marshlands Protection Act.

The industrial plants in Brunswick, while smaller than those in Savannah, were having no better effect on the environment. Nesmith used Eugene Odum to make the connection between the pollution and the endangered marsh. The marsh could eliminate small amounts of pollution, but "add a lot and you destroy vast areas of productivity," Odum said. The damage from pollution was so great that the state health department banned the harvest of oysters from the state's marshes.[38]

Despite increased attention to environmental issues, reporter Jeff Nesmith was not optimistic the Georgia legislature would change direction on environmental policy. Reviewing the "tide of abuse" heaped on Reid Harris by the Brunswick business establishment, Nesmith speculated that he could not win reelection in 1970. He also did not expect much from Al Holloway, who had HB 212 "locked in his Industry and Labor Committee." He saw little support coming from the "little men" in the fishing industry who should be in the battle to "save livelihood," but he did agree with advocates' strategy: rather than play the long game of changing public opinion, go straight to members of the General Assembly to create the needed change.

He highlighted the work of Odum, Robert Hanie, Dave Maney, the Georgia Conservancy, and the scientists of Sapelo and clearly hoped public opinion would shift to their side.[39] Nesmith and the *Atlanta Constitution*'s extensive and continuous coverage gave his readers facts they could use with their members of the legislature and gave encouragement to the organizations supporting the bill. The *Savannah Morning News* and the *Brunswick News* also had intense coverage of the legislative battle.

A project to dike 1,200 acres of marsh in McIntosh County caught Nesmith's attention. It also showed the urgent need for a regulatory body and raised the immediate issue of who owned the marsh. Marifarm, a Florida subsidiary of DuPont, claimed it had perfected shrimp farming and in 1969 was moving quickly to set up shop on the Georgia coast. Concerned about cutting off tidal water to other parts of the marsh, conservationists had a hard time arguing against food production from the sea when it was one of their arguments for preserving the coastal habitat. Under existing Georgia law, Marifarm needed approval only from the U.S. Army Corps of Engineers, which had jurisdiction over waterways, in order to create marsh lakes that could produce 1 million pounds of shrimp a year. The entire Georgia production was only 6 million pounds.[40] The Georgia Natural Areas Council wrote a letter opposing Marifarm's U.S. Army Corps of Engineers permit because there was no study enclosed of the effects of the dikes on the tidal flows critical to the health of marshlands.[41]

However, it was Attorney General Arthur Bolton who put a stop to the project. In a letter to the U.S. Army Corps of Engineers, he asserted the state's ownership of the marsh. He told Colonel John S. Egbert that the tidal lands between the high-water mark and the low-water mark "[constitute] a public trust administered by the State on behalf of the general public." Therefore, the permit asking to build a causeway across the marsh or to build dikes would need the approval of the General Assembly of Georgia, and the state was not consenting to the construction on its marshes.[42]

Meanwhile, with George Bagby's permission, Jim Morrison was filling the Game and Fish Department's monthly magazine and its radio feeds with discussion of the Coastal Marshlands Protection Act. His beloved "propaganda machine" produced some of the clearest coverage of the scientific value of the marsh. His readers were interested in sportfishing and hunting and Morrison helped them see how their sport was served by the conservation of the natural areas of the state. His summer issue reviewed the status of HB 212 and encouraged his readers not only to get ready for public hearings in the fall, but also "to get busy contacting their own local representative and senator to urge his support for a revitalized HB 212." He encouraged a letter-writing campaign directed at coastal members of the House and Senate, providing contact information for the members of the Committee on Industry and Labor.[43] Sportsmen were hearing from Jim Morrison and George Bagby what the women of the Garden Club of Georgia were hearing from Jane Yarn.

The Game and Fish Commission, with full voice, continued supporting coastal conservation efforts. *Georgia Game and Fish* published its five-point legislative agenda just before the 1970 session of the General Assembly. The Coastal Marshlands Protection Act headed the list. The commission supported a stronger bill with the restoration of the state agency that was part of the original, and it supported efforts to determine who owned the marsh. It requested support of a larger budget to include more biologists, more rangers to patrol the marsh, and positions "demanded by modern conservation programs." The fifth request for help to kill any gun control bills was probably not on the legislative agenda of conservationists, but it clearly shows the capacity of groups to work together on issues when they did find agreement.[44]

Back in the House, Paul Nessmith made plans for the joint House-Senate Georgia Coastal Islands Study Committee authorized by his HR 82-119. The Speaker appointed Nessmith as chair and Rep. Joe Battle as secretary; the lieutenant governor appointed Sen. William Searcey of Savannah as the vice chair. The eight other House and Senate members came largely from coastal districts, with Glynn County represented by Sen. Ronald Adams and Rep. Richard Scarlett. The appointments gave control of the committee to legislators from the coast or the near coast. There were six agency heads on the committee, including Reid Harris's most committed supporters: Rock Howard and George Bagby. There were two private-sector members: Alfred W. Jones Jr. of the Sea Island Company and Thornton Morris. The latter credited Reid Harris with helping to get him appointed to the committee. As a member, he was in a unique position to protect the interests of his clients and to provide them with progress reports on the work of the committee.[45]

The committee's mandate in the authorizing legislation was a direct challenge to those who wanted to preserve the natural environment of the coast. The resolution directed committee members to "study the feasibility of the State of Georgia acquiring said islands so that they may be developed for the greatest benefit and enjoyment of the Citizens of and visitors to our State." Supporters of the study aggressively highlighted that the islands were owned by a "few very wealthy non-resident families and enjoyed by these owners and some of their close friends." Development on the islands could add "hundreds of millions of dollars to our state's economy and revenue," Chairman Nessmith said.[46] The resolution was clearly influenced by Charles Fraser's vision of greater public access to the beaches and forests of the barrier islands and the hope that his Sea Pines Plantation–type development would be possible on the Georgia coast. There was, however, a broader appeal that average Georgians should be able to take their families to the beach. While the committee was looking for development opportunities on all the undeveloped islands, Cumberland was clearly in the crosshairs.

The private owners of all the undeveloped islands—Wassaw, Ossabaw, St. Catherines, Sapelo, and Cumberland—hosted the committee on their islands and expressed their hopes for the future of those islands. The committee held public hearings in St. Mary's, Savannah, and Atlanta and spent time on Hilton Head, where Fraser and his staff showed off Fraser's vision.[47]

When the Georgia Coastal Islands Study Committee visited Cumberland and held a public hearing in St. Mary's on October 8 and 9, members heard a clear division of opinion. At an evening meeting at Lucy Ferguson's newly opened Greyfield Inn on Cumberland, attended by Mary Bullard and Coley Perkins, the island owners told the committee "that at the present time the owners of Cumberland have no desire to sell any land to the State of Georgia." The next day, Thornton Morris, speaking at the public hearing in St. Marys for the island owners, said they opposed Robert Harrison's proposed bill to create the Camden Recreation Authority. They felt instead that the "National Park approach was the most realistic way to insure the long-term preservation of Cumberland Island." Opposition to the owners' views came from Rep. Robert Harrison, author of the authority legislation, and Camden County officials, who insisted they preferred the joint development of Cumberland by private individuals (i.e., Charles Fraser) and a governmental body like the proposed authority.[48]

Next the committee traveled to Savannah to hold a public hearing on November 10, right in the midst of the Wassaw Island sale controversy. The issue of the day for the business community in Savannah was Wassaw Island, and its sale to the Nature Conservancy dominated the hearing, with little interest expressed in the future of the other islands.[49] The visit to Ossabaw produced some conflicting opinions as well. Sandy West made it clear she had no interest in selling her island to the state and would be inviting college students to come there to study the environment. Rock Howard sided with West on the use of Ossabaw because it was distant from Savannah's industrial pollution, but he said that at some point the state should buy it and give it to the University of Georgia for education purposes. West wanted to turn the island over to "people who like snakes and birds," dismissively claimed Sen. William Searcey from Savannah, at a reception later that evening. He was more interested in the fellow who made $100 a week having access to the island. The next generation of owners will want to make some money, he said, and after all West "won't live forever."[50] Senator Searcey and Representatives Battle and Nessmith all agreed the state should own the islands. For Nessmith, access to the coast was the issue: "very few of our citizens have ever had the opportunity to visit and enjoy these islands," he claimed.[51]

While in the Savannah area for their hearing, the committee attended the dedication of the Richard J. Reynolds Wildlife Refuge on Sapelo. The final report of the Georgia Coastal Islands Study Committee recognized the state's ownership of Sapelo, and its use as a wildlife reserve settled the question.[52]

It was October when Senator Holloway's study committee finally came to the coast to look at the issues surrounding the Coastal Marshlands Protection Act. He planned a visit to the UGAMI for October 17 and his committee's public hearing on HB 212 the following day at Brunswick Community College. While the Holloway Study Committee was on Sapelo and in Brunswick, the Nessmith Coastal Islands Study Committee was enjoying a pleasant weekend at Sea Pines Plantation on Hilton Head. Nessmith planned a final, third public hearing day in Atlanta on December 9, with the committee scheduled to make its recommendations the very next day.

The cloistered scientists carefully planned for the visit by Holloway's committee. This was the most important opportunity to put to work the science they all believed in in order to protect their beloved marsh. They had stepped out of the cloistered life of the institute, taken the ferry to the mainland, and shared their knowledge at various public hearings. They had stopped legislators in the halls of the Capitol and spoken about their findings. All had participated in the outpouring of scientific information that helped the governor, the attorney general, Rock Howard, George Bagby, and other state officials understand the risk to the Georgia coast from the Kerr-McGee mining proposal. Now the scientists, Henry, Hoyt, Frankenberg, Linton, and Marland, all made carefully designed presentations to Holloway and his committee. They presented the UGAMI's scientific conclusions, reviewing the fragile nature of Georgia's barrier islands and the productive value of the marshlands that had developed from unique circumstances over millions of years. They highlighted the diversity of the plants and animals that surrounded the marshes. They identified the significance of the twice-daily flows of tidal water that take the marsh production out to coastal waters to sustain marine life in the ocean. Holloway was a quick study and, because of his childhood experiences in the Chesapeake Bay marshes, he grasped the data the scientists presented on the value of the marsh.[53] Not least, the beauty of the island and its surrounding marshes was apparent. Often in politics, what you see has the largest influence over what you do. The committee members could see and absorb the best evidence for the bill.

Another voice of authority came from John Teal, one of the first researchers at the UGAMI. As a researcher at the prestigious Woods Hole Oceanographic Institute in Massachusetts, he and his wife, Mildred, authored *The Life and Death of the Salt Marsh* in 1969. It was a review of the current scientific research on the salt marsh, made readable by the narrative writing Mildred added. Their book remains a guide to what other states had allowed to be done to destroy the marsh, how little remained in other states, and what a few states had done to preserve what remained. This popular study, which for many years remained the seminal work on the subject, helped cement in the public mind the simple idea: the marsh is valuable and very productive, more productive than the best midwestern corn farm.[54]

The next day, on their way off Sapelo Island, Harris and Holloway had an opportunity for a private conversation. Harris later characterized it as a "red-letter day" because Holloway confided that his father had been an "oysterman" on the Chesapeake Bay and pollution in the bay had destroyed the family business. The senator did not state a position on the bill, but at that moment Harris felt their goals were aligned.[55]

The crowd at the Brunswick Community College hearing on October 18 did not approach the raucous Kerr-McGee hearings in Savannah the previous year, but a respectable 125 people attended. At this public hearing on the bill, twenty-five people testified. Steven Johnson came from Athens to reiterate the Sierra Club's consistent position in support of the bill.[56] Hoyt Brown, chair of the Marshes of Glynn Society, argued that local governments on the coast were not capable of objective action to protect the marshes because they lacked the infrastructure and the will. A letter from Game and Fish commissioner George Bagby, read by the head of the commission's coastal fisheries program, reinforced Brown's main point. The counties and cities lack "trained technical personnel required to determine the effects of proposed filling and dredging activities on marine resources." Bagby maintained the authority over the marshes should rest with the state. The Georgia Game and Fish Commission was the best agency to take on this responsibility.[57] It is not enough to control the harvesting of marine life, he wrote, but there was a need to take "immediate steps to preserve the habitat which these species of life depend on for their very existence."[58]

A representative of the real estate industry said the bill was taking away another right from the property owner. Most interesting was the position taken by Rep. Richard Scarlett, who insisted that the process of getting title insurance would be too costly for the average person. He argued for flexibility. Not all of the marsh needed to be preserved: "Some should be used by industry, some for recreation and some should not be touched by man forever and ever. Amen." He didn't say how those zones would be created. The hearing did not produce the confrontation with local industry Harris had expected. They did not testify but "just took notes."[59] It is not clear why local opponents missed this opportunity to influence the committee.

The final hearing of Nessmith's Coastal Islands Study Committee on December 10, in Atlanta, would have delighted the producers of a present-day cable news show. The players in the drama over Cumberland were all crowded into the House Appropriations Committee room, the largest room in the Capitol apart from the two chambers. Conservation advocates at this hearing were focused on Cumberland's future, but in most cases they were the same core advocates supporting HB 212 and supporting the efforts of other island owners to preserve the natural environment of their islands. One whole row was filled with Cumberland owners. The presentations made on December 9 were widely covered by the state's newspapers and television stations; Andrew Sparks preserved much of the testimony in a delightfully written article for the *Atlanta Journal and Constitution Magazine*.[60]

Following the political hopes of James Earl "Jimmy" Carter, Sparks described him as a "sparkling-eyed" not-yet-announced Democratic candidate for governor who declared himself on the side of private property rights and, according to Sparks, "God, motherhood and apple pie." Taking people's land by condemnation, for "commercial development and profit" violated Carter's principles. He claimed the high ground of Georgia politics when he declared that people who own the land "ought to have a right to determine its future."[61]

The "evangelical" director of the Georgia Natural Areas Council, as Sparks described Bob Hanie, took the stand and gave the committee a small taste of his lyrical prose. The barrier islands needed to be seen as a whole: "the sea bass in Christmas Creek on Cumberland, a semi-tropical storm on Sapelo, the sight of 300 egrets nesting at Middle Place on Ossabaw, and the 'wild chowder smell of the marsh' after the tide has gone out." The point of his testimony was far less exciting than his poetic flourish. He wanted the committee to recommend a two-year plan for the whole coast, put together by planning and environmental experts, rather than legislators.[62]

Eugene Odum, who Sparks referred to as "the Billy Sunday or Clarence Darrow of the conservation movement," said the dunes and the marshes should be the most important target of preservation because the marsh and the beaches could not survive without the protection of the dunes. The islands themselves would be "buried by the sea" without the dunes. Founding his presentation on the theory of interdependence of the elements in a natural system, he skillfully made the scientific theory of ecology relevant to the decisions legislators needed to make about an island. The coastal ecosystem was in a delicate balance and humans could disastrously upset that balance.

He also supported Hanie in his call for a comprehensive plan for the coast and encouraged legislators to wait for the expert advice that would come from the planning process.[63]

By this point in the Cumberland discussion, the Georgia Conservancy had overcome its lukewarm support of the island owners, and fully backed their efforts to put the islands' future under the control of the National Park Service. It was still unclear if Congressman Bill Stuckey would help make this outcome a reality. The Georgia Conservancy had joined with the Cumberland owners, who by this time saw the National Seashore as their best option. To the disappointment of Savannah Rep. Joe Battle, William Griffin, representing the Georgia Conservancy, supported the transfer of Wassaw to the U.S. Bureau of Sport Fisheries and Wildlife.[64]

Mary Bullard, a third-generation descendant and Cumberland historian who had inherited a small plot on the island, stated her personal views: Cumberland should be part of the National Park Service, and building a causeway would be a "disaster" for the island. She had wanted to keep her property and build on it but over the last year had seen the efforts of private developers threaten the tranquility of the island. She became concerned at the possibility of legislation empowering the state to condemn her property and gave her support to the National Park Service proposal. William Warren, a Candler family owner, stated his support of the federal park and told Representative Battle the family rejected state control because it had "done a job on Jekyll that the people on Cumberland don't want."[65]

As the chair of the board of the newly created Ocean Science Center of the Atlantic, Laurie Abbott, a Savannah attorney, led the development argument. He was an outspoken opponent of the transfer of Wassaw to the U.S. Bureau of Sports Fisheries and Wildlife. He brought up his old argument that, to be legal, the transaction needed state approval. In the short history of the center, he had seen 9 miles of Georgia beaches become off-limits to the public and lamented that four of Georgia's coastal counties had no public ocean beaches. His argument for a delay in the decision process and support of a comprehensive plan sounded similar to the recommendations of Hanie and Odum, but his objective seemed more like a last stand for island development. Abbott opposed HB 212, he insisted, because there needed to be more time and study (a year of legislative delay wasn't enough) before the state put the marshlands off-limits.[66] It was a rear-guard "study" argument from the development advocates who saw the issue getting away from them.

The political highlight of the hearing came from Joseph Fraser, a "balding, tanned, slow talking man with none of the dramatic flair of his brother Charles." As vice president of Sea Pines Plantation, he stood in for his brother, the company's more well-known president. Charles was otherwise engaged in a meeting with the governor of South Carolina arguing against the BASF chemical plant upstream from Hilton Head. Joe said he agreed much of nature should be preserved for the next generation, but "we have some obligation to the current generation to provide clean recreation, the opportunity to get away from the city." He presented the well-honed company message of his brother, a belief in planning that needed to combine public recreation, private communities, and conservancy. But Joe was not ready for what happened next.[67]

Under the hearing rules set down by Chairman Nessmith, only Study Committee members could ask questions of the witnesses. Committee member Thornton Morris, who was representing the Cumberland Island Conservation Association (owners) and several branches of the Carnegie family, took this high-stakes moment to ask Joe Fraser if it was the Sea Pines Plantation lawyer who had *introduced* the Camden County Recreation Authority bills. Joe walked into that one, casually responding, why yes, and adding that the Sea Pines company supported the legislation.[68]

When the revelation hit the front page of the *Savannah Morning News* the next day, Rep. Robert Harrison was forced to explain his conflict of interest. He drew a small distinction: that his law firm of Harrison and Laseter had done real estate work for Fraser, but that he had not personally represented Fraser.[69] The disclosure took the leadership of the committee by surprise and put a cloud over the Camden County Recreation Authority legislation, still a live bill left from the 1969 session. It also energized discussions already under way in both houses regarding committee officers' conflicts of interest. Robert Harrison's legal work for Charles Fraser got the attention of the press following legislators' efforts to tighten the conflict rules. Perhaps the ethics work was a side effect of legislative independence. The power that came with independence from the governor also came with greater responsibility.[70]

The day following the hearing, Representative Nessmith reconvened the Coastal Islands Study Committee to determine its recommendations. The members all agreed to recommend that the attorney general determine who owned the marshlands. They further agreed steps should be taken to stop the erosion of Savannah Beach. However, there was disagreement on the central issue of the state's control of Cumberland. The report said there was no opposition to the development of Cumberland as a National Seashore, but the state should "at least have the opportunity to acquire one or more" islands if the situation presents itself. A majority of the members supported the expansion of the Jekyll Island State Park Authority and the appropriation of $3 million to support a general obligation bond of $36 million "for the purchase of one or more of the undeveloped coastal islands."[71] Thornton Morris reported to his clients that the vote on this issue of greatest importance was eight in favor and five against.[72]

Although the marshlands were not the focus of the committee's work, in the members' travels they had seen a lot and were clearly aware of HB 212. Nessmith was a cosigner of the bill and had helped it move out of the House. The committee had heard from scientists that the Georgia marshlands were the "richest and most productive marshlands in the world." They also heard Eugene Odum and Robert Hanie on the need to look comprehensively at both the islands and the marsh. These recommendations and those of Laurie Abbott provided an opportunity to sidestep a recommendation on the Coastal Marshlands Protection Act and recommend the creation of a permanent commission to develop a comprehensive plan. The plan would satisfy avid coastal developers by clearly leaving open the possibility of greater development. The final report stated "the marshlands should be controlled and regulated at the earliest possible time a comprehensive plan can be formulated and implemented."[73] With that recommendation, the committee dodged most of the important issues related to the marsh. It didn't pile up criticism on the bill, and didn't provide help to the Brunswick business opponents. It left the protection of the marshlands in the hands of some future commission or in the hands of the Holloway Senate Study Committee.

Reactions to the committee recommendations came quickly. Robert Hanie, in his usual hyperkinetic tone, said that "this could permit the rape of the Georgia coast." Bill Jones Jr. of the Sea Island Company and a member of the committee, was more measured in his prediction that the action "will further alienate the owners" and force them further away from any sale to the state. Rep. Leroy Simkins of Augusta labeled the committee action as "just poor politics." Committee member Thornton Morris, reflecting the views of his clients, added to the pile of complaints: "the good will of the State has been destroyed."[74]

One of the committee's "no" votes came from Sen. Roscoe Dean, whose district included Camden County and Cumberland Island. His "no" was at least in part payback for Sen. Ford Spinks and Representative Harrison messing in his Senate district. He didn't just vote no. He issued an unusual personal Minority Report laying out the details for his opposition. The state could not afford to issue new debt, he said, but his main opposition was the use of condemnation power to "abridge the sacred and valuable property rights of persons now holding lands on the coastal islands." The private property value came down on the side of preservation. He went beyond his opposition to the committee's recommendation to expand the jurisdiction of the Jekyll Island Authority. He called for the defeat of Representative Harrison's Camden County Recreation Authority Bill in the House, because there was so little difference between the committee recommendation on Jekyll and the Camden County Authority bill. Finally, he called out Harrison's conflict of interest as a reason to defeat the legislation.[75]

At the start of the 1970 session in Atlanta, Holloway worked with Rep. Reid Harris and Sen. Bob Walling on a Senate committee substitute. The substitute largely restored the bill to the original version Harris had introduced in the House the previous year. In his substitute he had made the important decision to exempt a few powerful business interests from the requirements of the bill. It would make Holloway's task a little easier if the bill avoided opposition from Georgia Power and allay Atlanta Gas Light's concerns for its statewide distribution network. He had made sure that the strong business interests that might need or want to put a telephone pole or a pipeline in the marsh could do so. He had also exempted the Highway Department from the bill and that lessened the possibility Sen. Hugh Gillis, whose father Jim Gillis headed that department, would oppose the bill.

After the 1970 session was gaveled to order, Holloway held one more Study Committee hearing on HB 212 on January 19. This is public hearing number three, if you are keeping track.

While it was an open public hearing, Holloway made sure the advocates for the bill were present. Steven Johnson again made a statement for the seventy-thousand-member Sierra Club. On behalf of the national organization and the Georgia chapter, he urged "the fullest protection be given to Georgia's coastal marshes."[76] Harris himself told the committee that the bill the House had passed was too "watered down" and hoped the committee would draft a bill that would give the state responsibility for "industrial and commercial development on the coast."[77] Twenty-one people gave testimony, including students and scientists from UGA. The three Glynn County commissioners in the room did not speak.[78]

Holloway extended a special invitation to Hoyt Brown. He was not a celebrity or a partner from a large firm, but a presenter that Governor Maddox liked to call the "little people." He had presented his views at the Brunswick hearing, but Holloway brought him to a bigger stage. He was a seventy-year-old retired shop superintendent from the Hercules Powder plant, who had worked to protect the marsh beginning with his participation in organizing the Marshes of Glynn Society in 1963. He helped revive the society in 1967 and had been a consistent supporter of the Coastal Marshlands Protection Act. What made his testimony important to the Senate committee was his service on the County Board of Health and the Brunswick / Glynn County Planning Commission. He believed the local government in his county was inadequately prepared to protect its marsh from local development pressures and pointed out that only two of the six coastal counties had full existing zoning laws. He pointed to a recent Glynn County Commission decision to rezone 27 acres of marsh from conservation-preservation to commercial without seeking Planning Commission approval. In fact, he said, the new 1969 county ordinance passed to protect the marsh did not require the Planning Commission's approval before the Glynn County Commission acted on the permit. It merely said the applicant had to submit plans before the dredging started. To Brown, the facts clearly showed "the fallacy of depending on local City or County Commissioners, or local Planning or Zoning Boards, in protecting the marshlands."[79]

The Marshlands Protection Agency, with its power over the final permit, was back in the bill. Holloway dispensed with a formal interim study committee report and instead, on January 29, with the 1970 session well under way, released a new and stronger draft of a full Senate Committee Substitute. He put supporters and opponents on a very short notice that the full committee would hold a public hearing on February 3.[80] The hearing on the newly revised Senate substitute to HB 212 was the fourth public hearing on the bill—possibly a record number of hearings on just one bill. This did not attract a packed house as had the third public hearing of the Coastal Islands Study Committee on December 9, but it gave supporters one more chance to educate the public and one more chance for friendly news coverage to spread knowledge and understanding of the science of the day. Those who closely followed the legislature could tell that this train was moving and that Holloway was at the controls.

The organized opposition from Brunswick, which had been silent at the hearing in their town, came to Atlanta looking for an opportunity to weaken the Senate committee draft. John Gaynor, a partner in the Gilbert law firm from Brunswick and Harris's boyhood friend, was the chief spokesperson for the opposition. Gaynor and Harris had been in the same high school class at Glynn Academy and had been debate partners on the school team. Later, as partners in the two largest law firms in Brunswick, they often had been on opposite sides in front of local judges. Gaynor went to Princeton and then to the UGA School of Law, where he was one of three students known to earn A's in all of his classes. He was very "bright" and had represented Brunswick in the Georgia Senate, where he was known as the "conscience of the Senate." He was the sponsor of the Georgia Administrative Procedures Act and was given credit for its passage during his time in the Senate. The clients of Gaynor's firm were the large industries of the city, including Hercules Powder, Brunswick Pulp and Paper, and the Sea Island Company. His father had come to Brunswick as the president of Brunswick Pulp and Paper, with the plant on the river and next to the marsh, making the company an opponent of HB 212.[81]

Gaynor spoke for an hour. In addition to his firm's local clients, he represented the Georgia Business and Industry Association, the Seaboard Coast Company, the Brunswick–Glynn County Chamber of Commerce, and the

Glynn County Real Estate Board. He stated that the Brunswick Central Labor Council was also opposed to the bill. He focused the attention of the committee on the marsh, which "all but surrounded" Brunswick and would limit its future industrial growth. Under the bill as drafted, "there could never be any use of the marshes in terms of commercial expansion or industrial development in Brunswick," he said.[82]

Again, Harris's supporters showed up. Fred Marland and John Hoyt came from Sapelo. Hoyt told the committee that unless the marshes trap the silt from the rivers, the silt "will build up in the water and make coastal waters so muddy that "fish, oysters, even shrimp will die." He said if we "start destroying a large amount of the marshes, you're in real trouble."[83] Eugene Odum came from Athens. At the Save the Marsh Committee teach-in the day before, he had made the point that a population increase was coming to Georgia. "The carpetbaggers are coming back and we are not prepared."[84] J. Furman Smith testified for the newly formed Planning Conservation League (later changed to SAVE under Jane Yarn). Smith argued the marshes belonged to the public and the "proper body to assume guardianship and protection of them is a state agency."[85] Eugenia Price traveled from St. Simons to deliver an aesthetic plea for the preservation of the marsh that surrounded her home.

Following the hearing, Senator Holloway invited Marland and Hoyt for a late-night discussion at his Atlanta apartment. They shared a nightcap and discussed the testimony presented at the hearing. They had to keep their voices low because George Busbee, an early-to-bed kind of guy, was asleep in the adjoining room. While Holloway did not say what would happen on the bill, the two scientists felt they had answered all of his questions and had full confidence the bill was on its way to passage in the Senate.[86]

While the three relaxed in conversation, Gaynor was working. He lobbied all the senators he could find. He knew he could not affect the core provisions of the bill, but he developed language for the "whereas" section or "findings" he hoped would show usable legislative intent. His addition said the General Assembly intended "that any use of the marshlands be balanced between the protection of the environment on the one hand and industrial and commercial development on the other."[87] Holloway added the provision to the released committee substitute. This gave Gaynor, his industry clients, and future developers an opportunity to argue before the Marshlands Protection Agency and the courts that their project was within the intent of the law.

The full committee met on February 5 to consider the substitute. In addition to the Gaynor language, Holloway had altered the membership on the Marshlands Protection Agency board to give slightly more influence to those interested in the state's economic development. He replaced the Council for the Preservation of Natural Areas with the executive director of the Ocean Science Center of the Atlantic, which had been given responsibility for coastal research. This was a small sign of waning support for the marine institute on Sapelo. He added the director of the Coastal Area Planning and Development Commission, who would connect the agency to the local coastal governments. The most significant shift in the balance was the addition of representatives of the Georgia Ports Authority and the Department of Industry and Trade. Harris's stalwart supporters from the Game and Fish Commission and from the Water Quality Control Board were still there. The Marshlands Protection Agency was placed in the state Game and Fish Commission for administrative purposes but as an autonomous agency was given control over its own decisions on applications. The attorney general filled out the seven-person board and held the deciding vote if there was an even split over a permit application.[88]

It passed the Industry and Labor Committee with little discussion; within minutes the Rules Committee, under Holloway's firm control, placed it on the calendar for the full Senate for the next day, February 6.[89] The swift movement of the bill to the Senate floor showed there was no significant opposition left with the need or the will to oppose a Holloway-endorsed bill.

Sen. Ronald Adams presented the bill. During his four years in the Senate he had lost most of his eyesight. He could not read a speech or a poem but, like many Georgia schoolchildren, had memorized several verses of Sidney Lanier's "The Marshes of Glynn" and recited the poem to his appreciative fellow members, who applauded his performance. He was likely pleased that, after a year, more people had come to understand the value of the marshland and the need to protect it from future development. He felt that time would bring consensus and had stayed out of the forefront of the legislative fight. He had been for the preservation of the marshes since the founding of the Marshes of Glynn Society in 1963, and he had hoped that increased understanding would yield increased preservation efforts.[90]

Holloway believed that "a majority of the people of Georgia want some control of the marshes," and he believed that the bill was the right policy for the state. Holloway admitted he had received more letters on this bill than he had for all other legislation in his whole time as a senator. Jane Yarn's garden club members had done their work. Fred Marland recalls that during his "educating of legislators" at the Capitol he met Sen. Sam McGill in the hall and asked, "what are you going to do on the Marshland bill?" McGill spoke of receiving letters from all those women; "I can't go home if I did not vote for the Coastal Marshlands Protection Act."[91]

The bill passed unanimously.

It is hard to analyze a unanimous vote. It means the two African American senators were for it; eight Republicans were for it; rural and urban Democrats were for it. The leadership of the Senate was for it. It is likely that a bill thoughtfully sponsored by a newly minted majority leader would have few opponents, but it remains remarkable there were no dissenting votes. Consensus is difficult to reach in any democratic process. In former Sen. Bobby Rowan's mind, it was about friendship. He recalled fifty years later, "why would anyone in good conscience vote against an Al Holloway bill?"[92] The vote also shows the state had reached a surprising degree of consensus on how it would protect the natural environment of its coast.

Reid Harris and Holloway believed that all the discussion of water pollution had created a genuine movement in public opinion. Others, including Senator Walling, worried that the public support for the environment was largely a "creation of the media."[93] Julian Bond, former spokesperson for the Student Non-Violent Coordinating Committee—who had to go to the U.S. Supreme Court to be seated in the House—said pollution was a serious business, but he speculated that the environmental cause was an easy way to "take the heat off the civil rights movement."[94] It would not be long, however, before the political leaders of the state would understand the reality of the public's commitment to the environment. They just had to wait for

Earth Day on April 22, less than a month after the session ended, and for the 1970 race for governor, to see environmental issues were not going away.

After the Senate, the Coastal Marshlands Protection Act had two more barriers to clear. To be a law there must be a vote in both bodies on exactly the same wording—the bill needed to come back for another House vote. Oh yes, and then the signature of the governor.

Harris spent the weekend of February 7–8 at home contemplating his next step. He studied the rule book and decided to gamble. He would try to bring the bill to the House floor during the period of unanimous consent, when most members are not fully attentive. It was a time in the proceedings when roll call was taken, prayers were said, the journal for the prior day approved, and new bills were read for the first time. There was also a usual calendar of "local" bills with support from the members of a county delegation that would be read and passed with unanimous consent of the full House. But if the Speaker recognized him during this lax time, he would have control of the floor and be able to make a motion. He would move to "accept the Senate Substitute to House Bill 212," and the bill would get a final vote immediately. This was legislative craft that came with his six years of experience. Although risky, this strategy would cut off the opposition's opportunity to flood the House with telegrams and phone calls. The Garden Club of Georgia letters to House members had been much fewer than to senators.

But the bill had to be physically present in the House in order for this to work. Very early in the morning of February 9, Harris talked to the secretary of the Senate, and the two agreed that the bill would be delivered to the House with the first messenger of the day in order to get there during unanimous consent. He waited and watched for the messenger. Finally, a young man with a wooden box filled with bills shouted his presence from the back of the room and was permitted to bring his bills to the clerk. Harris went to the clerk's desk, found HB 212 in the bottom of the box, and headed back to his seat. With mike in hand, he signaled the Speaker to be recognized.

What happened next is a little unclear. In the last fifty years, the Speaker has almost always queried the member, "and for what purpose does the gentleman rise?" If the member replies "to make a motion," the Speaker can decide whether or not to recognize the member for that purpose. But that was not always the practice under Speaker George L Smith. According to Tom Murphy, when he became Speaker Pro Tem in 1970 and Smith gave Murphy the gavel temporarily, he began questioning the gentleman's purpose in order to gain more control over the order of debate. Smith found this to be a good practice and began using it himself in later years.[95]

Smith may have wished he had used it with Harris, but according to Harris, Smith said, "the Gentleman from Glynn is recognized." Knowing he controlled the floor, Reid Harris called out, "Mr. Speaker, I move that the House agree to the Senate's amendments to House Bill 212." He recalled hearing the Speaker groan and saw him bow his head. The Speaker asked him to come down to the Speaker's podium and explained that the House needed to first finish with the Appropriations Bill. "I can't wait," Harris said. The pressure was too great. He had the experience and confidence to say no to the independent Speaker of the House, a person whom Harris helped make Speaker. As Harris walked back to his desk he heard the Speaker say, "the motion of the gentleman from Glynn is, that the House agree to the Senate amendments to House Bill 212. Is there objection?"[96]

Robert Harrison, after feverishly consulting his rule book, rose and said, "I object."

Speaker: "State your objections."

Harrison: "The members of the House have not seen the Senate amendments."

Speaker: "That is not a proper objection."

Harrison: "Well, in light of the fact that the Senate only passed its amendments last Friday . . . I move that HB 212 as amended be printed."

Speaker: "The gentleman has that right . . . a motion to print is not debatable."

Harris: "Point of inquiry, Mr. Speaker."

Speaker: "State your inquiry."

Harris: "Is it not true, Mr. Speaker, that the Senate merely changed the bill back to the form it had been in when introduced but changed many of the features previously objected to by the House?"

Speaker: "If the gentleman states these matters as facts, the Speaker, having no knowledge of them, has no reason to doubt the truth of your statement." The Speaker ordered the Clerk to unlock the machines and they all waited for the red and green lights.

Speaker: "On the motion to print the ayes are 41 and the nays are 78. The motion is lost."

The Speaker moved quickly to a final vote. The ayes were 103 and the nays were 21. "The House has agreed to the Senate amendments to House Bill 212." And probably with some relief in his voice he added "You can send this to the Governor, Mr. Clerk."[97]

Like the vote in the House on March 14, 1969, that passed the bill the first time, this vote was closer than expected. The bill received just five votes above the required ninety-eight. Only five votes to spare. The closeness of the vote came to some degree from Harris's unexpected and unusual motion at the end of the period of unanimous consent. Among the seventy-one members not voting were thirteen individuals who had voted for the bill in 1969. The nay votes were down because twenty-three of the nay votes in 1969 did not vote in 1970. It is likely that some of these members had felt the grassroots pressure and preferred to abstain rather than have a recorded vote. The most conspicuous abstention was Robert Harrison's, who had made the motion to print just moments before the final vote. Given his consistent opposition and feverish search for an alternative, it is hard to understand why he decided to abstain. The campaign for the Coastal Marshlands Protection Act had changed eleven votes from a nay to aye, while only five members changed from supporting the bill in 1969 to opposing it in 1970—enough to tip the balance.[98]

Reid Harris was very likely pleased his bill won the support of a majority of the members from the coastal counties. At the beginning of the session, Rep. Charles Jones, the Democratic Whip representing Macintosh and Liberty Counties, who worked against Harris in 1969, switched his position on the bill and stated a willingness to cosponsor the bill with Harris. Surprisingly, Rep. Joe Battle of Savannah, who had fought long and hard to give the state control over Wassaw and Cumberland Islands, joined Jones as a yes vote on the final passage. Those two switches gave the bill a solid seven-to-two majority of the coastal representatives. Only two Republicans voted against the bill, but an increase in abstentions left the total support from Republicans at thirteen.[99]

Applause followed the passage in the House, also from newspaperman Reginald Murphy. In his column titled "The System Works on Marshland Bill," he wrote that "a well to do businessman" and president of the Georgia Chamber, Senator Holloway, had opposed the bill in 1969 but helped pass a stronger bill in 1970. He had listened to the public will. To Reg Murphy this was evidence the system of representative government worked.[100] It was also enough to give Joyce Blackburn renewed faith that writing letters worked. She had written to Holloway and Lieutenant Governor George T. Smith and would write to Lester Maddox and ask him to sign the bill.[101]

The interim Coastal Islands Study Committee also had a success with one of its recommendations. The bill expanding the jurisdiction of the Jekyll Island Authority did not pass, but the bill to create a permanent commission to plan the coast's future passed with nearly a consensus behind it.

On March 27, 1970, Reid Harris picked his way across Capitol Avenue to the back entrance of the Capitol. The governor's chief of staff, Zell Miller, had requested he come to Atlanta for a meeting with his boss. There was no hint of what Governor Maddox would do. This was the day Harris would find out if his work over the last two years would result in a new law protecting his beloved coast. The Coastal Marshlands Protection Act was on the governor's desk, and today it would either get a veto or a signature, or become law the next day without a signature (the governor has thirty days from the time he receives a bill to take action). Harris knew that Brunswick business interests had continued their opposition with letters and high-level contacts with the governor, whom they had asked for a veto. The press reported the governor was leaning toward a veto.[102]

The governor was not close to Harris and had been a wild card throughout the legislative life of the bill. He had not stated his position on the bill, but was part of the political consensus prioritizing development, jobs, and the wealth that came to the state from economic activity. However, he had an unpredictable populist side and was proud of being with "the little people." When he thought about what Maddox might do now, Harris remembered in great detail the day in January 1967 when he had asked the General Assembly for a new runoff election and failed. Then, on the next vote, Harris voted not for Maddox but for Bo Callaway as governor.[103] Maddox also knew Harris was one of the conspirators who stripped the office of governor of his control of the House. Those were major votes that everyone in politics remembers in detail. Politically, Maddox owed Reid Harris nothing but punishment.

While Maddox was now the last barrier to be hurdled, the legislative independence movement that Harris helped start in 1966 had given him the opportunity to make his argument for the marsh in a legislative process no longer controlled by a governor. The open legislative process provided four separate public hearings at which citizens and scientists spoke directly to legislators. While they heard what the captains of Brunswick industry wanted, they also heard what Hoyt Brown wanted to happen with the marsh and the barrier islands. Harris didn't know how Governor Maddox felt about the reduction of the governor's power or his personal role in rebalancing that power. Democrats had elected George L. Smith to carry the power of the Speaker, and Smith had cast the supporting vote on the bill and given Harris the floor he needed for a vote on the final passage.

Harris was probably encouraged by the others already in the outer office on the second floor: Eugene Odum, Jane Yarn, and Rock Howard. He knew that without them there would have been no bill.[104] When the veto rumors started, these three were his first calls. He knew the letters were flowing to the governor from Garden Club of Georgia members and from the young scientists on Sapelo. The zoology students had traveled the state to deliver the new scientific knowledge to corners of Georgia that no politician could reach. Harris was proud of the way his scientific friends from the UGAMI on Sapelo stepped out of their cloistered scientific lives to bring their decades of research to the public, in language average people could understand in order to realize that the state needed to save the marshlands.

As he and the others waited in the outer reception room to be ushered into the governor's inner office, they chatted with members of the Capitol press corps who had turned out in unusually large numbers. The reporters had told Harris of the veto rumors. Two days before, they reported that only ten bills still remained on the governor's desk. On the marshland bill, Maddox had only said he would "consult with his advisors."[105]

A shy, scholarly lawyer, Harris was comfortable talking policy but, as his Maddox election vote showed, he was not necessarily good at picking winners and losers in a fight over power. Harris had spent many hours helping reporters understand the science behind the bill and the details of the new regulatory system that would control how Georgians could use coastal resources in the future. He made sure they understood the core legal concept of his bill that regulated the state's publicly owned marshlands. He had been disappointed Attorney General Bolton had waited until after the bill passed to rule on who owned the Georgia marshlands. He was good at the policy and the science and had a lawyer's capacity to keep the public debate out of the weeds, but he needed a lot of help from the masters of the state's politics.

George Bagby, one of those masters, was not in the room when they were ushered into the official office. Bagby, the Maddox "Fish Head," was critical to the governor's decision. He had a special relationship with the governor. He was one of the few Capitol politicos who was with Maddox from the start of his quixotic campaign for governor, and he had introduced him to the legislators who made him governor. Maddox had fought the independent Game and Fish Board to put Bagby at the head of the state's most important environmental department. Bagby had fought Kerr-McGee with all the words he could muster (thanks to his publicist, Jim Morrison), and Maddox had agreed that the marsh was more important than phosphate. Bagby was a fervent supporter of a permanent law to preserve the marshlands; it was he who made the deal with Mrs. Reynolds to purchase most of Sapelo. He brought with him the support of the sport fishermen and the hunters, who were the deep roots of Georgia's political culture and appreciation of the outdoors.

The governor entered the room with Bagby. He greeted Harris, Howard, Yarn, and Odum. Ferris Freeman, Holloway's Capitol secretary, was there to explain that Holloway could not attend because of a death in the family. Given who was in the room, it must have looked very good at that point.

Addressing Harris, Maddox said: "We've got us a controversial bill here. You know it's controversial, don't you Chief?"

Harris replied, "I know Governor. Nobody in the state knows better than I do."

"Tell you the truth, Chief, I've thought long and hard about a veto. Bagby here tells me I should sign it into law. You ought to see the letters and wires I've gotten on this. There must be three barrels full back there."

He asked for pens and started signing. He gave the first to Reid Harris.

"Hope I've done the right thing," said Maddox.[106]

Chapter 11

The Movement Continues

Dear Governor Busbee,
I hereby make available the amount of four million dollars.

—ROBERT W. WOODRUFF

The story does not end there. Once you start a stone rolling, it's hard to stop it.

Just ten days before Governor Maddox signed the Coastal Marshlands Protection Act, as we've seen, Arthur Bolton decided the state of Georgia owned the marsh and issued a position paper on March 17, 1970. Following extensive research, the attorney general expressed his agreement with Reid Harris that the king of England had owned the land under tidal waters. With the American Revolution, ownership passed to the states in trust for the people. The marshes "are not susceptible to private exploitation of conservation."[1] With some minor exceptions, where grants from the king specifically included the marshland, the 500,000 acres of coastal marsh were in the control of the state. Some landowners, led by Rep. Robert Harrison, disagreed, pointing to a complicated and convoluted provision in the 1945 Georgia Constitution. Owners threatened to sue the state to get back the taxes they had paid on the land they thought was theirs.[2] Private marsh "owners" went to the courts to assert their position, but in 1976, in *State v. Ashmore*, the Georgia Supreme Court confirmed Bolton's opinion. Thirty years later, the court's 2006 ruling in *Black v. Floyd* affirmed that the "soil between high-water mark and low-water mark was the property of the crown" and that Georgia now owned it unless specifically conveyed by a "Crown or state grant." The court pointed to the code in section 52-1-2 of the Official Code of Georgia Annotated, which read that the tidewater is "the sea and all rivers and arms of the sea that are affected by the tide, where the tide rises and falls, which are capable of use for fishing, passage, navigation, commerce, or transportation."[3]

The decision to keep the marsh in state ownership was reinforced by a gratuity clause of the Georgia Constitution, adopted after the 1795 Yazoo Land Fraud, which says the state cannot gift property to a private person. Bolton's position paper put an end to Kerr-McGee's phosphate and ocean real estate ambitions. The company admitted that its ownership to the tidal lands was "fuzzy" and said they were unlikely to try again to mine the marsh.[4]

The attorney general's conclusion confirmed the Coastal Marshlands Protection Act as protection of property rights, even though they were the state's property rights. Throughout the legislative battle over the bill, Harris had maintained that not one acre of or backyard of a private owner had been taken away by the legislation. While the bill enabled the state to regulate the use of the marsh, it was establishing a system for regulating the state's property. It clearly expanded the regulatory power of the state and for some opponents it carried the stink of big-government interference, but with the settlement of the ownership question it also fit into a conservative political philosophy that awarded highest respect for the rights of private property owners.

The reach of the act onto private property was tested again in a case that came before the Georgia Supreme Court in 2007. Environmental advocates, fearful that pollution from storm water runoff from upland developments was negatively affecting the marshlands, sought to expand the act's reach. The developer of Cumberland Harbour, a large proposed residential development near St. Mary's, on a 1,100-acre maritime peninsula, had been granted a permit for a dock and harbor at Point Peter. Conservation advocates believed the regulators must review the upland development, pointing to language in the act: "no person shall remove, fill, dredge, drain, *or otherwise alter* any marshlands" (emphasis added).[5]

Ironically, Reid Harris and Fred Marland were on the side of the developer. Patricia Barmeyer, who was an assistant attorney general and advised Fred Marland when he staffed the Marshlands Protection Agency, was also on the side of the developer as an attorney for King and Spalding. Harris wrote an amicus brief for the court and joined Marland in a letter to the editor of the *Savannah Morning News.* They argued that the legislative intent of the bill was to limit its reach to the clearly defined edge of the marsh. The other federal and state laws could be used to control nonpoint source pollution. Marland was concerned that the expansion of the marsh definition to private property could destroy the regulatory impact of the act.[6] The Supreme Court agreed with the developer, Harris, Marland, and Barmeyer.

The development stalled in the 2007–9 financial downturn, at which point the project fell into bankruptcy. Earlier, in 2005, when the U.S. Army Corps of Engineers required an archaeological survey, the remains of an historic fort from the War of 1812 were discovered. Excavation unearthed 67,000 artifacts from that war.[7] A few homes have recently been built, but many more lots are available in the development. To date, no further legal action has taken place to address the issue of nonpoint source pollution from the uplands.[8]

However, as sea level rise pushes the tide onto land that is now considered in private ownership, it is likely the court will need to review the state's ownership of the tidal lands again.

Less than a month after Governor Maddox signed the Coastal Marshlands Protection Act, college students at nearly every institution of higher learning in Georgia held public programs looking at the challenges facing the environment. The first Earth Day, held on April 22, 1970, quickly showed that public interest in the environment was not just the creation of the media, as Sen. Bob Walling had opined. Students at universities and schools across the state came out of their dorm rooms and rode their bicycles to the teach-ins organized by students, faculty, and enthusiastic citizens. The conservationist advocates, who had played a major part in the legislative and anti-mining campaigns, spread out across the state to make speeches. Rock Howard managed to speak at Emory University, Georgia State University, Georgia Tech, and Georgia Southern. In his speeches across the state, Howard pushed for a $300 million program to help local governments treat their sewage and clean up the state's rivers.[9] At Georgia Southern, Howard was joined by Fred Marland, Reid Harris, former congressman James Mackay, and Ogden Doremus. Steven Johnson was on the program at the Emory teach-in. Robert Hanie was the keynote speaker at Mercer University.[10] Eugene Odum drew the most attention and told the crowd of five thousand at the University of Georgia that speeches and study "must be followed by action." In addition to the major universities, there were programs at Brenau College, Atlanta University, and Agnes Scott College. The students at West Georgia College drew press attention when they held a special ceremony for the burial of an internal combustion engine.[11]

Perhaps the buildup to Earth Day and the beginning of the 1970 campaigns for governor can explain in part the unanimous vote in the Senate for the Coastal Marshlands Protection Act. It is clear the grassroots campaign for the bill laid the foundation for a widespread Earth Day celebration in Georgia.

The race for governor was off and running by Earth Day 1970. Both leading candidates claimed the mantle of environmentalism. While Jimmy Carter did not have coastal issues in his platform, he did say he would "prevent pollution of air and water and reduce the deterioration of our environment." In his speech at Georgia State University, he called for a "massive education project" on the environment.[12]

Carl Sanders used the day to kick off his official campaign with a fly-in around the state. He announced at Georgia Southern that every college in Georgia should have an ecology field of study. Sanders, who justifiably took credit for Rock Howard's Water Quality Control Board, embraced a Eugene Odum proposal backed by Bob Hanie for a Georgia "Department of the Environment." He pledged to protect the underground aquifer that supplied drinking water to the coast.[13] When he spoke to the Atlanta Rotary Club, his greatest applause came for the lines related to conservation.[14]

Implementing the Coastal Marshlands Protection Act was slow at first. Administrative responsibility was with the Department of Game and Fish, where Bagby gave his rangers responsibility for finding violators. However, the agency did not have dedicated staff for processing permits or sanctioning violators. Georgia would need new political leaders and new agency levers to implement the decision it made between 1968 and 1970, and the details of the policy would need continuous review.

Jimmy Carter won the election for governor, and in 1972, Governor Carter's Executive Reorganization Act put environmental agencies and their implementation authority into a new Department of Natural Resources (DNR). Parks and Recreation, Game and Fish, and the Water Quality Control Board were collected under the new department. Forestry managed to fly solo. Earlier the Marshlands Protection Agency had received its first dedicated staff in 1971, when the new Game and Fish commissioner, Joe Tanner, selected Fred Marland to head implementation efforts. The Marshlands Protection Agency also came under the umbrella of the DNR, which essentially was in charge of almost all things environmental. Another important organizational decision was the creation of the Coastal Resources Division of DNR under Governor Busbee in 1978. This decision brought together the DNR staff responsible for federal and state regulation of the coast to an office in Brunswick, close to the subject of their work. It concentrated the board of the Marshlands Protection Agency from seven to four, and put the DNR board more directly in charge: the commissioner and three other members selected by the DNR board.[15]

In 1988, while reviewing the implementation of the act, the Carl Vinson Institute found some interesting facts. The Marshlands Protection Agency granted 202 permits between 1970 and 1986, which together altered less than 450 acres of marsh. Half of this acreage was in the first two years, before a full administrative structure was in place. However, this did not count the exceptions granted for the construction of I-95, which amounted to a loss of 3,976 acres of marshland. The institute report concluded that the act was an efficient regulator of the marsh but would need to be coordinated with other concepts from time to time like the Georgia Vital Areas Act and the public-trust doctrine in Bolton's position paper.[16]

It would take decades—five at this writing—to implement the decision Georgia made to save the natural environment of its coastal marshlands and the islands' coast. Georgia passed other laws to extend that protection. In 1976, it amended the state constitution to expand the state's powers to "protect and preserve the natural resources, environment, and *vital areas* of the State."[17] The coast was clearly a "vital area." The Shore Assistance Act of 1979, regulating the sand sharing system, had the most implication for the future of the islands.

In the 1970s, the state saw help from a flurry of federal legislation driven by the burst of public support for responsible use of the environment: the National Environmental Policy Act (1970), the Clean Air Act (1972), the Clean Water Act (1972), the Endangered Species Act (1973), the National Forest Management Act (1976), the Federal Land Policy and Management

Act (1976), the Surface Mine Control and Reclamation Act (1977), and the Comprehensive Environmental Response, Compensation, and Liability Act of 1980 (1980). Each of these acts, like the Coastal Marshlands Protection Act, had a public-notice requirement and a provision for the public to be heard regarding their implementation.[18] The staff of U.S. senator "Scoop" Jackson, the principal author of the 1970 Environmental Policy Act, looked carefully at the work of the UGAMI scientists, the Kerr-McGee fight, and the Coastal Marshlands Protection Act when writing the bill.[19] The requirement for environmental impact statements for a wide range of federal projects followed closely the Georgia process requested by Governor Maddox.[20] In most cases, the state had significant responsibility for administering the new federal initiatives and had opportunities to receive grants to support the activities.

Protecting the Remaining Islands

In the years immediately following the passage of the Coastal Marshlands Protection Act, except for St. Catherines Island, the remaining barrier islands came under the protection of the state or the federal government. Currently 85 percent of Georgia land facing the Atlantic is under some level of state-administered protection.[21]

Cumberland

The political story of U.S. congressman Bill Stuckey's Cumberland Island National Seashore bill had many stops and starts and has been reviewed in detail by a number of thoughtful authors.[22] Although this book won't cover well-trodden ground, there are a few stories too good to leave on the sidelines.

The first is about the critical role played by Alfred Bill Jones Sr., who in 1968 sat silently during the two days of the Conference on the Future of the Marshlands at his Cloister resort. This is a story of connections and conversations. Jones knew Paul Mellon, who headed the Mellon Family Trust. Mellon's attorney, Stoddard Stevens, visited the Cloister on occasion, and Jones took him to see the beauty of Cumberland. Stevens, in turn, convinced Mellon to visit and had Jones conduct a private tour. These informal discussions resulted in a luncheon invitation with the secretary of the Department of the Interior, who learned Mellon would provide $7.5 million to the newly formed National Park Foundation to purchase land on Cumberland. The goal was to buy three-fifths of the remaining Carnegie land, which incidentally included the land owned by Charles Fraser. The National Park Service, with the help of Thornton Morris, worked out an agreement with Fraser, Joe Graves, and Colony Perkins, who controlled the Johnston family land. The Mellon commitment of funds and the agreement of critical Carnegie family members dropped into place before the federal legislation passed in 1973.

One other Cumberland political story that must be told is Stuckey's need for a "no-causeway" provision in his bill. Back in 1966, Stuckey had run hard against incumbent Congressman Jim Tuten. During the campaign he charged that Tuten reneged on a promise to support a Cumberland causeway. Stuckey knew the Department of the Interior would oppose any bill that included a causeway. He himself had concluded there should not be a causeway. However, he had to find a way out of his own causeway commitment to the Camden County commissioners. Two commissioners opposed the causeway, two were on the fence, and one would oppose any bill that did not allow the possibility of a causeway. When the commissioners met at the Greyfield Inn on Cumberland to discuss the issue, the County Commission executive secretary, who favored the National Seashore, bought rounds of whiskey at the bar for the one diehard, who missed dinner with the other four. Stuckey used that opportunity to convince the two on the fence to approve his bill without the causeway. That meeting took him off the hook.[23]

Ossabaw

After lengthy negotiations with Eleanor Torrey "Sandy" West, whose family purchased Ossabaw Island in 1924 for $150,000, the state, during George Busbee's governorship, purchased the island in 1978. The value of the island—which is about twelve times the size of Tybee Island—was estimated at $16 million, but it sold for $8 million, because West's first priority was to preserve the island in its natural state. She said she had been looking for a compatible buyer for sixteen years. Jane Yarn and DNR commissioner Joe Tanner teamed up to make the transaction work. The state did not have the money in its Historic Preservation Trust, but Yarn brought Boisfeuillet Jones of the Robert Woodruff Foundation for a weekend on the island

and Mr. Woodruff made a $4 million contribution to the fund. The donation was documented in Woodruff's handwriting on a high-rag note card to Governor Busbee.

> Dear Governor Busbee:
> I hereby make available the amount of four million dollars toward the purchase of Ossabaw Island for the enjoyment of the people of Georgia. Two million now and the remainder of two million on closing.
> Sincerely,
> Robert W. Woodruff
> Atlanta, GA 30303

The story goes, Governor Busbee stopped by the Trust Company Bank in Atlanta to cash the note. A flustered teller called the bank vice president upstairs. Supposedly, the $2 million was then deposited in the state bank account and the deal moved to a successful closing.[24]

Like other island transactions the Ossabaw purchase went through the Nature Conservancy, which imposed an environmental easement that met Sandy West's highest priority. Ossabaw became Georgia's first Heritage Preserve, to be used for "natural scientific and cultural study, research and dedication to environmentally sound preservation, conservation and management of the island's ecosystems." West, age sixty-five at the time of the transaction, continued to live on the 23-acre life estate until she left the island at the age of 103 in 2016. Since 1998 the state has turned to the Ossabaw Island Foundation to manage programs and facilities on the island.[25]

Little Tybee Island

When Kerr-McGee reviewed Arthur Bolton's position paper on the ownership of the marsh, it lost interest in Little Tybee and Cabbage Islands as phosphate mining sites. When Lester Maddox rejected the Kerr-McGee lease, Georgia dodged a large environmental bullet. The largest phosphate mine in the country is just outside the tiny town of Soda Springs, Idaho. That mine, owned by Monsanto, produces a critical ingredient in the world's most widely used herbicide: Roundup®. The use of the herbicide currently has its environmental problems, but pertinent to the Georgia coast, the EPA designated the Soda Springs mine a dangerously polluted Superfund site in 1990. Despite the EPA decision, the "oozing lava-like slag" from the refining plant is still today dumped off a cliff outside the town. Local people who faced personal economic disaster (loss of jobs and the wealth in their homes) agreed to keep the mine through a "decentralized" EPA process. At one point over the decades, the slag was used to pave streets and create cinder blocks for the construction of homes before it was found to be radioactive. The site continues to endanger the groundwater supply and the agriculture that dominates the surrounding landscape.[26] Additionally, juries have recently concluded Monsanto Roundup causes cancer (multimillion-dollar damages have been awarded); however, large building supply retailers continue to carry the product.[27]

It took another twenty years after Bolton's decision before Kerr-McGee relinquished ownership of the sliver of upland that faced the Atlantic. For that period it was left to the shorebirds, fiddler crabs, fishermen, canoers, and campers. In 1991, the company agreed to sell its islands to the Nature Conservancy, if they in turn, would agree to sell to the state for $1.5 million. Over two fiscal years, Governor Zell Miller set aside the funds. The money was used by the Nature Conservancy to purchase and protect 50,000 acres of prairie grass for an Oklahoma preserve.[28] Like Ossabaw, Little Tybee is protected by a Heritage designation by the Department of Natural Resources. It is still available for camping and day use, but no structures can be built on the upland or the marshes' many hammocks.[29]

What Happened to Our Coast Protectors and Their Institutions?

This story would not be complete without the personal histories of the main characters. We begin with Al Holloway, who steered the Coastal Marshlands Protection Act without a hitch to a unanimous vote in the Senate.

Albert Weston "Al" Holloway

Senator Holloway enjoyed his majority leader status until his friend and deskmate Jimmy Carter became governor in 1970. He became Carter's floor leader in the Senate, and in that role often clashed with Lieutenant Governor Lester Maddox and his Senate faction. In 1974, he helped his friend and former Atlanta housemate, George Busbee, become governor. Since Maddox was no longer lieutenant governor, and the number of his supporters had dwindled, Holloway was elected by his fellow senators to the number-two position in the body: Speaker Pro Tem. He acquired significant power as the leader of the Senate budget conferences and was one of the Committee of Three who selected committee chairs. He was pro tem until 1984, when he moved aside due to failing health. He died in office in 1985.[30]

Frederick Charles Marland

Fred Marland was offered a house and an academic position at the UGA Skidaway Institute of Oceanography but chose to remain on Sapelo for a time. After the election of 1970 and environmental agencies were reorganized under Governor Carter, the Marshlands Protection Agency found itself under the umbrella of the new Department of Natural Resources. In 1971, Joe Tanner, as commissioner of Game and Fish, selected Marland as the first professional staff of the Coastal Marshlands Protection Agency. Tanner later became DNR commissioner, and Marland continued to serve for a total of twenty-two years. From 1990, Marland was the research coordinator at the Sapelo Island National Estuarine Research Reserve, studying the ecology of the marsh, sea level rise, and the effects of global climate change. He and his wife, Sarita, live at the edge of the marsh in McIntosh County just north of Darien, and look across their backyard at Sapelo Island, where they lived with the cloistered scientists.

John Hoyt

Geologist John Hoyt was also a pilot who became interested in operating gliders. Soon after he testified in 1970 before Holloway's committee, his son was towing his glider at a small general-aviation airport near Darien when something went horribly wrong. He died in the crash.

George Talmadge Bagby

Under Governor Carter's reorganization of the state government, the Game and Fish Commission was put under the newly created Department of Natural Resources. Bagby asked newly appointed commissioner, Joe Tanner, where he fit into the organizational chart. "You choose," said Tanner. Bagby became deputy commissioner of DNR and kept the department closely connected to his traditional constituency in the legislature. He later served as a special assistant to House Speaker Tom Murphy for ten years. He often was the liaison to Lieutenant Governor Zell Miller, especially when the two state leaders were at odds over hotly contested decisions. Bagby kept his law practice (Bagby, Gajdos and Zachary) open, and when his daughter Patricia finished law school, she joined him in that practice. After his death in 1991, George T. Bagby State Park was named in his honor, as well as a DNR research boat.

R. S. "Rock" Howard

Rock Howard continued his fierce efforts to clean the state's rivers. He fought a brief battle with then Governor Carter to keep the Water Quality Control Board free of political interference. The first Carter Reorganization Bill put the newly named Environmental Protection Division directly under the control of the board of the newly created Department of Natural Resources. In the end, Howard got an independent division with its own policy-making board and became the first EPD director.[31] He retired from EPD in 1974 to fight his own final battle, with bone cancer. Shortly before his death in 1977, Howard spoke to a reporter for a story titled "What Happened to . . . ?" Still passionate about his work, Howard told the reporter he wished to slip quietly from life, serene in the knowledge that President Carter had "stuck it to American Cyanamide."[32]

Arthur Bolton

Bolton, who Carl Sanders originally appointed attorney general in 1965, was repeatedly elected to that office until he retired in 1981. He was credited with professionalizing the state law department and charting a path independent from whoever was governor. Wounds suffered at the hands of a German soldier in World War II caused him pain throughout his life. At his death in 1997, he was remembered for asserting the state's ownership of its marshlands and its beaches.

Robert Harrison

Representative Harrison stood for reelection in 1970 and was defeated. He never ran for public office again.

Robert Hanie

Robert Hanie was not shy about politics. Jim Morrison said he was an "odd ball" and a "crazy" on our side who did not "mind going after Goliath with a sling shot."[33] In the 1970 election he shared his idea for a new state Department of the Environment with Carl Sanders. Despite being a government employee, he openly backed Sanders in the race for governor. He brashly told the press that anyone not agreeing to the Department of the Environment "has a hole in their head."[34] When newly elected Governor Carter, who had been a member of the Georgia Natural Areas Council, in 1971 proposed consolidating state agencies, including those dealing with the environment, Hanie openly disagreed. What the attorney general had done with his ruling and what Reid Harris had done with his legislation was not enough for Hanie. He expanded his agenda to the cleanup of all fourteen rivers that fed the coast.[35] With the help of a supportive letter from the chair of the GNAC, Hanie kept his job for nearly a year after the election, but when he openly opposed Carter's "disastrous" reorganization, his end was near. The news articles that picked up the story said Hanie "expects the ax."[36] With the council's budget reduced and its duties absorbed by DNR, Hanie resigned on October 27, 1971.

Hanie never reached a position of leadership again. He got a new job in historic preservation in Springfield, Illinois, later returning to Atlanta to create a consulting firm focused on planning for human ecology in the twenty-first century. He died at age fifty-eight in 1979.

Jane Hurt Yarn

On Yarn's death in 1995 after a long bout with cancer, Charles Seabrook, the *Atlanta Journal and Constitution Magazine* columnist and coastal scholar, hailed her as a "Defender of the Wild."[37] For almost thirty years, beginning with her return from Africa in 1967, Yarn committed her energies to preserving the natural environment. She served on the national board of the Nature Conservancy and was responsible for the beginnings of the Georgia-based branch. Her desire to work directly with members of the legislature led to the creation of SAVE (Save Our Vital Environment), which for many years was the legislative lobbying arm of the environmental movement. As a close friend of Governor Jimmy Carter, Yarn is credited with starting the Georgia

Heritage Trust Commission. When Carter became president, she was one of three members of the Council on Environmental Quality directly advising the president. In later years she was an early supporter and board member of the Southern Center on Environmental Law. She garnered awards too numerous to name. Twice she received the Conservationist of the Year award from the Georgia Wildlife Federation and was the first recipient of the Department of Natural Resources' Rock Howard Award. Thirteen years after her death, her husband Charles, who preferred *her* meetings to his medical meetings, was still very much in love with her. A history of Georgia's environmental movement could be done in the form of a biography of Jane Hurt Yarn.[38] According to former governor Zell Miller, "no other single individual has done as much for conservation in Georgia as Jane Yarn."[39] She is memorialized in the naming of the Jane Hurt Yarn Interpretive Center at Tallulah Gorge State Park.

Lester Garfield Maddox

Limited to one gubernatorial term by state law, Maddox considered having his wife Virginia, who was the CEO of his businesses, run for governor, like Lurline Wallace had done in Alabama. Instead he ran for lieutenant governor in 1970 and won a four-year term. In that office he constantly battled Governor Carter. One of the more interesting conflicts between the two was the fight over the preservation of the Chattahoochee River in Atlanta. It was high on the priority list of conservationists. After securing a promise of no public comments from the supporters of the bill, Rep. Elliott Levitas quietly got it passed in the House. However, Maddox, as presiding officer of the Senate, took the bill, stuck it in his desk drawer, and held a news conference to say that is where it was going to stay for the duration of the 1973 session—he would not let it come to the floor of the Senate. House Speaker George L. Smith told Levitas not to worry. On the second visit, the Speaker showed Levitas the bills stashed in his desk drawer that Maddox wanted passed. He was also holding them as political ammunition. In the final days of the session, Maddox badly wanted one of those bills. They both opened their desk drawers, and both bills passed. With some quick maneuvering, Carter and his environmental advocates won the Chattahoochee bill battle with Maddox. This bill's effective date was immediately upon the governor's signature, and because Carter was available to sign the bill immediately, developers were precluded from filing for a permit before the bill became effective. After seeing those maneuvers close up, Levitas concluded that George L. was the "smartest politician I ever knew."[40]

Maddox left his lieutenant governor's position to run again for governor in 1974, but he was defeated by George Busbee. He ran several businesses that included a souvenir shop in Underground Atlanta and wrote an autobiography. After a long battle with lupus, his wife Virginia died in 1997 just after their sixty-first wedding anniversary. Maddox died at age eighty-five in 2003 after a long life and a long illness.[41]

The University of Georgia Marine Institute

The UGAMI on Sapelo lost most of its research grants and its staff to the newly created Ocean Science Center of the Atlantic, and the research, education, and planning would continue as the UGA Skidaway Institute of Oceanography. Once the bridge to Skidaway Island was completed, the Skidaway Institute was more accessible and attractive for scholars, students, and the public—indeed, it was more environmentally friendly to family life. It would grow and thrive.

The cloistered scientists of Sapelo spread out to other University System of Georgia schools. Jim Henry moved to Skidaway from Sapelo and had an extended research career and an opportunity to mentor young scientists, who today seek policies and programs that will continue to save the marsh. The marshes and estuaries around Sapelo became part of the National Estuarine Reserve, and scientists continue to come there to monitor their experiments. The UGAMI still exists as a research organization and its facilities are still used as a field station. Most of the research is done under the Georgia Coastal Ecosystems Long Term Ecological Research program. The former labs and accommodations of the UGAMI continue to support the scientists when they come in the summer and on short visits throughout the year. There are no year-round residents at the facility.[42]

Reid Walker Harris

Harris never ran for office again. The reasons he gave us in his 2008 book will have to stand. He felt he could win another election despite the opposition of the business leadership of Brunswick, but legislative life was hard on his wife and his children. His youngest was still in diapers. During his six years in the legislature, he had made eighty-four trips to Atlanta, 300 miles away on country roads or on a prop airplane. He "needed to get back to my law practice to make a living and be with my wife and our three boys." At one point he speculated he might like to go back to school. While serving in the legislature, there were clearly moments of high drama and great satisfaction, but "there were also times of loneliness, of missing my wife and children, particularly at day's end."[43] Another reason Harris gave was his interest in helping Jimmy Carter become the next governor.[44]

Harris, who for most of his adult life had been part of the established leadership of Brunswick, must have felt alienated from his close-knit community. Political wounds don't easily heal, and the passage of time doesn't always help. Don Hogan, who currently represents St. Simons in the Georgia House, observed that "politics is sometimes a brutal business."[45] There is no hint of personal disappointment or criticism of his mentor Charles Gowen, or his boyhood friend John Gaynor, who were on the other side of his deeply personal fight, but it is unlikely even a disciplined lawyer could ignore the personal hurt that disturbed those relationships.

Harris had wanted to be a concert pianist and a writer. He maintained his keyboard skills on a grand piano at his home and tried his hand at writing worthy projects. Thanks to the encouragement of two long-time friends, Jim Morrison and Fred Marland, Harris wrote a book on the Coastal Marshlands Protection Act of 1970. Harris's book presents us a unique and personal legislator's expression of what it takes for a bill to become a law. Harris also wrote a short unpublished history of the Georgia legislative independence movement and an unpublished novel, with the same title as his memoir, "And the Coastlands Wait."[46]

When he left the legislature, Harris continued to advocate for the coastal environment. Governor Carter appointed him chair of his new Environmental Council, and took his call when Harris spotted workers from the U.S. Army Corps of Engineers dredging the marsh along the St. Simons causeway. He served on a committee advising the Georgia Department of Transportation on the design of I-95, so that it would not prohibit the tidal flow to the marshes east of the highway. He served on a state commission studying the coastal environment that extended past I-95, along the shoreline and lowlands of the Altamaha River. He made a good living practicing real estate law alone, or occasionally with an associate. When his sons were older and there was no pressing work, he closed his office early and took them for a carefree afternoon of golf. Together he and his wife, Doris, traveled to interesting places around the world. Harris died on his beloved coast, St. Simons Island, in 2010.

The story of the Georgia coast is not over. The public policy accomplishments of an earlier generation of scientists, advocates, and public servants granted the coast stability for fifty years. It is clear the struggle to protect the natural environment is never over in a world of advancing technology, population growth, urbanization, and multiplying wealth. The challenges facing Georgia's fragile coastal environment are ongoing. Today, scientists expect the sea to rise over the next century. It will be a gradual process, but by the end of that period it could have risen 3 feet. It is hard to say if the threats to the marsh habitat were more severe in 1968 than they are today. Like most environmental issues, one battle won is not a predictor of the outcome of the next. The Georgia coast continues to be at risk.

Chapter 12

Today's Coastal Challenges

Honestly, managed retreat is the only way to deal with the issue in the long term.

—CLARK ALEXANDER, UGA Skidaway Institute of Oceanography

One, and only one, road takes you to Tybee Island. That one road is impass-able at a king tide . . . a king tide that inundates the road with more frequent regularity. A record thirty-eight times in 2016. Sea rise is today's most signif-icant challenge to the marshlands and the barrier islands that protect them.

Because of decisions made fifty years ago, Georgia still has the most salt marsh and the most productive salt marsh of any East Coast state. With it comes the responsibility for thousands of tiny inhabitants, the periwinkle snails, the migrating birds, and the four hundred right whales that visit the state's waters during winter months to deliver new members of their species. The ongoing challenge is the health of the most biologically productive land on the planet. If the sea rises at the rate predicted by scientists, the current marshlands may sooner or later be under the sea, no longer able to act as the spawning ground and the source of nutrients for sea life. Although the cause for concern is different, the issues of today are similar to those legislators confronted fifty years ago.

However, when faced with rising sea levels, regulating what the state cur-rently owns may not be enough to save the habitat that is still critical to marine life both small and large. Private development along the coast and private land intended for future development may need more local and state regulation. Regulating the use of private land, even though it may be under water at some point in the future, would exceed the reach of the Coastal Marshlands Protection Act of 1970. The state can respond to the threat by regulating the use of private land, or it can use a more conservative approach by purchasing endangered land.

Over the last half century, scientific research has confirmed the value of the marshland ecosystem to the health of the oceans. Clark Alexander, professor of marine geology and director of the UGA Skidaway Institute of Oceanography, says we now know more by "leaps and bounds" about how the marsh ecosystems work, and "we know what we need to do to help those systems."[1] However, the survival of the marshlands and the habitat they create is uncertain. Our greater scientific understanding of the global climate predicts that the ocean will rise gradually but defiantly over the next hundred years. The survival of the marshlands will depend on new public policy similar in intent and effect to the legislation passed to protect them in 1970. Georgians should celebrate the success of the decisions that gave the state the most protected coastal environment on the East Coast, but it is clear the task is not over. The decisions that prevented the development of marshes and islands have limited the damage that rising seas could do to real estate.

Like most environmental challenges, however, there must be new initiatives to secure the coastal environment for the next fifty years. Political and economic battles over the future of the coast will need to be won each year because decisions impacting the coastal environment cannot easily be reversed. No take backs. Historians seldom write about the present; that task is left to journalists. Digging into the state's decisions to protect Georgia's coast fifty years ago makes one curious about decisions the state is making today. As in the past, the debate over coastal regulation will need to balance the public's deep love for the marshlands, and their value to tourism and marine life, against the deeply held value of private property. Even Reid Harris and his supporters at the beginnings of the conservation efforts shied away from treading on private property. In the floor debate in the House, Reid Harris agreed to Rep. Robert Harrison's amendment exempting the upland from regulation under the bill. There are no easy answers today, and in some cases the questions are still forming; however, it is valuable to shed some light on the decisions the state is facing. Just a warning, this final chapter is more journalism than history, more personal observations, and more a search for answers than actual answers. What are scientists, advocates, and political leaders saying today? How are current political leaders responding to the new science of the day?

It bears repeating: sea rise is today's challenge to the future of the marshlands and the barrier islands that protect them. The evidence is in a lot of numbers and they are important markers. The sea level measured at the entrance to the Savannah River at Fort Pulaski has risen 9 inches since 1935. Doesn't seem like much. But using data from the Fort Pulaski gauge, the National Oceanic and Atmospheric Administration (NOAA) predicts that by 2100 the sea will continue to rise, somewhere between 1 foot and 6.6 feet, with the most likely range being from 1 to 4 feet. That is still a very wide range. The Fourth National Climate Assessment in 2018 reported that with a rapid loss of land ice from Greenland and Antarctica, a sea level rise of 8 feet cannot be ruled out.[2] NOAA predicts extreme flooding will begin in 2030, and flood days more severe than the "nuisance" level will happen 350 days a year by 2100. It recognizes that some models "project tidal flooding nearly every day of the year."[3] The UGA Marine Extension Service predicts there will be at least a 6-inch rise in sea level by 2050 that will put "barrier islands and coastal communities at risk for more frequent flooding, intensification of storm surges and saltwater intrusion into low lying areas."[4] Data from the Pulaski gauge showed a record-setting 38 flood days in 2016. The chart published in the Fourth National Climate Assessment shows 355 days of flooding in Savannah by 2050 under its extreme scenario.[5] It cites a 2012 study by Georgia Tech emeritus professor Larry Keating, who predicted that 420 square miles of the Georgia coast will be flooded by 2110.[6] But perhaps these predictions are too far in the future to stir immediate legislative action.

A personal story may bring it home, however. Scientist Fred Marland has lived on the marsh across from Sapelo in Darien for nearly forty years. The spring tides used to stop at the bottom of the 6- or 7-inch step up from the marsh to his backyard, but now they regularly flood the top of the step. If land-based glaciers are dramatically affected by rising average temperatures, he thinks sea levels could rise faster than NOAA predicts. Marland also agrees with many other scientists that in addition to melting glacial ice, the warming temperature of the oceans is contributing to sea rise because, as the water warms, it expands, thereby raising the level and covering more of the earth's surface.[7]

Distinguished emeritus professor Orrin Pilkey of Duke University has written several books on coastal challenges, including, in 2009 with Rob Young, *The Rising Sea*.[8] His research career connected with the Georgia coast when he was at the UGAMI from 1962 to 1965. In doing research in 2018 for a new book (*Retreat from a Rising Sea*), he found hundreds of scientists whose

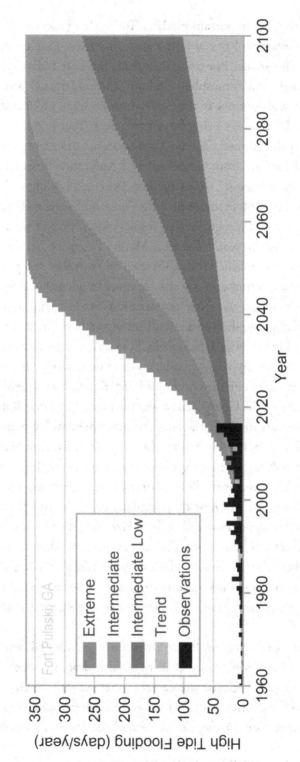

Future flood days projected for Fort Pulaski. (Fourth National Climate Assessment, 2018, https://si//nca.2018.globalchange.org/chapter18/19)

research confirms the effect of climate change. "It is now beyond any doubt," he wrote in an opinion piece for the *Charlotte Observer* in early September 2018, that "global climate change, including sea rise, is upon us. The longer we delay, the more difficult our response will be."[9] Following the devastation in North Carolina from Hurricane Florence in September 2018, he said the recent hurricanes of 2017 and 2018 were evidence "of a long predicted outcome from a warmer ocean. Warmer water energizes storms and causes more evaporation, making for a wetter storm." He is advising North Carolina to "recognize that sea level rise is going to force a retreat from storm-tossed, retreating shorelines."[10]

While the scientific predictions of the level of sea rise vary, it is certain that sea rise will change the edge between the ocean and habitable land, and it will change the marsh. For John Hoyt, who summarized Georgia's coastal geology for the 1968 Conference on the Future of the Marshlands, the coast always was a movable line of islands that traveled east and west over millions of years, depending on the level of the sea. The level of the sea in turn was dependent on Earth's temperature over the polar ice caps, which produced more or less ice from the ocean waters, and the location of the line was dependent on the level of the sea at any given point in the geological history of the state. On a map he presented at the conference, Hoyt located five ridges, or lines of high ground, which were dune-built islands (see map, p. 148).[11] The land between the barrier islands, he speculated, was former marshland that today has only an elevation of 1.5 feet above sea level. This Georgia lowland is now predominantly planted in rows of fast-growing slash and loblolly pine trees that feed timber to the pulp and paper mills along the Georgia and South Carolina coasts. Like Union Camp's development of its pine-forested Skidaway Island in the 1970s, pulp and paper conglomerates are now beginning to sell off large tracts of their timber holdings as real estate values exceed their value as timber.[12] The low-elevation forest lands of Southeast Georgia provide the best opportunity for the marsh habitat to migrate.

According to Clark Alexander, the current marshland "will be under the ocean, and the habitat it supports will have to move."[13] Alexander told *Atlanta Journal-Constitution* reporter Dan Chapman that "every storm that comes ashore will intrude further inland and become more dangerous, and we will have more days of nuisance flooding." Based on research then current, he speculated that two-thirds of Georgia's saltwater marsh could disappear.[14] The Fourth National Climate Assessment predicts that the salt marsh is likely to migrate up rivers and into freshwater wetlands.[15]

Mark Risse, who directs the UGA Sea Grant and Marine Extension service, agrees. He encourages the state to look for areas "where the marsh is allowed to migrate and protect those areas before they are developed."[16]

Geologist Chester Jackson of Georgia Southern University has a suggestion for where to look. At the height of a king tide, he says, you can fly over the coast, using cameras and software to record where the tidal waters have pushed inland. This approach could help guide the state in an effort to protect land for future marsh development before urban development makes state acquisition or regulation impossible.[17] The Sea Level Affecting Marsh Model (SLAMM), developed by Warren Pinnacle Consulting and incorporated into NOAA's Sea Level Rise Viewer, uses data and mapping software to predict where the fresh, brackish, and salt marshes will be in the future.[18] This model gives Georgia an opportunity to get ready.

The Georgia Conservancy coordinated a study of the effect of sea level rise on Chatham, McIntosh, and Liberty Counties that included scientists from the Georgia Institute of Technology and the University of Georgia. They used an estimated sea level rise of 1 meter by 2100. The results of the projection are startling: a decrease of one-eighth in the amount of dry land, a 10 percent increase in open water, and the current marshlands will be "permanently inundated." McIntosh will lose 20 percent of its dry land, Chatham 8,900 buildings, and Tybee Island 50 percent of its residential land; 13 miles of I-95 will be "impacted" as well. There will be a loss of one-third of the globally significant habitat (54.91 square miles), which currently supports threatened or endangered species in the state.[19]

According to the Georgia Conservancy, communities must consider both the impact on the human population and the environment and they "must plan well in advance in order to develop adequate adaptation strategies."[20] Given these dire predictions for less than a hundred years from now, strategies available to the state vary—full retreat, adaptations, land setasides, bulkheads, or seawalls.

The 2012 study completed by Georgia Tech's City and Regional Planning Studio and Professor Larry Keating includes a rare discussion of "full retreat" as a strategy for coastal communities. The study suggests that moving critical infrastructures and homes to higher safe ground and prohibiting building in vulnerable areas "may realize large savings as compared to the implementation of shoreline protection measures." It recognizes this approach is not popular with local governments or economic interests, but perhaps private market interests will migrate inland if they understand the risk. There would, however, continue to be current investments in structures like the facilities at the Port of Savannah that will justify the expenditure of protection funds.[21]

The University of Georgia has a Natural Resources Spatial Analysis Laboratory headed by Elizabeth Kramer. In 2017 the lab used scientific modeling and data collected by satellites to identify "sites for wetland protection, mitigation, restoration and migration along the coast." In a paper presented at the Georgia Water Resources Conference in 2017, Kramer pointed out it will be more cost-effective to use "natural hazard mitigation and coastal resilience" than expensive armament. Let nature do the work, she said. The lab's model projected that low-lying areas could add 124,000 acres of brackish and freshwater wetlands. Currently developed land will contribute 12,774 of those acres, and land that could be developed will contribute 5,871 acres. Georgia is fortunate to have undeveloped land to inexpensively contribute to a future marsh environment. Kramer argues that allowing the natural barrier to migrate will enhance the resilience of local communities from future flooding. She also worries that sea rise predictions used by coastal communities may be more conservative than the data indicate. Asked where Tybee Island will be in thirty years, she predicted, "if it is there, it will be on stilts."[22]

For local communities, the use of 2100 projections of sea level rise is so hard to absorb that the stark picture may shut down discussion. Public and private programs are giving technical advice to coastal cities and counties. Adaptation improvements can find support if steps are taken incrementally. Community planning assistance comes from nonprofits like the Georgia Conservancy and the Nature Conservancy that also work closely with programs within state agencies and the University System of Georgia. The UGA Marine Extension and Sea Grant and the UGA Carl Vinson Institute of Government, for example, assisted the city of Tybee Island in developing the first long-range sea-rise adaptation plan. Discussions started in 2011, and the

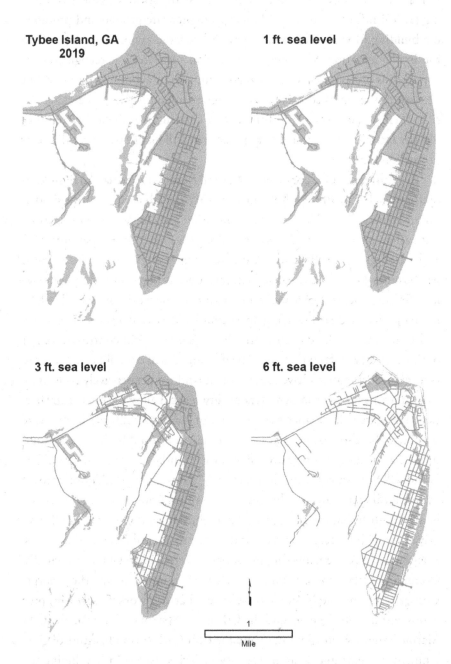

Land mass on Tybee Island at 3 feet and 6 feet of sea rise. (Courtesy of Chester Jackson, geologist, Georgia Southern University)

plan was adopted in April 2016. Its specific recommendations are based on available information, but it will be an ongoing "adaptive process actively incorporating new information into decision making."[23] Another example is a project at the Vinson Institute of Government to help lower flood insurance rates along the coast. The National Flood Insurance Program gives credits to communities for their work lowering the risk of coastal flooding and decreasing the damage that may come from future sea level rise. The institute published a detailed legal guide on how to earn those credits.[24]

Shana Jones, an attorney at the Carl Vinson Institute of Government, agrees with the incremental approach to change. Cities and counties, she says, are more likely to take action to set aside land from development when they see one or two examples of unusual flooding that make it clear that more flooding is coming to that location in the future. The Tybee plan, for example, recognizes that high tides flooded U.S. Highway 80, the only road onto Tybee, twenty-three times in 2015 and thirty-eight times in 2016, and called for raising the height of the causeway. It is obvious to citizens this problem needs to be fixed soon. It is also in the plan to raise the height of homes along Lewis Avenue on the Back River side of Tybee. The city of Savannah is clearing the way for future floods by purchasing properties clearly in harm's way. It has found funds to purchase five hundred such properties, and the city of Tybee Island has made similar purchases. Jones says that "cities can retreat little by little by acquiring land and limiting development rights, but a policy of retreat is hard to get their minds around."[25] Former Tybee councilman Paul Wolfe says they tried hard to depoliticize the issue of whether or why the climate is changing: "we're just here to talk about what we see, which is the road is underwater more often." But it is hard to keep a near-term actionable view when scientists from the Skidaway Institute of Oceanography have predicted what land will be left on Tybee by the end of this century. There is some livable space if the sea rise is 3 feet, but there is only a sliver of dry land left if the rise is 6 feet.[26] Southface Institute in Atlanta, a nonprofit focused on energy efficiency, also agrees that efforts should focus on impacts. In a recent paper it commended the strategy of Paul Hawken, who suggests omitting "battle words" from discussions. He wants advocates to acknowledge the "impacts" of climate change and focus on addressing them together to "rediscover balance with the natural world." While Southface sees change happening at a "faster pace," it also believes that creative energy coming from innovation can mitigate the changes.[27]

Some hope for the future of the marshlands comes from a 2018 study published by *Nature* the day before Hurricane Florence hit the North Carolina coast. The study, authored by scientists from around the world, says sea level rise could enhance the size of marshlands if they are permitted to migrate. The study concluded: "large-scale coastal wetland loss may be avoided if sufficient additional space can be created by increasing the number of innovative nature-based adaptation solutions to coastal management."[28] Let the marshlands migrate, they advise.

For those who expect nature to handle the changes on its own, there may be lessons to be learned from the marshlands and islands of the Mississippi Delta south of New Orleans. With the high-volume waters of the river contained within levies south of the city, the marshland that spread out from its banks has been denied the sediments that replenished the land. The channels cut through the marsh to serve the offshore oil industry have contributed to the shrinking of protective marshland. In fact, since the 1930s Louisiana has "shrunk by more than two thousand square miles" and the open waters of the Gulf of Mexico are 20 miles closer to New Orleans. In 2019, Mayor LaToya Cantrell speculated that the city of New Orleans could become an island in the future. Massive efforts will attempt to reverse the trend, but the destruction of these marshlands should be a warning to the policy makers in Georgia.[29]

One response to the rising sea and the force of waves from more powerful storms is to "build a wall." Armoring the coastline means the construction of bulkheads and seawalls made of rock and cement to absorb the force of the waves and prevent erosion of the land behind the wall. The number of permits to build bulkheads has risen in recent years and is expected to grow as the threat to private property increases. Scientists know that coastal armor sends the force of the waves downward, scraping out any marsh habitat that might have existed prior to the construction. These structures can also fail when wave action erodes foundations and the force of overflow floodwater comes back on them when returning to the sea. While armoring may protect private property from erosion in the short run, changing the gentle slope of the land with hard structures prevents the migration of the marsh.[30] "They could build a sea wall around Tybee but that would destroy the beach," says Paul Wolfe.[31]

In 2019 the National Center for Climate Integrity conducted a study to determine the cost of protecting the coast over the next twenty years. They determined that in Georgia, with 2,460 miles of seawalls, the cost would be $15 billion. The cost for the whole country would be $40 billion, which is the same as the cost of the entire interstate highway system. They were looking at sea rise predictions for 2040. When asked about the study, Clark Alexander, director of the Skidaway Institute of Oceanography, responded that the cost of the protection would exceed the "value of what you are protecting." He added, "honestly, managed retreat is the only way to deal with the issue in the long run."[32] The cost of sea walls gives hope for marsh migration onto current low-lying tree farms that used to be marsh. It is unlikely the state or federal government will build walls to protect trees.

Scientists and advocates lean toward the greater use of a living shoreline with natural barriers they believe have more sustainable resistance to the pressures of the sea. These barriers, designed to protect private property, would support the continued growth of marsh plants for a time.[33] Contrasts between the two approaches can be found on St. Simons Island. The south end of the island and its business village have for years been protected by the Johnson Rocks. As a result, no vegetation exists in front of the wall and only at the very lowest moments of the tide can you see bottom. The Johnson Rocks were a political commitment of a campaigning President Lyndon Johnson seeking his first full term in 1964. The barrier has recently shown signs of deterioration and may soon need repair. On the northern end, the St. Simons Land Trust has successfully used natural barriers consisting of a combination of oyster shells and shoreline vegetation to slow erosion on its Cannon's Point Preserve. The Georgia Conservancy and most coastal advocates urge the use of natural barriers and generally oppose armoring the coast.[34] A work group, which includes DNR's Coastal Resource Division, the Nature Conservancy, and the St. Simons Land Trust, monitors the results from installations on Sapelo Island and Cannon's Point on St. Simons. The seventh such installation in the works is on Little St. Simons.[35]

Ironically, under current state regulatory processes, it is more difficult to obtain a permit to construct a natural barrier than to get permission to construct a bulkhead. The U.S. Army Corps of Engineers has issued general permitting guidance for natural barriers, but Georgia has not followed its lead.[36] State Rep. Jesse Petrea, who grew up on the marsh and whose district covers the north end of the coastline, says he is interested in finding a legislative or administrative fix for the permitting problem, but the Coastal Resources Division of DNR has yet to endorse this strategy.[37] The Nature Conservancy supports the current go-slow-and-get-it-right process, and has had no problems getting permits on the demonstration projects. They feel there is a need to develop the methodology, which may require more than one design because of varying shoreline profiles. The Nature Conservancy likes the collaboration with DNR, which they think will produce the simplest cost effective design.[38]

The regulation of development on the edges of the current marshlands will determine if there is an adequate path for migration of their habitat. Land use or development setbacks from both the shoreline and the marsh will be important public-policy tools to assure sustainable marshlands. It is within these detailed issues that good science should mix with good politics. Often the process is messier than scientists would like. To some extent, the responsibility lies with local governments and their planning and zoning functions, but they will need the support of state decision makers. The fact that setbacks have been on the agenda for recent legislative sessions indirectly shows the importance of sea level rise and its future effect on the coastal environment. It is not, however, clear how effectively scientists and legislators are communicating with each other.

Marsh setbacks came first. On Earth Day 2014, the Georgia Environmental Protection Division got the full attention of marshland advocates when it declared that the 25-foot buffer between the marsh edge and development was no longer legally enforceable under the Georgia Erosion and Sedimentation Act against developers seeking permits. The Sedimentation Act was designed for rivers and streams and not marshlands that had no line of "wrested vegetation." The EPD had decided back in 2004 that it could substitute the Sedimentation Act's definition by using the definition of marsh edge found in the Coastal Marshlands Protection Act. But in 2014, the new EPD director decided that without new legislation he would no longer use the 25-foot setback when issuing permits.[39]

Scientists and advocates agreed a marsh buffer of vegetation and porous material is needed in order to filter out nonpoint source pollution from rainwater runoff into the marsh. The response from advocacy organizations was loud and, on the part of some, aggressive. Megan Desrosiers, director of the newly created nonprofit One Hundred Miles, said the EPD ruling was "a direct assault on Coastal Georgia." The absence of the 25-foot buffer would permit developers to build houses right on the edge of the marsh, eliminating the filtering a setback provided. Also the structures would be more vulnerable to "hurricanes, winds and storm surges," warned Bill Sapp, a senior attorney with the Southern Environmental Law Center.[40] Supporting his point is the fact that Georgia has not yet had any structures fall into the ocean, as has happened in other Atlantic-facing states.[41] Additionally, if the development line was the edge of the marsh, property owners could get permission for bulkheads or sea walls at the edge to protect their private properties and further restrict where the marsh could move.

In the 2015 legislative session, Sen. Ben Watson of Savannah introduced Senate Bill 101 to restore the 25-foot marsh buffer, using the definition of the marsh edge from the Coastal Marshlands Protection Act. Developers and environmentalists vigorously negotiated the number of exceptions in the original bill. Special focus was on the concern that EPD would have discretion to modify the setback line to accommodate development, resulting in an expansion of bulkheads constricting the movement of the marsh. Some environmental advocates wanted to push the buffer line back to 50 feet. The final version of the bill restored the 25-foot line and limited any maintenance of existing hardscapes to its original life expectancy and design. No extension of barriers would be permitted. In the debate over the details of the legislation, environmental advocates won a promise from EPD that it would prevent owners from building "makeshift bulkheads along the marsh."[42] In the end, the legislature appeared to have found a middle ground. Reps. Jesse Petrea and Jeff Jones, two House members who represent most of the coast, say they get an occasional call complaining about property taxes paid on the buffer land, but constituents are 99 percent in favor of action that protects the marshlands.[43] On the environmental side, the Georgia Conservancy was encouraged with what it considered a bipartisan success.[44]

Bill Sapp of the Southern Environmental Law Center was pleased the buffer was restored but continues to be concerned about how the Erosion and Sedimentation Act and the Coastal Marshlands Protection Act can be abused to allow unnecessary armoring of private property along the coast.[45] Megan Desrosiers of One Hundred Miles, who was in the forefront of the lobbying effort to restore the buffer, was satisfied with the final bill and felt the give-and-take showed the state really did want to protect the marsh. However, she sees the need to look carefully at the state and local levels for land where the future marsh may be able to live.[46] Her organization, in its 2019–20 Strategic Plan, recognizes "with each passing year, coastal Georgia is increasingly impacted by rising seas and intense storms."[47] Most advocates are concerned with how the new rules will be implemented by DNR, the impact of many small decisions, and the lack of public scrutiny.

The most recent setback fight involved the 1979 Shore Protection Act. The protection of the beaches of the state's barrier islands can provide insight into how decision makers will treat future efforts to protect the marsh. As Eugene Odum stated at the Conference on the Future of the Marshlands and the Sea Islands of Georgia in 1968, the islands are the first line of defense of the marshlands. The original Shore Protection Act was passed in order to make Georgia eligible for federal grants.[48] Rep. Dean Auten, the author of the bill, knew that the sand-sharing system—which included dunes, beaches, shoals, and sandbars—protected the islands from storms. The act authorized DNR to regulate any construction activities to seaward of a zigzag "jurisdiction line," created from existing stable ground and structures. A 20-foot-tall native tree existing in 1979 was the proxy for stable ground. The line of the state's authority went from tree to structure to oceanfront stabilization structures. In some cases, the line did not protect existing dunes. Where none of these points existed within 250 feet of another, it used the high-water mark determined during the most recent spring tide. Where there was no tree, structure, or sea wall, there was no setback. In 2016 the method was "archaic," declared Representative Petrea, and the Department of Natural Resources needed a line that was simpler to administer.[49] This seemed to be the main motivation for the bill.

Most scientists believe that available data and electronic technology could be used to develop a line limiting development in areas where flooding from king tides currently occurs and is likely to go in the future. The same technology can predict where the marsh will want to migrate in the future. Chester Jackson's software can produce data from a GPS flyover of the coast and then map the edges of the tide. He has been at the forefront of scientific efforts to determine coastal erosion rates, and he believes it is possible to determine a current rate that could be used to project the property likely to be affected by such tides in the future. He proposes a restriction on development of single-family homes to a line set at thirty times the current erosion rate, so that a new home would not be threatened during the life of its first mortgage. Commercial construction restrictions would be set to a line that is sixty times the current erosion rate. He would have the state update the line every five to seven years, but grandfather any structures built based on the prior line. This approach would rely on solid science that is "real and repeatable."[50] Some supporters believe Jackson's methodology to be too complex for most developers and way over the head of the average small-property owner, but perhaps the methodology can be simplified.[51] Advocates believe it is possible to use erosion rates to set the line, pointing to the use of this method in South Carolina and North Carolina. The 25-foot barrier, they point out, was "arbitrarily" taken from the setbacks from Georgia rivers and streams, which has little to do with the impact of storms and coastal tides.[52]

Aiming at a compromise between the rights of property owners and the public interest, the Coastal Division of the DNR drafted a bill and Representative Petrea introduced HB 271 in the 2017 session. His bill drew the "jurisdiction line" 25 feet back from the high-water mark or the most landward toe of a dune or the most shoreward point of a stabilization structure. The line would be 100 feet back from the high-water mark on state-owned land. Petrea was pleased his line protected every dune on the coast, but others expressed concern that the areas of the coast with no dunes were the least protected from overdevelopment. When some conservationists wanted to move the line landward to 100 feet where no dunes existed, Petrea felt some advocates were always wanting to go to the next level and seemed to forget "that's not their land. It is not their property. That the land belongs to someone else."[53] In 2017 the bill received a unanimous vote in the House but stalled in the Senate.

The Shore Protection bill drew the legislature's attention again in 2019. The wording in the 2017 bill, again with DNR support, was introduced by Rep. Don Hogan as HB 445.[54] It had one interesting exemption of 5,000 feet of beach on Sea Island in front of the Cloister and a narrow strip of land owned by the Sea Island Company.

The exemption came from high-profile battles over what has become known as the Spit. In 2015, the current corporate owner of Sea Island decided to build eight luxury homes called the Reserve on the narrow strip of land south of the Cloister. The lots alone were each estimated to be worth between $3.5 million and $5.5 million. To hold the south-moving sand in front of the future luxury homes, the owner proposed pumping sand from an offshore sandbar and constructing a 350-foot T-shaped rock groin perpendicular to the beach. According to most scientists and advocates, this new barrier would prevent the sand from moving south to the end of the Spit, which is a protected shorebird rest stop covered by an environmental easement, and to the East Beach of St. Simons Island. The sand has been piling up on East Beach for over forty years, and there are high-priced beach homes in the area. "This is exactly what the Shore Protection Act was supposed to do," says Neill Herring, a long-time environmental advocate and Sierra Club lobbyist. He remembers how a salt pool on the accreted beach became a freshwater pool and then the small maritime forest that is there today. If the sand is captured by the new groin, Herring and many others believe the natural area at the end of the Spit will disappear, and the East Beach, deprived of new sand, will erode rather than build. In 2017, Hurricane Irma nearly broke through the Spit in several places. Most believed that erosion from the hurricane would cause the Sea Island Company to abandon its plan. It didn't. Herring believes the big money behind the project doesn't care if the luxury homes are washed away in the future.[55]

The Spit issue has naturally spilled into local politics. When the Sea Island Company renewed its efforts in March 2018, Rep. Jeff Jones, who represents the area, renewed his opposition. Jones said he respected the right of people to develop their property, but not if my actions "would adversely affect my neighbor's property." Megan Desrosiers, of One Hundred Miles, and David Kyler of the Center for a Sustainable Coast have also continued their opposition.[56]

But the main issue—of setting development back from the sea—in the Shore Protection Act drew significant attention in the 2019 session. The language protecting "the Spit" on Sea Island was dropped from the bill in the Senate. On the last night of the session, Democrats lined up with environmental advocates, including the Sierra Club, to push an amendment that would increase the setback line to 100 feet from the new jurisdiction line. The amendment failed, and the bill passed largely along party lines by a narrow, two-vote margin. During the committee debate on the bill, there was no discussion of using scientifically determined erosion rates, as neighboring states have done.[57] The principal author of HB 445 was Don Hogan, the secretary of the committee. A long-time resident of St. Simons Island, he describes himself as a lover of the coast. In 2019 he also authored a DNR proposed bill to regulate the discharge of waste water in the state's estuaries from vessels with overnight sleeping capacity. But on the Shore Protection Act revision he said he had no discussions with scientists about different approaches to establishing the setback line.[58]

The lack of scientific data in the hands of legislators was disappointing to Chester Jackson, a geologist from Georgia Southern University. His extensive research on the effects of sea rise is funded by the DNR, but none of the data or the scientific techniques used to compile the data were used in constructing the shore protection policy. His approach to coastal development would draw a line based on erosion rates. In a forum conducted by *SavannahNow* after the passage of the legislation, Jackson pointed out there is no scientific basis for using 25 feet as the setback requirement. There are "good folks" at DNR who acknowledge sea rise, he said, but the result of scientific research is not finding its way into the policy process at the legislature.[59] David Kyler of the Center for a Sustainable Coast, who called on Governor Brian Kemp to veto the bill, agreed the 25-foot standard was "illogical." The state should use some form of Jackson's erosion rates to limit development. He believes the state does not move forward on issues related to climate change because people of wealth like the status quo.[60]

The protection of the state's beaches is certainly important to the economy of the coast and the people who earn their living from its tourism business. It is important to people who have money invested in fixed assets in the tourism industry. The fight over the Spit on Sea Island shows the impact of wealth on the policy process and gives us some insight into the current politics of saving the Georgia coast. However, the debate misses the more essential issue of what sea rise or the effects of climate change might do to the critical habitat of the marshlands and the significance of that habitat to the life of the sea.

Maybe legislators need more opportunity to understand the work scientists are doing. The UGA Carl Vinson Institute of Government has recognized that need and has annual "academies" for the members of the House and Senate Natural Resources Committees. The briefings include scientists and are private so legislators can feel free to ask questions. But the briefings haven't gotten into the sea rise issue—Rep. Debbie Buckner, a Democrat and member of the Natural Resources Committee, can't recall there being any discussion of the sea rise issue at these sessions.[61] Perhaps more discussion is needed that gives the public a chance to participate. Public hearings were one of the cornerstones of the movement that gave Georgia its Coastal Marshlands Protection Act. Without the opportunity to hear the public will, it is unlikely that legislators would have enacted it. The two legislative study committees operating in the summer of 1969 helped the state decide the future of the coast. Maybe it is time to try that process again.

Chapter 13

Hope for the Future and a Commentary

Marsh is a space of light, where grass grows in water, and water flows into the sky.
—DELIA OWENS, *Where the Crawdads Sing*

It is much easier for the state to acquire land than to regulate its use when someone else owns it. While regulation of the shoreline and the need to protect the long-term future of the marshlands have lagged behind the developing science, the story of the state's programs to acquire environmentally sensitive land is a more upbeat and optimistic story. The state's protection of critical habitat through purchase of land or environmental easements has moved forward rapidly in recent years. The program is not just about endangered land-based species. It is providing opportunity for the marsh to gradually migrate. Egg Island and Wolf Island, which sit at the mouth of the Altamaha River, were acquired with the help of Jane Yarn and the Nature Conservancy in 1969. These marsh islands have now been under the protection of the U.S. Fish and Wildlife Service for fifty years. Beginning with a Department of Natural Resources plan in 1978, the state, coordinating closely with nonprofits, has sought to control the environment along both sides of the Altamaha River going inland and north of Egg. This project has become the focus of the Southeast Conservation Adaptation Strategy that seeks to use "cost effective science to achieve a connected network of landscapes and seascapes."[1]

The Altamaha River has been the focus of habitat preservation since 2005. Occasionally called the Amazon of the South, the Altamaha travels 138 miles through the heart of Georgia and, joined by the Ogeechee and Oconee Rivers, drains more than a quarter of the state. One of its many origination points is the South River, which runs through residential neighborhoods in southeast Atlanta and carries pollution off the city's streets. The Altamaha delivers 100,000 gallons per second to the Atlantic and feeds a number of marsh islands in its delta between Darien and Brunswick. For centuries, it has delivered critical fresh water and sediments to build the coastal marshlands. Most of Georgia's longleaf pine forest was floated down the river on its way to world markets in the post–Civil War era, and at one time sawmills, shrimp boats, and oyster canneries dotted its banks at Darien.

The expenditures for these preservation lands have totaled $100 million since the program's energetic beginning in 2005. Strong partners include the Nature Conservancy, the Conservation Fund, the U.S. Department of Defense, the U.S. Fish and Wildlife Service, and private donors. The surprising partner is the Defense Department, which has an interest in preventing development under the path of Marine jet-fighter pilots flying F-18s, A-10s, and other warbirds to drop "inert" bombs on its Townsend Bombing Range on the north side of the river. This way, the Department of Defense avoids residential complaints about low-flying craft.[2]

While Georgia's political leaders and parties have not found it easy to openly discuss the causes of global warming, Hurricane Michael was the first known hurricane to cross into Georgia in over a century (1894 and 1896). It did extensive damage to homes, businesses, and crops, and forced the issue of climate change into politics just three weeks before Georgians were to vote on a new governor in November. While the Atlantic coast has seen hurricane damage many times in its history, including the double header of Hurricane Matthew in 2016 and Irma in 2017, Hurricane Michael in October 2018 was only the fifth major hurricane to hit Georgia since 1851. It was a category 5 when it roared into Florida and an unprecedented category 3 when it swept across South Georgia. Scientists from the National Center for Atmospheric Research said such storms will get worse "if the oceans are warmer, that's fuel for the storm . . . they also get bigger, they also last longer."[3] Democratic majority leader and 2018 gubernatorial candidate Stacey Abrams responded: "climate change is real." She vowed to strengthen environmental laws and address the pollution that is contributing to it, if elected. Republican gubernatorial candidate Brian Kemp, who won the election said, following Michael's damage he would ensure "fact based efforts" but then added that a lot of red tape is not the answer.[4] Although bipartisan politics were behind the

1970 passage of the Coastal Marshlands Protection Act, today the environment appears to be more of a partisan issue. Both candidates seemed willing to move climate issues higher on the state's political agenda, but at the end of his successful campaign, now Governor Kemp has yet to speak out on the issue of climate change or its visible effects.

One place where Georgia has openly addressed the effects of climate change is in its Wildlife Action Plan. Submitted every five years to the U.S. Fish and Wildlife Service, this plan establishes the basis for federal grants. The plan submitted in 2016 outlines a strategy for a state response to climate change. It notes that the greatest impact of climate change will be felt in the coastal regions and that the state "must acknowledge the need to protect coastal uplands, as well as wetlands, and provide opportunities for migration of habitats and species as sea levels and coast lines change." It also calls for "setbacks and buffers to provide protection for both wildlife and humans as sea levels and storm surge levels rise in the coming decades." The state has acquired 105,000 acres of sensitive habitat and gained control over another 290,000 acres through easements. The plan intends to "implement climate smart conservation."[5] This intent is backed most dramatically by the acquisition of land along the Altamaha River corridor.

According to Jason Lee of the DNR Coastal Division, who helped write the coastal part of the Wildlife Action Plan, future land acquisition will focus on the sand ridges identified in 1968 by John Hoyt.[6] Islands, previously identified as Trail Ridge in the Wicomico Formation, run along the eastern edge of the Okefenokee Swamp, and farther east the Talbot Formation has other sand hills sufficiently above sea level to resist the impact of sea rise for at least the next fifty years. Since the ridges parallel the coast, they create a path to connect with the Altamaha corridor to the sprawling Fort Stewart army base just outside Hinesville. Going south the ridges connect to the Okefenokee Swamp outside of Waycross and continue into Florida. The grand design of connecting these corridors would allow species at risk due to disappearing habitat to migrate over time and keep a healthy mix of DNA.[7] The completed link between Fort Stewart and the Okefenokee will create a 120-mile greenway with 1.5 million acres of protected land across the coastal plain of Georgia. "Now is the opportune moment to really build those corridors to protect all these species well out into the future," Jason Lee says.[8]

However, the Wildlife Plan faces a new threat. Twin Pines Minerals, LLC is seeking permission to slice through the Trail Ridge formation near the Okefenokee Swamp to extract titanium from the ancient sand. The Georgia Conservancy and other conservation advocates are alerting other advocates to the threat to the swamp. The Conservancy public comment letter called for a full environmental impact statement on the project. The proposed mining project is located in sparsely populated Charlton County on the Florida border where new jobs would be welcomed. The mining project would sever the greenway trail for migrating wildlife and threaten the Okefenokee.[9]

So, how can this grand design be completed? The state's completion of the Altamaha River corridor in 2017 with the acquisition of 19,500 acres of the former Sansavilla Plantation just north of Darien is an excellent example. This was accomplished through collaboration with the Conservation Fund, a national nonprofit committed to preserving land. The fund originally bought the land from a single owner in 2014 for $36 million and sold it to the state in phases, completed in 2017. The state funds came from a combination of donations from the Robert W. Woodruff Foundation, the Knobloch Family Foundation, grants from the U.S. Fish and Wildlife Service and the U.S. Forest Service, and bonds issued by the state. This land provides 10,000 acres of sand hill habitat for the critically important gopher tortoise, the endangered indigo snake, and the beginning of a new longleaf pine forest. It also reserves 9,000 acres of lowlands available for marsh migration. There are lowland gaps between the sand hills to accommodate the new marsh as it migrates inland along the river. The former plantation has an added advantage of deep connections to the history of the state that include the Timucua Native Americans, Spanish missionaries, and Mary Musgrove, but the diked fields of the rice plantation economy that prospered along its banks in the first century of Georgia's history may provide barriers to marsh migration.[10]

The acquisition of Sansavilla is a powerful present-day example of how the Conservation Fund, the Nature Conservancy, and similar organizations work closely in partnership with the state. The process starts when the state identifies the next piece of critical land. The nonprofit begins the discussion with landowners, who are often large corporations that own large tracts. The nonprofit contribution includes extra feet on the ground and the ability to move quickly when an owner is ready to sell. As a tax-exempt organization,

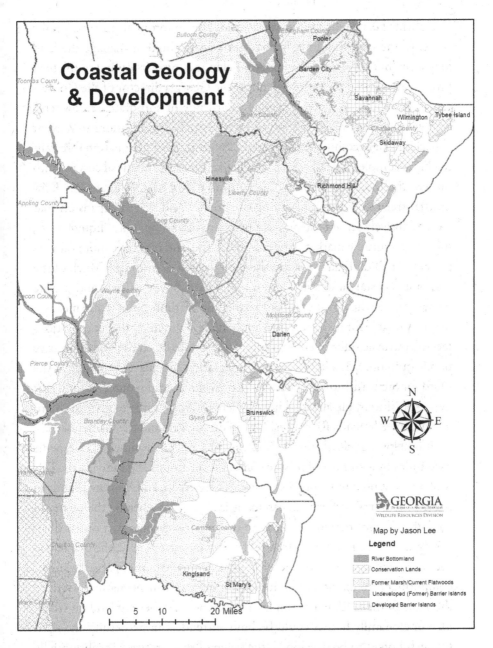

Coastal geology, 2019. (Courtesy of Jason Lee, earth ecologist, DNR Coastal Division, Brunswick, Georgia)

it can bring tax benefits to the transaction. The nonprofit also assures public access to the land acquired. It does not want to hold or manage the land long term, but would rather get out quickly and move its capital to the next project. According to Andrew Schock, the Georgia director of the Conservation Fund, "there is a real change in attitude of corporate landowners," who want to work with the state and conservation organizations to prevent a species from becoming "endangered." Preventing the designation forestalls the more complex federal rules that will likely increase financial cost to landowners and lessen their control. According to historian William Boyd, industrial tree farms acquired during the post–World War II expansion that have exclusively served the pulp industry are becoming more "liquid assets, subject to multiple market opportunities." The land may have more value as preserved habitat than it does in the supply chain of its mills.[11] Much of the corporate coastal land is just a foot and a half above sea level, and private owners can see the threat of sea rise to their use of timber. But it also means it may be valuable for real estate development. It is also likely that corporations feel the intrinsic value of conservation and want to be on the side of positive public opinion. Schock, like other conservation organizers, worked for the Outdoor Stewardship Fund because it provides a steady source of funds for new acquisitions. He already knows where the state wants to go next: "connecting the Altamaha River corridor to Fort Stewart and the Okefenokee."[12]

It is helpful to clearly understand the power of environmental easements used today by a number of private conservation groups and individuals. This tool was first used in Georgia to preserve Egg, Wolf, and Wassaw Islands in 1969. In its simplest form, an easement is a contract whereby the owner of land gives a right to another party to use or control some part of the owner's rights. If the intention is to keep land in its natural state, the owner can use an easement to grant the development rights to another party and make commitments to maintain it in its natural state. Easements naturally reduce the value of the land. For example, if the owner of a piece of land on which fifty single-family homes could be built surrenders in perpetuity the right for such homes to be developed, the value of that property is substantially reduced. If the development rights are deeded to a federally tax-exempt organization, the gift of the easement will most likely become a deduction on the owner's income tax return and the real estate property tax will decrease.

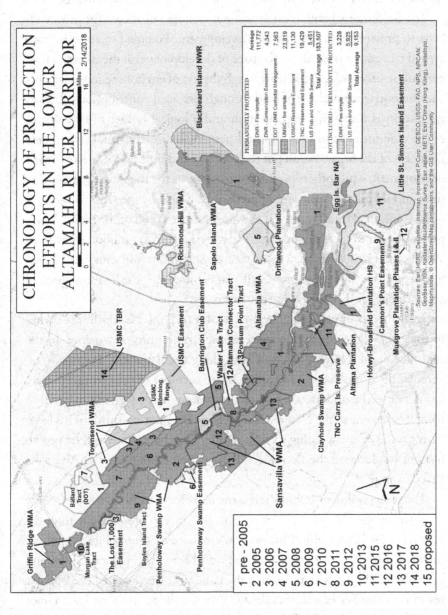

Altamaha land preservation history. (Courtesy of Jason Lee, earth ecologist, DNR Coastal Division, Brunswick, Georgia)

Georgia currently has no statutory law on the use of environmental easements, but it is recognized by both the state and federal governments.[13]

The St. Simons Land Trust is another example of successful private efforts to preserve land from future development. Founded in 2000 by concerned citizens worried about the pace of development on the island, it now controls in excess of 1,000 acres through the use of environmental easements and the outright purchase of land through financial contributions. The organization is a 501(c)(3) organization and a logical holder of or enforcer of the commitment to keep the land perpetually in its natural state. Some members of the organization put their money and time into it to slow urban development, while others participate to preserve the fragile ecosystems that surround the island.[14] The largest piece of land held by the trust (608 acres) is the Cannon's Point Preserve at the most northern end of the island. It was purchased for $25 million in 2012. The largest gift of $12 million came from Wendy and Hank Paulson, who own Little St. Simons just across the Hampton River from the former pre–Civil War plantation.[15] The Paulsons granted an easement for their island in 2015 (see p. 263).

A further example is the personal action of Dink NeSmith, the owner of the *Jessup Press-Sentinel*, a twice-weekly community newspaper. In the 1980s, he started buying tracts of land along the Altamaha, eventually accumulating 4,000 acres. As a former board member of the Georgia Nature Conservancy, he understood how to preserve his land by giving an environmental easement to the Nature Conservancy. He put two-thirds of his land, with 5 miles of the winding river shoreline, into the easement. If he gets to heaven, he declared, he hopes it will have "something like the Altamaha River Swamp."[16]

The preservation of Cabin Bluff is the most recent and dramatic example of a private organization partnering with the state to preserve environmentally sensitive land. Cabin Bluff was an exclusive men-only hunting retreat founded in 1827. It was purchased and refurbished by Howard Coffin and his nephew Bill Jones Sr. in 1928, at the same time they opened the Cloister resort hotel on Sea Island. President Calvin Coolidge and First Lady Grace Coolidge were two of Coffin's special guests. After the Sea Island Company bankruptcy in 2010, the property was owned by a succession of corporations until the Nature Conservancy—aided by a number of private foundations—announced in June 2018 the purchase from the WestRock Corporation.

With the Cabin Bluff resort come 11,172 acres of upland longleaf pine forest, marshes, forested hammocks, lowlands, and at-risk wildlife. The property is located across the Intracoastal Waterway from Cumberland Island National Seashore.[17] Like Sansavilla Plantation, much of this acreage is lowland and an opportunity for future marshlands.

The acquisition of Cabin Bluff was done in partnership with the state of Georgia, U.S. Fish and Wildlife Service, the Open Space Institute, and others. Georgia DNR had prioritized the entire 60,000-acre Harriet's Bluff (of which Cabin Bluff is a part), one of the largest unprotected yet developable areas on the East Coast. The sand ridges that were at one time barrier islands have an elevation up to 30 feet above sea level. This will likely keep them free of sea level rise for many decades. It will provide habitat for native species and will be managed with prescribed fire to encourage the regrowth of longleaf pine, which support an ecosystem as diverse as some tropical rainforests. Much like the phased acquisition of Sansavilla Plantation, the state is planning to acquire most of the Cabin Bluff land from the Nature Conservancy. According to Jason Lee, half of the property will become a Wildlife Management Area with trails open to the public. The other half will be under an environmental easement held by the U.S. Navy, which wants to protect the route to its Kings Bay submarine base.[18] Funds to purchase the land from the Nature Conservancy will likely come from the U.S. Department of Defense, private foundations, federal grants, and the state's new Outdoor Stewardship Fund. The Conservancy can reduce the cost by the sale of Cabin Bluff's existing resort and its golf course hotel accommodations, conference center, and dock on the Intracoastal Waterway. Its facilities and location make it a perfect project for an ecotourism-minded investor.[19] The preservation and management of this coastal land is an example of the public-private partnership that makes this kind of transaction possible. Like other acquisitions along the Altamaha, it provides opportunity for the marsh to migrate.

New state funding for land acquisition is right around the corner. The 2018 session of the General Assembly passed a constitutional amendment giving the state legislature power to designate sustainable revenues for the purchase of conservation land. The amendment passed overwhelmingly in the 2018 general election with the support of every conservation-focused organization. The legislation will commit 80 percent of the tax revenue from the sale of outdoor sporting goods to the Outdoor Stewardship Fund. Those funds will not go back to the general treasury at the end of the year. The funds can be used for the acquisition of fragile areas that will benefit clean water, outdoor game, wildlife, fisheries, or natural resource–based recreation and can be used to improve hiking trails in Wildlife Management Areas or purchase lowlands that give marshlands the opportunity to migrate.[20] While land acquisition will certainly help provide a future for Georgia's marshes, there may not be enough money to buy all the land needed to keep structures out of the way of a migrating marsh; the regulation of land may still be important for future marshlands.

Part of the economic picture of life on the coast is the decline of the oyster and shrimping industries. Oysters contribute significantly to the health of the marsh because they filter out pollutants, but they can also be overwhelmed by high levels of bacteria in the marsh water. Hope could be on the way. In the 1930s, Georgia led the nation in harvesting and packing oysters, but according to Mark Risse of the UGA Sea Grant program, the market has shifted from canned oysters on the restaurant menu to fresh oysters on the half shell, and Georgia's long, narrow, irregularly sized oysters no longer have market appeal. Because traditional seafood jobs will be needed on the coast, the state is doing something about it. With a $100,000 appropriation, the university opened its first oyster hatchery and has demonstrated how to grow caged oysters acceptable to the half-shell market. The hatchery is expected to produce 5 to 6 million baby oysters by 2018. A 1-acre oyster farm can produce as many oysters as 700 acres of open marsh, and the final harvest is worth several times more on the market.[21] Supporters feel the development of an oyster industry will take advantage of pollution-free areas of the marshlands that have come from the state's efforts to protect the marsh. Many of the estuaries and marsh rivers of the state are sufficiently clear of pollutants and therefore suitable for oyster farming.

The legislature tried to address the oyster issue in 2019. Brunswick Rep. Jeff Jones formed an Oyster Farming Stakeholders group to support legislation that would make it easier to put oyster cages into the water. He had support from the governor, the DNR commissioner, commercial fishermen, and environmental organizations. Prior to the 2019 session, Jones was optimistic the broad coalition of interested parties would get a bill passed supporting the new industry.[22] But HB 501, which did pass in 2019, was not without controversy. Critics, including Representative Jones, believe the bill puts too much control in the hands of DNR administrators and unnecessarily restricts who can farm the oysters. Jones and his oystermen complain the application process will be too expensive for small operators and too risky an investment because each successful applicant will have to win a farming license through a lottery. The process has too much risk for the little guy.[23]

The prospect for restoring the shrimping industry is not as hopeful. Frozen shrimp from Asia sell on Tybee Island cheaper than shrimp caught by the shrimp boats docked on the island. There has not been a new shrimp boat launched in the state in the last twenty years, and commercial dock space is harder to find. Darien bowed this year to residential growth and closed some of its shrimp boat docks to make room for a new condominium project. The UGA marine scientists are still searching for a remedy to the Black Girl parasite that lodges in the lungs and slows the growth of the shrimp.[24] It may not be as easy as the revival of the oyster industry, because shrimp farming in Asia has resulted in significant pollution issues.

Other Challenges and Opportunities

Managing the coastal environment today is accompanied by a number of hot political issues. Not all have a direct effect on the future of the marshlands, but will affect the economy of the region and as such have an indirect impact. The people of the coast will still look for ways to expand citizens' wealth and the number of jobs in the region and, as with the efforts fifty years ago, there will be conflicts that put the future of the marshlands at risk. Scientists clearly know more about the existing ecosystems today, and there are stronger academic institutions available to support new research and confirm earlier research. The electronic revolution has given them more tools to determine the real-time effects of climate change, sea rise, and storm surge flooding. They have more capacity to investigate the impact of human activity on the ecosystems along the coast. But is it enough? Is one tide gauge at Fort Pulaski enough to gather the data needed between the northernmost point on the Georgia coast and Fernandina, Florida? How do you measure the impact of spring tides or storms on affected parts of Chatham County with one gauge at the mouth of the Savannah River? Should there be an additional gauge to measure wave height? The question also remains of the ability of the political systems to listen to the science. It is clear that Georgia decision makers listened fifty years ago, but it is not clear if their hearing is as acute today.

Advocates for the coast will need to coordinate their message and their communication in a way that helps the public participate. When advocates disagree, the multiple voices on a singular issue become a formula for legislative inaction. In recent years, advocates have made significant progress in coordinating their message. In May 2017, twelve environmental organizations came together around shared goals and launched the Georgia Coast Collaborative. Each member of the collaborative has its own members and varying goals, but together they seek to maintain a unified front at the Capitol and in their cries for support from the public. Collectively they share the goals of land conservation, project advocacy, policy advocacy, and legal action. The collaborative's first report, in 2018, highlighted concerns for the impact of sea rise on coastal communities and habitats; the need to move shoreline development farther from the sea; and the need to accommodate growth while protecting special habitats and the species that depend on them.[25] The coordination was evident at the House committee hearing on the Shore Protection Act (HB 445). Eight organizations took their two minutes at the microphone, each stating their opposition to the language exempting the Spit on Sea Island from regulation under the bill. But in the final lobbying for amendments and against the final passage of the bill, the Sierra Club was opposed while the Georgia Conservancy stated its support for the bill.[26]

A few other important issues may be decided before this book goes to press, but since most do not directly affect the marshlands they will need to be explored in more detail by journalists. Just a few more warnings here.

Spaceport Camden

For several years, Camden County has been working to develop a spaceport, on a site just 4 miles from the Cumberland Island National Seashore. The site was number two when Cape Canaveral was selected for launch pads. They expect twelve rockets a year to be launched, flying over Cumberland, Little Cumberland, Cabin Bluff, and a few homes in the area. Property owners and environmentalists have teamed up in opposition to this project, while local officials and other county residents are enthusiastic about the jobs the project could bring to the area. According to a reporter for the *Atlanta Journal-Constitution*, "longtime residents, seeing the new property owners as elitists, have seen their hometowns dry up for lack of jobs and want to help their neighbors and children get work without having to move away."[27] State Rep. Jason Spencer, who supported the project for several years, was defeated in the Republican primary by Steven Sainz in 2018. Representing Woodbine in the legislature since January 2019, Sainz is less enthusiastic. He would support the spaceport if—and it is a big if—there is no violation of property rights and the environment is unharmed.[28]

In June 2018 the Georgia Conservancy submitted comments to the Federal Aviation Administration that express "significant ecological concerns" about the impact of the project on the fragile environment surrounding the spaceport site. The letter points out that the draft environmental impact statement contains very limited information and no discussion at all of the impact on the marshlands between the site and the island and impact on the habitat around the site. The surrounding habitat, which includes marshes and longleaf pine lands like Cabin Bluff, has "more threatened and endangered species than any other region of the state." The Georgia Conservancy also raised the issue of the rights of property owners who might be evacuated for a time on either side of every launch. The draft environmental impact statement also did not specify whether the National Park Service would be required to close Cumberland Island during launch periods because of the potential danger of a catastrophic failure. In considering the extent of the ecosystem that would be affected by the Camden spaceport, the conservancy argues that the ecosystem between the proposed spaceport and the ocean is highly integrated and interdependent and "vitally linked to Georgia's economy and quality of life."[29]

Cumberland Island Development

It is still an issue. There are 1,000 acres of privately owned land on Cumberland. The owners, most of whom are descendants of the Candler or the Carnegie families, have indicated that they want to have a right to build new homes on the land they own. The flash point of the controversy was an emergency zoning ordinance from the Camden County commissioners, which approved the subdivision of an 88-acre tract into 10-acre lots. Bill Sapp of the Southern Environmental Law Center is concerned that a substantial number of homes "may be a harbinger of future development on the iconic island, a place recognized internationally for its natural beauty and wild character."[30] To keep Cumberland's natural and wild character certainly was the objective of Rep. Bill Stuckey's 1972 act (Public Law 92-536, October 23, 1972) signed in the final days of the Nixon administration.

The Georgia Conservancy believes the "natural state of Cumberland is under threat," and the "the heart and soul of this incredible National Park [Cumberland Island National Seashore] is at stake." Camden County is moving forward to change the Conservation Preservation zoning for all 1,000 privately held acres. The conservancy urges the National Park Service, the conservation community, and the landowners to "work in concert" to support the original vision of the park.[31] The county began negotiations with environmental groups with the hope of a compromise on the issues, and the National Park Service has also stepped into the private discussions. No progress reports have been given to people outside the negotiations. Possible options include land exchanges and environmental easements. Charles McMillan, the Georgia Conservancy Coastal Division director, is "banking on the legacy families like the Candlers, to be good stewards of Cumberland." He hopes fewer homes will be built and there will be a final solution on an issue that has remained unsettled since 1972. Other Cumberland advocates—among them the Center for a Sustainable Coast, the Georgia Sierra Club, and Wild Cumberland—are skeptical about the closed-door negotiations.[32] The National Park Service director will clearly struggle to find a solution satisfying both public and private interests. The issue may be headed for a lengthy series of court cases.

The Rayonier Company and Pollution on the Altamaha

Discharge from the Rayonier AM (Advanced Materials) Company and pollution on the Altamaha needs to be addressed. The giant plant, built in Jessup in 1954, processes pulp wood from its trees and produces many products from the resulting cellulose. As did the pulp and paper industry of fifty years ago, it dumps the effluent into the Altamaha River about 40 miles from the complicated delta where it enters the Atlantic. The Altamaha Riverkeeper (ARK) has focused on this source of pollution since its founding in 1999. Beginning in 2011, Rayonier has made the Dirty Dozen list of the Georgia Water Coalition every year. An Atlanta high school teacher and his son, paddling the Altamaha, documented the immediate change in the color of the river just south of the Rayonier plant and continuing for 3 miles.[33] Aerial photographs and a video posted by the Riverkeepers clearly shows the discoloration of the river when it passes the plant and the pollution plume continues downstream.[34] Riverkeeper director Jen Hilburn says they do not know what is in the brown stinking discharge, but even fish caught downstream smell. According to Hutton Brown of the Southern Environmental Law Center, which represents ARK, no one has identified polluting elements in the discharge. There are no pending enforcement actions from the Georgia Environmental Protection Division. Unable to get voluntary cleanup from the plant and regulatory enforcement from the Department of Natural Resources, ARK is engaged in procedurally complex litigation to end the spewing of effluent into the river south of the plant, claiming that the compromised water quality is insufficient for fishing.[35] After a trip to the Georgia Court of Appeals, DNR changed its regulation to stipulate that the river's water quality cannot be "unreasonable" for sportfishing.[36] The integrity of the process is not enhanced by the presence of one of the Rayonier employees on the DNR board. The case, with all the procedural maneuvering of the company's King and Spalding lawyer, at this writing, is on appeal to the Georgia Supreme Court. Jen Hilburn of ARK is optimistic that new plant management will address the issue soon.[37] This is a case that makes one wonder what Rock Howard would do.

Oil Exploration

One House resolution introduced in 2018 and passed in 2019 gives an indication of how the state feels about the future of the coast. The resolution doesn't put in place a new state policy, create a new commission, or even have the force of law. It passed as an expression of the General Assembly's will and thus did not need the signature of the governor. But it also was not a unanimous consent resolution passed early in the morning after the daily prayer. It went to committee and was hotly debated.

In January 2018, the Trump administration lit a fire under Georgia's coastal residents, government representatives, and environmental advocates when it announced plans to open the nation's coastal areas, including the Georgia coast, to gas and oil testing and drilling. The Georgia Conservancy, which had opposed such leases in 1983, shifted to a "heightened level of concern" and sent appropriate letters to federal agencies stating its opposition.[38] Members of the Georgia Coastal Collaborative coordinated grassroots efforts of its memberships, and they spoke in a unified voice to local and state leaders.

In the 2018 General Assembly session, responding to voter concern, a bipartisan coalition of House and Senate members from coastal districts introduced resolutions in both chambers stating their opposition to offshore drilling and seismic testing. The "whereas" provisions of these identical resolutions (HR 1041 and SR 706) showed a uniform desire to protect tourism and fisheries against the dangers of a new extraction opportunity.[39] It was Kerr-McGee all over again. Their position reflected the list of reasons similar to those in opposition to Kerr-McGee's proposal to extract phosphate from the marsh. The resolutions expressed concern that the likely spills would impact the salt marsh responsible for most of the marine life along the coast. One paragraph expressed concern for the four hundred endangered North American right whales that birthed their young off the South Georgia coast. It said fishing and tourism was responsible for 21,000 jobs and contributed $1.1 billion to the state's gross domestic product. The Department of Economic Development weighed in later, noting that the contribution was more like $2.4 billion. However, there was no uniform state response: Governor Nathan Deal, in the last year of his second term, despite urging from advocates, expressed only "concern" about the impact of the resolution and legislators, responding to the governor's request, kept the resolutions in committee for the remainder of the 2018 session.[40] But the issue continued to focus the attention of advocates. In the 2018 election of a new governor, both party nominees committed to join other Atlantic coast governors in opposition to offshore gas and oil exploration.[41] Average people got involved. An all-day music concert, "Don't Drill GA" on October 20, 2018, was held in the parking lot of Tybee's North Beach Bar and Grill. It drew on grassroots organizing and support from Tybee Island Marine Science Center, the Dolphin Project, Environment Georgia, the Georgia Conservancy, One Hundred Miles, the Savannah Riverkeeper, and others.[42]

At the beginning of the 2019 session, both resolutions were introduced again and advocates expected them to pass since the new governor, Brian Kemp, had stated his opposition to offshore exploration. The Senate Resolution did not move. But Reps. Carl Gilliard (D-Savannah) and Don Hogan (R-Brunswick) pushed forward the House version of the identical resolutions despite efforts of the oil and gas interests lobbying to water down the resolution language. Industry lobbyists proposed a substitute limiting the effect on their exploration and calling for the investigation of all forms of energy in Georgia's coastal waters and beyond in the waters controlled by the federal government. In a tense meeting of the Committee on Natural Resources, the well-coordinated effort by coastal advocates paid off. The substitute failed five to four. The resolution moved through the full committee and came to the floor of the House on the last night of the session. HR 48 came out of the Rules Committee as a substitute, which concerned some observers. However, this last move only increased the number of towns, cities, and businesses that officially stated their opposition to offshore drilling and testing. In its final form, the resolution stated that two hundred towns and cities—among them Savannah, Tybee Island, Brunswick, St. Marys, Kingsland, Hinesville, Porterdale, Richmond Hill, Thunderbolt, Midway, and the city of Atlanta—had passed resolutions against oil drilling and seismic testing off the coast. Authors Gilliard and Hogan also presented a list of two hundred businesses that had taken similar positions. This was an expression of the people of Georgia as loud and clear as the people who showed up to speak against Kerr-McGee at the Desoto Hilton in 1968. Still, though not as close as the vote on the Coastal Marshlands Protection Act in 1970, the final vote on the resolution was not unanimous—125 to 36.[43]

Between 1968 and 1970, Georgia committed to the preservation of the natural coastal environment and to industries and jobs that could come from the thoughtful use of nature on the coast. The state would not support extraction industries or industrial plants not compatible with the natural environment. House Resolution 48 was a clear and somewhat remarkable statement of legislative intent to stick with the basic decision made a half-century ago.

Conclusions

This narrative has been about the actions taken and the decisions Georgia leaders made to preserve nature along the coast fifty years ago. It has been about the decision of an independent legislature when Rep. Reid Harris carefully framed a law that fit the political structure of the state.

It is a more complicated story and answer than I expected when I was sitting in my kayak in the Little Tybee marsh and asked myself who owns the marsh and this little barrier island between me and the ocean. How can there be this mile of clean, white sandy beach facing the Atlantic waves twice each day, and no one has built a fancy house on its upland? I didn't know the story would be filled with so many twisting trails of information that impacted the decisions. I didn't yet know the cast of characters I would encounter who helped save the coast from extractions, pollution, and development close to the edge of the sea. I have gone down many narrow paths to answer the how and why of the decision, and I regret I have not been able to fully follow them all. As the story of the past merges with the stories of today, it is clear there are still decisions being made that will determine the ultimate answer about the future of Georgia's coast. To a great extent, today's Georgia leaders face questions similar to the questions faced by Reid Harris, his friends and supporters, and his fellow legislators. As we face new questions, here is what I have learned from this study of the politics of the Coastal Marshlands Protection Act of 1970:

1. Dedicated and courageous political leaders make a difference. Rep. Reid Harris had a broad understanding of the law and a deep commitment to and appreciation for the place where he had lived from childhood to adulthood. Through many conversations with scientists he gained a thorough understanding of the importance of the marsh. He fought for and could communicate the importance of that place to others who would make the decision about its future. When the powerful business forces in his community turned against him, he had sufficient support from family and friends to move forward.

2. The state will make good decisions if it provides opportunities to hear from its citizens. When the decisions about the future of the coast were being made, nine well-attended public hearings were held. Two packed rooms, one in the House chamber and one in the DeSoto Hil-

ton ballroom in Savannah, focused on whether to mine the phosphate in the Wassaw Sound and the marshlands of Little Tybee Island. Four hearings allowed proponents and opponents to express their views on the proposed Coastal Marshlands Protection Act in both the House and the Senate. The Nessmith Committee, looking for support for developing the islands, held three public hearings. Those large, freely open public hearings seem to be missing from today's decision-making process.

3. Study commissions or committees were crucial information-seeking opportunities for legislators to engage with experts and the public. Both Representative Nessmith's bicameral committee on the future of the islands, and Senator Holloway's committee on HB 212 provided opportunities for members to interact with the public and scientists.

4. Neither the voting nor the debate fell along partisan lines. Legislators made up their minds based on constituents' letters and their own perception of the interest of their communities. Protecting the state's natural resources was a bipartisan effort. House Resolution 48 gives us hope it can continue to be so.

5. Advocacy organizations like the Georgia Conservancy, the Sierra Club, and SAVE were instrumental in getting information to supporters and coordinating communication to members of the legislature. The organizational capacity to closely follow today's complex policy decisions regarding the coast has grown far beyond the capacity of fifty years ago. Today these constitute a strong voice speaking for the natural environment of the coast.

6. Agency heads, like Rock Howard and George Bagby, had the freedom to speak boldly to the issues in front of the governor and the legislature. They had the opportunity because Governor Maddox "knew what he didn't know." When the future of the coast received its greatest challenge, the dedicated staff of those agencies stepped up to help the state make decisions to preserve the habitat of the coast. Will the state agencies today fight as hard for the preservation of the coast's natural environment?

7. Scientists were then and should be now an important resource in any decisions about Georgia's coast. In 1968–70, scientists had the research and the data proving the value of the marsh if left in its natural

state. They also had open lines of communication with state leaders. They kept agency heads informed, educated legislators, and spoke at public hearings. That process seems to be in stark contrast to today. Rep. Don Hogan, like Reid Harris, a lover of the natural environment of the coast and author of the amendments to the Shore Protection Act of 1979, did not take advantage of the coastal scientists before managing the passage of the bill in 2019. The knowledge of Chester Jackson, geologist from Georgia Southern who can use modern technology to predict erosion on a five-year or thirty-year time frame, had remained untapped.

8. Scientific investigation needs to continue. Data collection is essential, but, according to Fred Marland, one tide gauge (currently at Fort Pulaski) is insufficient to monitor sea levels, tidal surges, and the height of waves in the midst of storms.[44] Collaboration and coordination can make the data go further, so scientists from all of the state's institutions of higher learning are beginning to coordinate their research through the Georgia Climate Project. The steering committee, composed of representatives of Georgia universities, state and municipal leaders, and the private sector, asked researchers to submit critical questions needing more research. With Daniel Rochberg of Emory University as coordinator, scientists from across the state converged at Emory in May 2017 to write the "Georgia Climate Research Roadmap" that posits forty questions that should drive research. Five questions directly focus on the coast, while three more address the state's water resources.[45] The collaborative's 2019 Georgia Climate Conference in November focused on future steps.[46] Perhaps it is time for another Coastal Study Committee, so scientists can share the implications of their research.

9. Wealthy people and private foundations took action to preserve the natural environment of the property they owned in 1968. The coast between St. Simons Island and Tybee Island is undeveloped today because owners used their private property rights to preserve the islands they had come to love over generations. It could have been different. County recreation authorities could have condemned the land of wealthy private owners. The results encourage those who believe private initiatives that effectively use environmental easements can make significant and lasting contributions to the preservation of the natural environment of coastal

Georgia. However, there are ongoing concerns when wealth makes a decision to develop the Spit on Sea Island or argues today the right to subdivide and develop 1,000 acres of private land on what was to be a wild, natural experience for visitors of Cumberland Island, or wants to build within 25 feet of the coastline. The private impact of wealth unchecked by public policy can move decisions away from the interests of nature.

Some historians argue that environmental concerns can be resolved by action taken in the private market if done in cooperation with democratic institutions. Patrick Allitt, in his *Climate of Crisis*, argues that expansion of the nation's wealth will expand the capacity to address environmental concerns. He says that "industrial capitalism, the system that caused the problem of pollution, is better equipped to solve it than any alternative especially when linked with political Democracy." But he says it will take a "sufficiently aroused" public to get the attention of its political leaders.[47]

10. It could have been different if the political leaders of the state had decisively put short-term economic development ahead of the interests of the natural environment. But it was not a clear dichotomy. Some leaders clearly saw the public's demand for peaceful engagement with nature was an opportunity for gaining wealth and jobs from tourism. The 2019 passage of HR 48, in its broadest and most philosophical sense, confirms the decision made by state leaders fifty years ago. The resolution combines the desire to maintain the economic benefits of tourism, the income from fishing the sea, and the peaceful opportunity to wander on a deserted beach or paddle a kayak through a winding marsh river. It also recognizes the capacity of the marshlands to protect the developed coast from the rising threats of stronger storms and higher seas.

The narrative of this story is not complete, and hopefully it never will be. All the possible paths of research have not been followed, nor have all the possible questions been fully answered. The story should, like the little brooks, streams, and small rivers that combine to make the mighty Altamaha, follow more closely all the people who helped make the decision a half-century ago. But that task will be left to future historians curious about the full effect of today's decisions on the future of the coast and its natural environment. Documents now forgotten in attics and rusting cabinets may add more detail and insight to this political story. It might be possible to know more about the inspiring and persuasive Jane Yarn, the dogged and forceful Rock Howard, the determined and devoted George Bagby, the passionate and poetic Robert Hanie, or courageous and determined Reid Harris, the aspiring concert pianist turned legislator.

This narrative has been about the political process in 1969 and 1970 that was open to citizen participation. Like most contemporary commentaries it raises the question of what historians will say fifty years from now about the decisions being made today. One only hopes they will say that they listened to environmental experts and their impact studies. They listened to the citizens at public hearings.

And above all, they listened to the scientists.

Appendix

Coastal Advocacy Resources

(Courtesy of Altamaha Riverkeeper)

LOCAL/REGIONAL ENVIRONMENTAL GROUPS

Atlanta Audubon Society (http://www.atlantaaudubon.org/)

Center for a Sustainable Coast (http://www.sustainablecoast.org/)

Coastal Georgia Audubon (http://www.coastalgeorgiabirding.org/)

Coastal Wildscapes (http://www.coastalwildscapes.org/)

Environment Georgia (http://www.environmentgeorgia.org/home)

Georgia Climate Change Coalition (http://www.georgiaclimatecoalition.org/)

The Georgia Conservancy (http://www.georgiaconservancy.org/)

Georgia Environmental Action Network (http://www.protectgeorgia.net)

Georgia River Network (http://www.georgiarivers.org/)

Georgia Water Coalition (http://www.gwf.org/gawater/)

Georgia Wildlife Federation (http://www.gwf.org/)

GreenLaw (http://green-law.org/)

Glynn Environmental Coalition (http://www.glynnenvironmental.org/)

Initiative to Protect Jekyll Island (http://www.savejekyllisland.org/)

Nature Conservancy in Georgia (http://www.nature.org/en-us/about-us
/where-we-work/united-states/georgia/)

Ocmulgee Audubon (http://www.ocmulgeeaudubonsociety.blogspot.com/)

Ocmulgee River Water Trail (http://www.ocmulgeewatertrail.com/)

Oconee Rivers Audubon (http://www.oconeeriversaudubon.org/)

One Hundred Miles (http://www.onehundredmiles.org/)

Rivers Alive (http://www.riversalive.org/)

Save Our Cypress (http://www.saveourcypress.org/)

Sierra Club—Georgia Chapter (http://www.sierraclub.org/chapters/ga/)

Southern Environmental Law Center (https://www.southernenvironment.org/)

South River Watershed Alliance (http://www.southriverga.org/)
St. Simons Land Trust (http://www.sslt.org/)
Upper Oconee Watershed Network (http://www.uown.org/)
Vote Environment (http://www.voteenvironment.org?)

RIVERKEEPERS

Altamaha Riverkeeper (http://www.altamahariverkeeper.org/)
Chattahoochee Riverkeeper (http://www.chattahoochee.org/)
Coosa Riverkeeper (http://www.coosa.org/)
Flint Riverkeeper (http://www.flintriverkeeper.org/)
Ogeechee Riverkeeper (http://www.ogeecheeriverkeeper.org)
Satilla Riverkeeper (http://www.satillariverkeeper.org/)
Savannah Riverkeeper (http://www.savannahriverkeeper.org/)
Waterkeeper Alliance (http://www.waterkeeper.org/)

WEB RESOURCES

Author updates: paulbolster.com
Emory University developed site: georgiacoastalatlas.org

Notes

INTRODUCTION

1. Janisse Ray, "The Majestic Scene East-ward," in Sutter and Pressly, *Coastal Nature, Coastal Culture*, 310.

2. Wallace Stegner, quoted in ibid., 314.

3. John Muir, *Thousand-Mile Walk*, 13, quoted in ibid., 320.

4. Price, quoted in Reid Harris, *And the Coastlands Wait* (memoir), 99. The version quoted in text is from Eugenia Price, "From *At Home on St. Simons*," in *Georgia Voices*, vol. 2, *Nonfiction*, edited by Hugh Ruppersburg (Athens: University of Georgia Press, 1994), 486.

5. Sidney Lanier, "The Marshes of Glynn," in *American Poetry and Prose*, 5th ed., ll. 55–64, p. 939, edited by Norman Foerster et al. (Boston: Houghton Mifflin, 1970).

6. Teal and Teal, *Life and Death*, 3–4.

7. See discussion in Allitt, *Climate of Crisis*, 225–27.

8. Personal interview with Thomas Jackson McCollough, February 22, 2018.

9. Seabrook, *World of the Salt Marsh* is perhaps the most readable and comprehensive; for a recent readable scientific look behind the *spartina*, see Sheer, *Marsh Mud and Mummichogs*; for someone new to the topic Pearce's *The Low Country* has wonderful illustrations to help with identification.

10. Ray, "Majestic Scene East-ward," 319.

11. Ibid., 321.

12. Sparks, "Marshes of McIntosh."

13. "How Apollo 8 Astronauts Took the Famous 'Earthrise' Photograph," Witness, BBC news, video, 3:38 min., December 12, 2018, www.bbc.com/news/stories -46514930.

14. Reid Harris, "And the Coastlands Wait: A Novel" (unpublished), v, personal papers of Frederick C. Marland. There appears to be in existence only one partial copy of 174 pages. Although Harris's unpublished novel adds some insight, his

self-published memoir of the same title, *And the Coastlands Wait*, was integral to observations of the environmental legislative struggle, especially in chapters 9 and 10.

CHAPTER 1. BUILDING WEALTH ON THE BACK OF NATURE

1. Nelson, *Trembling Earth*, 7.
2. Stewart, *What Nature Suffers to Groe*, 246; Way, *Conserving Southern Long-leaf*, 9–10.
3. Stewart, *What Nature Suffers to Groe*, 246.
4. Coleman, *History of Georgia*, 18–26; Stewart, *What Nature Suffers to Groe*, 21–34; Nelson, *Trembling Earth*, 13.
5. Stewart, *What Nature Suffers to Groe*, 53–69.
6. Ibid., 91–99; Nelson, *Trembling Earth*, 21–22.
7. Fraser, *Lowcountry Hurricanes*, 255–65.
8. Ibid., 133, 252.
9. Way, *Conserving Southern Longleaf*, 7.
10. Ray, *Ecology of a Cracker Childhood*, 100. This autobiography combines stories of growing up on Georgia's southeast coastal plain with descriptions of the region's longleaf pines and the habitat they created.
11. Albert Way, "Longleaf Pine, from Forest to Fiber: Production, Consumption, and Cutover on Georgia's Coastal Plain, 1865–1900," in Sutter and Pressly, *Coastal Nature, Coastal Culture*, 235.
12. Stewart, *What Nature Suffers to Groe*, 97–107.
13. Boyd, *Slain Wood*, 5, 3.
14. Ibid., 9–10; Ray, *Ecology of a Cracker Childhood*, 66–67.
15. Nelson, *Trembling Earth*, 73–75; 90–100; Wharton, *Natural Environment of Georgia*, 89. Until very recent times, Wharton's scholarly review of diverse Georgia environments was the critical guide for the scientists of the Department of Natural Resources. It was a "physiographic" classification of all the regions of the state.
16. Nelson, *Trembling Earth*, 107–15.
17. Stewart, *What Nature Suffers to Groe*, 214–15.
18. Way, "Longleaf Pine, from Forest to Fiber," 209–41; for more extensive treatment, see Way, *Conserving Southern Longleaf*.
19. Way, *Conserving Southern Longleaf*, see esp. chapter 1.
20. Sullivan, *The First Conservationists?*, 11.
21. Ibid., 11–18.
22. Ibid., 13; "Little St. Simons Island History," Golden Isles Georgia website, www.goldenisles.com/discover/little-st-simons-island/history/.

23. M. Bullard, *Cumberland Island*, 245–48.

24. William Boyd, "Water Is for Fighting Over," in Sutter and Pressly, *Coastal Nature, Coastal Culture*, 243; see full treatment of the subject matter in Boyd, *Slain Wood*.

25. Boyd, "Water Is for Fighting Over," 251–58.

26. Boyd, *Slain Wood*, 220–26, quotations on 3, 215, 221, 227.

27. Ray, *Ecology of a Cracker Childhood*, 123.

28. Allitt, *Climate of Crisis*, 234–37.

CHAPTER 2. OF ARCHDRUIDS, CONSERVATIONISTS, AND DEVELOPERS

1. U.S. Census Bureau, 1950, 1970.

2. Claxton, *History of the Georgia Conservancy*, 7.

3. David Brower quoted in McPhee, *Encounters with the Archdruid*, 80 and 144, first published in the *New Yorker*, March 27, 1971.

4. David Brower quoted in McPhee, *Encounters with the Archdruid*, 80. Shortly after this conversation, Brower would be pushed out of the leadership of the Sierra Club and would go on to found the Friends of the Earth and the League of Conservation Voters.

5. See Allitt, *Climate of Crisis*, 80–82.

6. McPhee, *Encounters with the Archdruid*, 95–96, 100–12, quotations on 95, 103.

7. See Hays, *Conservation and the Gospel*.

8. McPhee, *Encounters with the Archdruid*, 104.

9. Ibid., 139, 141–44.

10. Ibid., 144–49.

11. Ibid., 139.

12. Ibid., 141.

13. Ibid., 107–11, quotations on 107, 110.

14. Ibid., 84–85, 142.

15. Ibid., 122.

16. S. Hays and B. Hays, *Beauty, Health, and Permanence*; Gottlieb, *Forcing the Spring*, 121–48; Rome, "Give the Earth a Chance"; Rome, *Genius of Earth Day*, 10–46.

17. Bolster, "Civil Rights Protests."

18. Ferguson, *This Is Our Land*, 12.

19. See Newfont, *Blue Ridge Commons*, 3.

20. Carson, *Silent Spring*, 5–6; Carson, who spent at least one summer on St.

Simons Island, didn't write about her Georgia experience but walked on the beach with children and collected samples of sea life, which she took back to her cottage. The parents of Jingle Davis, members of the local Audubon chapter, took her out into the estuaries and marshes surrounding the island. Personal interview with Jingle Davis, June 23, 2018.

21. Rome, *Genius of Earth Day*, 24–25.

22. Haq and Paul, *Environmentalism since 1945*, 41.

23. Personal interview with Fred Marland, September 5, 2019.

24. Seabrook, *World of the Salt Marsh*, 156–69.

25. Ibid., 166–68; Teal with his wife, Mildred, would draw in part on the research he did at the institute in Teal and Teal, *Life and Death*; reviewed by Pat Malone, *Atlanta Constitution*, September 14, 1969; Seabrook, *World of the Salt Marsh*, 159–60. According to Seabrook, the Teals' book remains the best treatment of how the marsh ecosystem functions.

26. Worster, *Nature's Economy*, vi.

27. Allitt, *Climate in Crisis*, 191–96.

28. Rome, *Genius of Earth Day*, 10–20.

29. Ibid., 29–37.

30. Ferguson, *This Is Our Land*, 6–8.

31. Ibid., 100–101.

32. William Cronon, foreword to Drake, *Loving Nature, Fearing the State*, xiii.

33. Drake, *Loving Nature, Fearing the State*, 13.

34. Ibid., 10.

35. Ibid., 11.

36. Drake, *Loving Nature, Fearing the State*, 80, 91. Drake writes that "we see Goldwater and the free-market environmentalists struggle to reconcile their environmental concerns with their ideological ones. . . .

" . . . Goldwater tried to carve out a place for federal environmental protection in the midst of his suspicions of regulation and his faith in unfettered capitalism. Not given to rigorous philosophical thinking, he was unable to fully reconcile the tension between the two" (16–17).

37. For a review of free-market environmentalism and the development of alternatives to government regulation of natural resources, see the contributions of two historians who seek to rebalance the environmental debate by looking at capital and wealth as a means to resolving environmental concerns of today: Drake, *Loving Nature, Fearing the State*, esp. "Tending Nature with the Invisible Hand" (114–37), and Allitt, *Climate of Crisis*, esp. "Anti-Counter-Environmentalists" (157–88).

The epigraph to this chapter is quoted in Reid W. Harris, "Memoirs for My Grandchildren, 1964–1971," 7, Reid Harris Papers.

1. Carl Sanders, interview by James F. Cook, August 5 and 12, 1986, P198606, series A, Georgia Governors, Georgia State Government Documentation Project, 25, 60, cited hereafter as Sanders interview with Cook.

2. Sanders, *Addresses and Public Papers*, 5–6; James Cook, "Carl Sanders and the Politics of the Future," in Henderson and Roberts, *Georgia Governors in an Age*, 172; Cook, *Carl Sanders*, 124; Bartley, *From Thurmond to Wallace*, 60.

3. Cook, *Carl Sanders*, 93.

4. Galphin, *Riddle of Lester Maddox*, 93–97.

5. Sanders interview with Cook, 23.

6. Cook, *Carl Sanders*, 60–71.

7. Henderson, *Politics of Change*, 223; Bullock, Buchanan, and Gaddis, *Three Governors Controversy*, 47.

8. Cook, *Carl Sanders*, 79–81.

9. Sanders interview with Cook, 40.

10. Key with Heard, *Southern Politics in State*, 665, 670.

11. Bartley and Graham, *Southern Politics*, 18, 22; Bartley, *From Thurmond to Wallace*, 12.

12. Cook, *Carl Sanders*, 159.

13. Ibid., 173; *Atlanta Journal and Constitution*, February 23, 1964.

14. Carl Sanders, "A Time of Progress," in Henderson and Roberts, *Georgia Governors in an Age*, 188.

15. Acts and Resolutions of the General Assembly, 1964, 416.

16. Gary Roberts, "Tradition and Consensus: An introduction to Gubernatorial Leadership in Georgia, 1943–1983," in Henderson and Roberts, *Georgia Governors in an Age of Change*, 11.

17. Bartley, "Georgia Governors in an Age of Change," in Henderson and Roberts, *Georgia Governors in an Age of Change*, 295.

18. Short, *Everything Is Pickrick*, 31–35.

19. Personal interview with Leonard Ledbetter, May 15, 2018.

20. Maddox, *Speaking Out*, 55.

21. Ibid., 2, 54.

22. Short, *Everything Is Pickrick*, 123.

23. Ibid., 17.

24. Ibid.

25. Lester Maddox, November 22, 1988, and July 26, 1989, p198822, series A, Georgia Governors, Georgia State Government Documentation Project.

26. Galphin, *Riddle of Lester Maddox*, 26–32.

27. For details of the confrontation at the Pickrick and the resulting legal action, see Short, *Everything Is Pickrick*, 53–66.

28. Ibid.; Short, *Everything Is Pickrick*, 45–51, 1–2, 111.

29. Ibid., 9; Short, *Reflections on Georgia Politics*, ROGP 000-01, Richard B. Russell Library.

30. Personal interview with Elliott Levitas, August 5, 2017. For a discussion of the factions within the one-party system, see Short, *Reflections on Georgia Politics*, ROGP 00-04.

31. Galphin, *Riddle of Lester Maddox*, 111, 139.

32. Bartley and Graham, *Southern Politics*, 109.

33. Galphin, *Riddle of Lester Maddox*, 106–7.

34. Ibid., 138–39, 132.

35. Bartley, *From Thurmond to Wallace*, 71–72.

36. Bullock et al., *Three Governor's Controversy*, 61.

37. Ibid., 62; Henderson, *Politics of Change in Georgia*, 243.

38. Ibid., 55–59.

39. Ibid., 59–61, 64.

40. Galphin, *Riddle of Lester Maddox*, 110.

41. Bartley, *From Thurman to Wallace*, 71; Cook, *Carl Sanders*, 277.

42. Bartley, *From Thurmond to Wallace*, 71–75; Bartley and Graham, *Southern Politics*, 114–15.

43. Galphin, *Riddle of Lester Maddox*, 133–36; Cook, *Carl Sanders*, 276–77.

44. Personal interview with Fred Marland, August 8, 2017.

45. Galphin, *Riddle of Lester Maddox*, 127.

46. Ibid., 151–52.

47. Ibid., 153.

48. Ibid., 163.

49. Harris, "Memoirs," 1.

50. Ibid.

51. Ibid., 1–19. See also Harris, *And the Coastlands Wait*, 8–9.

52. Hyatt, *Mr. Speaker*, 55.

53. Cook, *Carl Sanders*, 290.

54. Ibid., 129; Tom Murphy interview by Cliff Kuhn, March 28, 1988, series B, Georgia State Government Documentation Project; Hyatt, *Mr. Speaker*, 50; Levitas interview, August 5, 2017.

55. Murphy interview by Kuhn, May 5, 1988.

56. Ibid.

57. Harris, "Memoirs," 6–8, quotation on 6; Levitas interview, August 5, 2017; Elliott Levitas, *Reflections on Georgia Politics*, ROGP 042, interview by Bob Short, August 1, 2008, Richard B. Russell Library.

58. Harris, "Memoirs," 8; Lester Maddox to Roy Lambert, October 24, 1966, and Bo Callaway to Roy Lambert, November 12, 1966, both in box 1, House of Representatives Arrangement Committee, 1966–67 folder, E. Roy Lambert Papers.

59. Harris, "Memoirs," 15.

60. Sanders interview with Cook.

61. Murphy interview by Kuhn, March 28, 1988.

62. *Journal of the House*, 1967, 12.

63. Ibid., 54.

64. Harris, *And the Coastlands Wait*, 9. While the *Journal of the House* says Robin Harris of the 118th argued for a new runoff election from the floor, Elliott Levitas recalls that it was Reid Harris who made the presentation of their argument (Levitas interview, February 22, 2018). In Reid Harris's unpublished novel, "And the Coastlands Wait," the protagonist makes the speech (22), personal papers of Frederick C. Marland.

65. *Journal of the House*, 1967, 54.

66. Personal interview with Chris Lambert, February 23, 2018.

67. Levitas, *Reflections on Georgia Politics*; Levitas interview, August 5, 2017.

68. Galphin, *Riddle of Lester Maddox*, 165–66.

69. Ibid., 166; Harris, *And the Coastlands Wait*, 9.

70. Galphin, *Riddle of Lester Maddox*, 166–67.

CHAPTER 4. WHO WAS IN CHARGE?

1. Bradley R. Rice, "Lester Maddox and the Politics of Populism," in Henderson and Roberts, *Georgia Governors in an Age of Change*, 193.

2. Lester Maddox, "A Chance for the Truth," in Henderson and Roberts, *Georgia Governors in an Age of Change*, 217.

3. Cook, *Carl Sanders*, 160–62; Bowdoin, *Georgia's Third Force*.

4. Maddox, *Addresses and Public Papers*, 4.

5. Galphin, *Riddle of Lester Maddox*, 170–71; Maddox, *Addresses and Public Papers*, 3–11.

6. Maddox, *Addresses and Public Papers*, 9, 8.

7. Ibid., 4–5, 6, 10.

8. Lester Maddox to Roy Lambert, October 24, 1966, House of Representatives Arrangement Committee, 1966–67 folder, E. Roy Lambert Papers.

9. Hyatt, *Mr. Speaker*, 50.

10. Maddox, *Addresses and Public Papers*, 7.

11. Rice, "Lester Maddox and the Politics," 204.

12. Numan Bartley, "Georgia Governors in an Age of Change," in Henderson and Roberts, *Georgia Governors in an Age*, 295.

13. Thomas Murphy, interview by Clifford Kuhn, 5 May 1988, P1988-19 series B, Public Figures, Georgia State Government Documentation Project; Hyatt, *Mr. Speaker*, 60–61; Hoffman, *Speaker of the House*.

14. Hyatt, *Mr. Speaker*, 62.

15. Remer Tyson, "Rowan Is through 'Helping Lester,'" *Atlanta Journal and Constitution*, February 18, 1968.

16. Ibid.; Galphin, *Riddle of Lester Maddox*, 174; personal interview with Bobby Rowan, April 4, 2018.

17. Tyson, "Rowan Is through 'Helping Lester.'"

18. Eugene Patterson, "All's Not So Pickrick Now," *Atlanta Constitution*, February 19, 1968.

19. Galphin, *Riddle of Lester Maddox*, 177.

20. Rowan interview. Hyatt, *Zell*, 144.

21. Rowan interview. Personal interview with Shirley Miller, July 5, 2017.

22. Hyatt, *Zell*, 144.

23. Cook, *Carl Sanders*, 160–62; Bowdoin, *Georgia's Third Force*, 12.

24. Personal interview with Judith Bagby (daughter) and Tommy Bagby (son), September 5, 2018.

25. Judith Bagby interview.

26. Griffin acknowledged the story at a meeting of the Atlanta Press Club; *Atlanta Constitution*, April 14, 1967; Lee Walburn, "Politically Correct," *Atlanta*, June 2006, 231–32.

27. Tommy Bagby interview.

28. *Atlanta Constitution*, January 18, 1967.

29. Ibid.

30. Eugene Patterson, "Why Wildlife Migrates," *Atlanta Constitution*, January 27, 1967.

31. Sam Hopkins, "Bagby More First-Rate after Second Look," *Atlanta Constitution*, February 9, 1967.

32. *Atlanta Constitution*, January 27, 1967.

33. *Atlanta Constitution*, February 10, 1967. Fish Head was only one of many nicknames that followed Bagby through his colorful career. Howard Zeller soon left the Game and Fish Commission to become regional director of the Federal Water Quality Control Administration.

34. Judith Bagby interview.

35. Tommy Bagby interview.

36. *Atlanta Constitution*, February 10, 1967.

37. Personal interview with Leonard Ledbetter, May 15, 2018.

38. Crockford would become the head of the Game and Fish Division of the Department of Natural Resources for most of the 1970s.

39. Bureau of State Planning and Community Affairs, *Georgia Activities in the Field of Environment*, 1970, in the vertical files of the Bull Street Library, branch of Savannah Public Library.

CHAPTER 5. GATHERING THE TROOPS

1. Charles Seabrook, *World of the Salt Marsh*, 156–59; personal interview with Hans Neuhauser, March 9, 2018.

2. Seabrook, *World of the Salt Marsh*, 166; Teal, "Energy Flow." In Teal and Teal, *Life and Death of the Salt Marsh*, see "Marsh Production," 183–201, for a readable discussion of what is in the marsh and its productive capacity. Charles Seabrook sees this work as the classic study of the new science of the marsh, Seabrook, *World of the Salt Marsh*, 159.

3. Craige, *Eugene Odum*, xvi, 9.

4. Personal interviews with Steven Johnson, April 20, 2018, and September 8, 2019; "Report to the Atlantic Chapter of the Sierra Club," January 24, 1968, Sierra Club file—Steven Johnson, RCB 63710, Carnegie Family Trust; Ben Fortson to Steven Johnson, January 1968; *Georgia Sierran*, April 1968, folder 1968–71, Georgia Sierra Club Records.

5. Johnson interview.

6. Claxton, *History of the Georgia Conservancy*, 7–8.

7. Draft curriculum vitae, RCB 20340, GNAC Papers.

8. Claxton, *History of the Georgia Conservancy*, 7–8.

9. Lefkoff, "Voluntary Citizens' Group," 25–28. In his dissertation Lefkoff found the organization to be "extremely cautious in its activities" because of its decision to be a tax-exempt organization. He concluded the organization was "a group of well-educated, white collar, middle-to upper income people" with only four of seventy-one leaders lacking a college degree; none were from a blue-collar class, 52–53.

10. *Acts and Resolutions of the General Assembly*, 1966, 1:330.

11. Ingram Richardson, introduction, in Maney, Marland, and West, *Future of the Marshlands*, 5.

12. C. H. Wharton to Zell Miller, March 15, 1963, and C. H. Wharton to Sen. Brooks Pennington, February 11, 1963, both in Creation of the Council folder, RCB 20337, GNAC Papers.

13. Statement of Charles Wharton, Dr. Charles Wharton folder, RCB 20336, GNAC Papers; Wharton was quoted on his vision in John Pennington, "In Search for Unspoiled Georgia," *Atlanta Journal and Constitution Magazine*, November 21, 1971. Wharton wrote to Sen. Brooks Pennington, and he is also quoted in the story by journalist John Pennington.

14. *Acts and Resolutions of the General Assembly*, 1966, 1:330, 1:333.

15. Ibid., 1:331.

16. Personal interview with Leonard Ledbetter, May 15, 2018.

17. "Draft—Special Report," September–December 1967, "Quarterly Reports" folder, RCB 20348, GNAC Papers.

18. Maney, Marland, and West, *Future of the Marshlands*, 5.

19. Six Months Resume, April 8, 1968, RCB 20342, GNAC Papers.

20. Personal interview with Charles Yarn, December 6, 2017.

21. Ibid.; Lenz, "Jane Yarn," 24.

22. Yarn interview.

23. Ibid.

24. Lenz, "Jane Yarn," 23.

25. Yarn, "New Challenge." The *Garden Gate* is the bimonthly journal of the Garden Club of Georgia. As cochair of the Conservation Committee, Yarn had regular opportunities to inform the 21,000 members regarding conservation issues. These members provided Yarn with a base of support throughout the fight for the Coastal Marshlands Protection Act.

26. Charles Yarn interview.

27. Ibid.; Sparks, "Housewife Saves an Island."

28. Lenz, "Jane Yarn," 23.

29. Yarn, "New Challenge," 12–13; Yarn, "What Your Club Can Do," 16–17.

30. "What Your Club Can Do," 23.

31. *Acts and Resolutions of the General Assembly*, 1957, 264.

32. Sanders's biographer James Cook fails to mention this bill that was part of the governor's second year avalanche of legislation.

33. Acts and Resolutions of the General Assembly, 1964, 420–22, quotation on 417.

34. "Rock Howard Gets Water Board Post," *Atlanta Constitution*, November 10, 1964.

35. Ledbetter interview; *Atlanta Constitution*, July 26, 1977.

36. "The Pollution of Georgia's Environment," *Georgia's Health*.

37. Ledbetter interview.

38. Personal interview with Fred Marland, March 12, 2018.

39. Ibid.

40. Personal interview with Harold Reheis, April 26, 2018; Ledbetter interview.

41. "Pollution of Georgia's Environment."

42. Ibid.

43. "Water Quality Control Board Sets Standards," *Atlanta Constitution*, October 27, 1966.

44. Robert Hanie, Report of April 17 to February 14, RCB 20336, GNAC Papers; R. S. Howard, op-ed, *Atlanta Constitution*, December 11, 1968.

45. Ledbetter interview.

46. A board member of the Water Quality Control Board, who also represented the kaolin industry in central Georgia, saw field reports that no fish lived in the milky streams down from the mines operating there. He initiated a voluntary industry-wide effort to make the waters downstream free of clay. Ledbetter interview.

47. Ledbetter interview.

48. Ibid.

49. Ibid.

50. Fallows, *Water Lords*.

51. Ibid., 226.

52. Ibid., 225–26.

53. Ledbetter interview.

54. Ibid.

55. Mary R. Bullard, *Cumberland Island*, 269–71; Graves, *Cumberland Island Saved*, 25.

56. *Glynn High Tide* 1, no. 1 (Brunswick: Senior class, 1948).

57. Personal interview with Michael Harris, November 7, 2017.

58. Personal interview with Merry Tipton, March 13, 2018.

59. The story is described in detail in Reid Harris, "And the Coastlands Wait"

(unpublished novel), personal papers of Frederick C. Marland. Fred Marland confirms that the details of this story as told in Harris's novel are true.

60. Tipton interview.

61. Ibid.

62. Michael Harris interview.

63. Personal interview with Albert Fendig III, May 16, 2018.

CHAPTER 6. LET'S DIG UP THE MARSH

1. Harris, *And the Coastlands Wait*, 1.

2. Personal interview with Dean Auten, March 12, 2018.

3. Personal interview with Bill Brown, December 11, 2017.

4. Personal interview with Chris Lambert, February 23, 2018.

5. Personal interview with former state Rep. Peyton S. Hawes Jr., June 23, 2017.

6. Harris, *And the Coastlands Wait*, 19. Unless otherwise indicated, all *And the Coastlands Wait* notes refer to Harris's published memoir rather than his unpublished novel.

7. Ibid., 17; personal interview with Michael Harris, November 7, 2017.

8. Harris, *And the Coastlands Wait*, 17.

9. Ibid., 18.

10. House Resolution 86-209, Acts and Resolutions of the General Assembly, 1967, 519–21.

11. Harris, *And the Coastlands Wait*, 19; Bills and Resolutions 1967–68, HB 969, RCB 34884, Georgia Archives.

12. HB 969, Acts and Resolutions of the General Assembly, 1968, 1:1–8.

13. Ibid.

14. Notice in *Brunswick News*, May 31, 1968, 12.

15. Harris, *And the Coastlands Wait*, 20–21.

16. Ibid., 21–22.

17. Ibid., 22, 21.

18. Auten interview.

19. Personal interview with Albert Fendig III, May 16, 2018.

20. Ibid.

21. Bob Cohn, "Sea Mining Lease Sought in Chatham," *Savannah Morning News*, May 25, 1968; Duane Riner, "Oil Firm Makes Pitch for Offshore Phosphate," *Atlanta Constitution*, May 25, 1968.

22. Harris, *And the Coastlands Wait*, 23.

23. Berendt, *Midnight in the Garden*, 6.

24. Bob Cohn, "Geologist Had Contract with Kerr-McGee," *Savannah Morning News*, July 21, 1968.

25. Acts and Resolutions of the General Assembly of the State of Georgia, 1884–85, 125–27.

26. Minutes of the Natural Areas Council, July 8, 1968, RCB 20336, GNAC Papers.

27. *Atlanta Constitution*, March 1, 1968; Dr. Fred Marland to the Honorable Arthur K. Bolton, May 31, 1968, "Arthur Bolton" file, personal papers of Frederick C. Marland. Proceedings of the Jekyll Island meeting are at https://ntrl.ntis.gov/NTRL/dashboard/searchResults/titleDetail/PB230073.xhtml.

28. Personal interview with Fred Marland, July 21, 2018.

29. Cohn, "Sea Mining Lease Sought in Chatham." Most of Little Tybee Island's 6,780 acres is marsh. The marsh is protected from the ocean waves by a barrier island that has less than a mile of sandy beach, depending on how you count the sandbars that attach to the island, and depending on the impact of recent storms. It has sixty hammocks with upland vegetation.

30. Cohn, "Sea Mining Lease Sought in Chatham"; Riner, "Oil Firm Makes Pitch for Offshore Phosphate"; Harris, *And the Coastlands Wait*, 23–25.

31. Cohn, "Sea Mining Lease Sought in Chatham"; Riner, "Oil Firm Makes Pitch for Offshore Phosphate"; Harris, *And the Coastlands Wait*, 23–25.

32. Cohn, "Sea Mining Lease Sought in Chatham."

33. Ibid.

34. Riner, "Oil Firm Makes Pitch for Offshore Phosphate."

35. Ibid.; Cohn, "Sea Mining Lease Sought in Chatham"; Harris, *And the Coastlands Wait*, 25.

36. E. L. Cheatum, presentation to the Mineral Leasing Commission, June 20, 1968, "Phosphate Mining" file, Fred Marland unprocessed papers.

37. Personal interview with Jim Morrison, August 9, 2017.

38. Ibid.

39. Ibid.; Harris, *And the Coastlands Wait*, 75.

40. R. S. Howard to Arthur Bolton, May 28, 1968, RCB 29320, GNAC Papers.

41. *Savannah Morning News*, May 26, 1968, clippings in R. S. Howard Papers; Harris, *And the Coastlands Wait*, 27–28.

42. *Atlanta Constitution*, June 3, 1968, clippings in R. S. Howard Papers.

43. Personal interview with Leonard Ledbetter, May 15, 2018.

44. Charles Wharton to the Honorable Lester Maddox, June 19, 1968, RCB 20342, GNAC Papers. Notes in the file indicate that Hanie was in England until June 30; Wharton would complete a "physiographic" classification of all the regions

of the state published in 1978 by the Georgia Department of Natural Resources. His *Natural Environment of Georgia* was a guide to the diverse ecosystems of the state used extensively by the scientists of the department until recently.

45. Vernon Henry to Robert Hanie, May 28, 1968, "Marshlands Conference" file, Fred Marland unprocessed papers; also in RCB 36167, GNAC Papers.

46. Mrs. Clifford West to Robert Hanie, June 9, 1968, "Marshland Conference" file, Fred Marland unprocessed papers, and in "Phosphate Mining—Georgia Coast," RCB 20342, GNAC Papers.

47. *Savannah Morning News*, May 26, 1968, clippings in R. S. Howard Papers; personal interview with Fred Marland, May 5, 2018.

48. Marland interview, May 5, 2018.

49. The first staff members of the UGAMI on Sapelo Island were Eugene Odum, Don Scott, director Bob Rogotski, Larry Pomeroy, and George Lauff. They organized two conferences that drew scientists from around the world, and they established estuaries as a critical scientific subject for research. Fred Marland to author, e-mail November 21, 2018.

50. Marland interview, May 5, 2018.

51. Vernon Henry to Reid Harris, February 27, 1968, "Phosphate Mining—Georgia Coast" file, RCB 20342, GNAC Papers.

52. Charles Gowen to the State Leasing Commission, May 17, 1968, RCB36167, GNAC Papers.

53. Marland interview, November 8, 2017.

54. Ibid.

55. Morrison interview, August 9, 2017.

56. Drs. Fred Marland and Tom Linton to Dear Colleague, "Arthur Bolton" file, personal papers of Frederick C. Marland, also reproduced in Harris, *And the Coastlands Wait*, 26.

57. Marland to Bolton, May 31, 1968.

58. Ibid.

59. Dr. Fred Marland to Dr. Stanley A. Cain, May 27, 1968, "Arthur Bolton" file.

60. S. Fred Singer to Dr. Fred Marland, June 12, 1968, "Marshland Conference" file, Fred Marland unprocessed papers.

61. Invitation list, "Phosphate Mining" file, personal papers of Frederick C. Marland. The duties of the Bureau of Outdoor Recreation are now performed by the Heritage Conservation and Recreation Service in the Department of the Interior.

62. Personal interview with Charles Yarn, December 6, 2017.

63. *Atlanta Constitution*, June 14, 1968; Statement of the Georgia Conservancy, RCB 20342, GNAC Papers.

64. Personal interview with Jim Richardson, April 3, 2018.

65. Fred Marland to Reid Harris, August 5, 1968, "Arthur Bolton" file.

66. Marland interview, July 21, 2018.

67. Charles Gowen Papers, Richard B. Russell Library for Political Research and Studies.

68. Marland interview, May 5, 2018.

69. Ibid. Yazoo Land Fraud was a massive real-estate transaction in which large tracts of land, most of what are now Alabama and Mississippi, were sold to political insiders by Georgia governor George Matthews and the Georgia General Assembly.

70. Fred Marland to Reid Harris, August 5, 1968, personal papers of Frederick C. Marland.

71. John Hoyt to the Honorable Arthur K. Bolton, September 12, 1968, "Arthur Bolton" file.

72. Dr. Dirk Frankenberg to the Honorable Arthur K. Bolton, August 16, 1968, "Arthur Bolton" file.

73. James Howard to the Honorable Arthur K. Bolton, August 30, 1968, "Arthur Bolton" file.

CHAPTER 7. COMING IN LOUD AND CLEAR

1. Statement of George Bagby at the September 16, 1968, hearing, "Phosphate Mining" file, personal papers of Frederick C. Marland; also in "Marshland Hearings 9/16 and 9/30," RCB 20342, GNAC Papers. The commissioner's speech was published on the front page of the department magazine, *Georgia Game and Fish*, November 1968. Morrison put Bagby's colorful remarks into a press release from the commission and sent it to two hundred small-town newspapers and media outlets. Press release, Office of Public Information, Georgia Game and Fish Commission, September 16, 1968, "Phosphate Mining" file.

2. *Georgia Game and Fish*, November 1968.

3. George Bagby to Brooks Haisten (president, St. Simons Island Chamber of Commerce), August 22, 1968, "Marshland Hearings 9/16 and 9/30," RCB 29320, GNAC Papers.

4. Personal interview with Steven Johnson, April 20, 2018.

5. R. S. Howard Jr., "Statement of Georgia Water Quality Control Board Relative to Kerr-McGee Corporation's Proposal to Lease State Offshore Lands for Surface Mining and Land Developments in Chatham County Georgia," presented

September 16, 1968, in Atlanta and September 30 in Savannah, RCB20342, GNAC Papers.

6. Ibid., 5, 7, 8; *Savannah Morning News*, September 17, 1968, clippings in "Phosphate Mining" file, personal papers of Frederick C. Marland.

7. *Savannah Morning News*, September 17, 1968, clippings in "Phosphate Mining" file.

8. "People to Testify at the Public Hearing, September 16," on stationery of Mrs. Charles Yarn, RCB file 38334, GNAC Papers.

9. "Phosphate Public Hearings, September 16, Comments of Various Speakers," GNAC Papers.

10. Most commission members were elected officials appointed by their governing body to develop plans and policies affecting the entire region; "Resolution by the Coastal Area Planning and Development Commission," GNAC Papers.

11. David Maney, Statement to the Public Hearing, Atlanta, Georgia, September 16, 1968, RCB 20342, GNAC Papers, 9.

12. Statement of the Georgia League of Women Voters before the Mineral Leasing Commission on Phosphate Lease in Chatham County, September 16, 1968, "Phosphate Mining" file.

13. Minutes of the Board of Directors of the Garden Club of Georgia, January 16, 1969, archive room, state headquarters, Athens, Georgia; "Help Save Our Georgia Marshlands," *Garden Gate*, November/December, 1968, 11.

14. Personal interview with Charles Yarn, December 6, 2017.

15. Lester Maddox to Mr. Thomas Lowndes, June 7, 1968, "Phosphate Mining" file.

16. "People to Testify at the Public Hearing September 16"; personal interview with Thomas Lowndes, March 2, 2018; Tom Lowndes to Fred Marland, August 15, 1968, "Phosphate Mining" file.

17. Statement of Dr. Dirk Frankenberg to the Mineral Leasing Commission, September 16, 1968, "Phosphate Mining" file.

18. Testimony of John R. Thoman, "Marshland Conference" file, Fred Marland unprocessed papers.

19. *Savannah Morning News*, September 16, 1968, clippings in "Phosphate Mining" file.

20. Ibid.

21. *Savannah Morning News*, September 17, 1968, clippings in "Phosphate Mining" file.

22. *Savannah Morning News*, October 1, 1968, clippings in "Phosphate Mining" file.

23. *Atlanta Constitution*, October 2, 1968, clippings in "Phosphate Mining" file.

24. *Savannah Morning News*, October 2, 1968, clippings in "Phosphate Mining" file.

25. *Atlanta Constitution*, October 2, 1968, clippings in "Phosphate Mining" file.

26. George Bagby, "The Marshes of Chatham," *Georgia Game and Fish*, November 168, 5, original emphasis. Bagby's speech written by Morrison per interview with Jim Morrison, August 9, 2017.

27. Bagby, "The Marshes of Chatham," 8.

28. *Savannah Morning News*, October 1, 1968, clippings in "Phosphate Mining" file.

29. Bagby, "Marshes of Chatham," 8.

30. Statement of Dr. John H. Hoyt to the September 30 Hearing in Savannah, "Arthur Bolton" file, personal papers of Frederick C. Marland.

31. Minutes of the Council on Natural Areas, July 8, 1968, RCB 20336, GNAC Papers; personal interview with Fred Marland, May 5, 2018.

32. Ibid.; Statement of Dr. John H. Hoyt to the September 30 Hearing in Savannah, 3–4.

33. Fred Marland quoted in *Atlanta Constitution*, October 2, 1968, clippings in "Phosphate Mining" file.

34. Statement of Dr. Fredrick C. Marland to the Public Hearing for the Georgia Mineral Leasing Commission in Savannah, September 30, 1968, "Arthur Bolton" file.

35. *Savannah Morning News*, June 28, 1968. *Savannah Evening Press*, September 30, 1968.

36. *Savannah Morning News*, October 1, 1968.

37. Marland interview, July 21, 2018. Downing warned of the possible disaster in the hearing in Atlanta as well. *Atlanta Constitution*, September 17, 1968.

38. For a recent report on the efforts to recover the bomb, see Rob Hotakainen, "Lost Bombs and Buried Toxins," E&E News, Greenwire, May 3, 2018, https://www.eenews.net/stories/1060080761.

39. *Savannah Evening Press*, September 30, 1968; *Savannah Morning News*, October 5, 1968.

40. Bob Cohn, "Scientists' Testimony Impresses Mining Commission," *Savannah Morning News*, October 2, 1968.

41. University System Report on Proposed Leasing. A lengthy summary of the report was published by the *Savannah Morning News*, December 6, 1968. The report was not released for public review at the time but is now available: A Report on Proposed Leasing of State Owned Land for Phosphate Mining in Chatham

County, Georgia, November, 1968, https://dlg.usg.edu/, also at Hargrett Rare Book and Manuscript Library.

42. University System Report on Proposed Leasing.

43. Dr. Fred Marland to the Honorable Arthur K. Bolton, August 29, 1968, "Arthur Bolton" file; Fred Marland interview, March 12, 2018.

44. University System Report on Proposed Leasing, Environmental Affect, appendix C, 22; Eugene Odum authored this portion of the report.

45. University System Report on Proposed Leasing, Conclusions, 15–17.

46. Ibid., 17.

47. Ibid.

48. Ibid., 19.

49. Marland notes on a phone conversation, December 6, 1968, personal papers of Frederick C. Marland. Marland interview, May 5, 2018.

50. *Savannah Morning News*, December 12, 1969, clippings in "Phosphate Mining" file.

51. *Atlanta Constitution*, December 4, 1968, clippings in "Phosphate Mining" file.

52. *Atlanta Constitution*, December 6, 1968; *Savannah Morning News*, December 6, 1968, clippings in "Phosphate Mining" file.

CHAPTER 8. THE CONFERENCE ON THE FUTURE OF THE MARSHLANDS

1 Personal interview with Fred Marland, May 5, 2018.

2. Sparks, "Georgia's Wild Coast," 9.

3. Sullivan, *Sapelo*, 30–42.

4. Ibid., 11. The invitation list does not indicate that representatives of the Parsons heirs were present, but they would soon be briefed at a December meeting with other owners in New York City.

5. Sparks, "Georgia's Wild Coast," 63.

6. Ibid., 56; Sullivan, *First Conservationists*, 27–29.

7. Maney, Marland, and West, *Future of the Marshlands*, 67–68. The transcript of the conference proceedings was typed by Coastal Area Planning and Development Commission secretary Evelyn Smith and edited by Fred Marland and David Maney. Each speaker approved the final published version of their remarks before publication in 1970. Marland constructed the Odum paper from the recorded remarks, created the illustrations, and received approval from Odum to publish the paper. Marland made his copy of the publication available to the author. A copy is in "Future of the Marshland of Georgia, Oct. 13–14," folder, RCB 20342, GNAC Papers.

8. The crowning achievement of Wharton's distinguished career was the publication of his *Natural Environment of Georgia*, which became the state's environmental guide for many decades. He ended his academic career at the University of Georgia.

9. List of invitees in "Marshland Conference," file RCB 20342, GNAC Papers; also in "Cumberland folder," personal papers of Frederick C. Marland; Robert Hanie, Memo to Conferees, September 19, 1968, "Marshland Conference" file, Fred Marland unprocessed papers.

10. Maney, Marland, and West, *Future of the Marshlands*, 4; Robert Hanie, Annual Report, 1968, RCB 20340, GNAC Papers. Hanie led Governor Maddox on that hike. The governor pursued his plan to purchase the site although the work was not completed until 1972 when Maddox was Georgia's lieutenant governor. In addition to hiking trails, Sweetwater Creek State Park now boasts campsites, a lake, fishing docks, and yurts.

11. Maney, Marland, West, *Future of the Marshlands*, 7.

12. Ibid., 52–53.

13. Ibid., 53.

14. Ibid.

15. Ibid.

16. Ibid., 15–16. The scientists, primarily from the UGAMI on Sapelo and in Athens, favored conservation and wanted the state and its citizenry to take advantage of the new scientific theories of ecology. They became deeply engaged in the fight against Kerr-McGee. The geologists felt it would help if participants understood that the shoreline was never static and had moved during the ice ages of the last 2.6 million years. The scientists attending the conference included C. D. Clement, Dirk Frankenberg, Vernon Henry, James Howard, John H. Hoyt, Thomas Linton, Fred Marland, Eugene Odum, and Lawrence Pomeroy; also in attendance were graduate students Leonard Bahr, Richard Murlless, Steve Johnson, Hans Neuhauser, and James Richardson.

17. Maney, Marland, and West, *Future of the Marshlands*, 56; Sparks, "Georgia's Wild Coast," 57.

18. Maney, Marland, and West, *Future of the Marshlands*, 57.

19. Ibid., 18.

20. Ibid., 24–27. For a careful discussion of the geological difference between the recent formation of parts of Jekyll Island in the Holocene period five thousand years ago and the parts of the island formed fifty thousand years ago, see Davis and Galland, *Island Passages*, 1–10.

21. Maney, Marland, and West, *Future of the Marshlands*, 77.

22. Ibid., 83–84.

23. Ibid., 88, 92.

24. Sparks, "Georgia's Wild Coast," 63.

25. Sparks, "Housewife Saves an Island," 17.

26. Ibid., 20.

27. Ibid., 23.

28. Ibid., 24.

29. Joseph Parsons quoted in Sullivan, *First Conservationists*, 19–20.

30. Minutes of Georgia Islands and Marshland Owners Association, December 14 at the Cloister, RCB 20342, GNAC Papers.

31. "Public Statement" by the Parsons Trustees from Charles Ewing to Robert Hanie, Wassaw Island folder, RCB 20340, GNAC Papers; Robert Hanie, Report to the Council, December 10, 1968, "Conference" file, Fred Marland unprocessed papers.

32. *Atlanta Journal and Constitution Magazine*, June 2, 1968. Philip McMasters to Dr. Charles Wharton, July 21, 1968, and Charles Ewing to Lester Maddox, September 5, 1968; certificate pledges trustees "to protect and use the Isle for purposes consistent with the preservation of the natural integrity." All in "Wassaw Island" folder, RCB 20340,20342, GNAC Papers; also see Robert Hanie, Report, December 10, 1968, "Conference file," Marland unprocessed papers.

33. Kelly, *Short History of Skidaway Island*, 105.

34. Ibid., 108.

35. Ibid., 102–8.

36. Invitation from Charles M. Ewing, trustee, to Gov. Lester Maddox for visit to Wassaw on November 7, 1968, September 20, 1968, Governor Lester G. Maddox file, RCB 20338, GNAC Papers.

37. Fred Marland to Reid Harris, e-mail May 18, 2009, containing the paper delivered by Fred Marland in 2003 at the 50th anniversary of the Conference on the Future of the Marshlands, Jekyll Island, November 8, 2003, personal papers of Frederick C. Marland.

38. Duane Neergaard, "Chamber Position: Island Plans Are Assailed," *Savannah Morning News*, September 26, 1969.

39. *Savannah Morning News*, September 27, 1969, 4A.

40. *Savannah Morning News*, September, 27, 1969.

41. *Savannah Morning News*, September 30, 1969. There is no other record of an offer to sell an African island to the state.

42. *Savannah Evening Press*, June 5, 1968.

43. Ibid.

44. *Savannah Morning News*, October 18, 1969.

45. Fred Marland to Reid Harris, e-mail May 18, 2009, containing the paper delivered by Fred Marland in 2003 at the 50th anniversary of the Conference on the Future of the Marshlands, personal papers of Frederick C. Marland; *Atlanta Constitution*, October 22, 1969.

46. *Savannah Morning News*, November 20, 1969.

47. Ibid.

48. *Savannah Morning News*, December 19, 1969.

CHAPTER 9. A BILL TAKES A BREATH

Reid Harris's memoir, *And the Coastlands Wait*, was integral to reconstructing the legislative journey of HB 212. Unless otherwise indicated in this chapter and the next, Harris's recollections are from that work.

1. Mary R. Bullard, *Cumberland Island*, 277–78.

2. Teal and Teal, *Life and Death*, 240–55. The Teals found no permit process for disturbing the marsh in New York, New Jersey, Maryland, Virginia, North Carolina, South Carolina, Georgia, and Florida. Several states had programs to purchase the marsh from private owners. Only four New England states had some level of regulation: Maine, New Hampshire, Massachusetts, and Rhode Island had a process requiring a permit to disturb the marsh. The Teals said Massachusetts was the most advanced.

3. John R. Thoman et al. 1968, Clean Water for the Nation's Estuaries, Proceedings of the Georgia Public Meeting, Jekyll Island, Ga., February 1968. Proceedings of the Jekyll Island meeting are at https://ntrl.ntis.gov/NTRL/dashboard /searchResults/titleDetail/PB230073.xhtml.

4. Harris, *And the Coastlands Wait*, 43–44; Marland interview, August 7 and 8, 2017.

5. Teal and Teal, *Life and Death*, 246–48, 260–61. They said the future of the marshlands looks brighter in Massachusetts than anywhere on the East Coast, but after four centuries of development the commonwealth had little marsh remaining. All the marshland around Boston had been filled for commercial development or expanding docks. New Englanders love Fenway Park and their Red Sox but seldom think about the marsh on which the park was built. The Teals estimated only 48,000 acres of productive marshland was left in the state in 1964 and it had been losing marsh at 2.5 percent annually since 1955. Several other Atlantic coast states had small amounts of marsh remaining: New Hampshire 6,000 acres, Maine 15,500

acres, Connecticut 1,500, Delaware 115,000 but losing 4 percent per year. Only the Massachusetts 1965 law was found to be worthy of specific review in *The National Estuarine Pollution Study* (375–77, 399), which was authorized by Congress in the Clean Water Restoration Act of 1966.

6. The Florida management system was reviewed in *National Estuarine Pollution Study Report*, October 1970, 384–87.

7. Harris, *And the Coastlands Wait*, 43–44.

8. Ibid., 50; Maine has a similar problem with ownership of the intertidal zone, dating back to a 1641 Colonial Ordinance that established the parameters of private seashore property.

9. "Preserve the Marsh Now," *Georgia Game and Fish*, December 1968.

10. HB 212 with bill jacket as introduced, Bills and Resolutions 1969–70, RG 37-1-1, RCB 34892, Georgia Archives; the original HB 212 as introduced is not printed in the *Journal of the House* and can only be found in the Georgia Archives. The distance came from surveys Fred Marland of the UGAMI made on a summer trip up the East Coast from Florida to Maine with his wife Sarita Harris. Harris, *And the Coastlands Wait*, 50; personal interview with Fred Marland, November 8, 2017.

11. Original HB 212, *Journal of the House*, Georgia Archives.

12. Acts and Resolutions of the General Assembly, 1969–70, RG 37-1-1, RCB 34892, Georgia Archives; Harris, *And the Coastlands Wait*, 51–52.

13. "Preserve the Marsh Now"; Harris, *And the Coastlands Wait*, 51–52.

14. HB 212 in all of its forms, Acts and Resolutions of the General Assembly, 1970, 939–40; *Journal of the House*, 1969, 1329–30.

15. Bills and Resolutions, 1969–70, RG 37-1-1, RCB 34892.

16. Ibid.

17. Ibid.

18. Fred Marland to the author, e-mail November 2, 2017.

19. HB 212 with bill jacket as introduced.

20. Harris, *And the Coastlands Wait*, 54; Frederick Marland to Patricia Barmeyer, e-mail May 3, 2006, personal papers of Frederick C. Marland; *Atlanta Constitution*, March 7, 1969.

21. *Georgia's Official and Statistical Register, 1969–1970*, 470.

22. *Savannah Morning News*, February 19, 1969.

23. *Savannah Morning News*, February 12, 1969.

24. Jeff Nesmith, "Tide of Abuse Hits Conservation," *Atlanta Journal and Constitution*, November 2, 1969.

25. Harris, *And the Coastlands Wait*, 54–56.

26. *Atlanta Constitution*, February 5, 1969. *Atlanta Constitution*, February 12, 1969, 45.

27. "Silver Lining in Every Cloud," *Georgia Game and Fish*, May 1969.

28. *Savannah Morning News*, February 12, 1968.

29. Bills and Resolutions 1969–70, RG 37-1-1, RCB 34892, Georgia Archives.

30. *Atlanta Constitution*, January 23, 1969.

31. *Atlanta Constitution*, February 11, 1969.

32. Harris, *And the Coastlands Wait*, 52–53; *Atlanta Constitution*, February 11, 1969.

33. Harris, *And the Coastlands Wait*, 52.

34. Statement of Robert Hanie, February 11, 1969, RCB 20342, GNAC Papers; copy in possession of the author.

35. Fred Marland to author, e-mail August 6, 2018.

36. Price, *St. Simons Memoir*, 37.

37. Harris, *And the Coastlands Wait*, 61; Blackburn, *Earth Is the Lord's?*, 40–41; Blackburn's book featured a lengthy narration of the legislative history of HB 212 written by Harris. The book urged faith communities to get engaged in protecting the natural environment God had created.

38. Price, *St. Simons Memoir*, 191; Blackburn, *Earth Is the Lord's?*, 41.

39. *Brunswick News*, February 20, 1969.

40. *Savannah Morning News*, February 12, 1969.

41. Harris, *And the Coastlands Wait*, 59.

42. Ibid.; Fred Marland to the author, e-mail August 6, 2018.

43. Harris, *And the Coastlands Wait*, 59.

44. After Eugene Talmadge was elected governor, he died before the vote was certified. His son Herman argued that the General Assembly could choose him to replace his father because he was third in the election with a few write-in votes. M. E. Thompson, elected lieutenant governor, said he was the successor. And the sitting governor, Ellis Arnall, said he should stay as governor until there was a new election. For more details see Bullock, Buchannan, and Gaddie, *Three Governors Controversy*; and Scott Buchanan, "Three Governors Controversy," New Georgia Encyclopedia, www.georgiaencyclopedia.org.

45. Harris, *And the Coastlands Wait*, 59–61.

46. Ibid., 60–61; *Atlanta Constitution*, February 12, 1969.

47. *Georgia's Official and Statistical Register, 1969–1970*, 444.

48. House Standing Committee Minute Books 1969–70.

49. *Atlanta Constitution*, February 13, 1969.

50. Minutes of the Georgia Islands and Marshland Owners Association, February 15, 1969, RCB 63710, Carnegie Family Trust.

51. Harris, *And the Coastlands Wait*, 66–67; Harris does not identify the two members, but this is noted on the bill jacket as introduced, Acts and Resolutions of the General Assembly, 1969–70, RG 37-1-1, RCB 34892, Georgia Archives.

52. *Savannah Morning News*, February 19, 1969.

53. Harris, *And the Coastlands Wait*, 66–67. Jones's signature is not on the bill jacket.

54. Ibid., 63, 64.

55. *Journal of the House*, 1969, 2050.

56. Harris, *And the Coastlands Wait*, 81.

57. *Journal of the House*, 1969, 2053.

58. R. S. Howard Jr. to Leon Kirkland, January 14, 1969, Reid Harris Papers.

59. Harris, *And the Coastlands Wait*, 65.

60. House Standing Committee Minute Books 1969–70.

61. *Atlanta Constitution*, February 26, 1969.

62. Ibid.; *Atlanta Constitution*, February 25, 1969.

63. Eugene Odum to Reid Harris, February 28, 1969, Fred Marland unprocessed papers.

64. Fraser's plans are in a number of places: Sparks, "Cumberland Will Never Be the Same Again"; Charles Fraser, Thomas Richards, H. B. Masters, and John W Bright, "The Golden Isles of Georgia: Decision Time for Public Property," "Cumberland" folder, personal papers of Frederick C. Marland. In February and March 1969, Fraser promoted efforts for private planning of the island by sending a full proposal to each owner and inviting them to Sea Pines Plantation for a two-day discussion. He also proposed a conference that would highlight his development ideas.

65. Dilsaver, *Cumberland Island National Seashore*, 92; Dilsaver provides the best detailed treatment of the events that led to the National Park Service acquisition of Cumberland as a part of the National Seashore.

66. Mary R. Bullard, *Cumberland Island*, 279.

67. Senate Bills, 1969–70, RG 37-1-1, RCB 34927, Georgia Archives.

68. *Atlanta Constitution*, February 13, 1969.

69. *Atlanta Constitution*, March 2, 1969, B-18.

70. Senate Bills, 1969–70; Dilsaver, *Cumberland Island National Seashore*, 93–94; Mary R. Bullard, *Cumberland*, 269.

71. Dilsaver, *Cumberland Island National Seashore*, 1–93.

72. Graves, *Cumberland Island Saved*, 61.

73. Mary R. Bullard, *Cumberland Island*, 279.

74. Personal interview with Thornton Morris, July 23, 2018. The Thornton Morris memos are cited in Dilsaver, *Cumberland Island National Seashore*; Mary R. Bullard, *Cumberland Island*; and Graves, *Cumberland Island Saved*. Joe Graves represented the Johnston branch of the Carnegie family in all the family efforts to preserve the island; before he died in 2016, he placed all of his papers in the Georgia Archives as the papers of the Carnegie Family Trust. This collection has memos from Thornton Morris to the Cumberland Island Conservation Association and the early minutes of the association meetings. The Thornton Morris law firm files were lost when he closed his Atlanta office. Mary Bullard willed her research papers to the Cumberland Island National Seashore.

75. Joe Graves to Ingram Richardson, A. Steven Johnson, Richard Pugh, Norman Smith, and Robert Hanie, March 7, 1969, Georgia Sierra Club Records.

76. On Joe Graves's family connections, see Dilsaver, *Cumberland Island National Seashore*, 94.

77. Personal interview with Steven Johnson, April 2, 2018; Steven Johnson, "History of the Georgia Chapter of the Sierra Club," manuscript in possession of the author. Steven Johnson, Richard Murlless, Richard Bailey, and James Richardson, "The Proposed Cumberland Island National Sea Shore: Facts and Recommendations, A Report to the Atlantic Chapter of the Sierra Club," January 24, 1968, "Sierra Club," RCB 63710, Carnegie Family Trust.

78. Robert Schaefer to Steven Johnson, December 31, 1969, Georgia Sierra Club Records.

79. Sparks, "Tide of Change," 24.

80. Ibid., 22.

81. Morris to Cumberland Island Conservation Association, RCB63711, Carnegie Family Trust.

82. Morris interview, July 25, 2018.

83. Morris to Cumberland Island Conservation Association, April 23, 1969, "Cumberland Island Conservation Association" file, RCB 63711, Carnegie Family Trust.

84. Robert R. Jacobsen to Theodore Swem, March 7, 1969, Central Files, L58, Cumberland Island National Seashore; Dilsaver, *Cumberland Island National Seashore*, 94.

85. Morris interview, July 23, 2018.

86. *Savannah Morning News*, January 23, 1969.

87. Resolutions of the House, 1969–70, RG 37-1-1, RCB 34892, Georgia Archives.

88. *Savannah Morning News*, January 23, 1969; Bills and Resolutions, 1969–70, RG 37-1-1, RCB 34892, Georgia Archives; Acts and Resolutions of the General Assembly, 1969, 1:754–59. The board of the OSCA became more heavily peopled with individuals interested in coastal development.

89. *Brunswick News*, March, 5, 1969; Council Minutes, RCB 20336, GNAC Papers, also in Bills and Resolutions, 1969–70, RG 37-1-1, RCB 34892, Georgia Archives.

90. *Savannah Morning News*, February 22, 1969.

91. *Brunswick News*, March 5, 1969.

92. Harris, *And the Coastlands Wait*, 68.

93. Ibid., 69; *Brunswick News*, March 6, 1969; *Atlanta Constitution*, March 6, 1969.

94. Harris, *And the Coastlands Wait*, 69; *Atlanta Constitution*, March 6, 1969.

95. *Brunswick News*, March 6, 1969; *Atlanta Constitution*, March 6, 1969.

96. *Atlanta Constitution*, March 6, 1969.

97. Personal interview with Fred Marland, August 8, 2018. It took an unusual special request from Governor Sanders and Rock Howard. Leonard Ledbetter had laid out unprecedented strict requirements for the plant that they had not expected the paper company engineers would be able to meet. They were both surprised. Ledbetter interview, April 15, 2018.

98. *Journal of the House*, March 5, 1969, 1335. In *And the Coastlands Wait*, Harris recalled the amendment changed the effective date to July 1, but that was already part of his substitute. The journal records neither the nature of the amendment nor who objected.

99. *Journal of the House*, March 5, 1969, 1336–37.

100. Harris, *And the Coastlands Wait*, 70–72, 74.

101. *Journal of the House*, March 5, 1969, 1336–37; The vote count is reproduced in the *Journal*.

102. Harris, *And the Coastlands Wait*, 76–77.

103. Ibid., 77.

104. Ibid.

105. Ibid., 78.

106. Ibid., 78–79; *Journal of the House*, March 14, 1969, 2054.

107. *Atlanta Constitution*, March 15, 1969.

1. Harris, *And the Coastlands Wait*, 79.

2. Ibid.

3. Reginald Murphy, "The System Works on the Marshland Bill," *Atlanta Constitution*, February 12, 1970.

4. Personal interview with former Sen. Bobby Rowan, April 4 and November 18, 2018.

5. *Georgia's Official and Statistical Register, 1969–1970*, 372. Holloway's military service during World War II was typical of the members of the General Assembly during this term; most had leadership positions in one or another branch of the armed forces.

6. Personal interview with Fred Marland, November 8, 2017.

7. Personal interview with former Sen. George Hooks of Americus, September 28, 2017.

8. *Atlanta Constitution*, February 20, 1969; Hooks interview.

9. Hooks interview; *Atlanta Constitution*, February 20, 1969.

10. *Atlanta Constitution*, March 25, 169; *Georgia's Official and Statistical Register, 1969–1970*, 384–85.

11. Harris, *And the Coastlands Wait*, 79; Jeff Nesmith, "Marshland Bill Gets New Chance," *Atlanta Constitution*, March 19, 1969; Reginald Murphy, *Atlanta Constitution*, February 12, 1970.

12. Adopted March 24, 1969, Bills and Resolutions of the Senate, 1969–70, RG 8-1-1, RCB 63710, Georgia Archives; *Atlanta Constitution*, March 25, 1969. *Atlanta Constitution*, March 26, 1969.

13. *Brunswick News*, February 6, 1970.

14. Harris, *And the Coastlands Wait*, 82; Senate Resolution 138, Senate Journal, 1969, 1704. The resolution was drawn to authorize a joint study with the House but did not pass the House.

15. Mrs. Charles Yarn to Rep. Reid Harris, May 14, 1969, Fred Marland unprocessed papers, reproduced in Harris, *And the Coastlands Wait*, 81.

16. "One Message May Change the Vote," *Garden Gate*, January/February 1970, 50.

17. Minutes of the Board of Directors of the Garden Club of Georgia, April 16, 1970, 13, Club Headquarters, Athens.

18. *Atlanta Journal*, July 9, 1969, clipping in Fred Marland unprocessed papers.

19. Addes, "Length, Breadth and Sweep of Marshland Protection," MA thesis; flyer, Georgia Sierra Club Records; personal interview with Joyce Murlless, April 16, 2018.

20. Personal interview with Jim Morrison, August 9, 2017; *Garden Gate*, November/December 1969, 12.

21. *Atlanta Constitution*, September 21, 1969.

22. *Georgia Sierran*, January/February 1970, Georgia Sierra Club Records.

23. Ibid.; *Red and Black*, January 19, 170.

24. *Georgia Sierran*, January/February 1970.

25. Jane Yarn quoted in Bob Harrell, "Mrs. Yarn Sees Beauty in the World," *Atlanta Constitution*, January 8, 1970.

26. Ibid.; reprinted in Harris, *And the Coastlands Wait*, 102, 103.

27. Michael L. Jordan, "Jane Hurt Yarn (1924–1995)," *New Georgia Encyclopedia*, January 29, 2016; Morrison interview.

28. Minutes of the Board of Directors of the Garden Club of Georgia, January 13, 1970.

29. Morrison interview.

30. Minutes of the Board of Directors of the Garden Club of Georgia, April 16, 1970, 13.

31. Minutes of the Cumberland Island Conservation Association, February 7, 1970, RCB 63710-048-01-001, Carnegie Family Trust.

32. *Georgia Sierran*, January/February 1970, Georgia Sierra Club Records.

33. Unfortunately, neither the personal papers of Jane Yarn nor of SAVE have been located at this writing. The author hopes this history will encourage further efforts to identify collections of these papers.

34. Mrs. Ronald F. Adams to F. C. Marland, April 28, 1969, personal papers of Frederick C. Marland; Marland interview, August 7, 2017.

35. Program, May 9, 1969, Conference file, Fred Marland unprocessed papers.

36. "Howard Holds Firm on Pollution Plans," *Savannah Morning News*, September 12, 1969, 14B; "Get Tough Policy on Pollution Recommended by Federal Water Pollution Control Administration," *Savannah Morning News*, October 29, 1969, 1A; "Federal Officials Set 1972 for Pollution Curb, City Probably Unable to Meet Deadline," *Savannah Morning News*, October 30, 1969, 1A.

37. Boyd, *Slain Wood*, 165–68. Boyd says the Union Camp mill began implementing its $17 million upgrade to its waste treatment facilities in 1970, and by 1972 it had reduced the biological component of its waste by 85 percent and met the goals of the 1969 enforcement conference.

38. Jeff Nesmith, "Plants' Waste Equal to a Big City," *Atlanta Constitution*, November 4, 1969.

39. Jeff Nesmith, "Tide of Abuse Hits Conservation," *Atlanta Constitution*,

March 2, 1969; Jeff Nesmith, "'Little Men' Battle to Save Livelihood," *Atlanta Constitution*, November 3, 1969.

40. Jeff Nesmith, "Florida Firm Asks Marifarm to Develop Huge Coastal Shrimp Farm," *Atlanta Constitution*, November 6, 1969.

41. Sam Candler, assistant director of the Natural Areas Council, to Colonel John Egbert, January 6, 1970, RCB 20348, GNAC Papers.

42. Arthur K. Bolton to Colonel John C. Egbert, December 10, 1969, Fred Marland unprocessed papers.

43. "Money Changers Are Still in the Temple," *Georgia Game and Fish*, August 1969.

44. "General Assembly Conserves Wildlife," *Georgia Game and Fish*, January 1969.

45. Report of the Coastal Islands Study Committee; Morris interview, July 23, 2018.

46. *Savannah Morning News*, January 23, 1979.

47. Report of the Coastal Islands Study Committee, 1.

48. Thornton Morris to Cumberland Island Conservation Association, memo October 21, 1969, RCB 63711, Carnegie Family Trust.

49. Ibid.

50. Nancy Ancrum, "Ossabaw Is Not for Sale, Owner Informs Legislators," *Savannah Morning News*, November 11, 1969. Sandy West, who was fifty at the time of her conversation with the committee, sold the island to the state in 1973 under terms that protect it from development. She lived on the island until the age of 103, and at this writing is alive and well in a Savannah assisted living center. See *Savannah Morning News* and SavannahNow.com, "Sandy West celebrates 106 birthday."

51. Report of the Georgia Coastal Islands Study Committee, 4.

52. Ibid., 1.

53. Marland interview, August 8, 2017.

54. Pat Malone, review of *Life and Death*, by Teal and Teal, *Atlanta Constitution*, September 14, 1969; Seabrook, *World of the Salt Marsh*, 159–60. There is no evidence the Teals' book influenced the Georgia legislative effort, for it did not mention the campaign to pass the bill.

55. Harris, *And the Coastlands Wait*, 86.

56. Statement of Georgia Chapter of the Sierra Club, January 19, 1970, Georgia Sierra Club Records.

57. "Game and Fish Seeks Marsh Authority," *Georgia Game and Fish*, December 1969; *Savannah Morning News*, October 19, 1969.

58. "Game and Fish Seeks Marsh Authority." After the passage of the Coastal Marshlands Protection Act of 1970, Hoyt Brown, on behalf of his cousins, offered

the Nature Conservancy 3,500 acres of marsh they owned east of Highway 17, several miles southwest of Egg Island, and south of New Hope Plantation. F. C. Marland to Thomas Richards, Nature Conservancy president, March 10, 1971, "Cumberland" file, personal papers of Frederick C. Marland.

59. *Brunswick News*, October 18, 1969. Harris, *And the Coastlands Wait*, 87.

60. Sparks, "Day in the Life." Drafts of all Sparks's articles are available in Andrew H. Sparks Papers.

61. Sparks, "Day in the Life," 262. Carl Sanders, who by this point was planning his return to the governor's chair, missed this leadership opportunity for the environmental movement.

62. Sparks, "Day in the Life."

63. Ibid. He had a plan and purpose for each island and identified Little Tybee Island, to this author's disappointment, as an urban beach and entertainment center.

64. Sparks, "Day in the Life."

65. Ibid., 25–26.

66. Ibid., 26.

67. Ibid., 25.

68. Ibid., 25.

69. *Savannah Morning News*, December 10, 1969; *Atlanta Constitution*, December 10, 1969.

70. *Atlanta Constitution*, December 14, 1969.

71. Report of the Coastal Islands Study Committee, 10.

72. Thornton Morris to Cumberland Island Conservation Association, memo December 12, 1969, RG 048-01-001, RCB 63711, Carnegie Family Trust.

73. Report of the Coastal Islands Study Committee, 6.

74. *Savannah Morning News*, December 11, 1969.

75. Minority Report of Senator Roscoe Dean, Report of the Coastal Islands Study Committee, 12–15.

76. Statement of the Georgia Chapter of the Sierra Club, January 19, 1970, Georgia Sierra Club Records.

77. *Atlanta Constitution*, January 20, 1970.

78. Ibid.

79. Testimony of Hoyt Brown before the Senate Committee on Industry and Trade, February 3, 1969, Fred Marland unprocessed papers; Harris, *And the Coastlands Wait*, 96.

80. *Atlanta Constitution*, January 29, 1970.

81. Personal interview with Wallace Harrell Sr., June 1, 2018.

82. *Atlanta Constitution*, February 4, 1970; Harris, *And the Coastlands Wait*, 96.

83. *Atlanta Constitution*, February 4, 1970.

84. *Atlanta Constitution*, January 29, 1970.

85. *Atlanta Constitution*, February 4, 1970.

86. Marland interview, August 8, 2017; Harris, *And the Coastlands Wait*, 99.

87. Harris, *And the Coastlands Wait*; *Journal of the House*, February 9, 1970, 1208.

88. *Journal of the House*, February 9, 1970.

89. *Atlanta Constitution*, February 6, 1970.

90. Personal interview with Douglas Adams, April 20, 2018; *Atlanta Constitution*, February 7, 1970; Christopher J. Manganiello, "The Gold Standard," in Sutter and Pressly, *Costal Nature, Coastal Culture*, 279.

91. Jeff Nesmith, "Marshlands Bill Passed in Senate," *Atlanta Constitution*, February 7, 1970; Marland interview, July 21, 2018.

92. Personal interview with former Sen. Bobby Rowan, November 18, 2018.

93. Jeff Nesmith, "Marsh Bill Stirs Public," *Atlanta Constitution*, February 9, 1970.

94. *Atlanta Constitution*, February 9, 1970.

95. Thomas Murphy, interviewed by Clifford Kuhn, May 5, 1988, P1988-19, series B, Public Figures, Georgia Documentation Project.

96. Harris, *And the Coastlands Wait*, 108–9.

97. Although not recorded in the *Journal of the House*, February 9, 1970, the narrative of the final House vote is preserved in Harris, *And the Coastlands Wait*, 108–11.

98. Vote comparison from *Journal of the House*, March 5, 1969, 1336–38, and February 9, 1970, 1216–18.

99. *Atlanta Constitution*, January 16, 1970.

100. *Atlanta Constitution*, February 12, 1970.

101. Sen. Al Holloway to Joyce Blackburn, June 13, 1969, "St. Simons Concerned Citizen Association Correspondence 1971–75," Joyce Blackburn Papers.

102. Harris, *And the Coastlands Wait*, 113–15.

103. Ibid., 114.

104. Ibid., 116.

105. *Atlanta Constitution*, March 24 and 25, 1970.

106. The narrative and quotations from the signing meeting are preserved in Harris, *And the Coastlands Wait*, 115–17.

1. *Atlanta Constitution*, March 17, 1970. Harris reproduces Bolton's position paper as exhibit A in *And the Coastlands Wait* (118–20).

2. *Savannah Morning News*, March 18, 1970.

3. *State of Georgia v. Ashmore*, 236 Ga. 401, 413 (224 SE 2d 334) (1976). *Black v. Floyd*, 280 Ga. 525 (630 SE 2d 382) (2006).

4. *Savannah Morning News*, March 19, 1970.

5. Coastal Marshlands Protection Act of 1970, section 5A.

6. Personal interview with Fred Marland, July 5, 2018; e-mails and other material in personal papers of Frederick C. Marland.

7. Associated Press, "Archaeologists Find Relics at Georgia Fort," May 20, 2005, www.nbcnews.com.

8. Personal interview with Bill Sapp, December 10, 2018.

9. *Atlanta Journal*, April 10, 1970.

10. *Macon News*, April 9, 1970.

11. *Atlanta Constitution* April 17, 1970.

12. Carter 1970 Platform, "Marshland Areas Report" file, RCB 20341, GNAC Papers.

13. Marland interview, May 5, 2018.

14. Jeff Nesmith, "Marshland Bill Stirs Public," *Atlanta Constitution*, September 2, 1970.

15. Kundell and Little, *Management of Georgia's Marshlands*.

16. Ibid., 162.

17. Georgia Constitution, article 3, section 6, para. 2(a) (1); emphasis added.

18. Ferguson, *This Is Our Land*, 8; see also ch. 2, fn 14.

19. Marland interview, September 9, 2019.

20. Personal interview with Hans Neuhauser, March 9, 2018.

21. Georgia Coast Protected Lands, map created by Jason Lee, Earth Ecologist, DNR Coastal Division, Brunswick, Ga.; see p. xi.

22. For detailed accounts on Cumberland Island, see Mary R. Bullard, *Cumberland Island*; Dilsaver, *Cumberland Island National Seashore*; Graves, *Cumberland Island Saved*.

23. Mary R. Bullard, *Cumberland Island*; Dilsaver, *Cumberland Island National Seashore*; Neuhauser interview, March 9, 2018.

24. Fred Marland to Patricia Barmeyer, e-mail March 13, 2016, personal papers of Frederick C. Marland.

25. Mary Landers, "Ossabaw Preserve Celebrates Wild Status After 40 Years,"

SavannahNow, January 12, 2018. On January 19, 2019, Sandy West celebrated turning 106 years.

26. Elmore, "Roundup from the Ground Up."

27. *Atlanta Journal and Constitution*, April 4, 2019.

28. *Little Tybee and Cabbage Islands: Georgia's Newest Wildlife Lands*, Department of Natural Resources Outdoor Report, winter 1991; *Savannah Evening Press*, September 24, 1990. Oklahoma is the home of Kerr-McGee.

29. Personal interview with Jason Lee, DNR coastal staff, March 14, 2018.

30. The best political profile is David Morrison, "Major Power Rests in the Hands of a Few," *Atlanta Constitution*, April 15, 1977.

31. "Howard Hits Carter Water Plan," *Atlanta Constitution*, June 7, 172.

32. *Atlanta Constitution*, July 14, 1977.

33. Morrison interview, August 9, 2017.

34. *Savannah Morning News*, March 22, 1970; "Proposal for a Department of the Environment," RCB 20345, GNAC Papers.

35. *Columbus Ledger Enquirer*, May 17, 1970.

36. *Brunswick News*, September 23, 1971; *Atlanta Constitution*, October 8, 1971, both in clipping files, RCB 20342, GNAC Papers.

37. Patti Puckett and Charles Seabrook, "Defender of the Wild," *Atlanta Journal and Constitution Magazine*, June 20, 1995.

38. Such a biography would be difficult to write, however, since Yarn's personal papers, which could illuminate the details of her tireless advocacy, appear to be lost.

39. Michael L. Jordan, "Jane Hurt Yarn (1924–1995)," *New Georgia Encyclopedia*, January 29, 2016.

40. Personal interview with Elliott Levitas, August 5, 2017.

41. Justin Nystram, "Lester Maddox (1915–2003)," *New Georgia Encyclopedia*, August 10, 2018; Short, *Everything Is Pickrick*, 181–88.

42. Doug Samson (National Estuarine Reserve director, Sapelo) to the author, e-mail October 10, 2018.

43. Harris, *And the Coastlands Wait*, 94–95.

44. From a Harris essay included in Blackburn, *The Earth Is the Lords?*, 32.

45. Personal interview with Don Hogan, March 27, 2019.

46. Personal papers of Frederick C. Marland.

CHAPTER 12. TODAY'S COASTAL CHALLENGES

1. Personal interview with Clark Alexander, October 8, 2018.

2. USGCRP, *Impacts, Risks, and Adaptation in the United States*.

3. Frankson et al., *2017: Georgia State Climate Summary.*

4. "Sea Level Rise: UGA Marine Extension and Georgia Sea Grant Is Assisting Coastal Communities in Preparing for Sea Level Rise," Marine Extension and Georgia Sea Grant, University of Georgia, https://gacoast.uga.edu/research/major-projects/sea-level-rise/, retrieved November 1, 2018.

5. USGCRP, *Impacts, Risks, and Adaptation in the United States*, fig. 19.7, www.globalchange.gov.

6. Ibid.

7. Personal interview with Fred Marland, October 22, 2018.

8. Pilkey and Young, *Rising Sea.*

9. Orrin Pilkey, "Sea Level Rise Is Here. North Carolina Needs to Act," *News Observer* (Blue Ridge, GA), September 7, 2018, www.thenewsobserver.com.

10. Orrin Pilkey, "Business-as-Usual on Coast Can't Continue," Opinion, *JD-News* (Jacksonville, N.C.), October 20, 2018, www.jdnews.com/opinion/20181020/opinion-dr-orrin-pilkey-business-as-usual-on-coast-cant-continue.

11. Maney, Marland, and West, *Future of the Marshlands*, 18–34, map on p. 148.

12. Halfacre, *Delicate Balance*, 54.

13. Alexander interview.

14. Dan Chapman, "A Rising Tide of Concern," *Atlanta Journal-Constitution*, August 9, 2015.

15. USGCRP, *Impacts, Risks, and Adaptation in the United States*, fig. 19.7.

16. Personal interview with Mark Risse, October 16, 2018.

17. Personal interview with Chester Jackson, October 16, 2018.

18. "Sea Level Rise Viewer," NOAA Office for Coastal Management, http://coast.noaa.gov/digitalcoast/tools/slr.html, last modified August 26, 2019. Also see the Georgia Coastal Hazards Portal (https://gchp.skio.uga.edu/) for an interactive map that shows the effect on specific locations on the coast.

19. "*Blueprints*: Sea Level Rise on Georgia's Coast," Georgia Conservancy website, www.georgiaconservancy.org/blueprints/slr.

20. Ibid.

21. "Tracking the Effects of Sea Level Rise in Georgia's Coastal Communities," Georgia Institute of Technology City and Regional Planning Studio, Larry Keating coordinator, fall 2012, available at "*Blueprints*: Sea Level Rise on Georgia's Coast," Georgia Conservancy website, www.georgiaconservancy.org/sea level rise.

22. Elizabeth Kramer and Kevin Samples, "Adding Dynamic Information to Resilience Planning: Identifying and Reducing Future Conflicts from Wetland Migra-

tion Due to Sea Rise," in *Proceedings of the 2017 Georgia Water Resources Conference*, held April 19–20, 2017, University of Georgia, http://gwri.gatech.edu/sites/default /files/files/docs/2017/kramersamplesgwrc2017.pdf; personal interview with Elizabeth Kramer, December 10, 2018.

23. Joseph M. Evans et. al., "City of Tybee Island, Georgia, Sea-Level Rise Adaptation Plan," Adaptation Clearinghouse, April 17, 2016, www.adaptationclearinghouse.org/resources/city-of-tybee-island-georgia-sea-level-rise-adaptation-plan .html.

24. Jones, "How Planning for Sea Level Rise Creates Flood Insurance Reductions."

25. Personal interview with Shana Jones, UGA Carl Vinson Institute of Government, November 1, 2018.

26. Worley, "Georgia's Vanishing Coast."

27. Southface Staff, "Climate Change: A Way Forward," *Southface*, June 4, 2019, www.southface.org; Hawkins and Steyer, *Drawdown*.

28. See a review of the study in TerraDaily News about the Planet, September 24, 2018, www.terradaily.com.

29. Kolbert, "Control of Nature Under Water."

30. Alexander interview.

31. Worley, "Georgia's Vanishing Coast."

32. Emerson, "How Much Could It Cost to Protect Our Coastline?"; *New York Times*, June 22, 2019.

33. Chester Jackson interview.

34. Personal interview with David Pope, director of the St. Simons Land Trust, October 18, 2018; personal interview with Charles McMillan, coastal director for the Georgia Conservancy, October 1, 2018.

35. See "Shoreline Stabilization: Protecting Our Fragile Ecosystem," in "Changing Coastline: As Impacts from a Sea Level Rise Loom," onehundredmiles.org /changing-coastline.

36. Risse interview.

37. Personal interview with Jesse Petrea, October 17, 2018. Personal interview with Megan Desrosiers, October 25, 2018.

38. Shana Jones interview; personal interview with Christi Lambert, Nature Conservancy Coastal Division office, November 2, 2018.

39. Mary Landers, "Georgia Environmental Agency Eases Marsh Protection Rule," *Savannah Morning News*, April 22, 2014.

40. Ibid.

41. Marland interview, October 20, 2018.

42. *Atlanta Constitution*, March 30, 2015.

43. Petrea interview; personal interview with Rep. Jeff Jones, October 26, 2018.

44. "The Restoration of Coastal Marsh Buffers," Georgia Conservancy website, georgiaconservancy.org/marshbuffers.

45. Personal interview with Bill Sapp, October 16, 2018.

46. Desrosiers interview.

47. The link to the 2015 Strategic Plan is near the bottom of the page at onehundredmiles.org/coastal-vision-2050.

48. Personal interview with former Rep. Dean Auten, April 12, 2018.

49. Petrea interview.

50. Mary Landers, "Coastal Scientists Draw a Line in the Sand After New Shore Protection Act Passes House," *Savannah Morning News*, March 4, 2017; Jackson interview.

51. Personal interview with Mark Ressi, October 16, 2018.

52. David Kyler, "Georgians Deserve Better on Shoreline Protection," *Savannah Morning News*, April 15, 2019.

53. Petrea interview.

54. Search by year and bill number for the language and bills at the Georgia General Assembly website, www.legis.ga.gov/legislation.

55. Personal interview with Neill Herring, October 24, 2018.

56. *Brunswick News*, June 7 and October 18, 2018.

57. Observations of the author who followed the committee discussion.

58. Personal interview with Rep. Don Hogan, March 27, 2019.

59. Webcast video made at Moon River Brewing Company, *Savannah Morning News* Facebook page, April 24, 2019, www.facebook.com/savannahnow/videos /283846149218338.

60. Ibid.; Kyler, "Georgians Deserve Better."

61. Personal interview with Debbie Buckner, January 19, 2019.

CHAPTER 13. HOPE FOR THE FUTURE AND A COMMENTARY

1. See Southeast Conservation Adaptation Strategy website, secassoutheast.org, for more information.

2. See p. 263, Altamaha Land Preservation History, map by Jason Lee, earth ecologist, with Eamonn Leonard, DNR Coastal Division, Brunswick, Ga; personal interview with Jason Lee, September 25, 2018; Dan Chapman July 12, 2017, articles "The Military Embraces Conservation" and "A Gem for Hunters and Hikers Alike" on the U.S. Fish and Wildlife Service website, at https://www.fws.gov/southeast/.

3. Jennifer Brett, "Michael Marks a New Kind of Storm in Georgia," *Atlanta Constitution*, October 21, 2018.

4. Greg Bluestein, "Climate Change Barges into Governor's Race," *Atlanta Constitution*, October 21, 2013.

5. "State Wildlife Action Plan," 164, at Georgia DNR Wildlife Resources Division website, https://georgiawildlife.com/WildlifeActionPlan.

6. See p. 148 map by Dr. John Hoyt, geologist, UGAMI, in Maney, Marland, and West, *Future of the Marshlands*.

7. Lee interview, September 25, 2018.

8. Chapman, "Gem for Hunters and Hikers."

9. Charles H. McMillan III to Holly Ross, U.S. Corps of Engineers, August 29, 2019, in possession of the author.

10. Terry Dickson, "Georgia Now Protects 165,000 Acres Along the Altamaha River, Has Plans for More," *Florida Times-Union*, October 19, 2017; Jason Lee to the author, e-mail October 19, 2018.

11. Boyd, *Slain Wood*, 233.

12. Personal interview with Andrew Schock, October 26, 2018.

13. Personal interview with David Pope, executive director of the St. Simons Land Trust and former director of the Southeast Environmental Law Center, October 17, 2018.

14. Ibid.

15. St. Simons Land Trust website, www.sslt.org.

16. Dan Chapman, "Many Partners Work Together to Protect 'the Amazon of the South' for Generations to Come" (July 12, 2017), and "Local Landowner Fights for the Altamaha" (July 12, 2017), U.S. Fish and Wildlife Service website, https://www.fws.gov/southeast/.

17. Press release, WestRock Shared Services, June 28, 2018; Landvest.com; personal interview with Ashby Worley, October 5, 2018; personal interview with Christi Lambert, Nature Conservancy, November 2, 2018. WestRock succeeded the Mead Corporation, which had family connections to Bill Jones through his wife and was part of the partnership that brought Brunswick Pulp and Paper to the city of Brunswick.

18. Jason Lee interview, June 25, 2019.

19. Christi Lambert interview; Jason Lee to the author, e-mail November 26, 2018; Jason Lee interview, June 6, 2019.

20. See the Georgia General Assembly website, www.legis.ga.gov, for the full text of the bill.

21. "UGA Marine Extension First Oyster Hatchery," UGA Today, December 15,

2015, news.uga.edu/uga-marine-extension-first-oyster-hatchery; personal interview with Mark Risse, October 16, 2018.

22. Personal interview with Jeff Jones, October 26, 2018.

23. Jeff Jones interview, March 20, 2019.

24. Risse interview.

25. Georgia Coast Collaborative, "2017 Progress Report," March 30, 2018, One Hundred Miles website, http://www.onehundredmiles.org/wp-content /uploads/2017/05/GCC-2017-Progress-Report-PDF.pdf.

26. Personal observations of the author on April 2, 2019, the last night of the 2019 session; Georgia Conservancy, 2019 Legislative Session Recap at www.georgi-aconservancy.org/advocacy/update; personal interview with Leah Dixon, April 2, 2019.

27. Maya T. Prabhu, "Tensions Mount Over Spaceport," *Atlanta Journal-Constitution*, June 17, 2018; Maya T. Prabhu, "Residents Split on Coastal Spaceport" *Atlanta Journal-Constitution*, April 20, 2018.

28. Prabhu, "Tensions Mount Over Spaceport."

29. "Camden County Spaceport," Georgia Conservancy website, June 12, 2018, www.georgiaconservancy.org/spaceport.

30. Dan Chapman, "Battle Brewing Over Cumberland Proposal," *Atlanta Journal-Constitution*, December 10, 2016.

31. "The Rezoning of Private Property on Cumberland Island National Seashore," Georgia Conservancy website, www.georgiaconservancy.org/coast/cumberland/zoning.

32. Mary Landers, "Cumberland Island Development Talks Continue in Private," *Savannah Morning News*, September 19, 2018.

33. Personal interview with Scott Stephens, May 1, 2019.

34. The video is posted at https://www.youtube.com/watch?v=yAWNI1hknPo.

35. Personal interview with Hutton Brown, May 28, 2019. Personal interview with Jen Hilburn, February 15, 2019. See www.altmahariverkeeper.org for video on this problem and an available solution.

36. Wes Wolfe, "'Dirty Dozen' List Hits Rayonier AM, Sea Island, Spaceport," *Brunswick News*, November 14, 2018.

37. Hilburn interview.

38. "Seismic Testing and Offshore Drilling & Gas Exploration," Georgia Conservancy website, www.georgiaconservancy.org/offshore-drilling.

39. For resolutions by number see the Georgia General Assembly website, www .legis.ga.org, which provides all versions of the resolution and the legislative history.

40. Mary Landers, "Bipartisan Group of Coastal Georgia Lawmakers Leading Charge Against Offshore Drilling," *Savannah Morning News*, February 2, 2018.

41. Personal interview with Neill Herring, October 24, 2018.

42. Tybee Island Marine Science Center to the author, e-mail October 10, 2018. Rachel Flora, "Don't Drill GA," Connect Savannah, October 17, 2018.

43. For a final draft of the resolution, see HR 48 at ga.legis.gov.

44. Personal interview with Fred Marland, October 24, 2018.

45. Georgia Climate Project, "Georgia Climate Research Roadmap," https://roadmap.georgiaclimateproject.org; Rudd et al., "Climate Research Priorities."

46. Georgia Climate Project website, www.georgiaclimateproject.org.

47. Allitt, *Climate of Crisis*, 337.

Bibliography

PERSONAL INTERVIEWS

Douglas Adams, April 13 and July 19, 2018

Douglas Adams and Ronald Adams Jr., July 20, 2018

Dr. Clark Alexander, October 8, 2018

Rep. Dean Auten, March 12 and April 12, 2018

Judith and Tommy Bagby, September 5, 2018

Thomas Boller, April 4, 2018

Bill Brown, December 11, 2017

Hutton Brown, May 28, 2019

Rep. Debbie Buckner, January 19, 2019

Dan Chapman, October 2, 2018

Jingle Davis, February 6 and June 23, 2018

Megan Desrosiers, October 25 and December 10, 2018

Albert Fendig III, May 16, 2018

Brian Foster, October 8, 2018

Michael Hall, April 13, 2018

Wallace Harrell Sr., June 1, 2018

Duane Harris, July 13, 2018

Michael and Douglas Harris, November 7, 2017

Rep. Peyton S. Hawes Jr., June 23, 2017

Neill Herring, March 9, 2017, and October 24, 2018

Jen Hilburn, February 15, 2019

Rep. Don Hogan, March 27, 2019

James Holland, December 17, 2017

Sen. George Hooks, September 28, 2017

Dr. Chester Jackson, October 16, 2018

Steven Johnson, April 20, 2018

Rep. Jeff Jones, October 26, 2018, and March 20, 2019

Rep. Milton Jones, August 20, 2018

Shana Jones, November 1, 2018

William "Bill" Jones III, April 13, 2018

Bob Kerr, August 7, 2017, and November 3, 2018

Elizabeth Kramer, December 10, 2018

David Kyler, October 25, 2017

Chris Lambert, February 23, 2018

Christi Lambert, November 2, 2018

Buff Leavy, April 13, 2018

Leonard Ledbetter, April 26 and May 15, 2018

Jason Lee, March 14, 2018; September 25, 2018; June 6 and 25, 2019

Rep. Elliott H. Levitas, August 5, 2017

Thomas Lowndes, March 2, 2018

Thomas Jackson McCollough Jr., February 22, 2018

Charles McMillan, October 1, 2018

Dr. Fred Marland, February 8, 2017; August 7 and 8, 2017; August 25, 2017; November 8, 2017; February 6, 2018; March 12, 2018; May 5, 2018; July 5, 2018; July 21, 2018; October 22, 2018; October 24, 2018; April 26, 2019; September 9, 2019

Shirley Miller, July 5, 2017

Thornton Morris, July 23, 2018; October 8 and 13, 2018

Jim Morrison, August 9, 2017, and March 7, 2018

Joyce Murlless, April 16, 2018

Hans Neuhauser, November 15, 2016, and March 9, 2018

Jesse Petrea, October 17, 2018

David Pope, October 18, 2018

Harold Reheis, April 26, 2018

Dr. Jim Richardson, April 3,2018

Dr. Mark Risse, October 16, 2018

Sen. Bobby Rowan, April 4 and November 18, 2018

Doug Samson, October 10, 2018

Molly Samuel, September 26, 2018

Bill Sapp, October 16 and December 10, 2018

Andrew Schock, October 26, 2018

Charles Seabrook, October 29, 2018

Rep. Lillou Smith, March 13, 2018

Scott Stephens, May 1, 2019

Joseph Tanner, June 23, 2017

Merry Tipton, March 13, 2018
Thomas Whelchel, March 8, 2018
Woody Woodside, December 12, 2017
Ashley Worley, October 5, 2018
Dr. Charles Yarn, December 6, 2017

VIDEOS

Hoffman, Susan, writer. *Speaker of the House: The Thomas B. Murphy Story.* Video documentary. Aired March 17, 2002, on Georgia Public Television, a division of Georgia Public Broadcasting. 58:30 min.

Reid Harris, Elliott Levitas, and Milton Jones. *Reflections on Georgia Politics*, ROGP 042, interviews by Bob Short, Richard B. Russell Library for Political Research and Studies, Special Collections Libraries, University of Georgia Libraries, Athens.

Thomas B. Murphy, Carl Sanders, Lester Maddox. Georgia State Government Documentation Project, Special Collections and Archives, Georgia State University Library, Atlanta.

ARCHIVAL COLLECTIONS AND PERSONAL PAPERS

Cumberland Island National Seashore Archives, St. Mary's, Ga.

Georgia Archives, Morrow

Georgia Natural Areas Council Papers, State Parks and Historical Sites (of the Georgia Department of Natural Resources), Georgia Natural Areas Council Subject Files, RG 30-8-43. Cited in the notes as GNAC Papers.

Carnegie Family Trust, RG 048-01-001

Georgia Historical Society, Savannah

Buddy Sullivan Papers

R. S. Howard Papers (MS 4900)

Sea Island Company Papers

Hargrett Rare Book and Manuscript Library, University of Georgia Libraries

Andrew H. Sparks Papers

Georgia Sierra Club Records

Richard B. Russell Library for Political Research and Studies, Special Collections Library, University of Georgia Libraries

Eugene P. Odum Papers
Reid W. Harris Papers
E. Roy Lambert Papers
Arthur Bolton Papers
Fred Marland unprocessed papers

Robert W. Woodruff Library, Special Collections Department, Emory University

James A. Mackay Papers
Joyce Blackburn Papers

Papers in Possession of the Author

Personal papers of Frederick C. Marland

NEWSPAPERS AND PERIODICALS

Atlanta (Ga.) Journal
Atlanta (Ga.) Constitution
Atlanta Journal and Constitution Magazine
Brunswick (Ga.) News
Columbus (Ga.) Ledger Enquirer
Connect Savannah
Florida Times-Union
Georgia Game and Fish
Jacksonville Daily News
New York Times
Red and Black (UGA)
Savannah (Ga.) Morning News
Savannah (Ga.) Evening News

ARTICLES

Cobb, James C. "Beyond Planters and Industrialists: A New Perspective on the New South." *Journal of Southern History* 54, no. 1 (February 1988): 45–68.

Elmore, Bartow J. "Roundup from the Ground Up: A Supply-Side Story of the World's Most Widely Used Herbicide." *Agricultural History*, winter 2019, 104–24.

Emerson, Bo. "How Much Could It Cost to Protect Our Coastline?" *Atlanta Journal and Constitution Magazine*, June 23, 2019.

Jones, Hunter. "How Planning for Sea Level Rise Creates Flood Insurance Reductions: The Georgia Context." *Grant Law and Policy Journal* 7, no. 1 (2016).

Kolbert, Elizabeth. "The Control of Nature Under Water: Can Engineering Save Louisiana's Disappearing Coast?" *New Yorker*, April 1, 2019, 32–95.

Lenz, Richard. "Jane Yarn: The Grand Dame of Conservation." *Southern Wildlife* 1, no. 1 (1966): 23–30. Nature Conservancy records, CONS 245, Conservancy Collection, Denver Public Library.

Morris, Christopher. "A More Southern Environmental History." *Journal of Southern History* 75, no. 3 (August 2009): 581–98.

Rome, Adam W. "Give the Earth a Chance: The Environmental Movement and the Sixties." *Journal of American History* 90, no 2 (September 2003): 525–54.

Rudd, Murray A., et al. (41 authors). "Climate Research Priorities for Policy-makers, Practitioners, and Scientists in Georgia." *Environmental Management* 62, no. 2 (August 2018).

Sparks, Andrew. "Cumberland Will Never Be the Same Again." *Atlanta Journal and Constitution Magazine*, March 9, 1969.

———. "A Day in the Life of Cumberland Island." *Atlanta Journal and Constitution Magazine*, January 1, 1970.

———. "Georgia's Wild Coast . . . Can It Be Saved?" *Atlanta Journal and Constitution Magazine*, November 24, 1968.

———. "Housewife Saves an Island." *Atlanta Journal and Constitution Magazine*, November 2, 1969.

———. "Marshes of McIntosh." *Atlanta Journal and Constitution Magazine*, July 20, 1969, 19.

———. "A Tide of Change." *Atlanta Journal and Constitution Magazine*, March 9, 1969.

Teal, John M. "Energy Flow in the Salt Marsh System of Georgia." *Ecology* 43, no. 4 (1962): 614–24.

Worley, Sam. "Georgia's Vanishing Coast: With Stronger Storms, Higher Tides, and Rising Sea Levels, How High Will the Water Go?" *Atlanta* (July 5, 2018).

Yarn, Jane Hurt. "A New Challenge," *Garden Gate*, November–December 1968, 12–13.

———. "One Message May Change the Vote." *Garden Gate*, January–February 1970.

───. "What Your Club Can Do for Environmental Education." *Garden Gate*, March–April 1970, 16–17.

BOOKS

Allitt, Patrick. *A Climate of Crisis: America in the Age of Environmentalism.* New York: Penguin Press, 2014.

Bartley, Numan V. *From Thurmond to Wallace; Political Tendencies in Georgia, 1948–1968.* Baltimore, Md.: Johns Hopkins University Press, 1970.

───, and Hugh D. Graham. *Southern Politics and the Second Reconstruction.* Baltimore, Md.: Johns Hopkins University Press, 1975.

Berendt, John. *Midnight in the Garden of Good and Evil.* New York: Random House, 1994.

Blackburn, Joyce. *The Earth Is the Lord's?* Waco, Tex.: World Books, 1975.

Bowdoin, William R. *Georgia's Third Force.* Atlanta: Foote and Davis, 1968.

Boyd, William. *The Slain Wood: Papermaking and the Environmental Consequences in the South.* Baltimore, Md.: Johns Hopkins University Press, 2015.

Bullard, Mary R. *Cumberland Island: A History.* Athens: University of Georgia Press, 2005.

Bullock, Charles S., III, Scott E. Buchannan, and Ronald Keith Gaddie. *The Three Governors Controversy: Skullduggery, Machinations, and the Decline of Georgia's Progressive Politics.* Athens: University of Georgia Press, 2015.

Carson, Rachel. *Silent Spring.* Boston: Houghton Mifflin, 1962.

Claxton, Robert H. *The History of the Georgia Conservancy 1967–1981.* Atlanta: Georgia Conservancy, 1985.

Coleman, Kenneth, ed. *A History of Georgia.* Athens: University of Georgia Press, 1977.

Cook, James F. *Carl Sanders: Spokesman for the New South.* Macon, Ga.: Mercer University Press, 1994

Cowdrey, Albert E. *This Land, This South: An Environmental History.* Lexington: University Press of Kentucky, 1996.

Craige, Betty Jean. *Eugene Odum: Ecosystem Ecologist and Environmentalist.* Athens: University of Georgia Press, 2001.

Davis, Jingle. *Island Passages: An Illustrated History of Jekyll Island, Georgia.* Photographs by Benjamin Galland. Athens: University of Georgia Press, 2016.

───. *Island Time: An Illustrated History of St. Simons Island, Georgia.* Photographs by Benjamin Galland. Athens: University of Georgia Press, 2013.

Dilsaver, Larry. *Cumberland Island National Seashore: A History of Conservation Conflict.* Charlottesville, Va.: University of Virginia Press, 2004.

Drake, Brian Allen. *Loving Nature, Fearing the State: Environmentalism and Antigovernment Politics before Reagan.* Seattle: University of Washington Press, 2013.

Fallows, James M. *The Water Lords: Ralph Nader's Study Group Report on Industry and Environmental Crisis in Savannah, Georgia.* New York: Grossman, 1971.

Fancher, Betsy. *The Lost Legacy of Georgia's Golden Isles.* Garden City, N.Y.: Doubleday, 1971.

Ferguson, Cody. *This Is Our Land: Grassroots Environmentalism in the Late Twentieth Century.* New Brunswick, N.J.: Rutgers University Press, 2015.

Fraser, Walter, Jr. *Lowcountry Hurricanes: Three Centuries of Storms at Sea and Ashore.* Athens: University of Georgia Press, 2006.

Galphin, Bruce. *The Riddle of Lester Maddox.* Atlanta: Camelot Publishing, 1968.

Glynn High Tide. Vol 1, no. 1. Brunswick, Ga.: Senior Class, 1948.

Gottlieb, Robert. *Forcing the Spring: The Transformation of the American Environmental Movement.* Washington, D.C.: Island Press 1993.

Graves, Joe. *Cumberland Island Saved: How the Carnegies Helped Preserve a National Treasure.* Lexington, Ky.: Gravesend, 2009.

Halfacre, Angela. *A Delicate Balance: Constructing a Conservation Culture in the South Carolina Low Country.* Columbia: University of South Carolina Press, 2012.

Haq, Gary, and Alistair Paul. *Environmentalism since 1945.* London: Routledge, 2012.

Harris, Reid W. *And the Coastlands Wait: How a Small Group of Legislators, Scientists and Concerned Citizens Helped Save 500,000 Acres of the World's Most Productive Area.* [St. Simons Island, Ga.]: self-published, 2008.

Hawkins, Paul, ed. *Drawdown: The Most Comprehensive Plan Ever to Reverse Global Warming.* London: Penguin Books, 2017.

Hays, Samuel P. *Conservation and the Gospel of Efficiency: The Progressive Conservation Movement, 1890–1920.* Cambridge, Mass.: Harvard University Press, 1959.

———, in collaboration with Barbara D. Hays. *Beauty, Health, and Permanence: Environmental Politics in the United States, 1955–1985.* New York: Cambridge University Press, 1987.

Henderson, Harold Paulk. *The Politics of Change in Georgia: A Political Biography of Ellis Arnall.* Athens: University of Georgia Press, 1991.

———, and Gary L. Roberts, eds. *Georgia Governors in an Age of Change: From Ellis Arnall to George Busbee.* Athens: University of Georgia Press, 2007.

Howard, Robert M., Arnold Fleischmann, and Richard N. Engstrom. *Politics in Georgia.* Athens: University of Georgia Press, 2017.

Hyatt, Richard. *Mr. Speaker: The Biography of Tom Murphy.* Macon, Ga.: Mercer University Press, 1999.

———. *Zell: The Governor Who Gave Georgia Hope.* Macon, Ga.: Mercer University Press, 1997.

Kelly, V. E. *A Short History of Skidaway Island.* Savannah: V. E. Kelly and the Branigar Organization, 1994.

Key, V. O., Jr., with the assistance of Alexander Heard. *Southern Politics in State and Nation.* New York: Alfred A. Knopf, 1949.

Maddox, Lester. *Addresses and Public Papers of Lester Garfield Maddox.* Edited by Frank Daniel. Georgia Department of Archives and History, 1971.

———. *Speaking Out: The Autobiography of Lester Garfield Maddox.* Garden City, N.Y.: Doubleday, 1975.

Martin, Harold. *This Happy Isle: The Story of Sea Island and the Cloister.* Sea Island, Ga.: Sea Island Co., 1978.

McPhee, John. *Encounters with the Archdruid.* New York: Farrar, Straus, and Giroux, 1971.

Muir, John. *A Thousand-Mile Walk to the Gulf.* Houghton Mifflin, 1916.

Nelson, Megan Kate. *Trembling Earth: The Cultural History of the Okefenokee Swamp.* Athens: University of Georgia Press, 2009.

Newfont, Kathryn. *Blue Ridge Commons: Environmental Activism and Forest History in Western North Carolina.* Athens: University of Georgia Press, 2012.

Pearce, Mallory. *The Low Country, A Naturalist's Field Guide to Coastal Georgia, the Carolinas, and North Florida.* St. Simons Island: Salt Marsh Press, 2010.

Pilkey, Orrin, and Rob Young. *The Rising Sea.* Washington, D.C.: Island Press/ Shearwater Press, 2009.

Price, Eugenia. *St. Simons Memoir: The Personal Story of Finding the Island and Writing the St. Simons Trilogy of Novels.* Philadelphia: J. B. Lippincott, 1978.

Ray, Janisse. *Drifting into Darien: A Personal and Natural History of the Altamaha River.* Athens: University of Georgia Press, 2011.

———. *Ecology of a Cracker Childhood.* Minneapolis: Milkweed Editions, 1999.

Rome, Adam. *The Genius of Earth Day: How a 1970 Teach-In Unexpectedly Made the First Green Generation*. New York: Hill and Wang, 2014.

Sanders, Carl. *Addresses and Public Papers of Carl Edward Sanders, Governor of Georgia, 1963–1967*. Edited by Frank Daniel. Atlanta: B. W. Fortson and Georgia Department of Archives and History, 1968.

Seabrook, Charles. *The World of the Salt Marsh*. Athens: University of Georgia Press, 2012.

Sheer, Evelyn B. *Marsh Mud and Mummichogs: An Intimate Natural History of Coastal Georgia*. Athens: University of Georgia Press, 2015.

Short, Bob. *Everything Is Pickrick: The Life of Lester Maddox*. Macon, Ga.: Mercer University Press, 1999.

Stewart, Mart A. *"What Nature Suffers to Groe": Life, Labor, and Landscape on the Georgia Coast, 1680–1920*. Athens: University of Georgia Press. 2002.

Sullivan, Buddy. *Sapelo: A History*. Darien: Georgia Department of Natural Resources Wildlife Resources Division, 2010.

———. *The First Conservationists? Northern Money and Lowcountry Georgia, 1866–1930*. Self-published, 2016.

Sutter, Paul, and Christopher J. Manganiello, eds. *Environmental History and the American South: A Reader*. Athens: University of Georgia Press, 2009.

Sutter, Paul, and Paul M. Pressly, eds. *Coastal Nature, Coastal Culture: Environmental Histories of the Georgia Coast*. Athens: University of Georgia Press, 2018.

Teal, John, and Mildred Teal. *The Life and Death of the Salt Marsh*. Boston: Little, Brown, 1969.

Way, Albert G. *Conserving Southern Longleaf: Herbert Stoddard and the Rise of Ecological Land Management*. Athens: University of Georgia Press, 2011.

Wharton, Charles H. *The Natural Environment of Georgia*. Atlanta: Georgia Department of Natural Resources, 1978.

Worster, David. *Nature's Economy: The Roots of Ecology*. San Francisco: Sierra Club Books, 1977.

THESES AND DISSERTATIONS

Addes, Danyel Goldbarten. "The Length, Breadth, and Sweep of Marshland Protection in Georgia: Protection Afforded by Georgia's Coastal Marshlands Protection Act and Coastal Nonpoint Source Program." MS thesis, University of Georgia, 2012.

Bolster, Paul. "Civil Rights Protests in Twentieth Century Georgia." PhD dissertation, University of Georgia, 1971.

Lefkoff, Merle Schlesinger. "The Voluntary Citizens' Group as a Public Policy Alternative to the Political Party: A Case Study of the Georgia Conservancy." PhD dissertation, Emory University, 1975.

REPORTS AND OTHER SOURCES

Acts and Resolutions of the General Assembly of the State of Georgia. 1966, 1968, 1969–70. RG 37-1-1, Georgia Archives, Morrow, Ga.

Bills and Resolutions (House, Senate). 1969–70, RG 037-01-001, Georgia Archives, Morrow, Ga.

Frankson, R., K. Kunkel, L. Stevens, B. Stewart, W. Sweet, and B. Murphey. *2017: Georgia State Climate Summary.* NOAA Technical Report NESDIS 149-GA, 2017.

Georgia Laws. 1884–85, 1945, 1957.

Georgia's Health (newsletter, Georgia Department of Public Health) 50, no. 2 (February 1970): 2.

Georgia's Official and Statistical Register, 1969–70. Office of the Secretary of State.

Georgia Women of Achievement Honorees. *Jane Hurt Yarn, 1924–1995.*

House Standing Committee Minute Books 1969. RG 032-08-064, RCB 3538, Georgia Archives, Morrow.

Journal of the House. 1967, 1969. Available at the Georgia Archives, Morrow, on open shelves, and also at the Georgia Capitol, Atlanta.

Kundell, James E., and Alex Little. *Management of Georgia's Marshlands Under the Coastal Marshlands Protection Act of 1970.* Athens: Carl Vinson Institute of Government, University of Georgia. Reid Harris Papers.

Maney, David S., Frederick C. Marland, and Clifford B. West, eds. *The Future of the Marshlands and Sea Islands of Georgia: A Record of a Conference Convened by the Georgia Natural Areas Council and the Coastal Area Planning and Development Commission.* Brunswick, Ga.: Coastal Area Planning & Development Commission, 1970, cited in notes as Conference on the Future of the Marshlands.

The National Estuarine Pollution Study. Report of the Secretary of the Interior to the United States Congress, March 25, 1970.

"Position Paper Relating to the Georgia Coastal Marshlands." March 17, 1970, Attorney General Arthur K. Bolton.

Proceedings of the 2017 Georgia Water Resources Conference. April 19–20, 2017, University of Georgia.

Report of the Georgia Coastal Islands Study Committee (HR 82-219). January 1970, Summary of Committee Reports 1969–1972, acc. no. 1997-2525A, 37-8-35, Georgia Archives; cited in notes as Report of the Coastal Islands Study Committee. See also Minority Report of Sen. Roscoe Dean.

Senate Bills. 1969–70. Available at the Georgia Archives, Morrow, and also at the Georgia Capitol, Atlanta.

University System of Georgia Advisory Committee for Mineral Leasing. *Report on Proposed Leasing of State Owned Lands for Phosphate Mining in Chatham County, Georgia.* November 1968. Cited in notes as University System Report on Proposed Leasing. This report is available digitally at https://dlg.usg.edu/.

U.S. Census Bureau. 1950, 1970.

USGCRP. *Impacts, Risks, and Adaptation in the United States: Fourth National Climate Assessment.* Vol. 2. Edited by D. R. Reidmiller, C. W. Avery, D. R. Easterling, K. E. Kunkel, K. L. M. Lewis, T. K. Maycock, and B. C. Stewart. U.S. Global Change Research Program, Washington, D.C., 2018. doi: 10.7930/NCA4.2018.

Index

Candler, Sam: conversations with Brower and Fraser, 25–30, 37; Cumberland and, 178–179; GNAC and, 179, 195; Sierra Club and, 179

Candler family, 141–142, 175–176, 178, 269–270

Carnegie, Lucy, 94, 141–142

Carnegie, Thomas M., 20, 27, 141–142

Carnegie family heirs, and Cumberland, 27, 29, 94, 141–142, 160, 175–176, 178–179, 181, 209, 229, 269, 305n74

Carter, James Earl "Jimmy," 44, 192, 231; election of 1966, 48–51, 61, 64; election of 1970, 207, 226; GNAC board and, 83, 234; Reid Harris and, 237; Lester Maddox and, 235–236; reorganization, 71–72, 226, 232, 233, 234; Jane Yarn and, 234–235

cat clay, 133

Center for a Sustainable Coast, 254–255, 270

Chandler, Rep. Philip, 165, 170–172, 174

Chapman, Don, 243

Charlton County, 260

Chatham County, 154; Kerr-McGee and, 126–128; sea rise and, 244

Chesapeake Bay, 196, 205–206

civil rights movement, 31, 34, 40, 216; civil rights legislation and, 40, 45, 47, 68; election of 1966 and, 52; Write In Georgia, 52

Clean Water Act of 1966, 145, 199

climate change, 259

Climate of Crisis, A (Allitt), 277, 284n37

Cloister, 21, 94, 140–141, 151, 228, 254, 264

Coastal Area Planning and Development Commission, 124, 198. *See also* Maney, Dave

Coastal Islands Study Committee, 136, 155, 181–182, 202–204, 220; Roscoe

Dean, 211; Joseph Fraser, 209; hearings in Atlanta, 206–209, 213; Savannah and, 204; St. Marys and, 203. *See also* Nessmith, Rep. Paul

Coastal Marshlands Protection Act (CMPA), 159–174; in *Georgia Game and Fish*, 201–202; House vote, 183–188, 306n98; introduction and support for, 165; opposition efforts, 176–183; preamble, 163–164; signed into law, 225; to subcommittee, 172, 304n51; substitute, 173–174

—implementation, 226; *Black v. Floyd*, 223; Cumberland Harbor, 224–225; *State v. Ashmore*, 223. *See also* Marshlands Protection Agency

Coffin, Howard, 20–21, 140, 150; sale of Sapelo, 21

Colonel's Island Terminal Port, 93

Conference on the Future of the Marshlands and Islands of Georgia (Conference on the Future), 86, 138–152; CMPA and, 172, 181–182; Kerr-McGee mining and, 108; mentioned, 228, 243, 252

Conservation Fund, 258, 260, 263

Conserving Southern Longleaf (Way), 19

Coolidge, Pres. Calvin, 264

county unit system, 41–43, 48, 64, 68, 190, 192

Crockford, Jack, 71, 104–105, 108, 113, 114, 130, 289n38

Croft, Mayor Ralph, 167

Cumberland Harbour, 224–225

Cumberland Island, 140–143, 154, 160, 165; Carnegie Trust, 94; causeway and, 229; CMPA and, 160, 165, 172–182; Conservation Association and, 178, 209; development and, 175–182, 268–270, 304n64; Island Study Committee, 197, 203, 206–211, 219; National

hurricanes, 15; Florence, 243, 248; Irma, 254, 258; Matthew, 258; Michael, 258–259; response to, by gubernatorial candidates, 258

Interstate 95, 73, 129, 138–140, 153, 227; design, 237; effect of sea rise, 244
Intracoastal Waterway, 6, 265
Irvin, Tommy, 72
island owners, 19–21, 43, 138, 140, 142, 143; Reid Harris and, 160, 174; owners association, 149, 150, 152, 172, 174, 179
Izaac Walton League, 124, 171

Jackson, Chester: coastal erosion and, 244, 253, 255; Tybee Island sea rise maps, 246
Jackson, Sen. Henry M. "Scoop," 228
Jekyll Island, 8, 20, 115, 139, 146; Island Authority, 156, 208, 210–211, 220; Island Club, 20, 141; Water Quality Control Authority meeting in 1968, 161
Johnson, Sen. Leroy, 64
Johnson, Pres. Lyndon, 9, 35, 49, 249
Johnson, Steven: Cumberland proposal and, 80; Earth Day, 225; Kerr-McGee testimony, 122; Scenic Rivers and GNAC, 179; Sierra Club Georgia Group founding, 79–80, 117; testimony for CMPA, 195, 206, 212, 305n77
Jones, Albert "Bill," Jr., 202, 206, 211
Jones, Albert "Bill," Sr., 21, 117, 140, 150–152, 228; Cabin Bluff and, 264
Jones, Rep. Charles, 184–185; final vote and, 219
Jones, Rep. Herb, 172
Jones, Rep. Jeff, 251, 254, 266–267
Jones, Rep. Milton, 55, 58
Jones, Shana, 247

Keating, Larry, 241, 244

Kemp, Gov. Brian, 255, 258–259
Kerr, Sen. Robert, 116
Kerr-McGee, 24, 28, 228, 272; Coastal Marshlands Protection Act and, 205–206; Conference on the Future and, 139, 145, 153–157 passim; Little Tybee Island and, 104, 222, 230–231; mining phosphate, 103–110, 113, 133, 138, 159–160, 168; plan to convert marsh to bulkhead communities, 122; pollution, 199; proposed leasing area, 112; public hearings, 121–131 passim, 133; sale of islands, 224, 230–231; University System Report of Mineral Leasing, 134–137
Key, V. O., 43–44
King, Martin Luther, Jr., 9
King and Spalding, 105, 117, 145, 224; Cumberland Harbor and, 224–225; Rayonier and, 270. See also Gowen, Charles; Kerr-McGee
King's Grants, 12, 95, 145, 162, 223
Kirkland, Leon, 108, 114
Knobloch Family Foundation, 260
Kramer, Elizabeth, 245
Kyler, David, 254–255

Lambert, Rep. Roy, 97; legislative independence, 39, 55–59, 62; Maddox vote, 58; support for CMPA, 165
land acquisition, 149, 163, 173, 257; Egg Island, 150–151; Outdoor Stewardship Fund, 265–266. See also Nature Conservancy
Landscape Architects and Appraisers, 143, 168
Lanier, Sidney, 1, 4, 174, 215
League of Women Voters, 125, 194
Ledbetter, Leonard, 83, 88, 91, 109, 115, 198
Lee, Jason, 259, 265; Altamaha land preservation, 263; coastal geology 2019, 259; Georgia coast protected lands, xii
legislative independence: beginnings of,

marshland value, 123, 126, 239–240; habitat migration and, 259, 260, 265–266, 268

marsh ownership, 145, 160, 162, 302n8; House resolution and, 168; state ownership, 183, 201, 210, 222–223; who owns the marsh?, 171–172, 173, 304n63

Massachusetts, 161–162

Masters, Hugh B., 177

Mather, Mrs. Alan, 125

Matthews, Rep. Dorsey, 165

McGill, Sen. Sam, 216

McIntosh County, 139, 184

McMasters, Philip B., 154

McNicol, John, 167

McPhee, John, 25–30, 37

Mellinger, Marie, 169

Mellon, Paul, 228

Miller, Shirley, 60, 66

Miller, Zell: as lieutenant governor, 233; Lester Maddox and, 66, 72, 82; purchase of Little Tybee and, 231; signing of CMPA and, 220–222

Mineral Leasing Commission, 75; Kerr-McGee and, 103, 105, 106, 113, 114

Mississippi River, 248

Monkey Wrench Gang, The (Abbey), 6

Moon River, 153

Morgan, J. P., 20

Morris, Charles, 114

Morris, Thornton, 178, 180–181, 305n74; Carnegie heirs and, 202–203, 209–211, 229

Morrison, Jim: Game and Fish Commission, 71, 108–109, 113, 114, 162; Kerr-McGee testimony and, 121–122, 125, 129; support for CMPA, 162–163, 197, 201–202, 222

Muir, John, 3–4

Murlless, Joyce, 195

Murlless, Richard, 80, 196

Murphy, Reginald, 219

Murphy, Rep. Thomas B: George Bagby and, 233; legislative independence and, 53, 55, 56, 58; as Maddox floor leader, 58, 63–66; Carl Sanders and, 53; as Speaker Pro Tem, 217–218; vote on CMPA, 186, 192, 218

Musgrave, Mary, 260

National Center for Atmospheric Research, 258

National Climate Assessment, 241, 244

National Estuarine Pollution Study, 161

National Estuarine Reserve, 236

National Oceanic and Atmospheric Administration (NOAA), 241, 244, 314nm18

National Park Service, 208, 229

National Seashore, 208, 210

Native Americans, 12, 15, 17; Timucua, 260

Nature Conservancy: Altamaha River land preservation, 258, 264; Cabin Bluff, 264–265; Egg Island, 150–151, 257; Little Tybee and Cabbage Islands, 231; Ossabaw Island, 230; Sansavilla Plantation, 260; sea level rise and, 245, 249–250; use of environmental easements and, 138, 141, 143, 149–152; Wassaw Island, 154–157; Wolf Island, 196, 257

Nature's Economy (Worster), 33

Nelms, Doris, 95, 102

NeSmith, Dink, 264

Nesmith, Jeff, 198, 200–201

Nessmith, Rep. Paul: Coastal Islands Study Committee, 154, 181, 201–211 passim, 275; support for CMPA 165, 167–168, 172–174, 181–182; Surface Mining Act, 99–100; Wassaw Island and, 154–155, 157

New Deal, 43, 49, 50

New Orleans, 248

New Jersey coastal development, 105, 139, 161

Niles, Mrs. George, 151

Nixon, Pres. Richard, 35, 72, 270

Noble, Edwin J., 20, 141

nonpoint source pollution, 225

North Carolina, and hurricanes, 243, 248

northern industrialists, 15–17, 23; in Thomasville, 19

Nunn, Sen. Sam, 186

Ocean Science Center of the Atlantic, 135, 137, 157, 182–183, 208, 215, 306n88. *See also* Skidaway Island: Institute of Oceanography

Oconee River, 257

Odum, Eugene, 72, 92; Conference on the Future, 143, 146–150, 153, 252, 298n7; Department of Ecology, 221–226; Earth Day, 225; *Fundamentals of Ecology*, 33, 77; Kerr-NcGee and, 105, 115–116; Sapelo and UGAMI, 32–33, 77–79; School of Ecology, 79; support for CMPA, 170, 174, 182, 194–195, 201, 207–208, 210, 214; University System Report on Mining, 127, 130–137, 297n41, 298n44

Odum, Howard, 33, 77

Ogeechee River, 141, 257

Oglethorpe, James, and the Georgia Trustees, 12–16, 24

oil and gas offshore exploration, 271–273; House Resolution 48 against, 271, 273, 275; Brian Kemp and, 273

Okefenokee Swamp: timber harvest, 17–18; Trail Ridge, 147; Twin Pines mining threat, 260; Wildlife Action Plan, 259, 262

Oklahoma, 116, 231

One Hundred Miles, 251–252, 254; oil and gas and, 273

Ossabaw Island, 20, 105, 117, 141–143, 194, 203–204, 207, 309n50; Heritage Preserve, 23; Ossabaw Island Foundation, 230; sale of, 229–230. *See also* West, Eleanor Torrey "Sandy"

Outdoor Stewardship Fund, 262, 265–266, 317n20

overburden, 132, 133

oysters, 126, 135, 150, 191, 200; farming legislation and, 266–267

Palmer, Rep. Thomas, 126

Parsons, George, 19, 141, 152

Paulding County, 67, 70

Paulson, Hank and Wendy, 264

Perkins, Coley, 203

Petrea, Rep. Jesse: marsh setbacks, 250–251; Shore Protection Act, 252–253

phosphate mining, 99–104, 119; Act of 1885, 159; Roundup®, 230–231

Pickrick Cafeteria, 45–47. *See also* Maddox, Gov. Lester

Pilkey, Orrin, 241–242

Planning and Conservation League, 197, 214

Price, Eugenia, 3; support for CMPA, 169–170, 175–178, 180, 184, 214

private property, 131, 167–170, 184, 187; impact of sea rise, 239, 245–256; opposition to CMPA, 172–173, 181, 207, 208, 211, 224, 239–240; rights with Spaceport, 269

public hearings, 11, 62, 107; Coastal Islands Study Committee, 203, 204, 206–209; House, on CMPA 165–172; on Kerr-McGee, 121–131, 164; need for, 256, 274; requirement of, 164–165, 228; Senate, on CMPA, 196, 204–206, 212–213

Pulitzer, Joseph, 20

pulp industries, 21–24, 73, 199–200, 243, 270–271

St. Johns River, 26

St. Marys, 167, 175, 182, 224; opposition to oil and gas exploration, 273; Senate hearing, 203

St. Marys River, 16; Okefenokee and, 17

Stoddard, Steven, 228

St. Simons Island: Canon's Point Preserve, 249, 264; Reid Harris and, 7, 95, 98, 237–238; Don Hogan, 255; Johnson Rocks, 249; Land Trust and, 249, 264; Eugenia Price, 169, 214; sea rise mitigation, 249; the Spit, 268; mentioned, 8, 16, 18, 140, 143, 151

Stuckey, Rep. William, 208, 228–229, 270

Student Nonviolent Coordinating Committee (SNCC), 216

Students from UGA, 159, 179, 195–196, 198

study committees: House, 181, 198, 203, 204, 206–209; Senate, 193, 196, 204–206, 212–213; Surface Mining Act, 100, 109, 146; value of, 25

Surface Mining Act, 99–101, 130, 146

Suwanee Canal Company, 17

Sweetwater Creek, 81, 144

Talmadge, Eugene, 48, 50, 121, 303n44

Talmadge Faction, 41, 42, 43, 67; anti-Talmadge, 40, 48; election of 1966, 48–51, 121

Tanner, Joe, 227; as DNR Commissioner, 232; Ossabaw and, 229–230

Taylor, Mayor William H., 128

Teal, John: *Life and Death of the Salt Marsh* (with Mildred), 5, 161, 205; Salt Marsh Conference, 33, 78, 284n25, 289n2

Thomas and Hutton, 122, 131

Thompson, Gov. M. E., 67

Thousand-Mile Walk to the Gulf, A (Muir), 3–4

tides, 2; king tides, 239, 244, 253

timber capitalists, 15–18

Torrey, Bill, 117

tourism, 18–19, 25, 140, 143; effect of oil exploration and drilling on, 272–273; value of coastland to, 240, 255, 277. *See also* Fraser, Charles

Trail Ridge, 147, 259–260

Trump, Pres. Donald J., 272

Tuten, Rep. Jim, 229

Twitty, Frank, 42

Tybee Island, 8, 19, 140, 229; causeway, 239, 247; "Don't Drill GA," 272; hotels on coast, 19; Kerr-McGee and, 140; sea rise at, 244; sea rise mitigation, 245–247; shrimp, 267; Paul Wolfe and, 247, 249

Tybee Island Marine Science Center, 272

UGA Marine Institute (UGAMI), 5, 32, 72; Conference on the Future and, 139, 145–147, 156, 299n16; continuing research, 236; Kerr-McGee and, 77, 110, 126, 132, 135; reduced role of, 236; reorganization, 228; support for CMPA, 163, 170, 204–206, 215. *See also* Reynolds, R. J., II

UGA Natural Resources and Spatial Analysis Laboratory, 245

UGA Sea Grant and Marine Extension Service, 241, 244–245

Underwood, Judge John W., 128

Unicoi State Park, 175

Union Camp, 22, 89, 92, 200, 308n37; Skidaway Island and, 153, 199–200, 243

universities and colleges: Duke University, 241–242; Earth Day at, 225–226; Emory University, 225; Georgia Institute of Technology, 225, 241, 244; Georgia

Southern University, 226, 244, 255; Georgia State University, 183, 226; University of West Georgia, 52, 67, 110, 226. *See also* Georgia Natural Areas Council; Wharton, Charles

University of Georgia: Carl Vinson Institute of Government, 245, 246, 256; Sea Grant and Marine Extension Service, 266; Skidaway Institute of Oceanography, 232, 236; Zoology Department and School of Ecology, 77–79. *See also* Odum, Eugene; Scott, Don; UGA Marine Institute

University System of Georgia, 63, 74; Kerr-McGee plan to convert marsh to bulkhead communities, 122; Kerr-McGee proposed leasing area, 112; Report on Mineral Leasing, 107, 120, 127, 131–137, 145, 181, 198, 297n41; scientists to schools, 236; sea rise research, 245

U.S. Army Corp of Engineers, 88, 92, 114, 115, 201, 225; dredging without permit, 237; sea rise mitigation, 250

U.S. Department of Defense, 258, 265

U.S. Department of Interior, 115, 145, 154, 157, 161, 169; Cumberland Island, 229

U.S. Fish and Wildlife Service, 115, 154, 157, 180, 208, 257–259; land acquisition, 260, 265

U.S. Forest Service, 260

U.S. Geological Survey, 115, 123

U.S. Navy, 265

U.S. Supreme Court, 40–45, 50, 53, 57

U.S. Water Pollution Control Authority, 115, 126, 143; Act of 1965, 123, 199

Vanderbilt, William, 2

Vandiver, Gov. Ernest, 42, 48–49, 61, 68, 73, 77, 86

vital areas legislation, 227

Wallace, Gov. George, 235

Walling, Sen. Bob, 190, 193, 211, 216, 225

Wanamaker, John, 20

Wassaw Island: Coastal Islands Study Committee and, 203–204, 208, 219; GNAC and, 144; Kerr-McGee and, 126, 130, 132; Lester Maddox and, 152, 155–158; owners, 19; protection of, 139, 150–158, 180, 300n41

Water Quality Control Board (WQCB), 44, 71–72, 74, 83, 193; clean river work, 87–93; election of 1970, 226; Kerr-McGee mining and, 100–101, 109, reorganization of, 226. *See also* Howard, R. S. "Rock"

Watson, Sen. Ben, 251

Way, Albert, 19

West, Clifford, 142, 194, 298n7

West, Eleanor Torrey "Sandy": future of Ossabaw, 141–142, 204, 309n50; Islands Study Committee, 204, 309n50; Kerr-McGee and, 110; sale of Ossabaw, 229–230

WestRock Corporation, 264, 317n17

Wharton, Charles, 82, 109, 143, 153, 291n44, 299n8

Wicomico Formation, 259

Wild Cumberland, 270

Wildlife Action Plan, 259

Wildlife Management Area, 265

Williams, Hosea, 52

Williams, Jim, 104

Wilmington Island, 103

Wolfe, Paul, 247, 249

Wolf Island, 151, 154, 196, 257

Woodruff, Robert W., and Foundation, 260

CPSIA information can be obtained
at www.ICGtesting.com
Printed in the USA
LVHW090802250322
714273LV00008B/540